W9-BBD-884

North American Reference Encyclopedia of Women's Liberation

North American Reference Encyclopedia of Women's Liberation

EDITOR

William White Jr., Ph.D.

North American Publishing Company

Philadelphia, Pennsylvania

Copyright 1972

Library of Congress Catalogue Card Number: 72-84737
ISBN: 0-912920-02-5

Our Number: 7210

Staff:
Editor-Director: Dr. William White Jr.
Research Editors: Ms. Virginia Lamb
                 Ms. Bernie McGauley
Writer: Mr. Robert Tuten
Writing Assistant: Ms. Bonnie Greene

Irvin J. Borowsky, Publisher
North American Publishing Co.
134 North Thirteenth Street
Philadelphia, Pa. 19107

CONTENTS

Preface

This introductory volume of the North American Reference Library incorporates some radical departures from reference sources of the past. In our rapidly changing world, to describe a subject is virtually to both define it and advance it. Since all social movements have both historical roots and on-going goals it is necessary to combine the presentation of the facts about the movement with the citations to the sources in one volume.

The *Reference Encyclopedia of Women's Liberation* not only presents thousands of citations and cross-references but also defines all the terms generated and defined by the feminists in the context of their writings. The contributors to the volume represent every type of individual involved with the movement. It is the editor's belief that the members of a movement must be heard if anything is to be understood about the principles of the movement. Criticism, refinement, and academic study can then be based upon a fully rounded comprehension. The paragraphic index numbers in the articles do not indicate logical breaks in the articles, they are for the convenience of referencing the material.

The editor wishes to acknowledge the cooperation of the Philadelphia Free Library, The Temple University Library, The Library of the University of Pennsylvania, The New York Public Library, the Columbia University Library, the Bryn Mawr College Library, and numerous other public and private repositories of books and informational media. Additional acknowledgements are directed to Random House for permission to quote from Miriam Schneir's *Feminism: The Essential Historical Writings,* N.Y. (1972) pp. 40, 47, & 48 and to Massachusetts Institute of Technology Press for permission to quote from E. H. Erickson's "Concluding Remarks," in J. Mattfeld and C. Van Aken's *Women and the Scientific Professions,* Cambridge, Mass. (1965) pp. 244-245..

The editor would also like to thank Ms. Gloria Steinem, Ms. Shulamith Firestone, and Dr. Sylvia Tucker for their help and encouragement in the preparation of this reference work.

BUNNIES
ARE
FOR
BABBITT

BUNNIES NEED LIBERATION FROM THE ANIMAL WORLD

Chapter 1

Introduction

Women comprise over half of the number of human beings, although the statistics vary from time to time and from locality to locality. In the United States the 1970 census showed 104.3 million women over the age of one year to 98.9 million men over the age of one year. The female life expectancy as of 1968 was 74.0 years as compared to the male expectancy of 66.6 years, this is usually attributed to the greater resistance of women to many of the systemic diseases and their greater ability to cope with normal stress. If current patterns of fatality through military and civil strife, accident and drug abuse continue it is expected that the number of females over males will continue to increase. From antiquity up until approximately 1850 the biggest threat to women's lives was childbirth and resultant complications but world-wide medical care has reduced this threat in all the industrialized and many of the developing countries. Aside from the social dislocation caused by political conditions, this trend is expected to continue through the twenty-first century.

Five innovations based on new or necessary technologies have profoundly affected the position and roles of women in modern society. These are in historical order:

1. The *Industrial Revolution* beginning with the improved model of the steam engine introduced by James Watt in 1765. Throughout the three hundred years from 1450 to 1750 the cottage industry had been the mainstay of European and later colonial production. The populace had begun to move off the land and into the towns and villages after the Renaissance and skilled tradesmen passed on the traditions of their craft through their extended families. The cottage industry tended to keep the extended family together as a unit of production in which each member had a part. All members, old and young, male and female, engaged in some contribution to the family product. Each member could see the visible sign of the fruits of his labors and benefit directly from their barter. With the centralization and separation of the processes of production made possible by the steam power plant a vast new labor market opened up. One aspect of it was the enormous number of laborers needed to supply the machines with raw materials, coal, sand, wood, iron ore, and fiber. The other was the need for large numbers of unskilled and semiskilled workers to handle the materials for the machines and tend their output. As the cottage industries were brought to demise large numbers of women and girls moved into the towns and new industrial cities to work in the mills. The newly unattached women were thus both forced and able to make their own decisions. The immediate effects of the new exploitation were only slowed by the organization of trade unions after the pattern of the Wesleyan conventicles and the passage of labor legislation. The study of the social and economic effects of these changes became the background for the socialist theories of Saint-Simon (c. 1820)[1] and the communist theories of Marx (c. 1867)[2] which quickly became influential in the European labor movement. The plight of the mill girls was the first rallying point for feminism in America.

2. The perfecting of a practical *typewriter* by Christopher L. Sholes in 1868 and the invention of the *telephone* by Alexander Graham Bell in 1876 formulated the new women's role of the secretary-typist. While freeing woman from the need to seek employment in sweatshop industrial facilities it also opened up a socially acceptable employment for the Victorian middle-class woman. It in effect freed hundreds of thousands of unmarried girls from the bonds of the family and set a standard for women in the managerial middle class. However as with many seeming liberating technological innovations it soon became a defined occupation when the technology began to pale.

3. Although indirect, the technical innovations of *mechanized warfare* created another vacuum for personnel into which women rushed. From the end of the Franco-Prussian War (1870) until the outbreak of the First World War on June 28th, 1914, all of the industrialized nations had been pushing the new mechanical and chemical techniques to the limit in their quest for war machines to protect and advance the interests of their national states. As the demands on machines

grew to enormous proportions so did the demands for manpower to guide and resist the machines. England and the United States followed Germany, Austria, and France in utilizing women factory workers to turn the wheels of war. The coming of the century of total war in which civilian production and efficiency outweighed in effect the ability of the armies in the field brought every woman and man into the industrial-marketing machinery of the modern state. The worker-women were now not only producers, but consumers upon which whole new post-war markets opened up for commercial exploitation. Although the Second World War lacked the romantic patriotism of the First, it drew even more women into the offices and factories. The economic boom which was brought about by the war continued in the United States and Canada throughout the 1940's and 50's with only a slight recession during the Eisenhower Administration. Feminine production, feminine earnings, and feminine consumption were major factors in the economic progression toward the trillion dollar gross national product. The fact is, that only a relatively small proportion of the women who went to work during the First or Second World Wars went back to homemaking when the hostilities ended. The daughters of the upper income families of the era 1750 rarely took up careers, the daughters of the 1850's were permitted to do so, the daughters of the 1950's were expected to do so.

4. The *electronic media,* radio, television, and the computer, have had a catastrophic effect upon the society of the present century. This effect is so new and so pervasive that it is still very difficult to assess. It has for one, allowed an individualization of cultures within the dominant culture. Whereas in time past all the members of a family were mixed into one cultural synthesis by locale it is now possible for each small sector, youth, middle-aged, elderly, male, female, contemporary, traditional, white, black, and so on, to participate in his subcultural norms and patterns through the electronic media. Instant empathy in all segments of the global village is thus probable.[3] Cross-social alignments and influences have come into being which wreck havoc with the traditional institutions. A clear example is the evident difficulties of the two major political parties in trying to define themselves and to obtain a mandate from their constituents. It is no accident that each of the prime movers in the popular image of the women's liberation movement can fill the role of a television celebrity. The message of women's liberation can thus be spread through the medium of the television message. The control of T.V. news and information content will become increasingly important to the political party in power. The American dream of consumption is being rejected by more and more of the young who have found it increasingly more difficult to find places in society which will afford them the income they expect or feel their social class warrants. This motive has been coupled with a general shift in the U.S. industrial scene away from the production enterprises toward the service enterprises. The end result of this trend is coming to rest in concerns whose only product is information. It is the control of those means of information rather than the means of production that the women's movement must ultimately win. The startling success of women in the computer/information-science fields and in the educational institutions indicates their ability to compete. With the transfer of financial power in the American society away from the hard labor industries such as mining, smelting, rolling, and farming, to software based industries such as information processors, investors, and banks, the man is no more capable of successful competition by reason of his heavier frame than the women. Some have seen the effect of the electronic media to be a feminizing of society but this is a speculative judgement based on many cultural assumptions. The usual erroneous distinction between masculine and feminine as active and passive has been applied to the electronizing of modern life which is characterized as a passive enterprise. Both distinctions are wrong, what is correct is that in such a work environment both men and women must continually *learn* their jobs rather than merely process them. This learning process however goes against all the standards of a dynamic competitive capitalism. One of the stresses of this problem is the place and security of the worker in the company. This is a major concern to all sectors of the women's liberation movement. In the long run, the financial power of an electronic society, one assuming a thermodynamicized world-view, will be in the hands of the technical elite who can control the information-input to the cybernetic system. Conceivably the education requisite for this input function will have to be apportioned to the various subsections of a multi-form society by some government bureau and on the basis of some democratically acceptable policy.

5. No other technical innovation has so altered the roles of women than the commercialization of a chemical *fertility control agent* by the G. D. Searle

organization in 1961. The compound sold as Enovid was highly successful and popularized the whole notion of birth control. The full ramifications, sexual freedom from fear of illicit or unwanted conception, sex education, and sexual expression in other social contexts, are a long way from being understood or known. In the normal woman the use of such contraceptive agents can allow her to plan, space, or forego child bearing. This newly acquired freedom has made the other situation, unwanted pregnancy and coerced delivery, a greater psychological burden than ever before. Women of many different viewpoints are united in their insistence upon reform of abortion laws. Many desire the same degree of personal autonomy over their post-conception child bearing that the pill has provided their pre-conception. Other factors entering the decision are drawn from the recognition that environmental pollution is a function of population and that unrestricted child bearing has extremely adverse effects upon the quality of life a family enjoys. There is the additional psychological fact that as the median U.S. income arose on the basis of the working wife/mother, the subsistence level also rose and so the women who wanted to work to improve her family's economic position now must work to maintain it. In a society in which the number of workers per jobs available ratio is cooling down, job-security becomes more important than advancement or remuneration. The woman who is now able to control her child bearing, and thus her absence from work for pregnancy and delivery, is seeking to win the two remaining needs to obtain full-status job security with men, pregnancy-leave and day-care. In a democratic society the time-honored way to achieve these goals is through mass political pressure and concerted lobbying.

Along with, and partially dependent upon, the technical alterations in the state of women have come several major ideological upheavals which have influenced the way in which the new techniques were accepted and handled. One important insight in any consideration of such philosophical changes is the historical phenomenon that any given historical period always sees itself in the terms and through the norms of the period immediately gone before. On occasion it may reject that period, in some Hegelian sense, and select a period in the shorter or longer past it would like to emulate. In the period of swiftest technical change, 1860 to 1960, three alterations or revolutions in thought took place. Each of these

soon found expression in the opinions of women and aspects of all are tightly bound up with the three waves of feminism and the opinions all feminist writers and spokeswomen profess.

1. The dominant philosophical outlook of the nineteenth century was romanticism. This was the notion that reason was limited in its ability and that humanity possessed a more important faculty, intuition, derived from experience. Human affairs were not reducible to neat physical statements in mathematical formulae but coincidence, fate, feeling, and emotion, were the basic things that determined the life of humanity. Nowhere did romanticism shine brighter than in defining the roles of the sexes and moralizing on the passions and prides of sexuality. The great romantic philosophical thinkers, starting with Immanuel Kant (1724–1804)[4] and going through the works of Georg W. F. Hegel (1770–1831)[5] Arthur Schopenhauer (1788–1860)[6] Friedrich W. Nietzsche (1844–1900)[7] who stood at the threshold of a new age of thought, all had very pronounced and quite often negative estimates of women. Most of their followers in Germany and around the world thought of femininity and sexuality as lurid and wicked and placed womankind on a pedestal to protect her from their own animalistic and rationalistic instincts. In popular culture this was seen in the "gothic romance," that type of literature in which the pure and moral knight braves torment and terror to rescue the damsel in dire distress.[8] This plotline is the backbone of American "westerns," and detective stories. Long after the difficult Germanic writings of the philosophers who had founded the movement were relegated to college classrooms, the plots carried on, reaching their heyday in the movies of the twenties and thirties. This dream world came to collapse in Europe and among the literate classes in America in the shock of World War I. A deep mood of pessimism came upon Europe and art and literature fled from the horrors of reality into surrealism, Dadaism, and the jazz age. Freud and his interpretation of sexuality became popular and the grosser writings of D. H. Lawrence, James Joyce, and Henry Miller were read by the avant garde on both sides of the Atlantic. In the agony of European civilization the romantic heroine had gone and in her place were the existential antiheroines. The quiet frustration and unrequited love of Emily Dickinson and the Brontës gave way to the women of Gertrude Stein, Ernest Hemingway and F. Scott Fitzgerald. Behind this new, more human awareness was the brooding figure of one of the greatest misogynists of all time, the Dane, Soren Kierkegaard. He lived and wrote his strangely mystical works from 1813 to 1855 but his incredible dialectic of suffering and sensitivity to pain was thought repulsive in his own time.[9] It was only after all was quiet on the western front and 14 million had died that the world could stomach Kierkegaard. By the time his eerie brand of Christianity was popular the state churches, crowns, and establishments of Europe had crashed into dust. After an orgy which lasted a decade the U.S. slid uneasily into the depression and turned its intellectual leadership toward the brooding Dane. His melancholy view of life found sympathizers in Nietzsche, and the Russian novelist, Dostoevski[10] and later Americans such as John Dos Passos and John Steinbeck. The role of women, the old and the new, were placed in fine juxtaposition in Tennesse Williams' *A Streetcar Named Desire.* Thus the first change in thought was accomplished. While in Europe it was the complex existential philosophy of Kierkegaard and his followers Martin Heidegger and J. P. Sartre that had wide appeal, in the U.S. it was their emphasis on psychology that prevailed.

2. The second change in thought was the innovation of pragmatism by the American thinkers, John Dewey (1859–1952)[11] and Charles S. Peirce (1839–1914)[12], and the division of that pragmatism into a utilitarian mode in the social sciences and a positivistic mode in the exact and industrial sciences. While in almost all European philosophies truth is attainable by either reason or reflection upon the immediate situation, in the pragmatists, truth is verified only for the moment and only by experiment and experience. Therefore truth may be arrived at by a committee or through scientific authorization, a type of communal certainty.[13] The main proposition of a practical, workable solution to every problem with no long term commitments to a system fit the American national character as nothing before or since. While Dewey was scorned by the academicians and professional philosophical scholars, his views were raised to canon in the American Public Schools. Since whatever men and women learn about philosophy and life in American society is usually gotten from the public educational experience, his adoption by public education has made *his* virtually *the* American school of thought. The pragmatic woman is the jack-of-all-trades who appears in commercial advertising, the mother, wife, nurse, teacher, advisor, shopper, chauffeur. This image is especially attractive and malleable for the vendor of a product whose pitch always promises release from one of her many roles and chores with the help of his product. Strange to say, only a few women writers of the current movement have seen the link between Madison Avenue and Deweyism. But the hold of orthodox-dewey is beginning to fade. Even though it seriously effected the idea of science in the U.S. it had to make peace with the notion of positivism. Originally stemming from the writings of the French mathematician, Auguste Comte (1798–1857)[14] it became the underlying assumption of most natural and social scientists up to the present crisis, number 3 below. Comte taught that science based upon pure research and experimental validation led to truth about humanity and the cosmos. The ultimate comprehension of reality came with being able to construct mathematical laws and models of the functions of any process whether it was the fermentation of grapes or the voting patterns of the citizens of Paris. This notion that if science can lead to truth then more science can yield greater truth has dominated almost all of the industrialized west. It is what the Dutch Jurist, H. Dooyeweerd calls, "the science-ideal."[15] All this was too difficult for the educationist to follow and so there came a division between the scientist looking for scientific truth and the educator looking for the greatest, most favorable aspect to teach according to its utility to society. The second change came about with the birth of Dewey's system and its immediate splintering and loss of favored status. Many women who have been trained in educational methodology will appeal to education as the best method to liberate women, especially to raise their consciousness about themselves. Others, educated in the exact or natural sciences will seek to liberate women by the application of scientific investigation to the myths which hold women in check. If however, history repeats education alone will not alter attitudes and science alone will not bring about changes in status. And, there is the added problem of the rejection of Dewey's practical woman by many in the movement.

3. The third alteration, in the opinion of many, has been the rejection of both romanticism and pragmatism. The United States survived the Second World War unscathed by actual aggression and able to return to something like the social conditions and class structures of the pre-war period. However as world communism began to shift to peaceful production, the European powers had difficulty with their recalcitrant colonies, and the former enemies Japan and Germany began to make their entrance upon the world economic stage, optimistic pragmatism and idealistic positivism showed signs of strain. It became obvious throughout the 1950's and 60's that no amount of American social engineering would remake the world into the democratic image. It also became obvious that increased competition abroad and the children of the baby-boom at home were bringing about immense strains on the time-honored institutions. By 1965 the process called by Evan Runner, "rapidization,"[16] was taking place. Economic processes which had taken a century previously would run their course from innovation, to production, to spin-off, to collapse or acquisition, in a matter of years. The chief characteristic of the new society was mobility. Women became as mobile in personal relationships, education, and job opportunities, as men and both traded on an expanding market at home and abroad. As the mobility became more difficult and the hard facts of economic reality and the limits of the power structure were reached, it became apparent that many social problems could not be solved in the acceptable American way. That is, it was necessary to find a single application of either technical or marketing principles, in a word, to design a new product. For an example, the answer to the drug problem in the U.S. is viewed by many to be the development of a simple, inexpensive pill which will satisfy the craving for drugs and make further drug use unrewarding. The far more difficult method of restructuring the social conditions that lead to drug abuse is set aside. However the long-range method is the only real solution to the problem.[17] The immediate results of this pragmatic action and reaction is to solve many types of simple problems, however the overall result is to produce a crazy-quilt of stop-gap measures which one-day prove too unwieldy to function. This has been the fate of most government programs launched during the thirties and of all bureaucracies such as the nightmarish civil court system. It is against this phantastically interwoven and mutually dependent system that most of the protest of the sixties was launched. Much more appealing to the idealists of whatever age is a clean, linear system with built-in simplicity. Theoretical analysis and long range planning are impossible on the basis of pragmatism. However many feel that the world-wide problems of the modern age are amenable only to root-research and total structuring. The result of their quests has been the rise of isms, (European "-isme"), the carrying of legitimate methods of thinking about aspects of reality, for example: psychology, community and the like, to the extreme that they become the only insights to truth. Thus, psychology becomes psychologism, community becomes communism and so on. The absolutizing of ideas has led to the radicalism and radicalizing found on every hand. Unfortunately although pragmatic capitalism is a very pleasant and acceptable way to allow for individual freedom, it does not offer a basis for long-range theory, many thinkers and writers have turned to the dialectic and social models based upon it. The dialectic is the concept developed by Kant upon reflection on Plato and Aristotle, and modified by almost every modern thinker. It is basically the idea that any given situation is a tension between two opposing notions or forces which are equally true, opposite, and which define each other. When applied to social problems this means that progress in civil rights can only come about according to this theory by violent antagonism until a new situation is reached. Thus the pragmatic idea of evolution becomes the dialectic idea of revolution. This notion and its ramifications and interpretations underlies all radical revolutionary schemes. Since revolution and the founding of a new system is so appealing, many young people in the western nations have accepted it and contributed to the so-called new left. A certain minority of the women's movement has come out of this radical experience and accept all of its methods for the liberation of women. Like all such movements, the real philosophic basis is not understood by more than a handful of the leaders while a host of youths hang-on believing a mass of mythology and conjuring up terrors and threats on every hand. The final failure of pragmatic utilitarianism and positivism with a large number of thinking Americans is the chief source of the current "generation gap." Even within the women's movement this division is noted between the group 35 to 60 years of age who accept the pragmatic methods and want to work within the system and the group 16 to 30 who believe in dialectic principles and who want to wreck it. This second group should perhaps better be denoted as the "Third wave of feminism."

In collecting and studying the thousands of pages of documents for this research source it became apparent that the literature and media of the women's liberation movement falls into about six classes each representing a group within the movement and each geared for a special purpose. This six-part breakdown which you will find apparent in the various articles and the bibliographies is as follows:

- Academic theses, studies, papers and research notes. These originate from students and scholars as work for college degrees or publications for academic audiences. Although they are wordy and difficult they often are the most carefully researched studies of the place of women in society and the degree of specific exploitation. These can originate from any one of the three phases of feminism: suffragete, organizational, or new left.
- Position papers, group studies, surveys, institutional reports, published and funded by the women's groups which have status and acceptance in American society. These papers are often the ones upon which reforms in the laws and policies of institutions will be innovated. They are usually written by group authorship or by social task-forces and are never at odds with the methods by which the establishment brings about change. They invariably call for new regulations and increased funds and programming.
- Magazines, newsletters, newsbriefs, and pamphlets published by local groups and usually consisting of two parts: one or two general articles on abortion, child-care, consciousness raising or some other current concern of all women in the movement, and local news and events. In some cases this last local section gets bogged down in the same parlimentary and petty political disputes that characterize the great institutions against which the papers attempt to speak. These newsletters vary very widely in quality and frequency of issue. They are the most difficult documents to acquire and catalogue.
- Publicity releases and broadsides. As more commercial publishers become involved in direct distribution of books on and about women's liberation, the number of professionally written and distributed publicity releases is increasing. They fall into two categories, those advertising a new book by popularizing its author and those publicizing movement positions. As the women's

magazines shift to an image more acceptable to the movement, more of these documents will be appearing. Some of these are coming from the directly opposite source, the new left, they are often picked up by the local newsletters with the result that the same basic story line will appear in a great many different publications.

- Papers of all types originating from new left sources. These are difficult to divide, the temptation is to try and separate those which are truly representative of the women's liberation movement from those which are proposing long terms leftists projects but on the basis of a new appeal to the women's movement. However this is somewhat illegitimate as practical Marxism has always attempted to utilize the crisis situations, whatever their cause, as instances of establishment breakdown and socialist hope. There is a minority within the movement that have grown up in the radical movements and for whom crisis, conflict, and protest, are a way of life. There is no doubt that many of these women are able provocateurs and pamphleteers and their established habits of protest are a strong boost to the local groups where they are found. In their writings a wide range of neo-maoist jargon is utilized with constant references to "collectives," "communes," "third world comrades," and the like.
- The most cohesive writing and argument appears in the few publications of the lesbians. These women are trying to obtain two goals: first to have their relationships and life style accepted by society as an alternate but legitimate form of sexual expression, and second to unite their rather minor voice with that of the major voice of women's liberation. They pursue this aim by arguing that their role is that of the totally liberated woman, the woman free of the need for masculine sexuality. In popular culture their point of view has become equated with that of the other five groups delineated above. However in actual fact their writings comprise less than 5% of the available material and their membership or sponsorship still less.

REFERENCES

1. Saint-Simon, Claude, Henri de Rouvroy., *Systeme Industriel,* Paris (1821)
2. Marx, Karl., *Das Kapital* (1867 ff.), eng. tr. (1891)
3. McLuhan, Marshall, & Q. Fiore., *War and Peace in the Global Village* (1969)
4. Kant, Immanuel., *Kritik der Reinen Vernunft* (1781), and *Kritik der praktischen Vernunft* (1788), see also the writings on Kant and his followers by Richard Kroner.
5. Hegel, Georg Wilhelm Friedrich., *Werke . . .* Berlin (1832 ff.)
6. Schopenhauer, Arthur., *The World as Will and as Idea* (1884)
7. Nietzsche, Friedrich Wilhem., *The Philosophy of Nietzsche,* in the Modern Library edition. A philosopher between two worlds of thought his own views on women have been widely studied.

8. Tuchman, Barbara W., *The Proud Tower,* N.Y. (1962)
9. Lowrie, Walter., *Kierkegaard,* 2 vols. (1948), a prolific writer of great ability, a vast bibliography about Kierkegaard has arisen.
10. Dostoevski, Feyodor M., *Crime and Punishment* (1866) and *The Brothers Karamazov* (1880) see also, Wellek, Rene., ed. *Dostoevsky: a collection of critical essays,* N.Y. (1962)
11. Dewey, John., *Democracy and Education;* an introduction to the philosophy of education, N.Y. (1916)
12. Peirce, Charles S., *The Philosophy of Peirce,* N.Y. (1965)
13. Hart, Hendrik., *Communal Certainty and Authorized Truth,* Amsterdam (1966), an expert discussion and critique of pragmatism.
14. Comte, Isidore Auguste Marie Francois., *Cours du Philosophie Positive,* 6 vols. Paris (1840 ff.)
15. Dooyeweerd, Herman., *A New Critique of Theoretical Thought,* translation of *De Wijsbegeerte Der Wetsidee,* Amsterdam (1958) Consult index in volume 4.
16. Runner, Evan., in personal correspondence.
17. Grieco, F., ''The Drug Addict and the Drug Scene,'' *The Reference Encyclopedia of Drugs and Drug Abuse,* Philadelphia (1972)

William White Jr., Ph.D.
Editor

Chapter 2

Women in Politics

The current movement for women's rights or women's liberation is related in one way or another to the popular women's movements of the past in American history. Many advocates of the movement like to call it the "second wave of feminism." The long struggle for the woman's right to vote began at "the rights convention" of 1848 held in Seneca Falls, New York. The chief spokeswoman, Elizabeth Cady Stanton, proclaimed a number of the rights that should be afforded to women. From the founding of the democracy most men had firmly believed that women were fully represented in the machinery and deliberations of government by their fathers, husbands, and sons. It is possible that in a rural America dotted with cottage industries this may have been partly true. By the coming of the industrial revolution after 1800 it was less true and by the era of full industrial exploitation it was no longer true. The same economic and social pressures which brought about the freedom and enfranchisement of the slaves also forced the enfranchisement of women. However, because many women held a comfortable stake in the *status quo,* the movement for women's suffrage took longer and was far less violent than that for the emancipation of the slaves. In the past half century since full universal suffrage of women was enacted into law, there have been relatively few changes in the political sector. The dire predictions of moral collapse and the utopian promises of new moral strength supposed to come about when women got the vote did not materialize. In fact the conservative middle class continued to vote for conservatives, while the newer immigrant working class continued to vote for liberals, and the minorities were alternately bought and sold on the block of political compromise and expediency, in a phrase, nothing changed. One of the most sincerely held myths of the nineteenth century romantics had been the notion that women were purer although weaker than men, and that as voters they would pressure the political bosses for social reforms. There is no evidence that they were a deciding factor in pushing for such social reforms. It is more likely that they sought reforms which were immediately connected to their needs and interests as women. Much of the legal and political action of the current movement may be viewed in the same light. It is clear and obvious that women will demand and receive an ever increasing share of the authority and responsibility for the government of our society. However, until women see their unity in their sisterhood as a stronger tie than their social and economic class consciousness there is no reason to expect their political voice will represent their majority power at the poles.

WOMEN AND POLITICS

2.1 The feminists of the late Nineteenth Century were primarily interested in the legal and political rights of women. Their point of view is shared most closely by those women who hold elected political office today. For this reason many of the leaders of women's political action are also interested in the women's liberation movement. Few are as able and as vocal as representative Bella Abzug. She, and others who share her views, see women's liberation as the next and most necessary logical step in the course of American liberal political thinking. She ascribes to the cherished beliefs of democratic liberals who have often had outstanding women leaders such as Jeannette Rankin and Eleanor Roosevelt. As social services have grown to be a larger and larger item of federal government concern and spending women have felt more and more involved with government. Such vital concerns as abortion, birth control, women's rights in the labor market, and the education of girls, have now challenged ever larger segments of the female population. In the face of the increased interest in political affairs, there has been a steady decline in the number of women elected to public office. Congresswoman Abzug's article is new in its outlook and excitement, however, it also represents a strong bridge to the efforts for political power and responsibility on the part of feminists of the past. It is a good transition from the successes of the 1920's to the needs of the 70's and beyond, for the dignity of women in the political arena.

2.1.1 When a movement is as energetic and daring in its scope and vision as is this second wave of women's liberation, there is bound to be as much disagreement among those within the movement as among those outside of it. Most of these internal differences of opinion are healthy, and if we deal with them creatively and with a sense of proportion, they will help us grow. But there is one major point of dissension which is so basic, widespread and shortsighted that it worries me. It is between those women in the movement who are passionately devoted to liberation through political action and those who just as passionately affirm that politics "is simply not where it's at." Now it is certainly the option of the individual to choose a certain life orientation and to prefer one mode of endeavor to another, but to deny the interconnection and mutual dependence of political and personal or social goals is to dedicate oneself to nothing but frustration and fatigue. Perhaps some women feel that their own problems are purely emotional or spiritual. I would not want to argue this, but I do think that such a feeling is a luxury that very few can afford. Millions cannot begin to think about such problems, not until they have an hour to themselves, some autonomy and a certain perspective by which they can view themselves by their own standards and not those of Wall Street, Madison Avenue or Capitol Hill. Not until, shall we say, they have "a room of their own." Woman's liberation must come from her own efforts and this means power and power means politics. It doesn't necessarily mean domination, manipulation and mudslinging (although it is easy to understand how it got this reputation), but it does mean *true* representation, true sharing in the creation and administration of the policies, laws and programs which affect all of us. Perhaps I'm just saying something that has been said many times before, i.e., "man is a political animal." But I want to make one slight turn of the screw, i.e., "woman is a political animal too." Active recognition of this fact is not only essential for the liberation of women, it is essential for the rejuvenation of our whole distorted and demoralized society.

2.1.2 The call for "Womanpower" has been greeted with both mockery and fear. This reaction is in reality a mere cover-up for the shame that comes with the realization that a large part of our population has remained powerless for so long. But these reactions are transparent. There is really nothing funny or outrageous about our demands. I am not proselytizing for a female-dominated society, Congress or judicial system, but I do want a share of political power proportionate to our numbers in the population. Nothing more, nothing less. I am not fighting for this in order to satisfy some abstract, vacuous principle of justice. I make this demand because I want a society where women can be active, respected and fulfilled human beings; and where other now under-represented groups—Blacks, Chicanos, Indians, Puerto Ricans, youths (male and female) can be so also.

2.1.3 I guess it is unfair to say I "want nothing more." My demand for a truly representative Congress should not surprise anyone who puts faith in the democratic system. And yet this demand is revolutionary. It has never yet been met. Whatever are the intentions of our elite white, male, middle-aged rulers, good, bad or misguided, such a select group cannot be expected to *represent* all the people of this country. I have great faith that a truly representative Congress (and that means several hundred women instead of a dozen) would make for a truly different America.

2.1.4 I am not elevating women or other "minority" members to sainthood, nor am I suggesting that all women share the same views, or that they all think and act alike. Women have screamed for war, stoned Black children, have been prejudiced, narrowminded, reactionary, and even violent. SOME women. They, of course, have a right to vote and to run for office. I will defend that right, but I will not vote for them or support them.

2.1.5 On the other hand, there is a kind of snowballing sense of solidarity among women around certain issues. There is a lot we don't know about how and why men and women behave differently. We are discovering more and more that certain characteristics we thought to be biological are really social or historical. But, for whatever reason, there certainly seems to be a definite relationship between "masculinity," or rather "machismo," and violence and war. I am very optimistic that the full entry of women into political life will add qualities of humanism, compassion and creativity to our society.

2.1.6 I have dealt in very general terms with how I believe women's entry into politics can affect our whole society. Now I'd like to return to what effect this new expression of power will have on the individual woman and on women as a group. It is not my place here to enumerate the many ways in which women are oppressed. But I do want to emphasize that this oppression is very real. It has absolutely nothing to do with whether women in the movement wear bras or burn their bras, or whether they sleep with men or women. Much of women's oppression can be considered "psychological," "social," or "cultural." It is subtle, often unconscious. But much of it is institutionalized. It is blatant and deliberate. We know there is a very close connection between a society's institutions, its formal laws and structures, and its myths, customs and ethos. And it just so happens that in our society, these institutions, laws and structures have been created and administered primarily by men, while women have waited out their lives in the kitchens, bedrooms and backrooms of business and political offices. Discrimination has an economic base. Women get the lower paying jobs. They may perform the same work as men but they don't get the same title or the same pay. In fact, women as a rule earn one-third less than men.

2.1.7 Of course we are not the first women to have cried out in rebellion. Susan B. Anthony, Lucretia Mott and Elizabeth Cady Stanton dared to speak in public when it was considered to be a very un-ladylike thing to do. They made the first inroad, but we were left wandering in the woods for years before we realized how dark it was in there. Yes, we have had the "right" to vote and run for office for many years now, but our political and economic system, and the deep cultural biases it perpetuates, acts to keep women out of public office; to prevent them from ever running; to silence them. We women are the real silent majority.

2.1.8 The first rumblings may be muffled and ignored. My own experience has not been easy, but it has made me face up to what must be faced. Do not think that I was greeted with open arms. I am a mature citizen and a lawyer. I was a leader of the New Democratic Coalition, a national legislature representative of Women Strike for Peace, an organizer of Taxpayer's Campaign for Urban Priorities and a very aware and involved member of the New York community. But during my campaign, the media ignored these qualifications which might have indicated that I was a serious candidate. The press preferred to treat me as a joke. They portrayed me as a character: tough, noisy, a prize fighter, a Jewish Mother, a Mother Courage. And still, many find me entertaining, but they also now know that I am a serious Representative.

2.1.9 The battle is by no means over as soon as that big old door to Congress is forced open.

The few women who fight their way in are greeted with discrimination. Disbelieving eyes beneath highly raised eyebrows look upon my primarily female professional staff. Obviously they are not the norm. It is also interesting to note the way in which women members are given committee assignments. Of the twelve women in Congress, five are on the Education and Labor Committees. Could this be a reflection of the male view that women can only deal with problems of children and youth, but they cannot be expected to deal with decisions which send children and youth off to war in Asia?

2.1.10 Let's also look a moment at what happened when there was an opening in the Supreme Court. Certainly the time was long overdue for at least one woman to be seated on that sacred bench. One can learn a lot by examining the Supreme Court records. Take for example the cases guaranteeing women the right to work even if they have children. You will find that the court records are marked by frequent interruptions of laughter. I doubt that a Supreme Court Justice who has had to fight her way through all the obstacles of a male-dominated profession would find anything very funny in the efforts of women to get legal redress for their just grievances. I think her presence would have a salutory effect on the prejudices of her colleagues.

2.1.11 The National Women's Political Caucus submitted ten distinguished names. But President Nixon chose to play hide and seek. He secretly hinted that he had another woman in mind. In fact, he was considering a woman who was grossly unqualified. When she was finally rejected, the implication was that he couldn't find one woman in the United States good enough to be on the Supreme Court. The real problem was that he couldn't find one bad enough!

2.1.12 So where do we begin? We begin, first of all, together. We need each other's support. Courage, like cowardice, is contagious. Among us there are many differences which we must recognize and tackle. But, more important, we have much in common. Women have been in the forefront of the civil rights movement, the environment and consumer movements, the child care movement, the movements to reclaim our cities, neighborhoods and bodies. We are overwhelmingly against the Pentagon tapeworm that has been feeding off our society for a quarter of a century and depriving us of our most elementary needs.

2.1.13 We may be told that we cannot run for

office unless we have held some previous office; that we are not qualified because we are not experienced. But, actually, women as a whole, have more organizational experience and know-how than men have. We are the ones who organize and run the health drives, the charity drives, the church suppers and religious benefits. We run the P.T.A.s and the hundreds of other voluntary organizations that sustain our society. And more than that, we do the dirty work in the political campaigns: licking stamps, stuffing envelopes, raising funds, telephoning, doorbell ringing and poll watching. In fact, most of the techniques used in modern political campaigns were developed by women in their long struggle for the passage of the women's suffrage amendment. In those eighty years, suffragettes accumulated a lot of experience and wisdom; but after they won the vote in 1920 they made the mistake of thinking that their struggle was over. The result has been that women have been using their vote to elect men, because men were the only candidates there were. Well, they won't be the only ones any more.

2.1.14   In July 1971, women from all over the country and almost every minority group gathered in Washington to set up the National Women's Political Caucus. Our purpose was manifold but basically we wanted to "rally national and local support for the campaigns of women candidates— federal, state and local—who declare themselves ready to fight for the rights and needs of women, and of all under-represented groups." And we wanted to bring our campaign home: to train women to organize caucuses on a state and local level. We listed many specific issues on which we felt ready to take a common stand. They are too lengthy to list here. But we all had an overwhelming concern which I do want to emphasize. Paula Page of the National Student's Association put it this way: "We don't want to imitate the male pattern, by seeking power for its own sake. We don't want to elect Uncle Toms who, once in power, keep their sisters down . . ." As women become more and more prominent in politics, they run the danger of being co-opted by male politicians who seek to use them to perpetuate the kind of old party politics that we want to abolish.

2.1.15   Finally, athough our own interests as women are ever-present in our minds, we must recognize that oppressions are inter-connected. This is what makes our struggle so difficult. But it also makes it so exciting and promising. Our demands cannot be met without a total re-ordering of our nation's priorities. The National Women's Political Caucus aims to coordinate the organizing ability, courage and commitment of women, and to thrust women into political power at *all* levels. We will begin by running women as convention delegates. Much of our effort will be based on the local level where we are already somewhat involved: perhaps in the city council, school boards or state legislature. We are going to become mayors, governors, members of Congress, Cabinet officers, Supreme Court Justices, and eventually there will be a woman President. We may have to be pushy. No one will hand us the nominations just because we happen to be the most qualified in many cases. But I believe that if we demonstrate creativity, activism and courage, people will respond.

2.1.16   Most of all, whether or not we win the first time around, as Paula puts it, "a real victory of the Caucus lies in the education which women would receive from setting up and carrying out their own programs and actions, without direction from men." We are bound to make some mistakes, but I am very optimistic. Not because I believe women are necessarily smarter or more moral than men, but because we are in fact a tremendous source of as yet unused talent and energy. More important, because we have been oppressed, and because we are relatively new to politics, we bring to it special qualities: a unique sense of solidarity, vision, daring, imagination, self-respect, ideals and commitment.

We have among us a kind of auspicious innocence. Not the kind of innocence that is associated with naïvéte, but the kind that is associated with incipient health, growth and fertility. *This* is Womanpower.

Representative, Bella S. Abzug
Democrat, New York

THE POLITICS OF LIBERATION

2.2   The climate of opinion regarding human social activities has changed rapidly since the end of the Second World War. While the American culture revitalized its faith in progress and man's capacity for improvement, European attitudes were becoming engrossed with existentialism and insisting upon human culpability. The optimistic picture of the future was especially furthered by the American and

Canadian public education systems. Pragmatism, the principle of verifying truth through experience, became the order of the day throughout the vast educational establishment which came into being to meet the demands of the post-war baby boom. But as rising population surged against shrinking frontiers and diminished colonies, the quest for knowledge about the human condition was turned inward and a new horizon of exploration was uncovered in the behavior and sensibilities. Two further shifts came about, the first was the deemphasis of external, organizational subjection to moral and ethical standards. This meant that an individual's ethical behavior was dictated by psychological need more than social custom and institutional standard. The second, was the transfer of the domain of the political from the external and societal to the personal. What is meant by *political* in the writings of the youthful activists of the 60's is closer to what was meant by *religious,* or *metaphysical* in the writings of an earlier day. Indeed, the two strongest political philosophies of the Twentieth Century, democratic capitalism and dialectic materialism both deal fundamentally with politics at a level of commitment and dedication which is stronger than the traditionally religious.

While some of those engaged in the women's movement see their tasks in the light of traditional political action and reaction, others see it as beginning with a personal reconsideration of values, as a personal restructuring of the individual's self-image. In the terms of modern existential involvement, this is termed "consciousness raising." It can best be accomplished with the psychological methods of mutual interaction and group dynamics. In professor Andreas' article, the liberation of the individual from her political suppression is made possible through group action not necessarily directed towards the outside environment or intending to effect that environment. It is activity for the good of the activists, it aids them to become themselves. The interesting similarity between this goal and that of the Hasidic Rabbis or the early church is very striking and points to another assumption of modern acculturated youth, the total sterility and irrelevancy of organized religion in contemporary society. It has been said that Americans ascribe messianic character to education, it may be said that many now seek salvation in political activity. The liberation of which the author speaks is a spiritual and moral liberation, it is approached for her by political means. Through her eyes, both women and men can catch a glimpse of what is lost for both in sexist society.

2.2.1   There is an understanding within the women's movement in the United States that we are not merely a group of people asking for our share of the power and glory. Our purpose and our strength are revealed in the political style that is emerging out of our experience. My own experience in the movement has occurred primarily in the state of Michigan, but I have, like many active participants, kept in touch with the experiences of women in other parts of the country. I am presently living in California. In clarifying my own thoughts on paper, I think I speak for others as well. One thing seems certain. Very few of us want to be men. Nor do we want males to strive for "Manhood" as it has been defined in the past. This has been said so many times that it sounds already like a cliché, yet many men and some women who claim to be sympathetic to the notion of "women's lib", as they call it, continue to be baffled by the unwillingness of women to assume the prerogatives of men, and many of us who are struggling to develop alternative ways of relating to each other are baffled by the stubborn persistence in ourselves of "masculine" assumptions and characteristics. What are some of these assumptions and characteristics? And to what extent is it possible to rid ourselves of these and to deny "feminine" prerogatives while we attempt to survive and grow in a still-male-defined world?

2.2.2   Masculinity in the Western world involves role-prescriptions which are unattainable and attitudes which are impossible to hold without the development of elaborate defenses against reason and human sensitivity, but it nevertheless exists as an ideal toward which most of us have deferred for most of our lives. It involves, as I see it, a belief that there is an answer to every question, that finding the right answer depends on locating the infallible person, that infallible persons exist, that privileges must be accorded as a reward for effort or achievement, that the most important privilege is power, and that life exists primarily as a struggle for individual power.

Women have been watching men pretend to believe these propositions for a very long time, and they have been watching men act on such pretenses with disastrous consequences. Women who realize their own "femininity" are just as caught up in the "masculine" belief system, but they carefully exclude themselves from participation, or from becoming actors in it. They are, or want to be, the ultimate beneficiaries of masculine infallibility and power. Both women and men would, it seems, naturally fear acting in such a way as to deny themselves the rewards society promises for "good behavior" . . . unless the costs are too high. Women are sensitive to the price we all pay for accepting masculine ideals, and many of us want to have no part of them. What evidence is there that women are beginning to define their liberation not in terms of developing their power as individuals over others or in terms of dominating nature, but in terms of control of their *own* lives as cooperating members of a human society and as part of a natural environment that exists for its own sake as well as for theirs? We can look several places for evidence. We can look at the priorities that women who are asserting themselves in the struggle for liberation are placing on their time, and we can look at the way they conduct themselves when they are together. It is the priorities that baffle the observers. Why, they say, are so many women spending so much time talking among themselves rather than *doing* something?

2.2.3 What seems apparent to me is that the criticism comes from those who are less concerned about the *lack* of action than they are fearful about its revolutionary quality. When women are constantly engaging in self-examination and mutual support of a highly personal sort, they gain the strength and insight to move in directions that would be unlikely to emerge from public discussion and debate. The relatively "safe" territory of legislative lobbying or assertion of political power in male-defined organizations is less likely to concern them than the creation of new institutions to meet their own real and immediate needs, and the realization of personal autonomy which can be so threatening to those on whom they have been dependent.

Those who are irritated with the "small-group" phenomenon are especially put off by its unpredictable results. How can there be any long-term credibility for people who say they want abortion legislation reform one day, then emerge six months later with demands for repeal of all abortion legislation, and then drop that effort altogether to establish a network of free services run by women without regard for legality (or illegality)? How can there be any credibility for people who say they want to be allowed to teach in the universities and chair departments and then, after they win this right, decide that the universities are irredeemable, that their degrees

are rubbish, and that their own authority over students must be destroyed so that mutual learning can occur? For people who insist that men share in child-rearing and then fight custody battles with their ex-husbands? For people who criticize The Media for failure to present issues focusing on women and then refuse to appear on television panels to debate those issues? For people who invite participation of Third World women and then accept denunciation by Third World sisters who decide to create new modes of organization to fight male chauvinism as they experience it? For people who claim revulsion at lesbianism in the movement, assuring their husbands or lovers that *that* is not what women's liberation is all about, then gradually find that they can love each other in ways that make possible for the first time the development of their own real potential as human beings?

These apparent contradictions are the product of honest appraisal of personal and collective experience at a particular moment in history. They are a recognition of the power that existing institutions have over our lives, power to subvert our movement, to channel it, or to neutralize it. Out of the small group and the activity generated by it come new levels of awareness. Only by continually testing our own direction and developing confidence in ourselves can we grow so much in strength that society as it is presently constructed will become obsolete . . . that those who fear and belittle our movement, or seek to control it, will also be forced to change.

2.2.4 Women who are active in the small-group movement are not entirely happy about their activity. Individuals experience crises in their personal lives as vision of their potential grows, and sisters are often unsure of themselves in providing help at such times. Much of the frustration arises from the very real need for leadership and the ambivalence of women about exerting it. I have personally experienced the exhilaration of discovering my own talent for analysis and verbalization only to be cautioned that such skills come at least in part from the possession of class advantages and must not be used irresponsibly or without regard for the validity of the experiences of others whose talents may not be so easily recognized.

To learn humility at the same time that one is learning to develop long-suppressed talents is a difficult process, but the rewards are great. In learning to remain vulnerable and to exercise only those powers which are legitimized by group consent, we risk less the corruption of our personalities and of our politics that is so common in male-defined society. If sisters are not always able to achieve the balance between assertion and assimilation that is necessary to use their own resources well, they are at least willing to discuss these shortcomings among themselves, recognizing that leadership problems cannot be denied, nor can they be resolved by doing away with leaders.

Women who have participated in small-group organizing like to think that they are only responding to what is happening around them, that they are not themselves defining issues or determining policy. We would like to think that our movement is characterized by a lack of "directives," that we are uniquely without an "elite" body. However, at every level subtle pressures are felt by women who have not symbolically and substantively changed their appearance and their behavior to conform with the expectations of sisters whose "consciousness" has been raised to levels not yet experienced by everyone .The wisdom of committed activists should perhaps be more openly conceded, but there is another form of pressure exerted by those whose "conversion" to women's liberation is recent and still somewhat superficial. The wearing of overalls, the denial of interest in cooking, the mocking of romances with men, can be important steps in personal liberation for some women and unimportant or unnecessary for others. It is not always easy to check ourselves against false pride.

Again, the recognition of such problems and the open discussion of these in evaluation sessions (usually occurring at the end of each women's meeting, large or small) is part of the new politics of self-criticism that characterizes the small-group movement. The giving of support for the exercise of new freedoms and the offering of criticism to encourage continued growth can easily degenerate into a kind of mindless pressure to imitate each other . . . and this, we are coming to realize, is not where our liberation lies.

2.2.5 So there are some real reasons to appraise the small-group movement critically even if one is committed to liberation. One of the ways individuals have dealt with these realities has been to seek participation in small groups only with others who claim no power over them. And this more often than not means that men can not successfully meet with women, that blacks can not successfully meet with whites, that young can not successfully meet with old (in the case of

women, youth more often means power), that formally educated can not successfully meet with those who are not formally educated, et cetera. This is not an article of faith. This is just the way it seems to work out. Divisions that the wealthy rulers of America have created to keep us apart are doing just that. We are, therefore, working each in our own ways, and we find to our astonishment that we are moving in the same direction.

When we do find power games occurring in our groups, some have devised techniques for undoing them. For instance, many groups choose a facilitator for each meeting so that new leaders can replace "natural" leaders . . . usually to everyone's benefit. One group put slips of paper in a hat, to be withdrawn one at a time as each member spoke. No more than a given number could be withdrawn by anyone until the process was repeated.

2.2.6 Out of the small groups, working collectives are often born. Many of the newspapers and journals which circulate among movement women are written by people who did not have previous experience as professional writers but whose talents had been used dutifully reporting family activities to in-laws or writing letters and memos which appeared under the names of their husbands or bosses. When women put out newsletters and compile anthologies on women's liberation, they cannot depend on any one of their group to perform the secretarial function. It is assumed that if one can write, one can also paste and cut, and the end product is less important than the process by which it is achieved. The art of printing, and of repairing printing machines, is becoming common knowledge among women who come out of the small-group movement. Activity is seen as a reward in itself when it is self-directed, and sisters try not to accord special privileges to those who have the time and talent to produce creatively.

What about the conduct of such women when they come together in larger and more heterogeneous groups for discussion and action? I have attended perhaps half a dozen regional conferences of such women and have participated in the formation of several "coalitions," one in Detroit and another in Berkeley. In all of these gatherings the small-group experience was carried over into the larger meeting. Women met together in small discussion groups around issues that anyone felt to be important. Often signs would be put up in a given space to declare an interest and women who shared such an interest would come together and find a quiet place to meet. Or, alternatively, "issues for discussion" would be posted centrally and people would break up into small groups to discuss all of them before coming together in a larger meeting to decide on actions. In both cases, reporters would be designated in each group to report back to the larger meeting. When more formal panels were planned (as at regional conferences), or when workshops were planned in advance, notice would be sent out to everyone on the mailing list inviting the participation of all women who felt they had something to share on a given topic. There was no screening process. In the rare cases where specific women were invited to speak to the entire gathering, they were given respect but no special treatment or honor. Their appearance was seen as an opportunity to hear a point of view not well represented in the gathering rather than as a recognition of special service to the movement. People brought written material with them for distribution, again without screening, and anyone could use duplicating equipment.

2.2.7 In no case have I seen coalition groups or conferences that grew out of small-group activity elect officers for the organizations that grew out of their meetings. Usually people volunteer to carry out specific responsibilities (i.e. planning of particular actions or of another meeting, or publication of a newsletter or other communication). Collectives already in existence in one locale sometimes undertake a specific function one time around, with the expectation that new collectives can replace them in the future. If a chairwoman is needed (as for a local coalition meeting) to facilitate the next meeting, she is usually chosen by lot. If speakers or organizers are needed to meet with new groups or to appear at public gatherings, experienced women are paired with those who are less experienced so that many people are given a chance to develop their leadership skills.

The activity of caucusing is rare at women's liberation meetings or conferences. Instead, women with common interests simply meet together to plan their own actions, and attempt to persuade others to join them. Critiques of the activities of particular collectives sometimes resemble caucusing behavior, but when these have taken the form of hostile response and counter-response it has usually been, in my observation, an activity carried on by an organization originating outside the small-group

movement in opposition to the less-structured and less-ideological feminists, or vice versa. An example of such a battle was the critique that small-group women around the country made of the "Vancouver Conference" with Vietnamese women, a conference that was organized by "anti-imperialist" women who were working in white-male-left groups, or who retained the ideology from these groups and sought to share this with selected (specially invited) feminists.

2.2.8 In Detroit, women who disagreed with the approach of the "anti-imperialist" women, but who also disagreed with its total repudiation as published by local sisters in the *Fourth World Manifesto*, called a meeting of interested women to discuss the question of the relationship between Marxism and feminism. A smaller group has continued since then to discuss this question weekly, and intends to publish a statement of their analysis. Such disciplined activity growing out of a basically anarchist structure is not unusual in the women's movement.

Never have I seen any effort to squelch spontaneity at a large meeting called by small-group women. Women will bring plays they have written in the hope that someone will volunteer to practice and present them to the gathering, and the play is subjected to rewriting up until the last minute. After the play has been given, it is duplicated for distribution to those who saw it, identified as that performed at such-and-such-a-time-and-place, with others invited to take it from there. Sometimes the original author is credited and sometimes not. Women are not all of one mind about credit for authorship, having been "deprived" of such for so long, and having recognized the need for individuals to take responsibility for their own views. There is a gradual move, however, toward identification by first name only, or toward collective authorship. Women who write are not prone to endlessly quote each other to establish authority for their views, but footnote their material only when sources of new information need to be identified. Exceptions to these practices exist mainly in cases where women are dependent for a living on what they sell to the media.

Which brings us to the question of survival. Few of us manage to live our daily lives with complete devotion to learning rather than to Truth, with trust in the collective intelligence, and with a desire to draw out rather than to put down. But this is because our lives are not self-contained within the movement. Some of us are poor, some of us are angry; some of us hate our children and our bosses and our parents and our husbands and the lawyers and doctors and corporations that feed on our misery. Beyond survival, we need to exercise collective power in restructuring the institutions that produced those hatreds, and we have much to learn about that effort. But in our own comradely relationships we are working our way beyond the politics that grow out of hatred and fear and we are creating our own style of interaction. The promise of that style is the only real faith that we possess.

Carol Andreas, Ph.D.
Merritt College
Oakland, California

THE CASE FOR A WOMAN PRESIDENT

2.3 The ultimate political office in the United States is that of President. As proof of equality the woman candidate for political office can like her male counterpart, consider it the ultimate and final goal of any career in elective office. Caroline Bird, a widely published author and editor, gives a detailed historical account of attempts to elect women candidates to the presidency. The key consideration is whether the success of a woman candidate would best be served by her running as the head of a third party appealing to the natural majority of women voters over men, or running as the nominee of the Democratic or Republican parties.

The objections raised against the candidacy of a woman are interesting as they depict the various attitudes in the society as a whole and specifically the views of those active and interested in the political sphere. With the other changes in the role and status of women coming about in society the candidacy of a woman is a topic of concern to many members of the women's liberation movement. It will become increasingly important to the politicians and the planning agencies of the major political parties.

2.3.1 The possibility of a woman becoming President of the United States in the latter half of the 20th century has become not a question of "if" but "when." One factor has been the success of Golda Meir and Indira Gandhi, Prime Ministers of Israel and India. Their triumphant leadership through wars and crises of all kinds has done much to dispel misgivings about entrusting women with power. American women, as this is written, have attained every stronghold in our government except the Supreme Court and the White House. With women an actual numerical majority, most of them favoring "the thrust for equality," and the National Women's Political Caucus functioning, even the most conservative males concede that it is only a matter of time before these doors are also open to them.

The year 1972 saw three Congresswomen, Reps. Shirley Chisholm and Bella Abzug of New York and Patsy T. Mink of Hawaii, aspire to the Democratic nomination. Mrs. Chisholm, the first black Congresswoman, waged a valiant primary campaign with slender resources. All of which was in considerable contrast to the improbable humor with which many, especially males, long had associated the idea of a woman President.

There was a woman candidate for President, of course, exactly a century earlier. She was Mrs. Victoria Woodhull. Born Claflin in Ohio, she and her sister, Tennessee dabbled in clairvoyance, journalism and finally suffrage. Under the sponsorship of Commodore Cornelius Vanderbilt, they arrived in New York, started a stock brokerage firm, and then *Woodhull and Claflin's Weekly*. Of Victoria, sometimes called "the siren of Wall Street", Ishbel Ross, a leading authority on the history of the Period, wrote: "She was magnetic raffish, eerie, heralding the freedom of women, preaching free love, basking in the counsels of the great financiers and using the honest craft of journalism for her own strange ends. . . . Her editorials urged independence in woman. All manifestations of feminism were applauded." In 1871, she became the first woman to address a Congressional Committee, presenting a "Memorial" to the Senate Judiciary Committee, contending the 14th Amendment gave women the right to vote. Before she concluded, two surprised suffrage leaders, Susan B. Anthony and Isabella Beecher Hooker (a sister of the Rev. Henry Ward Beecher) having read of Victoria's plans in a newspaper, also appeared. Victoria was nominated for President next year by the Equal Rights Party which nominated Frederick Douglass, the black leader, for Vice President. Victoria's effort split the suffrage movement. Susan B. Anthony and 15 women were arrested after voting not for Victoria but for General U. S. Grant who also defeated

Horace Greeley. In revenge for slights by the Beecher family, Victoria exposed in *Woodhull and Claflin's Weekly*, the great scandal of the generation, the Rev. Henry Ward Beecher's love affair with Elizabeth Tilton, the wife of one of his church members. In 1892, Victoria returned to the United States from England, where she had started a magazine, the *Humanitarian*. A group of 50 women nominated her as the Presidential candidate of the Humanitarian Party. Grover Cleveland triumphed in the election. Victoria went back to England and, while women won suffrage and advanced on many fronts, many years passed before there was again talk of a woman for President.

2.3.2   The office is an awesome one, in the words of Prof. Harold J. Laski, a British observer, "both more and less than king: both more and less than a prime minister." In 1934, Eleanor Roosevelt said: "I do not think we have yet reached the point where the majority of our people would feel satisfied to follow the leadership and trust the judgment of a woman as President." In 1952, Maine's Senator Margaret Chase Smith was asked what she would do if she awoke one morning in the White House. She replied: "I'd go straight to Mrs. Truman and apologize. Then I would go home." In 1960, Mrs. Smith declined the second place on the Republican ticket because campaigning would mean breaking her near-perfect record of attendance at Senate roll calls. But times change. In 1964, the lady from Maine opened a campaign for the Republican nomination for the Presidency of the United States. Her name was put in nomination at the Republican National Convention and she polled votes second only to the landslide nomination of Richard Nixon, with whom she steadfastly refused to run in second place. Since she was the first woman to be put in nomination for the Presidency at the national convention of a major party, and came closer to the Presidency than any other American woman, I asked her in 1972 how she felt about a woman President. Margaret Smith is cool and alert. She has beaten arthritis with artificial hip joints. A former secretary herself, she runs a quiet, super-efficient office that manages to get everyone in to see the Senator without wasting a single moment of her time. "I'm not a feminist," she told me. "I don't hold with Women's Liberation. I announced in 1964 because I wanted to be President. I don't think the sex of a President matters. A woman President would have the same

interests and objectives as any other President. Sex doesn't matter in politics."

2.3.3   When you think about it, this is equal opportunity, and as such, squarely down the track of American democracy. When Gallup polls ask, "If your party nominated a generally well-qualified woman for President, would you vote for her?" it sounds like a civics test, and most people say "yes". The trouble is that a high proportion of those who say "yes" to the general principle can't think of a single woman who is well qualified.

Still, it's something to get approval in the abstract. It leaves the White House door ajar for some not impossible she of the future. In a statement intended to mollify feminists, President Nixon once said he thought there might be a woman president in 50 years—a date with the signal political advantage of being too far in the future for anyone then active to take seriously. Far more hopeful is the steady increase in the majority who would vote for a woman president whenever the poll has been repeated and a 1972 survey of women found 37 per cent who thought a woman could be elected President in the next decade. The growing majority who would vote for a woman President shows that the hoary objections to a woman President are evaporating. Many of them now get into the news only when they are being refuted. Let's take a look at the leading objections:

2.3.4   1. *Women aren't physically or emotionally strong enough to stand the strain of the Presidency.* In 1968, no less an insider on the subject than Margaret Truman said she didn't think most women were physically able to take the "kind of beating a President must take, day after day" and she went on to add that most women were too emotional and not logical enough for the job. Nothing happened. In 1970, all hell broke loose when Dr. Edgar F. Berman, a member of the Democratic Party's Committee on National Priorities, remarked that "raging hormonal storms" disqualified women from the Presidency and was so indiscreet as to wonder aloud what might happen to the nation if tough decisions like the one President Kennedy had to make at the Bay of Pigs were entrusted to a menopausal woman "subject to the curious mental aberrations of that age group." Women were outraged. Physicians both male and female pointed out that medically speaking, women can stand more stress than men, and that in any case the "raging hormonal storms" Dr. Berman feared were neither universal, necessary, nor as hazardous as the ailments affecting men of Presidential age. Dr. Berman was kicked off the Democratic Party Committee.

2.3.5 2. *A woman President couldn't fulfill her obligation as Commander in Chief of the Armed Forces.* There's plenty of evidence that women can and do whatever has to be done in war. Israeli women soldiers have distinguished themselves in combat and the Israeli Army hasn't suffered because it takes orders from a woman head of state. In our own Congress, one of the most respected military specialists is Senator Margaret Chase Smith, who once had defense Secretary Charles Wilson on the griddle for refusing to tell who ordered the Air Force cut from 143 to 120 wings.

2.3.6 3. *A real woman wouldn't want to be President.* This is what President Eisenhower must have had in mind when he said that there was no reason why a woman couldn't be President of the United States, but "most women had better sense than to want the job." Lurking behind the cryptic crack is the assumption that a woman couldn't function as President and still maintain a normal sex life, the theme of a 1964 movie. The silliness of this position is apparent when it is stated explicitly. A great many women now realize that it is just as easy for a woman to be aggressive in public and sexy in private as it has always been for men.

2.3.7 4. *Women won't follow a woman President.* This simply applies to the Presidency the objection that you can't make a woman the boss because the other women won't work for her. The Gallup polls show that more men than women say they would vote for a well-qualified woman for President, but the sex gap in opinion on this, is steadily collapsing. The reason is simple. The resentment of successful women is strongest among the declining group of women of limited education and/or work experience. Men in general are more apt to favor a woman president than women in general simply because more men than women have an opportunity to see women performing competently outside the home. There are some unsuspected assets in the traditional image of what women are like that could make the job of a woman President easier in some ways than if she were a man. Whether it's true or not, women are generally credited with being the peace makers, the mediators. They are free from the limitations as well as the advantages of membership in the ruling establishment. They are permitted to be more candid, more unpredictable, and more compassionate with the underdog than men. Finally, a woman who succeeded in becoming

President would strike people as so specially gifted that she would pack more weight than an equally well qualified man.

It is no more cynical for a woman to use these "image" advantages than it is for a politician to capitalize on the accident of birth in a log cabin. On the contrary, image-making is the name of the political game. If it is to be reformed, let it be reformed after women get enough political power under the present system to share in the job of changing it. Margaret Chase Smith owes her enviable reputation for independence in part to the fact that she keeps out of smokefilled rooms, or, for that matter, Washington parties. She spends the time she saves on her home work, making her a formidable opponent in committee action. When asked what she would do if she were President, she said she would abolish national conventions in favor of primaries as a method of choosing each party's candidate for the presidency, and she would also abolish the electoral college in favor of direct election of the President. Both reforms would sweep away complexities which permit backroom politicians to make secret deals. Maurine Neuberger, the former Democratic Senator from Oregon had similar proposals. The first thing she would do if elected President would be to change the system of financing Presidential campaigns so that the next President would come into office free of any obligations to his contributors.

2.3.8 *A woman can "get away with murder" in public life.* This is, of course, an overhang from the notion that women are to be forgiven for lapses from decorum because they don't know the rules, but smart women have used it to good advantage. Sex shouldn't make a difference in politics, but of course it does, and females have some unexpected advantages. Should a woman use her sex on the job? Just you watch. When we get a woman President, she's going to behave just like every other President. She's going to use everything she's got.

"Could you be President?" a woman's magazine in 1972 asked its readers saying "the possibility seems very real." Those who replied to the male-concocted questions with "honest and straight forward" answers without making "a major item" of your femininity or attacking (and thus antagonizing) men, were told "you have an excellent chance to gain the White House!"

Caroline Bird
Consulting Editor
The New Woman
Poughkeepsie, New York

WOMEN IN WORLD POLITICS

2.4 There is a principle of history which teaches that no great, new idea exists in a vacuum, it comes to fruition at the time humanity is ready for it in many places and through many minds. By this means innovations come about in the ebb and flow of human events. Certainly the awakening consciousness of women is not limited to the western world. Dr. Gruberg lists the many women around the world who hold both the responsibility and authority for guiding their nations destinies. Few of these women are in their positions by force of the liberation movement, however, all of them are aware of it and most are in sympathy with it. If the movement succeeds in challenging a majority of women to their political and economic potential, these leaders will be joined by many more of their sisters. What the total effect will be on world alignments and international affairs is impossible to state. However, since the liberation movement calls for a rejection of traditional masculine establishment roles it will certainly make alternatives to the traditional impasses of international relations more feasible.

2.4.1 One of the perplexing tasks of one who wishes to assess the accomplishments of women in American politics is the culling of numerous sources to come up with a tally on the significant political offices held by American women. For a table of this data see below §2.4.26. Perhaps even more difficult is the construction of a record of the attainments of women in the political life of other nations. Cross-cultural study will help to separate those factors which are nurtural from those that are natural. It will help to answer the question: To what extent is the subordinate political status of women in the United States the result of the fact that they are women? As our survey shifts from country to country and region to region, we'll encounter considerable variance in women's place in the traditional, transitional, modern, and revolutionary societies. For the most part, though, our report will record the limited extent to which women have occupied high-level elective and appointive positions.

2.4.2 There have always been female dynasts of distinction, from Boadicea to Matilda, Elizabeth I, and Victoria, from Cleopatra to Maria Theresa, and Catherine. There have also been the female grey eminences like Catherine di Medici, Lady Wu, and the Empress Tzu-Hsi, and the kings' mistresses, especially those who dominated French diplomacy in the reign of Louis XV. Women rulers in the Renaissance were as talented in intrigue as their male counterparts. Throughout history there have also been charismatic, legendary female leaders like Joan of Arc. An accident of birth or a crisis has often enabled a woman of ability to shine in a male society. Even in recent years, Elizabeth II of the United Kingdom, Wilhelmina and Juliana of the Netherlands, and Charlotte of Luxembourg have been chiefs of state in countries where few women achieve high governmental positions.

2.4.3 In a new country, where those with professional training are few or where there are no incumbents to be dislodged and the political situation is fluid, women stand a better chance to attain office. In the Weimar Republic, Germany, where women got the vote at the same time as in the United States, the first Reichstag contained 41 women, whereas only five women were elected to the U.S. Congress between 1916 and 1924. In the first general election in Japan after World War II, 39 females won election to the House of Representatives. Women found it easier to succeed politically in the western United States than in the long-settled states. Perhaps it was the frontier reality, where women did not lead sheltered lives, together with the need for and recognition of women's contributions, and possibly a spirit of egalitarianism and chivalry, or even a desire to induce migration of eligible women to the Rocky Mountain West that brought a number of western states to award the ballot to women earlier than they were enfranchised elsewhere. Fourteen countries besides the United States gave women political rights about the time of World War I. Yet, according to a writer in 1947, the U.S. lagged behind in the percentage of women in 10 of 12 national legislatures. These post-war events, however, were somewhat misleading. Sometimes, as in France, there was a new constitution and a desire for a fresh start after years of occupation and war. There may even have been an electoral feature, such as proportional representation or reserved seats, which made it easier for women to be elected.

United Kingdom

2.4.4 Even in a fairly traditional country like England, women are making a more important contribution to the public welfare than in America.

There have been less than 90 women in Commons since American-born Lady Astor blazed the way in 1919. However, they have played a more significant part in the governing of Britain than their American counterparts.

As was true in the U.S., a number of lady M.P.'s, such as Lady Astor who inherited her seat when her husband moved to the House of Lords, were abetted by voter familiarity with the family name. However, much more than in the U.S., these female lawmakers such as Lady Megan Lloyd George and Nye Bevan's Jennie Lee, established their own bases of political power. At present 26 women sit in the 630-member House of Commons and 38 peeresses in the 1,063-seat House of Lords.

Only twice have women made the American cabinet. Franklin Roosevelt appointed Frances Perkins his Secretary of Labor (ranking ninth in a cabinet of nine) and Dwight Eisenhower's first Secretary of Health, Education, and Welfare was Ovita Culp Hobby, number ten in a cabinet of ten.

In Britain five women have attained cabinet rank and even more have held non-cabinet ministries. Margaret Bondfield, a charter member of the Labour Party, was elected to Parliament in 1923, the same year she was elected Chairman of the Trades Union Congress (a position equivalent to that of George Meaney in the U.S.). From 1929 to 1931 she was Minister of Labour. In 1945 Ellen Wilkinson became the second woman to reach Cabinet rank when she was named Minister of Education. Florence Horsbrugh (later Lady Horsbrugh), a Conservative, was during World War II Parliamentary Secretary to the Ministry of Health. In 1945 she held this position for the Ministry of Food and in 1951, when her party returned to power, she became Minister of Education.

The most successful of the female M.P.'s has been Barbara Castle. Former Prime Minister Harold Wilson once called her "the best man in the Cabinet." She entered the Cabinet in 1964 as Minister of Overseas Development, ranking 23rd in a cabinet of 23. By 1965 she had moved up to be Minister of Transport. After doing a fine job of reducing road deaths (a 1968 public opinion poll into the popularity of government ministers placed her at the top) she was promoted to the newly created post of Secretary of State for Employment and Productivity, in charge of enforcing controls on wages and prices. This made her number three in the government. Mrs. Castle used the latter post to promote female equality. She announced that she would introduce legislation guaranteeing equal pay for women workers by the end of 1975. Mrs. Castle, the wife of a newspaper editor, stood a very good chance of succeeding Harold Wilson as leader of the Labour Party. She had already been Chairman of the party. Whereas in the U.S. neither major party has ever had a woman national chairman—the best they've gotten has been the auxiliary role of Assistant or Vice Chairman—from 1926 to 1966, 18 women served one-year terms as chairmen of the three British parties. In 1969, though, Mrs. Castle was the Wilson Administration's scapegoat when an effort to regulate wildcat strikes through legislation ran into strong union and party opposition. The Conservative government, which won the election of 1970, had Mrs. Margaret Thatcher as Minister of Education and Science and Lady Tweedsmuir in the sub-cabinet office of Secretary of State for Scotland. Mrs. Thatcher, whose husband is an oil executive, entered Parliament in 1959. She's popular in the Conservative party and is one of the three or four best known members of the Heath government, in part because of her support for birching of unruly pupils and capital punishment. In the wings, as the Labour Party's shadow cabinet Home Secretary is Mrs. Shirley Williams. In 1971 Mrs. Castle had lost her seat in the shadow cabinet. Two female civil servants, Dame Mary Smieton and Dame Evelyn Sharp, rose to be permanent secretaries of ministries. Miss Sharp in Housing was an expert on town and country planning and a champion of green belts. She had a reputation, very rare in British bureaucracy, for calling a spade a spade.

British women have also moved ahead of their American sisters in the judiciary. In the mid-sixties Elizabeth K. Lane became the United Kingdom's first female High Court Judge. Yet, a study of the status of British women concluded that "female social awareness is still too limited . . . apathy, diffidence and inhibitions . . . still handicap women after centuries of subjection. Only when a great band of women have learned to accept the challenge of responsibility, and from every class and neighborhood demand a share in policymaking as they once demanded the vote, is the proportion of men and women in politics likely to reach a reasonable equality." Though eight million British women are now working, only 2.7 per cent are in managerial positions of any kind. While 42 per cent of the men earn £15 a week or more, only 1% of women do so.

The Second Sex in Scandinavia

2.4.5 Scandinavian women are among the most emancipated in the Western World. Legally there are almost no distinctions between them and the males. Despite this, though, there is discrimination and stereotyping. Theoretically women have a chance to reach the top of the social ladder. In practice few do. Part of the limitations on female advancement stem from male and female traditional notions of the division of responsibilities of the sexes. As long as women are content with the traditional female roles, there will be demarcated areas that are predominately male and others that are essentially female. A ''sex-role debate'' has been going on in Scandinavia over the loss to society caused by adherence to the customary patterns. Young people especially are conscious of the discrimination. Everywhere women are seen in atypical occupations. Women's rights groups, trade unions, and political parties are contributing to the breakdown of the old arrangements.

2.4.6 Finland elected 19 women to Parliament in 1906. By 1967 there were 34 (17%). The entrance of the first woman in the Finnish cabinet occurred in 1927. Since then, seven other women have served.

2.4.7 Denmark was the first Scandinavian country to have a woman cabinet member (Mrs. Nina Bang, Minister of Education, 1924–26). After World War II it became customary to have at least one female cabinet member (usually assigned to social welfare, education, health, family relations or religious activities—that is, to women's traditional spheres—rather than to economics, industry, trade, agriculture or international relations. In 1963 Denmark had women as Minister of Ecclesiastical Affairs, Permanent Under-Secretary to the Ministry of Education, Justice of the Supreme Court, Ambassador to Switzerland, and Counselor to the Permanent Mission to the United Nations. Nineteen out of 171 members (11.2%) of the Danish Parliament are female.

2.4.8 Norway has about 10% of its lawmakers who are female. Norwegian women, like their counterparts elsewhere, have strengthened the conservative elements in politics with their votes, yet most of the women in the Storting came from the Social Democratic party. In 1966 Mrs. Schweigard-Selmer became Norwegian Minister of Justice. Quite a change from the customary post of Minister for Family and Consumer Affairs. Swedish women have gone the furthest of women in the region. About 15% of Parliament are

women (48 of 350 seats). Mrs. Alva Myrdal, wife of the noted economist, was Minister for Disarmament Questions and is now Minister of Church Affairs. She headed the Swedish delegation to Geneva disarmament talks, played a prominent part in U.N. arms debates and helped negotiate the nuclear test ban treaty. Mrs. Myrdal also served five years as Sweden's Ambassador to India. Another woman, Camilla Odhnoff, is Consultative Minister for Family Affairs.

In 1968 Mrs. Ingrid Gaerde-Widemar was appointed a Swedish Supreme Court Judge. Eva Remens was chairman of the Stockholm City Council. Her predecessor, Mrs. Inga Thorsson, the first woman elected to the City Council, became mayor in 1959. Even Icelandic women have played a part in politics. In 1963 Miss Ragnhildur Helgadottir became Iceland's first woman speaker of Parliament.

Women Under European Communism

2.4.9 Contrary to the popular impression, while women play a much larger part in the professions such as medicine, engineering, law, etc., in the Soviet world than in the West, they exercise a relatively weak influence on the life of the State and the Party. Leadership, even in the lowest rungs of the Soviet system, almost always remains in the hands of men. *Pravda* in 1965 deplored the fact that the percentage of women in leading positions in Soviet economic and political life was decreasing instead of getting larger. Though over 20 per cent of the Communist party membership are female, women play only a very modest part in the work of the Party Congresses. In 1962, for example, only 10 women were among the 330 members and candidates for membership elected to the Central Committee of the Party. Female representation seems better on the governmental bodies but their purpose under democratic centralism is for a demonstrative (symbolic) rather than a legislative function. Women make up about 40% of the deputies in the village Soviets, about one-third of the membership in the Supreme Soviets of the member Republics of the USSR, and about 27 per cent of the Supreme Soviet of the USSR. Yet, as indicative of where the power rests, women are rare in the 33-member Presidium of the Supreme Soviet. Under Khrushchev, a longtime friend, Mme. Ekaterina A. Furtseva was Minister of Culture and Maria Kovrigina was Minister of Health.

Mme. Furtseva was dropped from the party Politburo but is still Minister of Culture. She is the wife of a deputy minister of foreign affairs, Nikolai P. Firyubin.

The only exception to women's limited participation is their role in the law courts and people's courts. Women are about a third of the judges in the people's courts. They are about 40% of the judges in the law courts. One female judge sits on the 20-member Soviet Supreme Court, which does not equal its U.S. counterpart in importance or power.

2.4.10　As for women's role in the other European Communist countries: Women are 12 per cent of the deputies in Poland. At the local level women constituted about 15 per cent of the councillors. One woman was a member of the Council of State, 10 directed departments in various ministries, and three were judges on the Supreme Court. In Czechoslovakia, 70% of the district court judges and 30% of the counselors are women. Hungary has 65 female deputies, Bulgaria 71, and Rumania 67. Right after the Second World War, Ana Pauker was the most powerful Communist in Rumania. Probably the second most important Communist in East Germany in the fifties was Hilda Benjamin. The wife of the present East German Communist Party's First Secretary, Erich Honecker, is Margot Feist, now Minister of National Education, the only woman member of the Cabinet. Yugoslavia has had several female ministers and three ambassadors. However, Yugoslav women would like to gain more representation in the government and Communist party. Despite having almost 20% of the seats in the Federal Assembly, there is no woman in the presidium and only 5 women out of the 190 members of the powerful Central Committee. Yet there are many more women than men in the country.

Women Under Asian Communism

2.4.11　China has had several powerful women in recent years, including the sisters, Mme. Sun Yat-Sen and Mme. Chiang Kai-shek. The latest to derive authority from her husband's image is the wife of Chairman Mao Tse-tung, Chiang Ching. This former actress and private secretary to the Communist leader emerged in 1966 from years of obscurity, to assume a key role in the Great Proletarian Cultural Revolution. Prior to the

Cultural Revolution, women were not conspicuous in the Chinese Communist hierarchy. Soong Ching-ling, the widow of Dr. Sun Yat-sen, and honorary chairman of the All-China Democratic Women's Federation, and Tung Pi-wu were deputy heads of state but without significant political influence. There were only 14 women in the 279-member central committee, five of them because they were wives of "senior comrades." Women occupied 17% of the 3,037 seats in the National People's Congress. The last Congress adjourned seven years ago. They were 2.8 per cent of the mayors and magistrates and 3 per cent of the department heads and bureau directors. At the local level women deputies made up 20% of all people's deputies. Women were 10% of the Communist Party membership.

2.4.12　In the wake of the purges and power struggles, the wives of five Communist leaders ranked as powerful political personalities in their own right. The most important was Chiang Ching, sole adviser to the People's Liberation Army purge group. In October, 1967, she was in the 19th position on the presidium list. By May Day, 1968, she was ninth and later she was listed in sixth place. The wife of Defense Minister Lin Piao, Mao's heir, Yeh Chun, rose from complete obscurity to the No. 12 position. Miss Yeh owed her rise to power to a friendship that developed between her and Miss Chiang concurrently with the alliance forged between their husbands against the chief of state, Liu Shao-chi. Throughout the Cultural Revolution, Premier Chou En-lai's wife, Teng Ying-chao, who had been prominent long before Mao's wife emerged as a major political figure, remained withdrawn from the public eye, as if not wanting to compete with Miss Chiang. The wives of two other senior officials, Tsai Chang, married to Li Fu-chun, and Tsao Yi-ou, married to Kang Sheng, are also members of the presidium of the party congress. Miss Tsao rose to political prominence since the Cultural Revolution whereas Miss Tsai like Miss Teng had worked with their husbands to form a Paris branch of the Chinese Communist Party in the nineteen twenties. It was said that Kang may have owed his rise to power to the fact that he befriended Chiang Ching when she was being virtually ostracized by other party officials. Other Asian Communist governments have also had some conspicuous women leaders. The head of the Viet Cong's delegation to the Paris peace talks is Mrs. Nguyen Thi Binh. In North Vietnam women constitute about one-fourth of the parliament.

Women in Western Europe

2.4.13   Despite the importance of the female vote, women have continued to operate on the fringes of power in Western Europe. Most voters, male and female, believe that women belong in the home. In such traditionalist countries as Portugal and Spain, women legislators are rare. Yet even in modern countries such as France and West Germany, women play a marginal political role. There were more women elected under the Spanish Republic than subsequently. (Women under Franco have had the vote only since 1967 and they vote only for so-called family representatives.) Neither Spain nor Portugal, with only five and three females respectively in their national legislature, have women in high-level administrative positions. The cultural model for a woman is to be what a man wants her to be. Adjacent Andorra in 1971 let women vote for the first time but they still could not run for public office.

2.4.14   The number of women elected to the National Assembly in France has steadily decreased, from 40 in 1946 to a low of 11 in 1967. In 1936 under the Popular Front, France had three women secretaries of state but in the Fourth Republic (1946–58), there were only one female minister and two secretaries of state. A major factor in the reduction of the number of women deputies was the setback of the Communist party in the first Assembly of the Fifth Republic. Among those not returned were 18 women. Following de Gaulle's election as President in 1959, the first Government of the Fifth Republic had a woman, Mademoiselle Nafissa Sid Cara, an Algerian Muslim, as Secretary for Algerian Affairs. De Gaulle's second government did not include any woman of cabinet rank. The present Cabinet includes one woman. Sometimes there is publicity given to there being over 400 local councils in France headed by women mayors. However, this is out of 38,000 such positions. Yet there were some instances of advancement. Though women could become lawyers since 1900, it was only since 1946 that they could be judges. In the mid-sixties, out of 6,639 lawyers practicing before the Court of Appeals, 1,408 were women. Five per cent of the judges in the Superior Courts were women as were 10% of the judges in the courts of the first instance.

2.4.15   In West Germany women are 55% of the eligible voters, about a quarter of the members of political parties, but only 6.6% of the members of the Bundestag, a 2.1% drop since 1919, and only

6 to 8% of those in state assemblies. In 1966 the Dutch Finance Minister, Anne Vondeling, was a woman.

Throughout Europe it appears that the percentage of women officials as against men is inversely proportionate to the importance of the positions they occupy. The first post-war Italian Parliament had 43 women. By 1963 there were only 25 female deputies out of 596 and three women senators out of 249. The only high post held by an Italian woman was under secretary of the Ministry of Public Education. In 1971 there were 16 women in the 630-member Chamber of Deputies and 8 in the 322-member Senate. The Italian distaff lawmakers, nevertheless, were able to spearhead some changes in legislation. Nilde Jotti, a Communist and widow of the late party leader Palmiro Togliatti, and Maria Eletta Martini, a Christian Democrat, took leading parts in writing the 1971 reform of Italian family law which did away with child marriages, the dowry, discrimination against children born out of wedlock, and other archaic provisions which were still in force. Senator Tullia Carettoni of the Independent Left party, wife of Rome's Superintendent of Antiquities, and a Socialist Senator introduced in 1971 Italy's first bill for the regulation of false ancient coins. She had previously campaigned for legislation to combat forging, altering or reproducing art works for illegal profit.

2.4.16   Ireland's legislature also has a female corporal's guard though a woman has served as Minister of Labor, two have been Lord Mayor of Dublin, and one was Eire's Minister to Switzerland. Switzerland, a masculine stronghold, did not give women the right to vote nationally till 1971, though a few cantons had earlier enfranchised females. Nevertheless, in 1968 Mrs. Lise Girardin was elected Mayor of Geneva, the first woman city mayor in the history of the country. In 1971 Mrs. Girardin was the only female elected to the 44-member house of the Swiss parliament along with seven women elected to the 200-member National Council, the lower house out of 263 female candidates. The turnout of women was far less than the men's though women were 55% of the expanded electorate. Prior to the liquidation of Greek democracy by the military, four women were elected to Parliament in 1958 out of 300 seats, two in 1961, one in 1963, and one in 1964. The leading political parties were reluctant to include women candidates on their electoral lists. In 1970 Miss Colette Flesch became mayor of the capital city of the Grand Duchy of Luxembourg. Before entering politics in 1968, when she was elected to Parliament, she had served on the staff of the European Common Market.

Women in the Moslem World

2.4.17   While it is hard to generalize about countries which range from traditional to transitional, modern, and revolutionary, one common element is the subordinate role accorded women. In Turkey the number of women in Parliament has been decreasing with each election. In 1935, under Ataturk's one-party regime, there were 35 women in the Grand National Assembly. By 1963 there were only three in the Assembly and two in the Senate and by 1967 the number had "bounded back" to 8 in the Assembly and 3 in the Senate. Dr. Turkan Akyol became Turkey's first woman Cabinet member in 1971, Minister of Health. As a nonpolitical member of the government, she won praise for promoting birth control and public health programs. The bylaws of Turkey's major political parties require the setting up of women's auxiliaries and the election of at least one woman to the executive council of each party. In 1954 Madama Malahat Ruacan became the first woman appointed judge of the Turkish Supreme Court. The next year she was joined by Nezakat Gorele. The United Arab Republic's first woman minister (for Social Affairs) was appointed in 1963. Iraq also had a woman with the rank of cabinet minister. Algeria's first 190-member Parliament had 10 women deputies. The September 1964 election cut the number to two, one of them the widow of the late Foreign Minister Mohammed Khemisti. Outside the major cities, the National Women's Union is non-existent. On the local level in Algeria, the ruling National Liberation Front discourages women from signing up as members. When they are admitted, they are segregated. No women hold cabinet posts or membership on the 101-member party Central Committee. In 1970 Moroccan women formed a National Union. Among its supporters is Princess Lalla Fatima Zohra. The major problem, according to the princess' private secretary, is that in practice Moroccan women have no legal rights, even though by law they have more rights than European women. Neighboring Tunisia has one woman in its 190-member National Assembly. Women have no vote and are not eligible for election in Jordan, Kuwait, the Northern Region of Nigeria, Saudi Arabia, and Yemen. They

are limited politically by law in Syria.

2.4.18   Pakistan reserved a few seats in its National Assembly for women, 3 from West Pakistan, 3 from East Pakistan. Five seats were set aside for women in each of the Provincial Assemblies. The 1971 election to the ill-fated National Assembly had seven seats allotted to women. The Begum Liaquat Khan, widow of an assassinated Prime Minister, was appointed Pakistani Ambassador to the Netherlands in 1954—the first woman ambassador from a Moslem country. Pakistan has also had a woman as ambassador to Italy. In 1964 Miss Fatima Jinnah, 71-year-old sister of the late Mohamed Ali Jinnah, father of his nation's independence, ran unsuccessfully for the presidency against the incumbent, Mohamed Ayub Khan. Few village women voted in the recent elections for Afghanistan's second democratically chosen Parliament. The reason was that all voters had to produce an identification card with their picture on it, and orthodox Muslim women (and men) refused to be photographed. All four women who had served in the first Parliament were defeated. In 1965 Miss Kobra Noorzai was named Afghanistan's Minister of Public Health, the first woman cabinet member in Afghan history. Indonesian women numbered 20 in a Parliament of 261. They were 40 out of 522 in the Constituent Assembly. Indonesia has had a woman as Minister of Social Affairs and as Minister to Belgium.

Women in Israel

2.4.19   There are only three countries in the world that have women as prime ministers. India's Indira Gandhi; Ceylon's Sirimavo Bandaranaike; and Israel's Golda Meir. All three are democracies and all three premiers are widows. Mrs. Meir has long wielded enormous influence in backstage Israeli politics. Had she been a man she might have attained the premiership earlier. There are few women in the Israeli Knesset (Parliament). In 1965 there were only ten out of 120 members though four of the eight Deputy Speakers were female. Mrs. Meir grew up in Milwaukee and became a schoolteacher. She settled in Palestine after her marriage. She rose from a community council to executive duties with Histradrud, the Zionist general federation of labor. In 1946 she became director of the Jewish Agency's political department, then a sort of shadow foreign ministry. With independence in

1948, Mrs. Meir was sent as Ambassador to Moscow. In 1954–56 she was Minister of Labor. From 1956 to 1966 she was Minister for Foreign Affairs. Mrs. Meir headed Israeli's U.N. delegation several times. As Foreign Minister she formulated the policy of wooing emerging African states and established ties with West Germany. She resigned her governmental post in 1966 and became Secretary General of the majority party, Mapai. She resigned from this position in 1968 after Mapai merged with the other Socialist factions to form the United Labor party. Her political prestige plummeted on the eve of the 1967 Arab-Israeli War when she backed Yigol Allan for Defense Minister instead of Moshe Dayan.

In 1969 she was named Premier, at the age of 70, with the expectation that she would serve only a caretaker term until after the Fall, 1969, elections. However, she proved to be more than a match for her responsibilities. Despite her credentials, though, a letter to *Time* magazine still had to argue in 1969: "Sir: Re: Israeli's New Premier, I resent your necessity to refer to the leader of a nation as the '70 year old grandmother.' Did you ever refer to Johnson by saying 'so said the grandfather'?" There were a lot of "Jewish mother" jokes. Just as novel as a woman prime minister are women in the armed forces. The Commander of Israeli's women's army, Colonel Stella Levy, said: "We're not a bunch of Amazons and we're not off shooting in the fields. We're schooled in the art of self defense, first and foremost. Certainly, it's important for a woman to know how to handle a gun, but most of our girls are rear-guard supportive workers, such as clerks, hospital or signal aides, or teachers."

Asia's Two Women Premiers

2.4.20   A famous Indian writer said when Indira Gandhi first came to power, "Indira is the only man in a Cabinet of old women." The daughter of Nehru was brought up to be in command. Her father's eminence gave her the advantage of an excellent education and personal contact with influential citizens. Like her father she has an imperious will. However, while he was lauded as a statesman, she has been criticized for "acting like a woman, changeable and unpredictable." In 1959 she was elected President of the Indian National Congress Party. In the government of Premier Shastri she was Minister of Iinformation. After Shastri's death in 1966, she was handpicked

by the party leaders to be Prime Minister. The syndicate of power-wielders thought she would be their pliable front. Before long, she had turned the tables on them and crushed their opposition. The party's fortunes had declined from her father's time and, though still unchallenged nationally, decay had set in at the state level. While she blamed the patriarchs for the stagnation, they criticized her flirtation with the left and her undermining of party discipline. The Congress party split with Mrs. Gandhi retaining the support of all but 60 of the 282 party members in the lower house of parliament. In the next national election she won a landslide victory.

Mrs. Gandhi isn't the only woman to hold important political office in India. Her aunt, Mrs. Vijaya Lakshmi Pandit, had been Indian Ambassador to the U.S.S.R., the U.S., and the U.K., and U.N. General Assembly President. In Mrs. Gandhi's cabinet is Mrs. Nandini Satapathy, Minister of State and Deputy Minister attached to the Prime Minister. In the Shastri Government, Mrs. Suchila Nayar was Minister of Health. Nehru's Minister of Health was Rajkumari Amrit Kaur. A number of women have been state governors. Mrs. Sarojini Naidu was governor of the United Provinces. Padmaja Naidu was governor of West Bengal. Mrs. Suchetra Kripalani was elected leader of the Congress legislative party (that is, chief minister) in the state of Uttar Pradesh (population 75 million) in 1963. She was the first woman to serve as chief minister of an Indian state. Women have also held important posts in local government. In 1956 Srimati Sulochana Modi became mayor of Bombay. Three years later Mrs. Aruna Asaf Ali was elected to her second term as mayor of Delhi. By law every village council must have a woman member. Because of the relatively limited number of lawyers in India, women are quite common as magistrates and judges.

2.4.20   After the assassination of her husband in 1959, Mrs. Sirimayo Bandaranaike became Prime Minister of Ceylon, Minister of Defense and External Affairs, and President of the Sri Lanka Freedom Party. From 1946 to 1960 she had been treasurer, vice president, and president of the women's organization of the party. There were two women, including Mrs. Bandaranaike, in the 30-member Senate and two in the 157-member House of Representatives. She was not the first woman in the Ceylanese cabinet. Mrs. Vimala Wijeyewardene, who was appointed Minister of Health in 1956 and Minister of Housing and Local Government in 1959, had that honor. Mrs.

1793699

Bandaranaike's party lost control of the government in the 1965 election but she returned to the premiership in 1970. Before she demonstrated her iron will, she was known along the campaign trail as the "weeping widow." However, a key Western diplomat remarked, "she is a poised, strong-willed, intelligent woman, with charisma for the masses, and her influence over the coalition is enormous."

Women in Asia

2.4.21 We've already looked at the role of women in China, India, Ceylon, and Islamic Asia, but what about female participation elsewhere in Asia? Let's turn our attention to Japan and the Philippines. In the first general election after World War II, 82 women entered races for seats in the Japanese Diet. Thirty-nine won election. Since this initial success, fewer women have attained office, usually about ten each time. Today there are seven female members in the 491-member lower house and 13 in the 252-member upper house. Perhaps the most spectacular thing women did with their vote was lead the fight that abolished legalized prostitution. Two women have served briefly as cabinet members. The first Japanese woman to hold a cabinet position was Mrs. Masa Nakayama, who became Minister of Welfare in 1960. She held the post for four months, until the Premier reshuffled his cabinet. Another woman served as Minister of Science and Technology. Since 1947 a steadily growing proportion of women have been elected to local government assembly seats in prefectures, cities, wards, towns and villages. There are 6 women in the 104-member Philippine House of Representatives and 3 in the 24-member Senate. Locally about 6 per cent of the governors, vice-governors, municipal mayors and vice mayors, and members of legislative bodies are female. Women have held the posts of social welfare administrator, under secretary of commerce, minister-counselor to Italy, and minister-counselor to the Federal Republic of Germany as well as one other ambassadorship.

At present there is speculation that the wife of the Philippine President, Imelda R. Marcos, a former beauty queen, Miss Manila of 1954, will run for the presidency in 1973. Her husband was the first president ever to win re-election. She projects the image of a tireless, charming and effective campaigner by her husband's side and is an indefatigable fund-raiser, a pace-setter in fashion, a patroness of arts and culture, and a crusader for social welfare projects. Marcos himself repeatedly has described his wife as his "secret weapon" in politics and has said that she was worth at least two million votes—just about his margin of victory in the 1969 elections. The two appeared together singing love duets.

Women in Latin America

2.4.22 Latin countries, whether in the Americas or in Europe, have tended to use a double standard in defining the rights and responsibilities of the sexes. Few women have counted for much in the man's world. One possible exception to the last statement was the role of Eva Peron, wife of the Argentinian strongman. She was not a typical first lady. Evita was important in Juan Peron's attaining leadership and helped to keep him there. Her ties with the masses' affection surpassed his. Brazil at last count had only one woman in its 326-member Chamber of Deputies. One of its state governors has been a woman, as have its ambassadors to Costa Rica and Portugal. Two women have served in the Chilean cabinet, in the Ministries of Justice and Education. The province of Yungay has had a woman governor and the city of Santiago two women mayors. A woman has also been Minister to the Netherlands. President Allende's sister, Laura, is a member of the Central Committee of the Chilean Socialist party and is serving her second term in Congress. Women make up 5 per cent of parliament, a percentage which has not varied much in a decade. Sra. Josefina Valencia de Hubach has had an illustrious career in Colombia. She was governor of Cauca Province, one of the first women members of the Constituent Assembly, and a delegate to UNESCO. In 1956 she was named Minister of National Education.

Costa Rica had a single woman in its 57-member Legislative Assembly. Its ambassador to the United Kingdom was also a female. In 1966 President Joaquin Balaguer named a woman as governor of each of the Dominican Republic's 26 provinces. The governorships are more ceremonial than political. A number of women have been mayors of municipalities in Haiti and Peru including Lima, the capital. One measure of modernization in Mexico is the rate at which women are participating in public life. The ruling Party of the Institutionalized Revolution does have a female auxiliary. Women won the franchise in 1952. However, Mexico a few years ago did not have a single woman delegate in its Senate and only six women among the 178 members of the Chamber of Deputies. Today two of the 59 Senators are female as are 11 of the 211 Representatives. A woman was chairman of the Mexican Federal Board of Conciliation and Arbitration. Two women were magistrates on the Supreme Court of Justice. Today Christina Salmoran de Tomayo serves with four male judges. Mrs. Amalia de Castillo Ledon became the first woman to hold a ministerial post when she became under secretary in the Department of Education in 1960. Another woman was under secretary of Cultural Affairs. Women have represented Mexico as ambassadors to Sweden, Finland, and Denmark. The U.S. also has tended to assign its female ambassadors to Scandinavian countries. Two women have served as Panamanian Ministers of Labor, Social Welfare, and Public Health. The Venezuelan National Congress had five women among its 184 members in 1963. Venezuela also had a female Ambassador to Uruguay. A woman was mayor for many years of a Latin American city of half a million. She was Dona Felisa Rincon de Gautier of San Juan, Puerto Rico, the oldest city under the American flag.

In 1938 she became president of the San Juan Committee of the fledgling Popular Democratic Party. In 1940 she married a lawyer. He forbade her accepting the mayoral nomination in 1940 and 1944. But she filled a vacancy in 1946 and won re-election in 1948, 1952, 1956, 1960, and 1964, by vote of the San Juan Board of Commissioners. Senora de Gautier's main concerns were health, sanitation, housing, education, fiestas and celebrations, and acting as a goodwill ambassador. She was a champion of the poor.

Women in the British Commonwealth

2.4.23 Our neighbor to the north, Canada, has had even less of a representation of women in public life than the United States. Both countries enfranchised women at about the same time, although women didn't get the vote in the province of Quebec till 1940. By 1966 there were only four women in the Parliament as Senators, an appointed position, and three as members of Commons, out of 265 seats, making a total since the federal suffrage of 8 and 18. Today there are 6 in the 102-member Senate and only one in the 264-seat House of Commons. Miss Agnes C. Macphail (Labor), the first woman member,

entered the House of Commons in 1921 and was still there in 1940. She had been a teacher. The second woman, Mrs. George Black, did not arrive until 1935 when she succeeded her husband, a former Speaker who had become ill. It wasn't till 1930 that the first woman was appointed to the Senate. Cairine Wilson, whose father had been a Senator and her husband an M.P., was honorary president of the National Federation of Liberal Women of Canada. In 1971 when there were five women in the Senate, a Canadian Royal Commission on the Rights of Women recommended that women be appointed to the Senate on a quota basis. That is, as seats became open, two women from each province should be appointed until a more equitable membership mix is reached.

In 1966 there were only ten women among the 586 members of the provincial (state) legislatures. As in the U.S., women found it easier to win office in the western region. Mrs. Mary Ellen Smith, the widow of a liberal labor leader, became the first widow to succeed to her husband's seat in the provincial legislature of British Columbia. She also became the first woman cabinet minister in the British Empire or on the North American continent and the first woman to serve as Speaker of a legislative house. The first woman to hold cabinet rank in the central government was Mrs. Ellen Fairclough, who was appointed Secretary of State in 1957. The next year she became Minister of Citizenship and Immigration. In 1963 Miss Judy La Marsh was named Minister of National Health and Welfare. She played a major role in shaping important pension and welfare legislation. For much of the period since 1950, the civic affairs of Canada's capital city, Ottawa, were dominated by Miss Charlotte Whitton. She had been executive director of the Canadian Welfare Council when she entered politics to set an example for other women. With loyal female support at the polls she was elected to the four-member Board of Control and from there became deputy mayor and mayor. Canadian women have also held the posts of postmaster-general, civil service commissioner, and ambassador to Austria. Negotiations with Communist China were conducted by Canada's Ambassador to Sweden, Miss Margaret Meagher. Dr. Hilda Bynoe, a practicing physician and mother of two teen-age sons, became the first woman governor of a British Commonwealth when she was named Governor of Grenada in 1968. New Zealand, the first country in the world to give women equal voting rights with men, introduced adult suffrage in 1893 but 40 years passed before a woman was elected to the House of Representatives. At present there are 6 females out of 80 members. Several women have been cabinet members.

Australian women received equal political rights in 1902. However, there are only 2 women (2 senators, no representatives) out of 182 members of the two houses of Parliament (down from the 4 and 1 of a few years before). One Senator, Dame Annabella Rankin, became Minister for Housing in 1966, the first woman in Australian history to administer a federal department. Australia's first woman judge was Justice Roma Mitchell of the Supreme Court of South Australia. There are few women in the Parliament of South Africa but they are conspicuous in their opposition to apartheid. The most outspoken critic of the Government is Mrs. Helen Suzman. Another oppositionist is Catherine Taylor. Miss Leonara Van den Heever, whose father had been judge of Appeal and of the Supreme Court, was appointed an acting judge on the Supreme Court.

Women in Africa

2.4.24   In tribal days women often had great power in many African communities. They sometimes controlled the crown or maneuvered behind the scene. As late as the 19th century about one-third of the Dahomian army consisted of dreaded "Amazon" soldiers, who were forbidden to marry. This contingent was disbanded by the French in 1894 along with the rest of the army. Even today in Ghana, women (the "Mammies") control marketing of commodities.

A familiar tale today in Africa and elsewhere in the developing world is that of Rabia Abdelkader. Like most of Ethiopia's Moslem women, she was illiterate, obedient, and secluded until she came into contact with the Ethiopian Women's Welfare Association. Against her husband's will, she went to the Association's adult vocational school. Her independence so troubled her husband that they were divorced. She studied law at night and became one of the most active members of the Association. Finally, in 1961, she ran for the Chamber of Deputies. She lost but won the next time, in 1965, and was re-elected in 1970. She is one of the three women in the Chamber of Deputies (out of 251 members). Ghana reserves 10 seats for women in its National Assembly of 104 members. One woman, Mrs. Annie Baeta Jiagge, was appointed judge on the high court in

1962 after serving as a circuit judge. Justice Jiagge went on to become Chairman of the United Nations' Commission on the Status of Women. More typical, though, of the status of women in tropical Africa is Nigeria's one woman in its 52-member Senate or Cameroon's one woman in its 100-member National Assembly or Chad's one in 85 or Mali's one in 79 or Sierra Leone's one in 74 or Upper Volta's one in 50. For the first time, in 1969, a woman was elected to the Kenyan Parliament, Mrs. Grace Oniyago, a former mayor of Kisimu on Lake Victoria. The president of the juvenile court in Tananarive, Malagasy Republic, is a woman, as has been the mayor of Freetown, Sierra Leone. Miss Angie Brooks, assistant secretary of state for Liberia, has had a remarkable career at the United Nations, capped by her presidency of the Trusteeship Council and General Assembly. A U.N. report has stated: "In most countries, as in the United States, the percentage of women in high-level official positions is not large in relation to the total number of women in the population." Newly independent and some socially democratic countries have substantial female representation. Traditionalist cultures tend to have few women in prominent or responsible positions.

Women at the U.N.

2.4.25   As we have seen in our stocktaking of women's role around the world, several have represented their nation ably on the international stage.

In 1953 Mrs. Vijaya Lakshmi Pandit, sister of Pandit Nehru, was President of the U.N. General Assembly. In 1969, when it was Africa's geographical turn for the General Assembly presidency, Miss Angie Brooks of Liberia campaigned successfully for the post. In the 15 years that she had represented Liberia at the U.N., Miss Brooks became one of the more familiar and respected diplomats in the body. In various committees and as President of the Trusteeship Council in 1966–67, she championed the new African states. Her candor was regarded by many as refreshing in a forum where nuance is the usual style. Women have also been named to U.S. delegations to the United Nations. The only woman U.S. delegate to the 1945 San Francisco Conference was Dr. Virginia C. Gildersleeve, dean of Barnard College. Miss Gildersleeve had worked with the League of Nations Association and was a founder and two-time president of the International Federation of University Women. The first woman named U.S. Representative to the General Assembly was Mrs. Eleanor Roosevelt in 1946. From 1947 to 1952 she served as U.S. Representative to the U.N. Human Rights Commission and the Economic and Social Council. Mrs. Roosevelt's alternate from 1950 to 1952 was Mrs. Edith S. Sampson of Chicago. She had moved from social worker to probation officer to trial lawyer and had served as chairman of the Executive Committee of the National Council of Negro Women. Other women to serve as alternates in the Truman years were Ruth Bryan Owen Rohde (William Jennings Bryan's daughter, a former Congresswoman and ambassador). Congresswoman Helen Gahagen Douglas, and Anna Lord Strauss, President of the League of Women Voters. Hollywood star Myrna Loy was appointed in 1950 to the U.S. delegation to UNESCO. She served for three and a half years.

President Eisenhower appointed Mrs. Mary Pillsbury Lord to be U.S. Representative to the Commission on Human Rights and alternate to the General Assembly. She served from 1953 to 1961. Mrs. Lord, a social worker whose family had held a number of political offices in Minnesota, was chairman of the U.S. Committee for the U.N. International Children's Emergency Fund and president of the National Health Council. Congresswoman Frances Bolton was a U.N. alternate delegate under Eisenhower, as were actress Irene Dunne and singer Marian Anderson.

The Kennedy-Johnson female U.N. representative was Mrs. Marietta Tree. In 1964 she was given the rank of ambassador and was our representative to the Trusteeship Council and to the Human Rights Commission of the Economic and Social Council. She had long been active in civil rights activities. Her successor in 1965 as U.S. representative to the U.N. Trusteeship Council was Mrs. Eugenie Anderson, former Ambassador to Denmark and Bulgaria. Dr. Belma W. George served as a U.N. alternate under Eisenhower and Kennedy, 1960–62. She had been a social case worker, probation officer, college teacher, educational administrator, community center director, singer, and a newspaper columnist. Mrs. Edison Dick, a board member of many social welfare and foreign relations organizations, was our representative to the Social Commission of the Economic and Social Council. Mrs. Carmel Carrington Marr, a Negro lawyer, was an adviser to the U.S. Mission to the U.N. In 1966, Mrs. Patricia Roberts Harris, Howard University law professor and ambassador to Luxembourg, was named to represent the U.S. on both the Social and Legal Committees. In 1968 Mrs. Katie S. Louchheim, a Deputy Assistant Secretary of State and former deputy chairman of the Democratic National Committee, was named to represent the U.S. at UNESCO.

President Nixon named to succeed Mrs. Louchheim Mrs. Shirley Temple Black, the former motion picture star. Other Nixon appointments to U.N. posts included Mrs. Elizabeth Koontz, former President of the National Education Association and director of the U.S. Women's Bureau (U.S. representative to the Status of Women Commission), Mrs. Rita Hauser, a lawyer (ambassador to the Commission on Human Rights), and Mrs. Jean Picker (U.S. representative to the Social Commission of the Economic and Social Council).

SIGNIFICANT POLITICAL OFFICES HELD BY AMERICAN WOMEN

National

A. Legislative
   Congresswomen (69 women served in the House of Representative from 1917 to 1971; 10 served in the U.S. Senate) (The most at one time was in 1961-62 when there were 17 in the House and 2 in the Senate. In 1971 there were a dozen in the House and 1 in the Senate out of 435 and 100 members.)
B. Executive
   Head, Children's Bureau (a post held by women since 1912)
   Member, U.S. Employees' Compensation Commission (since 1917)
   Head, Women's Bureau (a post held by women since 1919)
   Member, U.S. Civil Service Commission (since 1920)
   Secretary of Labor (Frances Perkins, 1933-45)
   Secretary of Health, Education & Welfare (Mrs. Oveta Culp Hobby, 1953-55)

Head, Bureau of Home Economics (since 1924)
Member, Social Security Board (since 1937)
Chief, Passport Office (since 1928)
Director of the Mint (since 1933)
Assistant Attorney General (1920-33)
Assistant Secretary of the Treasury (Miss Josephine Roche, 1934-37)
Treasurer of the United States (since 1951) (with the exception of 1967-68)
Assistant Secretary of Defense for Manpower (Mrs. Anna Rosenberg, 1950-53)
Asst. Sec. of Labor for Women's Affairs (since 1953)
Asst. Secretary of Agriculture (Mrs. Dorothy Jacobson, 1964-68)
Asst. Secretary of Health, Education & Welfare (Mrs. Patricia Hitt, 1969-)
Member, Federal Communications Commissions (Frieda B. Hennock, 1948-55; Mrs. Charlotte Reid, 1971-)
Member, Federal Trade Commission (Mary G. Jones, 1964-)

Member, Atomic Energy Commission (Dr. Mary Bunting, 1964-)

Member, Interstate Commerce Commission (Mrs. Virginia Mae Brown, 1964-; Mrs. Brown became ICC Chairman in 1969)

Member, U.S. Equal Opportunity Commission (since 1965)

Chairman, U.S. Maritime Commission (Mrs. Helen D. Bentley, 1969-)

Chairman, U.S. Tariff Commission (Mrs. Catherine May Bedell, 1971-)

Presidential Adviser on Consumer Problems (since 1964)

Administrator, Bureau of Security and Consular Affairs, U.S. State Dept. (Barbara Watson, 1968-)

Member, President's Council of Economic Advisors (Dr. Marina Whitman, 1972-)

Ministers and Ambassadors (only about a dozen woman have ever served as a U.S. Minister or Ambassador to a country. A number of others have been regularly included as part of our mission to the U.N.) (Our female diplomats have headed our representation to Denmark, Norway, Bulgaria, Luxembourg, Italy, Switzerland, Barbados, Ceylon, and Nepal.) (At the present time we have envoys to over 100 nations.)

C. Judicial

Various judges in Washington, D.C.

U.S. Customs Court (Genevieve R. Cline, 1928-54; Mary H. Donlon, 1955-56)

U.S. Board of Tax Appeal (Annabel Matthews, 1930-36; Dr. Marion Herron, 1936-60; Mrs. Irene Scott, 1960-)

U.S. Courts of Appeals (Florence E. Allen, 1934-59; Mrs. Shirley M. Hufstedler, 1968-)

U.S. District Courts (The first one, Mrs. Bernita Matthews, was appointed in 1950. The second in 1951. The third in 1961. The fourth in 1966. The fifth in 1969. A sixth in 1970.)

State

A. Legislative

Approximately 300 state legislators (out of 7500 positions) (Down from a pre-redistricting high of 370 in 1965)

Mrs. Consuelo Northrop Bailey of Vermont was chosen Speaker of the House in 1953 (The first woman speaker of a state house was Mrs. Minnie D. Craig of North Dakota, elected in 1933.) Mrs. Bailey in 1955 was the first woman ever to be elected a Lieutenant Governor, 1955-56).

B. Executive

Governor—Three women have been governors, all succeeding husbands who preceded them in that post. (Mrs. Nellie Tayloe Ross of Wyoming, 1925-28; Mrs. Miriam A. Ferguson of Texas, 1925-26; 1933-34; Mrs. Lurleen Wallace of Alabama, 1967-68)

Attorney General (Only one woman, Anne X. Alpern of Pennsylvania, has ever been named state attorney general. She served around 1960.)

Lieutenant Governor (Aside from Mrs. Bailey of Vt., two women were appointed to fill out expiring terms, Matilda R. Wilson of Michigan in 1940 and Maude Frazier of Nevada in 1962.)

Secretary of State (Since 1922, this office in New Mexico was held by women. A similar tendency has taken place in South Dakota, Alabama, and Connecticut. Other states have had women Secretaries on occasion.)

Treasurer, Auditor, and Other Financial Offices (Arizona and Alabama have had a string of women in these positions. In Alabama, North Dakota and Pennsylvania women have moved from treasurer to auditor and vice versa.)

Superintendent of Public Instruction (Estelle Reel was elected to this office in Wyoming in 1894. Women have held the office in Colorado almost continuously since the 1890's. A number of other states have had women as Superintendents of Public Instruction. Women have headed all sorts of state departments, boards and agencies.)

C. Judicial

State Supreme Court (The first to be elected to a state supreme court judgeship was Florence E. Allen of Ohio in 1922. In 1934, she became a U.S. Circuit Court judge.) (The Second woman to be elected to a state's highest court, Lorna Lockwood of Arizona, was seated in 1960. By 1965 her colleagues chose her to be chief justice. Other women to sit in state supreme courts in the 1960's were Susie M. Sharp of North Carolina, Rhoda V. Lewis of Hawaii and Anne X. Alpern of Pennsylvania.

Local

Mayor of the following large cities: Seattle, Wash. (Mrs. Bertha K. Landes, 1927-28); Portland, Ore. (Mrs. Dorothy M. Lee, 1949-52); Sacramento, Calif. (Bell Cooledge, 1948-50); Yonkers, N.Y. (Mrs. Edith P. Welty, 1949-50); Hartford, Conn. (Ann Ucello, 1967-70); Oklahoma City ,Okla. (Mrs. Patience Latting, 1971-).

City Council and County Board members (Some women have chaired councils and boards.)

Borough President of Manhattan (Mrs. Constance Baker Motley, 1965-66.)

Women have headed all sorts of local government departments and agencies.

They have also sat on boards and been judges.

Party

The Republicans and the Democrats have each had women's divisions since before the Nineteenth Amendment. The ranking female held the post of vice chairman, vice president, or associate chairman of the National Committee. No woman has ever been chairman (though India Edwards declined the chairmanship of the Democratic National Committee in 1952). Several women have served as state chairmen and as campaign managers.

However, typically women have been recognized in auxiliary positions: Assistant chairman, co-chairmen, deputy chairman, vice chairman, secretary, committee-woman (with usually far less power than the committeeman), etc.

In recent years women have held about one seventh of the seats at the top national conventions. A serious effort is underway to give women, young people, and other minorities greater representation at the 1972 conventions.

Martin Gruberg, Ph.D.
University of Wisconsin
at Oshkosh.

Chapter 3

Women and the Law

Few people are aware that along with all the other radical changes which have come about in the twentieth century there has come about a redefinition of the concept of law. Of all of the cultural activities of humanity, certainly the promulgation of laws and their interpretation is one of the oldest. Law codes and law cases can be dated back into deep antiquity at thousands of years before Christ. But throughout most of those long ages, it was believed that law was a thing in itself, it had an existence apart from those who formulated it.

In the middle ages this was called realism, it defined the laws of state and church as being in and of themselves real and binding. Under such a system, women were before the law as the law givers saw them. Combined with the feudalistic system which placed all human beings in a vast triangular hierarchy with God and the King at the apex and all others subserviently below, women had no rights or responsibilities other than what had been defined for them by their fathers, husbands or sons as their representatives before the law. A woman without a man to take her place in the eyes of the court was in effect exlectic, outside the law. Even in the later rational and romantic codes, the U.S. Constitution and state papers, and the Code Napoleon, women were still excluded from specific, individual rights, certainly from having any voice in those rights.

In the twentieth century however, legal realism has given way to legal nominalism, the notion that the law only represents a social statement of behavior to which the majority adhere. This notion is gaining momentum in almost all western democratic countries and there are but few who attempt to find a deeper and possibly more satisfying meaning. It is easy to see the immense number of contradictions in statutes and precedents that have come about due to the application of two exclusive and opposed methods to the law. Since the United States is a country which recognizes the rule of law it is necessary to examine the place of women before those laws which define and effect their status as citizens.

The laws deal with actions and rights of citizens as a class and are often based upon the roles those citizens or the specific class of citizens fulfill in the general society. The proper definition and insight into roles thus adds or detracts from the body of the law and its usefulness. Although some small number of radical feminists have espoused anarchism as a philosophy, most of the advocates of women's rights are determined to work within the system, to humanize it, modernize it, and make it responsive to their wider roles.

Sex Roles and the Status of Women

3.1 The Masculine centered authority pattern is a source of a great deal of the difference in status according to many feminists. The roots of this patriarchal system is found in pre-classical antiquity. Since law changes very slowly over the centuries the structure of the law in almost all western nations is bounded if not founded upon these patriarchal concepts. Prof. Mc Clelland and her colleagues have studied the political science and sociology of sex-roles and authority patterns very extensively. Her insights add much to the understanding of the social structures under which men and women live and which repress the status and rights of women.

3.1.1 Men lead, women follow. Men order, women obey. There is nothing surprising in these observations, indeed, they function as truisms. So deeply ingrained is the doctrine of male domination, or, to put it another way, female subordination, that it is much more unusual to question the basis of women's legal, political, and social inferiority than it is to accept inferior status as a fact and way of life. Attempts to shake the foundations of male domination have resulted in small concessions which appeared as earth-shaking changes at the time of their enactment. Female suffrage, for example, a hard-won battle, has made very little difference in the long run. But while past efforts have altered laws and removed the more glaring injustices, social norms and practices have remained intact, for the most part. Whether dramatic changes can be realized within the context of the current feminist movement depends largely on the development of an ideology and program which not only accounts for, but will break down, patterns of social organization that have been impervious to change for centuries.

"Public or simply social authority always belongs to men." This is the conclusion Claude Levi-Strauss reached after his intensive study of primitive societies, a conclusion no one would challenge. The most universally observable pattern of social interaction between the sexes is one in which males are superordinates and females subordinates. This pattern is typically referred to as patriarchy, a term originally used to define rule by the male head of a family or tribe (usually the oldest male), but now taken to mean male supremacy generally.

3.1.2 Aristotle enunciated the doctrine of patriarchy as a form of social (and political) organization. As the founder of a general science of politics that was both empirical and descriptive, as opposed to merely ethical, he focused his attentions on the primary social unit in a society—the household—and observed that in that unit the head man rules over slaves, women and children. The rationale for the rule over slaves is found in natural law, since by nature some men are superior, others inferior. The basis for male subordination of females is never clearly elucidated. Aristotle states that the husband's rule over the wife is a constitutional rule, based on a consensual contract, which implies "that the natures of the citizens are equal and do not differ at all." But the case of women is an exception for the philosopher, because the legitimating principle for female subordination also lies in natural law: "Again," declares Aristotle, "the male is by nature superior, and the female inferior; and the one rules, and the other is ruled; this principle, of necessity, extends to all mankind." The virtue of the male is in commanding, of the female in obeying.

The significance of socialization in the family, for inculcating appropriate sex role behavior, is not overlooked. Insofar as the relationships Aristotle describes are part of a family, and every family is part of the state, "the virtue of the part must have regard to the virtue of the whole, women and children must be trained by education with an eye to the constitution, if the virtues of either of them are supposed to make any difference in the

virtues of the state. And they must make a difference: for the children grow up to be citizens, and half the free persons in a state are women."

Aristotle's interest in women as political subjects, and in the household as a political unit, ends there. The only connection between the authority of the patriarch and civil authority is in terms of the socialization process. Everything else that refers to the status of women is muddled. Women do possess a deliberative faculty (unlike slaves), but it is without authority. Their inequality is permanent. In sum, women are both free and bound, equal but unequal, the same but different. It is simply sufficient to establish the basis for male domination. The doctrine of patriarchy, then, legitimates the personal authority of individual males over females, a domination which existed long before Aristotle put it into words. Observable differences in the various statuses of women under a patriarchal system of rule result from the consensual contracts (which tend to follow class lines), contracts which in essence set down conditions not very different from those established by indenture.

Patriarchy has been subsumed in legal codes. Roman law, to give just one example, recognized the estate as the unitary basis of society, in effect, concentrating the rights of the patriarch. In Roman law, as in Aristotelian precepts, male supremacy was an aspect of natural law, based on the natural inferiority of women. The legal status of women underwent several transitions during the course of the empire—from the guardianship of the patriarch or male relatives, to a divided authority of both husband and father, finally ending in a guardianship by the state. But no changes in the principles and application of patriarchy, the ideology of the ruling class, resulted. Simone de Beauvoir has called this last stage a false emancipation. Roman women were awarded some civil rights, and were relieved of some of the private tyranny, but there remained nothing to which they could aspire.

Even if patriarchy did not require shoring, it received it in the form of a dynamic religious ethic. Christianity, while denying sex and race distinctions in the eyes of God, permitted such motes to exist in the eyes of men, at least as far as women were concerned. Christianity in no way countered the laws of the state, and openly supported patriarchal authority in the family. Wives are exhorted to submit to their husbands; the husband is head of the wife, wives are subject to their husbands "in everything." "Let the women learn in silence with all subjection," Paul writes, "but I suffer not a woman to teach, nor to usurp authority over a man, but to be in silence." (I Timothy 2:11, 12)

3.1.3 Patriarchy has come down to us in essentially unchanged form. The hold that patriarchal authority has over women has been mitigated for some women at some times, but then only at rare historic interludes. Women, individually or as members of a class, have emerged at several points in European history, voicing demands for an improvement in the social and political condition of their sex. The Italian Renaissance represented such a period for high-born females, as did the French Enlightenment, but gains made then did not permeate all society and were relatively short-lived. In more recent times, the reassertion of patriarchy and a return to traditional sex role definitions were underscored by Victorian norms, cutting the ground out from under eighteenth-century egalitarianism.

We can look almost anywhere to find manifestations of patriarchy today; and not only in its most natural habitat, the home. Wherever women and men interact patriarchy is operative. Harry Eckstein's model for the description and analysis of authority and authority patterns (i.e., the interactions which result from the exercise of authority), in various social units, is useful here. In families, occupational settings, voluntary associations, educational institutions—wherever the membership comprises adults of both sexes—generally women are subordinated to males either directly or ultimately. Males are superordinates, and females are subordinates. Males occupy positions of power; women lack authority. Exceptions to male domination of positions of authority exist, but—and this is almost true by definition—usually when men are not present in the unit or are in a small minority. In the United States, units where females dominate males are rare. Even in female professions, such as elementary school teaching and nursing, positions of authority tend to go to the few males who are members of the unit.

The family is often cited as an example of "matriarchal" rule, but this is false. Women may have a stronger influence in this unit than in any other, but their authority is delegated to them by patriarchs. One needs only to examine legal codes to expose this fallacy. We tend to think of the position of women in the United States as an enviable one, and it probably is, compared to alternatives. But social norms and laws blatantly reinforce traditional sex roles and patriarchy even in this country. Wives, and particularly working wives, are more discriminated against than women generally: tax, property, and contract laws are just a few of many examples. In most cases, a woman cannot bring a charge of rape against her husband. Recently, President Nixon vetoed a bill providing for day care for children of working mothers on the grounds that such an act would be dysfunctional to family life in the United States.

The Eckstein model provides for a breakdown of authority patterns along a number of dimensions, for example, social distance, deportment, legitimacy, influence dimensions such as compliance, permissiveness, responsiveness, and participation, and others. Although the model is not as sophisticated as some would hope, it does provide a basis for the analysis of authority. This scheme is most valuable for an analysis of patriarchy because it allows for cross-cultural and intra-cultural comparisons of authority relationships, which would take into account racial, religious, and socio-economic variables. The most obvious authority relationship, and the one most worthy of investigation, is the one which half the human population holds over the other half, males over females—patriarchy. A systematic application of this model to that universal authority pattern would yield extremely interesting results.

Take just one dimension: social distance. This is defined as how distant the superordinate and subordinate perceive themselves to be from each other. At one end of the continuum, women are considered not merely biologically different from males, but subhuman, compared to the humanness of males, i.e. another order of being. Moslems, for example, are taught it is better to be born a stone than female. Moving along the continuum, females and males may be considered equally human, but subject to immutable sex role differentiation which dictates separate spheres of activity and influence—the separate but equal argument, expressed more simply as "women are different." In no political system are women entirely equal (or superior) to males. The opposite end of the continuum—equality of the sexes—has only been approached, and then only in terms of enormous social upheaval, as examples in the socialist world show.

3.1.4 The other dimensions of an authority pattern center on aspects of behavior which are well known to be sexually differentiated. It has been repeatedly shown that even the most impersonal exchanges between a (male) superordinate and (female) subordinate evidence marked differences in verbal patterns, physical contact, ways of responding to directives, and so on. The passive-compliant nature of females, status distinctions, and education values (including socialization) have also been touchstones for many feminist writers. An empirical study of patriarchy as an authority pattern would show conclusively that authority and sex role perceptions overlap: men, and women, tend to attribute the exercise of authority to men and subordination to authority to women. Such a study would also show that patriarchy has left the boundaries of the household and now is the prevailing pattern in all bi-sexual social units.

What is perhaps most interesting about even a cursory analysis of patriarchy as an authority pattern, in which males are generally super-ordinates and females subordinates, is that while females are cast in subordinate or inferior roles, they are not conscious of the authority relationship. Few women perceive themselves to be inferior to males, only subordinates to super-ordinate roles occupied by males. The social and political subjugation of women is cloaked in whatever terms make their status as inferiors less perceptible—in semantics, cliches, and stereotypes (women are "different" which ultimately means women are inferior), in secular and religious ethics ("a woman's place") in myths, (romantic love), in biology ("anatomy is destiny") and in tradition ("it has always been the case").

It is true, the experience of the last one hundred and fifty years in particular has so numbed our brains that we think patriarchy has been and always will be the only authority pattern, and the nuclear family the only primary social organization. Clearly patriarchy has been the dominant theme in human history, but anthropologists, historians, sociologists, feminists, and social engineers, past and present, draw our attention to other possible social configurations.

In fact, patriarchy has not always been the only alternative, real or imagined. It is now perhaps commonplace to state that matriarchal societies, with power concentrated in female hands (such as the Iroquois), have been exceedingly rare. But there were, and are, other lines of human development besides a pattern of strict matriarchy or patriarchy. Early nomads and pre-classical agricultural societies were often matrilineal, tracing descendants through the mother. Matrilineal and matrilocal patterns, with wide variation in sex role differentiation, were observed by Mead in her studies among South Pacific tribes. The role of

women under theocratic rule in ancient Egypt was a favored one, probably because of the absence of private ownership and patriarchy.

In communalistic societies, such as Sparta, males and females were equally valued (and educated) for the services they could perform for the good of the state. The sexes lived apart, a Spartan husband visiting his wife stealthily. Again, patriarchy was noted for its absence: women were under the yoke of neither husband nor father. Plato, viewed as holding amazingly liberal attitudes towards women (they would probably be considered radical today), envisioned a communalistic society in which both men and women were equally socialized to the same end, as responsible guardians of the state. To effect this end, Plato prescribed group marriage with children held in common; he also proposed an end to patrimony and, hence, patriarchy. Contemporary socialist societies, such as the Soviet Union and China, have had limited success in their attempts to abolish patriarchy. In the case of the former, efforts to restructure the family and redefine sex roles failed. Russian women today lament that the revolution freed them to perform two jobs, one inside, the other outside the home. The Chinese have had better success to date.

Not only have there been authority patterns other than patriarchy, but it has been shown that patriarchal rule loses its effect under certain political and economic conditions. A review of patriarchy and the historical role of women and sex role conditioning generally raises a number of significant questions and inspires several generalizations. All these themes are worthy topics for feminist studies, each deserving much more consideration than the mere mention it will receive here.

3.1.5 First, women apparently fare better, in terms of expanded role definitions, during times of social upheaval than during times of relative stability. The reasons for this are not so obvious. Is it because men are directing attention elsewhere? Is the cooperation of women so necessary at these times that traditional norms about women's place and about behavior relative to the female role are overcome? Has the state intervened to a greater extent to diminish the power of the individual patriarch? Or is it merely that historians, naturally attracted to periods of disorder, have overlooked the continuous role of women (and of non-elites generally) in the less turbulent periods?

Second, it is foolish to speak of a continuous line leading towards female emancipation.

Repressions often seem to follow periods in which female roles have expanded. And often these regressions are not so much conservative as downright reactionary. Bearing this observation in mind, it is perhaps easier to see why women have advanced so little in absolute terms. It is not so easy to see why women themselves have allowed these setbacks to occur, because certainly the abrogation of gains could not have been made without their complicity.

Third, and probably most important for the current movement, is the relationship between civil authority and patriarchal authority. A review of the history of women reveals that virtually the only way the status of women advances at all is when the authority of the state is placed between the authority of the individual patriarch, who rules his home as he would a feudal kingdom, in which his wife and children occupy dependent roles. It is not misguided for women to work within the system to change the legal code, because ultimately laws do influence norms and practices by guaranteeing rights to women, or, to put it another way, in limiting the power of individual patriarchs. But the substitution of civil authority for patriarchal authority can be a two-edged sword. One need only to recall the Nazi "*Kinder, Kuche, Kirche*" dictum for women of the Third Reich (as ineffective as it was in reality) to conclude that the state is not necessarily the best guarantor of women's rights. Questions about the freedom of the individual are also justifiably raised in this context—is it, in fact, a desirable change of rule? Perhaps the only advantage lies in equal application: men, too, would have to sacrifice autonomy, hopefully to the same degree, for the greater good. Unfortunately, the experience of the past is that the intercession of the state may provide the only solution, since individual patriarchs have shown no inclination willingly to surrender the power they have over women. Female emancipation for males has always been a zero-sum proposition (nothing to gain, something to lose).

If, indeed, the enemy of women's liberation is a political ordering whereby half the human race rules the other half—whether we call this pattern patriarchy, male domination, male supremacy, chauvinism, whatever—what are the alternatives?

Two already crumbling institutions, marriage and the family, particularly the nuclear family, have come under severe attacks from feminists. In the case of the family, alternatives range from its total abolition to modifications of the structure, such as extended families, the members of which would qualify by affinity and not by blood. Proposals on this subject have been advanced by movement spokeswomen Germaine Greer and Shulamith Firestone, and there will undoubtedly be more to come.

Another alternative is inherent in the attack on the institution of marriage. Women should stay single to maintain their independence. Simone de Beauvoir has observed that throughout history there are examples of women who have existed outside of the context of marriage; they are not under the personal authority of a patriarch, and their status (not to mention their freedom) in a society rises accordingly. Men look to these women as companions, even equals. This is not the case for all single women at all times, as one is painfully reminded by the example of prostitution today.

A third possibility for negating the conditioning of women and the effect of patriarchy is in socialization. A radical change in definitions of sex roles and sex role models inside and outside the home will not have immediate effects, but it could make life different for our children, particularly our girl children.

But is the equation of the family and patriarchy the same thing? Commune women have complained that instead of being the exclusive property of one male they become the property of all males—and still wind up barefoot, pregnant, and in a kitchen. For all the ideals about rearing children in common, when the commune dissolves the child rarely belongs to anyone except its biological mother. Is the enemy really the family or the rule within the family and elsewhere, i.e. patriarchy? By challenging the family and marriage are we concentrating on a symptom instead of the disease?

3.1.6 Short of feminist revolution, and we are far from it, or a unifying program which would bring all the disparate elements of the movement together so that we will hear the one loud voice of a truly feminist rebellion, what action can members of a subjugated class take when all the power resides in the other side? Other subjugated peoples, some just as enslaved, have responded to challenges almost as great with such weapons as passive resistance, proselytization, guerrilla tactics, and fifth columns, all of which could have widespread applications in this liberation movement.

There is enough evidence to suggest that women are already well enough versed in the use of passive resistance, but perhaps this could be expanded to include non-violent strikes in the home and place of work. Active resistance would include attempts to relinquish the security of enclaves such as the home and the typing pool for something more adventurous. There is nothing to preclude forays into occupations traditionally thought of as male bailiwicks: why not women plumbers? [There are exceptions to the escape from traditional female roles: with what we now know about early childhood rearing and the effects of early socialization, the education of children, always a part of the female domain, would appear to be a prime target for feminists, and one that should be actively and not reluctantly pursued.] Professional women, instead of guarding their few entrenched positions, should make every effort to open doors for other women. Radical feminists could expand the list of means further.

Aristotle and the Church concurred in the view that "Silence is a woman's glory." For patriarchy, more than anything else, the principle of Roman law, *quis tacet consentire videtur*, has a chilling reality today: "Whoever keeps quiet is assumed to approve."

Prof. Muriel McClelland
Philadelphia, Penna.

THE DOUBLE STANDARD OF JUSTICE: WOMEN'S RIGHTS UNDER THE CONSTITUTION*

3.2 The fact that the women's liberation movement, or second wave of feminism came quickly upon the heals of the civil rights movement has given it some very valuable insights from experience. The major victories won by the organizations struggling for Black liberation from political and economic oppression have been won in the courts. There the hot winds of controversy and political turmoil are set aside in somewhat dispassionate consideration of the constitution and laws of the United States. With a bigger potential strength in the legal profession than the blacks, the women have been able to bring the consideration of the courts to bear upon their concerns with far less street activity and much reduced notoriety. Many grievances never attracted much public sentiment but were taken directly to the courts. In a carefully reasoned presentation, counselor Eastwood, points to the manifold ways in which sex differentiation based only on custom and socialization have become part of the structure of the law itself. There is no doubt that each and every aspect of the constitutional difficulties which she demonstrates will be tested in the courts in the near future. In the recent history of the United States, the federal judiciary has been innovative and more often liberal than conservative in its interpretation of the constitution. There is no doubt that sweeping changes in the legal position of various segments of society and the individual citizen are coming about. The reasons for these changes and the laws regarding them are carefully set forth by Ms. Eastwood.

3.2.1 Women frequently are subjected to different rules than are men, in the law as well as socially. There are still some federal and state laws that either treat men and women differently or apply only to one sex.[1] Government agencies sometimes administer laws designed to protect women from sex discrimination differently than those designed to protect blacks from racial discrimination.[2] Courts not only have approved laws distinguishing between men and women but generally have used a different criterion for determining whether constitutional protections against sex discrimination have been violated than is used with respect to racial discrimination. Thus, a double standard of justice is applied to the classes of men and women and the classes of women and blacks.

The failure of the courts to interpret the equal protection and due process guarantees of the fifth and fourteenth amendments[3] as prohibiting discrimination against women in the law has caused women to seek adoption of the Equal Rights Amendment: "Equality of rights under the law shall not be denied or abridged by the United States or by any State on account of sex."[4] The single purpose of the proposed amendment is to require the equal treatment of men and women under the law and to restrain the courts from applying different rules to women under the Constitution. The problem of sex discrimination does not lie in any limited scope of the fifth and fourteenth amendments to protect women from discrimination in the law, but from the refusal of the courts to regard women as fully human "persons" under these amendments.[5] As Representative Martha Griffiths explained on August 10, 1970, the first time in the 47 year history

* This article originally appeared in the *Valparaiso University Law Review*. Eastwood, The Double Standard of Justice: Women's Rights under the Constitution, 5 Val. U.L. Rev. 281 (1971).

of the Equal Rights Amendment that it passed the House of Representatives:[6]

> There never was a time when decisions of the Supreme Court could not have done everything we ask today . . . The Court has held for 98 years that women, as a class, are not entitled to equal protection of the laws. They are not "persons" within the meaning of the Constitution.[7]

Advocates of equal rights for men and women regard proper interpretation of the existing constitutional protections against sex discrimination as meaning the same as the Equal Rights Amendment. This position was first stated by the President's Commission on the Status of Women in 1963:

> Equality of rights under the law for all persons, male or female, is so basic to democracy and its commitment to the ultimate value of the individual that it must be reflected in the fundamental law of the land. The Commission believes that this principle of equality is embodied in the Fifth and Fourteenth Amendments to the Constitution of the United States.[8]

For this reason, the Commission concluded that an additional amendment was not at that time needed, "[b]ut judicial clarification is imperative in order that remaining ambiguities with respect to the constitutional protection of women's rights be eliminated."[9]

This article first sets forth the judicial standards that have been applied with respect to sex discrimination cases under the fifth and fourteenth amendments, as compared to other types of class discrimination cases, and secondly, analyzes the effect the Equal Rights Amendment would have upon existing differences in treatment of men and women in the law.

UNEQUAL PROTECTION
Constitutional Tests for Class Distinctions

3.2.2 Two standards have been developed by the courts to determine whether laws differentiating between classes of persons violate constitutional guarantees of equal protection of the laws.[10] One such standard is that the law is valid if the class distinction is based upon some "reasonable" ground. The other is that the class distinction is constitutional only if it is shown that the government has a "compelling interest" in making the class distinction. The reasonableness test has generally been applied with respect to laws treating women as inferiors or restricting their liberties. The stricter compelling state interest test has been applied with respect to racial classifications and situations involving fundamental constitutionally protected liberties.[11] There is, however, an additional distinction between the two standards: the burden is upon the person challenging a law to show that it is unreasonable; the burden is upon the state to show that it has a compelling interest.

The more lax reasonableness standard applied by the courts in equal protection cases is that the classification must be based on "some differences which bears a just and proper relation to the attempted classification—and not a mere arbitrary selection."[12] Under the stricter standard, the mere showing of some rational basis for the classification is not sufficient to support its constitutionality. Racial classifications are subject to the stricter test since "[a]ll legal restrictions which curtail the civil rights of a single racial group are immediately suspect and . . . courts must subject them to the most rigid scrutiny."[13] Thus, in holding unconstitutional Virginia's anti-miscegenation law, the Supreme Court found "no legitimate overriding purpose independent of invidious racial discrimination" to justify the classification.[14] The showing of an overriding and compelling state interest is also required where the law affects fundamental individual liberties, such as freedom of religion,[15] freedom of association,[16] and the right to travel,[17] to vote,[18] to have offspring[19] and to assert familial relationship.[20]

CLASSIFYING PERSONS BY SEX

3.2.3 The 98 years of inequality under the fourteenth amendment mentioned by Representative Griffiths[21] dates back to the 1872 Supreme Court Decision in Bradwell v. Illinois which upheld the refusal of the Supreme Court of Illinois[22] to admit women to practice law. Three of the United States Supreme Court justices based their decision in part on religion:

> The natural and proper timidity and delicacy which belongs to the female sex evidently unfits it for many of the occupations of civil life. The constitution of the family organization, which is founded in the divine ordinance, as well as in the nature of things, indicates the domestic sphere as that which properly belongs to the domain and functions of womanhood. . . .

... The paramount destiny and mission of woman are to fulfil the noble and benign offices of wife and mother. This is the law of the Creator.[23]

That woman's place is ordained to be in the home is one of several assumptions that the courts have relied upon as justifying laws discriminating against women. The other assumptions are related to "woman's place" and are only slightly more sophisticated. They are, in essence:

1. Since women are the only humans who can give birth, they are reproductive instruments who may be specially restricted, protected or controlled by the law in the interest of preserving the race.

2. Since women have special responsibilities in homemaking (housekeeping) and child rearing, and men do not have such responsibilities, women's rights as citizens outside the home may be curtailed to allow them to do their home chores.

3. Since women as a class are generally inferior to men in physical strength, it is assumed that a woman has less endurance and must be limited in her activities outside the home to save her strength.

4. In some situations women (but not men) are a danger to morality and need to be supervised by men.

5. Men are in power; they have established their control, and it should stay that way.

As will be shown, the courts have relied on either one or a combination of these rationales in cases upholding laws distinguishing on the basis of sex, and frequently they are no more subtly stated than as set forth above.

The BRANDWELL case was decided under the privileges and immunities clause of the fourteenth amendment rather than under the due process or equal protection clauses. Two years later, the Supreme Court held in MINOR v. HAPPERSETT[24] that the privileges and immunities clause did not confer on women citizens the right to vote. However, the Court stated specifically that "[w]omen and children are ... 'persons' " under the Constitution and reasoned that "[i]f the right of suffrage were one of the necessary privileges of a citizen of the United States, then the Constitution[25] and laws of Missouri confining it to men [would be] in violation of the Constitution of the United States."[26]

3.2.4 The rule that the law may properly single out women for special treatment was developed in connection with the enactment of special restrictions on the employment of women around the turn of the century.[27] Laws restricting the hours of work of both men and women were held violative of the fourteenth amendment due process right to liberty of contract for employment in LOCHNER v. NEW YORK.[28] In MULLER v. OREGON,[29] the Supreme Court upheld the validity of an Oregon maximum hours law that applied only to women,[30] distinguishing it from LOCHNER on that ground:

Differentiated ... from the other sex, she is properly placed in a class by herself, and legislation designed for her protection may be sustained, even when like legislation is not necessary for men and could not be sustained. It is impossible to close one's eyes to the fact that she still looks to her brother and depends upon him.[31]

Since hours legislation for both sexes was upheld in 1917 in BUNTING v. OREGON,[32] the utility of the doctrine that sex is a reasonable basis for legislative classification in upholding the constitutionality of labor standards legislation was short-lived. The theory of legitimacy of sex differentiation, however, became entrenched in the law.[33]

3.2.5 The justification in MULLER for special restrictions applicable to women was, in essence, that women are inferior to men in physical endurance and that, since women are instruments of reproduction of the race, the state has a special interest in protecting their health. Thus, the Court stated:

That woman's physical structure and the performance of maternal functions place her at a disadvantage in the struggle for subsistence is obvious. This is especially true when the burdens of motherhood are upon her. Even when they are not, by abundant testimony of the medical fraternity continuance for a long time on her feet at work, repeating this from day to day, tends to injurious effects upon the body, and as healthy mothers are essential to vigorous offspring, the physical well-being of woman becomes an object of public interest and care in order to preserve the strength and vigor of the race.[34]

The constitutionality of night work restrictions[35] and special minimum wage laws[36] for women was also upheld. In TRUAX v. RAICH, the Supreme Court stated that the right to work in legitimate occupations without discrimination on grounds of race or nationality "is of the very essence of the personal freedom and opportunity that it was the purpose of the 14th Amendment to secure."[38] In that case, an Arizona law requiring employers to employ not less than 80 per cent native-born citizens was held violative of the fourteenth amendment rights of an Austrian cook. In YICK WO v. HOPKINS,[39] a San Francisco ordinance administered to deny Chinese the right to operate laundries was found to be an unconstitutional denial of the right to learn a living. Similarly, in TAKAHASHI v. FISH AND GAME COMMISSION[40] a California statute forbidding issuance of commercial fishing licenses to aliens ineligible for citizenship was held to be violative of the rights of aliens to the equal protection of the laws.

However, in the same year as TAKAHASHI, the Supreme Court ruled in GOESAERT v. CLEARY[41] that a Michigan statute forbidding the licensing of any female to act as bartender unless she is the wife or daughter of the male owner was not violative of the fourteenth amendment, justifying the discrimination primarily on moral grounds:

> The fact that women may now have achieved the virtues that men have long claimed as their perogative and now indulge in vices that men have long practiced, does not preclude the States from drawing a sharp line between the sexes, certainly in such matters as the regulation of the liquor traffic.[42]

Bartending by women may "give rise to moral and social problems."[43] The fact that Michigan permitted women to serve as (lower paid) waitresses where liquor was dispensed was not thought by the Court to be inconsistent inasmuch as there the "man's ownership provides control."[44] Control over women is proper, but the kind of restriction in YICK WO (matural origin) was characterized as "the essence of slavery itself."[45]

The validity of a Chicago ordinance prohibiting employment of women bartenders was recently challenged. The ordinance was similar to the law found constitutional in GOESAERT except that female licensees as well as male licensees and their female relatives were exempt from the restriction. The Court of Appeals for the Seventh Circuit, in reversing the district court's dismissal of the case, stated that the additional exemption for female licensees might make the ordinance distinguishable from GOESAERT in that the justification of masculine control was not present. Where there is a female licensee involved, "there would be no protective male in the background."[46] On remand, the district court held the ordinance void on its face as denying women property rights without due process of law.[47] A New Jersey court

recently found it unnecessary to pursue the constitutional question raised in GOESAERT, finding simply that a prohibition on women working as bartenders served no public purpose.[48] The legality of special drinking places for men has also been successfully attacked by women.[49]

The moral danger of mixing women and liquor appears to have subsided. But "the woman's place is in the home" theme continues. As recently as 1961, the Supreme Court in HOYT v. FLORIDA[50] upheld the constitutionality of a Florida statute providing that no female be selected for jury service unless she has registered with the clerk of the circuit court her desire to be placed on the jury list:

> Despite the enlightened emancipation of women from the restrictions and protections of bygone years, and their entry into many parts of community life formerly considered to be reserved to men, WOMAN IS STILL REGARDED AS THE CENTER OF HOME AND FAMILY LIFE. We cannot say that it is constitutionally impermissible for a State, acting in pursuit of the general welfare, to conclude that a woman should be relieved from the civic duty of jury service unless she herself determines that such service is consistent with her own SPECIAL RESPON-SIBILITIES.[51]

Women have "special responsibilities" in homemaking and child rearing, but the "housewife and mother" role is an occupation not protected by labor standards legislation. A housewife has no legal right to claim wages, only room and board (support), and even that, as a practical matter, is largely dependent on the sufferance of her husband. The fact that the work in many situations can be pleasant is irrelevant. It is labor with no legal right to remuneration, and it is foisted upon women as their proper function—to serve not only their husbands, but also, by rearing children, society.

Because women are legally recognized as a particular kind of servant class, the denial of equal civic rights such as jury service is regarded as justified. This concept does not represent a fair arrangement between the sexes; it is a dual discrimination against women. It has even been asserted that the special responsibilities of mothers may justify discrimination against women in employment under Title VII of the Civil Rights Act of 1964.[52]

3.2.6 A more enlightened view of women's rights is reflected in the 1966 three-judge federal court decision of WHITE v. CROOK,[53] which held an Alabama statute barring women from jury duty unconstitutional. The court unequivocally applied the fourteenth amendment stating:

> The Constitution of the United States must be read as embodying general principles meant to govern society and the institutions of government as they evolve through time. It is therefore this Court's function to apply the Constitution as a living document to the legal cases and controversies of contemporary society. . . .
> . . . The Alabama statute that denies women the right to serve on juries . . . violates that provision of the Fourteenth Amendment to the Constitution of the United States that forbids any state to "deny to any person within its jurisdiction the equal protection of the laws." The plain effect of this constitutional provision is to prohibit prejudicial disparities before the law. This means prejudicial disparities for all citizens—including women.[54]

Similarly, in a fifth amendment case, the United States Court of Appeals for the Sixth Circuit reversed a conviction because the trial judge had dismissed women jurors from the panel on the ground that evidence in the case would require testimony concerning cancer of the male genitals:

> It is common knowledge that society no longer coddles women from the very real and sometimes brutal facts of life. Women, moreover, do not seek such oblivion . . .
> The District Judge's desire to avoid embarrassment to the women jurors is understandable and commendable but such sentiments must be subordinated to constitutional or congressional mandates.[55]

The reasoning in WHITE v. CROOK was rejected in a recent Mississippi decision.[56]

> The legislature has the right to exclude women SO THEY MAY CONTINUE THEIR SERVICES AS MOTHERS, WIVES, AND HOMEMAKERS, and also to protect them (in some areas, they are still upon a pedestal) from filth, obscenity, and noxious atmosphere that so often pervades a courtroom during a jury trial.[57]

Mississippi, however, no longer excludes women from jury service.[58]

Courts have also held that women are entitled to equal treatment in the penalties they are subject to for conviction of crimes.[59] This progress, of course, affects comparatively few women. As of December 31, 1967, only 3.2 per cent of the sentenced prisoners in federal and state institutions were women.[60]

In KIRSTEIN v. RECTOR AND VISITORS OF THE UNIVERSITY OF VIRGINIA,[61] a federal court held that the exclusion of women-plaintiffs from the University of Virginia at Charlottesville "denied their constitutional right to an education equal with that offered men at Charlottesville and that such discrimination on the basis of sex violates the Equal Protection Clause of the Fourteenth Amendment."[62]

3.2.7 However, in other recent cases approving sex discrimination in computing social security benefits and in imposing obligations for military service, courts have harped back to woman's physical weakness and her "place" in the home as supplying justification for the difference in treatment. Thus, in finding beneficial treatment of women in computing amounts of retirement benefits constitutionally valid, the Court of Appeals for the Second Circuit stated that the objective of the difference was "to reduce the disparity between the economic and physical capabilities of a man and a woman."[63] There is some logic in the reference to the economic inferiority of women workers, but the reference to "physical capabilities" of retired male and female workers would seem to cut the other way since women live longer, i.e., are physically stronger, not weaker. Even if it were possible to balance out discriminations against men and women by sex, giving benefits to one sex in one area and to the other in a different area, there is no certainty that the perfect balance between the classes of men and women would result in INDIVIDUAL justice which presumably is the goal. Only the elimination of sex distinctions in the law can accomplish this.

In UNITED STATES v. ST. CLAIR,[64] involving a challenge under the fifth amendment to the constitutionality of the Military Selective Service Act of 1967,[65] the court stated:

> In providing for involuntary service for men and voluntary service for women, Congress followed the teachings of history that if a nation is to survive, men must provide the first line of defense while women keep the home fires burning.[66]

3.2.8 Military service, like jury duty, is a right and obligation of citizenship. The Supreme Court has stated that "the duty of citizens by force of arms to defend our government against enemies whenever necessity arises is a fundamental principle of the Constitution."[67] Similarly, in WHITE v. CROOK, the Court stated that "jury service is a form of participation in the processes of government, a responsibility and right that should be shared by all citizens, regardless of sex."[68] WHITE v. CROOK and UNITED STATES v. ST. CLAIR are distinguishable. In the former case, the Alabama law totally excluded women from jury service, whereas in ST. CLAIR women were not totally excluded from military service and could volunteer.[69] In addition, women challenged their exclusion from the jury law in WHITE v. CROOK, whereas the attack on the Military Selective Service Act was made by a man, but it is not likely that it would have made any difference if it had been a woman in view of the Court's nostalgic view of women keeping the home fires burning.

MENGELKOCH v. INDUSTRIAL WELFARE COMMISSION

3.2.9 Perhaps the most extreme example of applying a double standard of justice to women is the district court decision in MENGELKOCH v. INDUSTRIAL WELFARE COMMISSION.[70] The case challenged the constitutionality under the fourteenth amendment and the consistency with Title VII of the Civil Rights Act of 1964[71] of California's maximum hours law for women.[72] The suit was a class action brought by employees of North American Aviation, Inc. (now North American Rockwell Corporation). The women sought an injunction against the California Industrial Welfare Commission to prevent enforcement of the hours restriction, alleging that the effect of the law was to deny women the opportunity to work at higher paid and supervisory jobs that might occasionally require overtime work and to deny them additional premium overtime pay.

The complaint was filed in October, 1966. A three-judge court was convened pursuant to 28 U.S.C. #2281, 2284 which requires that an action to enjoin state officials from enforcing a state law on the ground that such law is unconstitutional be heard by a three-judge district court. A year and a half later in May, 1968, the three-judge court dissolved itself, stating it lacked jurisdiction because there was no substantial constitutional issue. Since the constitutionality of state hours restrictions on women had been upheld by the Supreme Court in MULLER v. OREGON[73] and MILLER v. WILSON[74] and by the California courts in EXPARTE MILLER,[75]

the three-judge court reasoned that the question of constitutionality was foreclosed. The case was returned to a single judge who then dismissed the case, invoking the doctrine of abstention.[76]

Since state courts have no jurisdiction in Title VII cases (federal courts have exclusive jurisdiction),[77] the effect was that women simply could not pursue their remedies under the federal statute. This would read "sex" out of Title VII as effectively as if it were repealed. A direct appeal was taken to the Supreme Court pursuant to 28 U.S.C. #1253. The court vacated the three-judge order and remanded the case for entry of a fresh decree from which a timely appeal could be taken to the Ninth Circuit, holding that where a three-judge court dissolves itself, the appeal lies to the appropriate court of appeals.[78] The appellants had argued that the three-judge court's dissolution after deliberating the question for over a year in effect denied the injunction[79] and resulted in a decision on the merits of whether the state law was constitutional so that a direct appeal would lie under 28 U.S.C. #1253.[80] The Supreme Court, however, treated the case as one involving the threshold question of whether a three-judge court should be convened (whether the constitutional question was insubstantial). Threshold questions of jurisdiction under the three-judge statute are appealable to the court of appeals rather than to the Supreme Court.[81]

The Court of Appeals for the Ninth Circuit reversed and remanded the case to the three-judge court holding that a determination that MULLER and MILLER require rejection of new attacks on the constitutionality of the hours restriction "is not so obvious and beyond reasonable debate that the constitutional attack must be regarded as insubstantial."[82]

The court of appeals opinion in MENGELKOCH strikes a blow at the continued viability of MULLER, noting several distinguishing factors:

1. That the relevancy and importance of some of the conditions discussed in MULLER "today may not be the same;"[83]

2. That in MULLER the primary issue was whether restricting work hours of women was a "wise" exercise of the police power under the due process clause standards applied then and that the constitutional attack was by the employer, not the women employees;[84]

3. "In MULLER the statute was upheld in part because it was thought to be a necessary way of safeguarding women's competitive position. Here the statute is attacked on the ground that it gives

male employees an unfair advantage over females."[85]

4. By emphasizing differences of the sexes, the Supreme Court in MULLER was able to uphold the statute despite its decision in LOCHNER v. NEW YORK.[86] This emphasis is no longer necessary.[87]

The court, however, took pains to make clear it was not pre-judging the substantive issue of constitutionality but only showing that the constitutional issue was not insubstantial and that the three-judge court therefore had jurisdiction to decide the case.[88]

It took from October, 1966, to January, 1971, for the federal courts to determine that a three-judge district court has jurisdiction to hear Mrs. Mengelkoch's complaint that the California hours restriction on women workers violates their rights to equal protection of the laws under the Constitution and their right to pursue remedies afforded by a federal civil rights law. In the meantime, decisions in cases brought by other women under Title VII of the Civil Rights Act of 1964[89] have generally established that special restrictions on women workers are inconsistent with and superseded by that Act.[90]

SEX AS A PROHIBITED CLASSIFICATION

3.2.10 Arguments have been made in sex discrimination cases that laws classifying persons by sex should be subjected to the stricter standard of constitutionality as opposed to the more lax reasonableness test and that the state should be required to show a compelling interest in the classification.[91] In UNITED STATES ex rel. ROBINSON v. YORK,[92] a federal district court held unconstitutional a Connecticut law requiring longer prison terms for women than for men convicted of the same crimes. The court recognized that

> [w]hile the Supreme Court has not explicitly determined whether equal protection rights of women should be tested by this rigid standard, it is difficult to find any reason why adult women, as one of the specific groups that compose humanity, should have a lesser measure of protection than a racial group.[93]

Nevertheless, the court in dictum went out of the way to approve the rationale of cases upholding sex classification in employment and jury service.[94] It is doubtful that the law in question in ROBINSON could be upheld under any test no matter how lax.

Even under the stricter compelling state interest standard, there is no assurance that it would be applied to strike down legal discrimination against women in the same way as have laws discriminating on the basis of race. Regardless of the test applied, as Professor Kanowitz has noted, "the result will inevitably depend upon a court's visceral rather than its cerrebral behavior."[95]

The Supreme Court stated in HARPER v. VIRGINIA BOARD OF ELECTIONS:

> [T]he Equal Protection Clause is not shackled to the political theory of a political era. In determining what lines are unconstitutionally discriminatory, we have never been confined to historic notions of equality, any more than we have restricted due process to a fixed catalogue of what was at a given time deemed to be the limits of fundamental rights. . . . Notions of what constitutes equal treatment for purposes of the Equal Protection Clause DO change.[96]

It is suggested that any differentiation based on sex should no longer be tolerated under the equal protection clause and that courts turn their attention in a given case to the issues of whether there is a DIFFERENTIATION, and, if so, whether the differentiation is based on SEX. These latter issues are discussed in connection with the interpretation of the proposed Equal Rights Amendment.

3.2.11 Women constitute a political class in part because the law has made them so by treating the class differently. The fact that women are integrated into all economic classes and that many women do not serve the function of homemaking and childrearing has not been deemed relevant. The entire class of women is treated differently from the class of men for some purposes on the basis of those functions.

It is difficult to reconcile laws classifying persons by the permanent class of their birth with the basic democratic concept that "all men are created equal."[97] Classifications that treat persons differently simply because they were born into a class are antithetical to democracy because the individual is permanently condemned to legal restrictions by virtue of a status over which he or she has no control. In this respect, sex, race, national origin and legitimacy differ from other classifications.[98] For example, the AGE of a person changes; so might his religion, economic status or citizenship. If classifications by birth were prohibited, attention would shift from the question "can government discriminate between men and women by this rule" to the question "does the rule under attack, though superficially neutral, result in different treatment of the sexes?"

To interpret constitutional guarantees of equal protection as prohibiting all distinctions in the law based on permanent birth castes is particularly necessary where the class that is treated differently lacks power, as in the case of women. There are no women on the Supreme Court. Only one of 97 United States Court of Appeal judgeships is filled by a woman[99] and only four of the 402 federal district court judges are women.[100] Only one woman is in the Senate[101] and only 12 of 435 members of the House of Representatives are women. The President, Vice President and the Cabinet are all males. As the Supreme Court stated in MULLER:

> [H]istory discloses the fact that woman has always been dependent upon man. He established his control at the outset by superior strength, and this control in various forms, with diminishing intensity, has continued to the present.[102]

Masculine control (or raw power) was similarly given by the Oregon Supreme Court as partial justification for barring women from participating in wrestling competitions.[103]

> We believe that we are justified in taking judicial notice of the fact that the membership of the legislative assembly which enacted this statute was predominantly masculine. That fact is important in determining what the legislature might have had in mind with respect to this particular statute, in addition to its concern for the public weal. It seems to us that its purpose, although somewhat selfish in nature, stands out in the statute like a sore thumb. Obviously it intended that there should be at least one island on the sea of life reserved for man that would be impregnable to the assault of woman.[104]

Men make, enforce and interpret the laws that apply to women. AS A CLASS, women are still under the control of men and dependent, for the most part, on male judges to define the degree of protection against discrimination afforded by the Constitution.

Disappointed with the court's interpretations of the fourteenth amendment, women have sought, albeit unsuccessfully, congressional approval of the Equal Rights Amendment in the hopes that the more restrictive language of the amendment will restrain the judiciary from approving sex discrimination in the law. But unless women play a greater role in all forms of government, there is no assurance that their lack of equal status under the law will not continue indefinitely despite new constitutional mandates. Although women have the ultimate political power of the vote, suffrage has not brought about great improvement in women's legal position. As one feminist has quipped, "If we gave the dog the vote it wouldn't change anything." The reasons why women have not brought themselves into self determination are what the women's liberation movement basically is about.

THE EQUAL RIGHTS AMENDMENT
Language and History

3.2.12 For nearly a half-century women have sought congressional approval of a constitutional amendment to guarantee equal rights under the law. As introduced in 1923, the Equal Rights Amendment read: "Men and women shall have equal rights throughout the United States and every place subject to its jurisdiction."[105] The language was partially changed in 1943 because it was thought the above language might be interpreted to require geographic uniformity.[106] Modified, the proposal read: "Equality of rights under the law shall not be denied or abridged by the United States or by any State on account of sex." It has since been introduced in that form.[107]

When it became apparent that the amendment would not be approved by the Senate after it had already passed the House in the 91st Congress, Senator Birch Bayh offered a substitute amendment: "Neither the United States nor any State shall, on account of sex, deny to any person within its jurisdiction the equal protection of the laws."[108] As stated by Senator Bayh, the purpose of the language, which was taken from the fourteenth amendment, was in part to "make absolutely clear that the Congress and the country do not agree with the implications of the Supreme Court's decisions in this area."[109] Senator Bayh also stated that his substitute proposal would "prevent the kind of restrictive interpretation and disruptive application which the critics have feared."[110] Because the substitute was designed as a compromise and would afford something less than absolute equality, it was not supported by the women's movement and the amendment died a quiet death in the 91st Congress.

Numerous hearings have been held on the Equal Rights Amendment from 1924 to 1970.[111]

The Equal Rights Amendment has frequently been reported favorably by the Senate Judiciary Committee.[112]. It passed the Senate in 1950[113] and 1953,[114] but it was saddled with an obviously killing rider providing that the amendment not "be construed to impair any rights, benefits, or exemptions now or hereafter conferred by law, upon persons of the female sex." As noted above, it passed the House of Representatives in 1970.[115]

The Equal Rights Amendment was originally introduced in 1923 at the instigation of the National Woman's Party. This organization has been the most persistent group in continuously pressing for congressional approval of the amendment since that time.[116]

The stepped-up interest in the amendment in 1970 was probably the result of)1 increased publicity of the women's liberation movement in the popular press which had the effect of making the potential political power of women felt by Congress and 2) the endorsement and support of the amendment by two official bodies, the Citizen's Advisory Council on the Status of Women[117] and the President's Task Force on Women's Rights and Responsibilities.[118]

The Citizens' Advisory Council published a MEMORANDUM ON THE PROPOSED EQUAL RIGHTS AMENDMENT TO THE UNITED STATES CONSTITUTION in March, 1970.[119] The MEMO-RANDUM contains a five-point analysis[120] by which to determine the effect of the Equal Rights Amendment on various laws differentiating on the basis of sex. An elaboration of that analysis in light of issues raised in connection with the 1970 Senate hearings and the debate in the 92nd Congress is set forth below.

It has been asserted by opponents of the amendment that "at one fell swoop this amendment would wipe out all those protective laws that we, after arduous toil, sought to put on the statute books."[121] It is true that the Equal Rights Amendment would be largely self-implementing and in "one fell swoop" would require equal treatment of men and women under the law. But it would not wipe all the unequal laws off the books. Some laws which apply to one sex only would be rendered unconstitutional by the amendment; others would be extended to the other sex.

The language of the amendment parallels that of the fifteenth and nineteenth amendment except that those amendments refer to "[t]he right of citizens of the United States to vote" instead of "[e]quality of rights under the law." Under the fifteenth and nineteenth amendments, state voting

laws were not wiped off the books; they were extended to apply to Negroes and women, respectively.[122] Instead of the right to vote, the Equal Rights Amendment is concerned with the right to equal treatment in the law without differentiation because of sex.

The five-point guide for determining the constitutionality of laws that distinguish on the basis of sex could likewise be utilized in cases brought under the fifth and fourteenth amendments. The battle for the Equal Rights Amendment, whether or not it ever becomes a written part of the Constitution, may serve to encourage proper interpretation of existing constitutional equal protection guarantees.

It is of course assumed that there is no such thing as "good discrimination" based on sex and that complete legal equality of men and women is desirable. If these assumptions are not valid, if it is desirable that the law treat men and women differently, then women must be represented in government in proportion to their population so that they have equal power to make the laws that apply to them and to determine when the law should be unequal.[123] The only third alternative is for women to accept their lot as a subspecies and to be ruled by a superior class.[124]

INTERPRETATION OF THE EQUAL RIGHTS AMENDMENT—THE 5-POINT GUIDE

3.2.13 1. Laws That Confer a Benefit, Privilege or Obligation of Citizenship on One Sex: Strike the Words of Sex Identification and Extend the Benefit, Privilege or Obligation to Both Sexes

(a) PROTECTIVE LABOR LAWS. Minimum wage laws and laws requiring meal periods, rest periods or seating facilities for women but not for men workers[125] confer a legal right on women workers. To give men equality of rights under the amendment to extend these benefits to men. It should be noted, however, that most minimum wage laws apply to men as well as to women.[126]

(b) SOCIAL SECURITY AND OTHER SOCIAL BENEFIT LAWS. Social Security and other types of public insurance which confer greater benefits on one sex than the other would have to be equalized by giving the greater benefit to both sexes. The additional cost involved is the measure of the extent to which the law presently discriminates against one sex and gives a special preference to the other.

One contingency for eligibility for a husband's

insurance benefit under the Social Security Act is that he must have received at least one-half his support from his wife, but no such contingency is required for a wife to secure benefits.[127] As a matter of the principle of equal rights, the benefits are equalized upward; as a matter of policy, perhaps the assumption in the law that all married women are economically dependent on their husbands should be removed by legislation. Thus, wives of individuals included under the Act would be subjected to the same contingencies that are presently applied to husbands of included individuals.

(c) ALIMONY. State laws that authorize courts to award alimony only to women in effect authorize courts to confer benefits to women but not to men.[128] The effect of the Equal Rights Amendment on these laws would be to authorize award of alimony to men. As a practical matter, alimony is sometimes awarded instead of child support so that the mother instead of the father pays the federal income tax.[129]

(d) CHILD SUPPORT. Children are legally entitled to support from both mother and father[130] despite the common assumption that the father is the breadwinner. The law pertaining to child support applies only where there is marital dissolution. Where the marriage is intact, it does not matter what the law says. In many families both parents contribute to the financial support of the family. In some, the mother devotes full time to homemaking and child care in lieu of a financial contribution. None of these arrangements would in any way be affected by the amendment.

In the case of divorce, separation or desertion, the mother is most frequently granted, or left with, custody of the children. There is no escape from her responsibility for providing food, shelter, medical care, education and upbringing for her children. She must rely on the law and, perhaps to a greater degree, on the father's goodwill for some financial assistance for the children. Women generally bear the greater burden of supporting and raising children and the Equal Rights Amendment, although requiring equality of obligations, would not make that burden heavier. It would not preclude requiring one parent to make child support payments while the other parent makes her (or his) contribution in the form of care.

(e) CHILD CUSTODY. In a few states, the law gives the mother preference in child custody matters.[131] The presumption that men are not as fit to raise the next generation is, of course, unfair.[132] As against third parties seeking custody,

the Equal Rights Amendment would extend legal preferences now accorded to women to fathers as well.

(f) DIVORCE GROUNDS. The same grounds for divorce are generally available to either party to the marriage. Exceptions in some states are "nonsupport" available to the wife,[133] or the pregnancy of the wife without knowledge of the husband at the time of the marriage, available to the husband.[134] Under the amendment, the right to support from a spouse would extend equally to both spouses; it is possible that non-support might in some circumstances be available to the husband. However, in a case where the wife works as housekeeper for her husband, such contribution should be a defense to a divorce action brought by the husband on non-support grounds.

Where pregnancy of the wife at marriage is a grounds for divorce by the husband, expectant paternity of the husband would be equally available to the wife seeking divorce. Because of problems of proof, this extension of divorce grounds to the wife would probably have practical application only where the husband subsequently acknowledges his paternity of another woman's child.[135]

(g) COMMUNITY PROPERTY CONTROL. In seven of the eight community property states,[136] the husband has control that community property including property and income contributed by the wife.[137] In Texas, however, each spouse manages and controls that community property he or she would have owned if single. Where the property contributed by the two spouses is mixed or combined, it is jointly controlled unless the spouses agree to a different arrangement.[138]

Under the Equal Rights Amendment, the husband's power in the seven other states to manage the community property would extend to the wife as well, i.e., it would be jointly managed unless otherwise agreed upon. The legislatures of those states could, of course, provide for other nondiscriminatory management of community property such as that provided in the Texas law.

(h) INHERITANCE RIGHTS. To the extent that sex distinctions in laws pertaining to inheritance and administration of descendents' estates remain,[139] the higher benefits would apply to both sexes.

In upholding the constitutionality of an Idaho statute providing that "of several persons claiming and equally entitled to administer [decedents' estates], males must be preferred to females,"[140] that state's highest court noted that it could be argued that the law discriminated against women on the basis of sex. The court explained, however, that "[n]ature itself has established the distinction and this statute is not designed to discriminate, but is only designed to alleviate the problem of holding hearings by the court to determine eligibility to administer."[141] It is doubtful that expediency should justify discrimination against women. The drawing of lots and flipping of coins are also efficient methods of decision-making and certainly preferable to the admittedly arbitrary discrimination in the Idaho law.

(i) CONSORTIUM. In some jurisdictions, only the husband has a right to sue for loss of consortium where his spouse is injured. Consortium is the right to the spouse's services.[142] Once lost, the wife's services have sudden economic value—to the husband. Under the Equal Rights Amendment, the right to sue for loss of consortium would be extended to the wife in case of actionable injury to her husband.[143]

(j) JURY SERVICE. The Women's Bureau has summarized the state laws on jury service as follows:

> In 28 States women serve under the same terms and conditions as men, with the same qualifications, disqualifications, and exemptions. In 22 States and the District of Columbia, women may be excused on grounds not available to men. Of these, 11 States permit a woman to be excused solely on the basis of her sex. An additional 10 States . . . and Puerto Rico permit women to claim an exemption because of child care or family responsibilities. Rhode Island further provides that women shall be included for jury service only when court house facilities permit. In 1967 Florida and New Hampshire removed their requirement that women register before they may be considered for jury service. Louisiana is now the only state with this requirement.[144]

Since jury service is a right and obligation of citizenship,[145] the obligation to serve imposed upon men would be extended to women. In order to extend full rights to women, IMPEDIMENTS TO SELECTION would be nullified by the amendment. Preconditions that women register or that the courthouse facilities are appropriate or a rule encouraging non-service by reason of sex would therefore be void. EXCUSES from jury service, (other than excuse for being a woman) such as for hardship, child care or family responsibilities, should be regarded as an individual privilege and extended to men in like circumstances. Thus, with

respect to jury service, the goal would be equal rights to be selected and equal rights in the excuses allowed in individual hardship cases.[146]

(k) MILITARY SERVICE. The Military Selective Service Act of 1967, as amended, makes only men liable for compulsory military service.[147] In the House debate on the Equal Rights Amendment on August 10, 1970, Representative Griffiths pointed out that women would under the amendment be equally subject to the draft but "would not be required to serve—in the Armed Forces—where they are not fitted any more than men are required to so serve. The real effect . . . would probably be to permit both sexes to volunteer on an equal basis, which is not now the case."[148]

Women have served in the armed forces for nearly 30 years.[149] There are presently more than 40,000 women in military service.[150] In 1967 special restrictions placing a ceiling on the rank to which women in military service could be promoted were removed,[151] and there are now two women generals.[152] Differences in treatment between men and women in military service parallel those in civilian life. As one woman officer stated:

> [M]ilitary women have generally fallen into the same patterns of employment that prevail in the private sector—that is a concentration in the jobs traditionally classified as "women's work" and in the skill/grade levels. To date, top level management and executive positions are, for all practical purposes, closed to military women except those directly involved with women's programs.[153]

The practice of discharging women who become pregnant (but not discharging expectant fathers) also parallels discriminatory practices of some private employers.[154]

The number of women volunteers allowed in the military is also limited. For example, the authorized strength of the Women's Army Corps is prescribed by the Secretary of Defense and is currently limited to approximately one per cent of that of the regular army.[155] In 1967, the President's National Advisory Commission on Selective Service recommended that opportunities be made available for more women to serve in the armed forces, thereby reducing the number of men who must be called involuntarily.[156]

Before the end of World War II, consideration was given to drafting women nurses.[157] However, the end of the war in Europe lessened the need for drafting nurses and the proposal was not pressed. Not all nurses are women, of course, but there are not enough male nurses to eliminate the necessity of assigning women nurses to the front. The Office of Public Affairs, Department of Defense, reports that as of January 1, 1971, the number of women, including nurses, serving in Vietnam was a little over 800.

Women are not required to train for or to serve in combat. To the extent that the exemption of women from combat duty increases the chances of such duty for men in service, it should be regarded as discriminating against men. However, in upholding the constitutionality of excluding women from the draft, a federal district court in UNITED STATES v. COOK stated that

> [w]hile each of the sexes has its own innate characteristics, for the most part physical strength in a male characteristic, and so long as this is so, the United States will be compelled to establish and maintain armed forces of males which may at least physically be equal to the armed forces of other nations, likewise composed of males, with which it must compete.[158]

Men as a class have greater muscular strength than women as a class, but big men as a group are also stronger than little men. Moreover, private employers under Title VII of the Civil Rights Act of 1964[159] are not allowed to exclude women from work requiring weight lifting.[160] Equal responsibility simply requires that people be treated as individuals and not classified by sex.

The Senate attached an amendment to the proposed Equal Rights Amendment in the 91st Congress that would have allowed Congress to exempt women from military service.[161] In expressing opposition to the draft exemption rider, the Citizens' Advisory Council on the Status of Women pointed out that there are benefits, as well as disadvantages, in serving in the armed forces:

> The opportunities for education and training afford our young people advantages for upward mobility instead of being locked into any particular economic stratum. . .
> . . . The young women of this country should not be denied the opportunity for complete training for the defense of themselves and their families, and for the preservation of their homes and their country.[162]

A group of young women of draft age also expressed opposition to the draft exemption rider. George Washington University Women's Liberation issued a statement during the Senate debate on the amendment in the 91st Congress:

> Sex exemption from the draft is a negation of our ability to face the most onerous self-determination question of our time. We are not asking to be spared from making critical decisions. If the passage of the Equal Rights Amendment means that both men and women will be subject to involuntary induction, we claim the right to answer for ourselves.
> For long enough we have been given an easy out solely because we are females. We did not ask for this easy out, and we will accept it no longer. Neither will we have our credibility diminished, our need for equal rights demeaned by senators who seek to deny us this equality with the tactic of fear.[163]

3.2.14   2. Laws That Restrict or Deny Freedom or Opportunities to One Sex: Rendered Unconstitutional

(a) PROHIBITIVE OR RESTRICTIVE LABOR LAWS. Prohibitive occupations for women under state laws are basically of two types: working in mines or other specified hazardous occupations and bartending.[164] Obviously, no one can be forced into any occupation, and the nullification of all laws closing certain work to women would not force or encourage any woman into any line of work. It would only permit women to make their own decisions without state interference. Laws prohibiting women from working in certain jobs are an obvious restriction upon their liberty and would be rendered void by the Equal Rights Amendment.

Laws in a few states still limit the weights which women can lift.[165] Such laws violate the rights of women to equal employment opportunity under Title VII of the Civil Rights Act of 1964.[166] Irrespective of Title VII, such laws also limit the freedom of a woman to choose certain types of work and would deny women equal rights under the amendment.

It might be argued that weight lifting laws confer a benefit upon women workers by protecting them from having to lift heavier objects, and therefore, the "benefit" could be extended to men workers under the amendment. The amounts of the restrictions range from 10 to 50 pounds.[167] If these restrictions were imposed upon men as well as women, some jobs simply could not be performed.[168] If the law applied to housewives, most would have to quit.

The same is true of hours restrictions, still on the books in most of the states, and laws prohibiting night work by women in certain occupations.[169] To extend such restrictions on hours to men workers would require drastic changes in the operation of most businesses and would cause an abrupt reduction in national output. A constitutional requirement of equality of the sexes does not carry with it any correlative requirement that industry restructure, no matter how desirable that ultimately might be.

(b) DOMICILE LIMITATIONS. One's domicile or legal residence can determine in which state one may vote, run for public office, serve on juries, pay taxes or have one's estate administered. The traditional rule has been that by operation of law a married woman's legal domicile automatically is that of her husband and is determined by him regardless of her intentions or where she lives. In five states married women have the right to establish their own domicile.[170] In addition to these five, three states allow a married woman to establish her own domicile for purposes of running for public office, two for purposes of jury service, three for probate purposes and thirteen for voting.[171] The Equal Rights Amendment would have the effect of removing remaining restrictions on the freedom of married women to establish their own domicile.

(c) OTHER RESTRICTIONS ON MARRIED WOMEN. The Women's Bureau of the Department of Labor reports that in three states a married woman does not have the legal capacity to become a surety or a guarantor,[172] and in four states she may not go into business for herself without court sanction.[173] These remaining legal disabilities imposed upon married women would be nullified by the amendment.

3.2.15 3. Laws Making Age Distinctions on the Basis of Sex: Equalize Up or Down.

Different ages specified for men and women or boys and girls in the same law would be equalized under the Equal Rights Amendment. Where the two different ages specified in the law are ages at which a right terminates, the HIGHER age would apply to both sexes. This would be consistent with the rationale of extending the rights, benefits and privileges accorded to one sex under the law to the other sex.[174] Where the ages are those at which limitations or disabilities are terminated, the limitations are nullified with respect to persons between the two ages by applying the LOWER age to both sexes.[175]

In a few western states the age at which a child's right to parental support terminates is 18 for girls and 21 for boys.[176] Under such laws, boys between the ages of 18 and 21 have a right which girls do not have, and the effect of the amendment would be to extend that right to girls and make the cut off

age 21 for all children.

Similarly, some laws provide the juvenile court jurisdiction may extend to girls at a higher age than boys.[177] Under the amendment the advantages accorded to one sex would be extended to the other by applying the higher age of juvenile court jurisdiction to both sexes.

In some states the age at which marriage can be contracted with parental consent and the age below which parental consent is required for marriage is higher for boys than for girls.[178] By contrast, some child labor laws provide a higher age for girls than for boys. The right to marry[179] and the right to engage in labor[180] are restricted for persons between the two ages—boys in the case of marriage and girls in the case of the child labor laws. The restriction would be removed by the amendment, and the lower age applied in both cases.

3.2.16 4. Laws Which Involve Difference in Sexual or Reproductive Capacity

(a) MATERNITY. Since men do not bear children, a law which applies to pregnancy and childbirth and which refers only to women is not making a sex classification. Despite its terminology, the law would apply in the same way and have the same effect if it referred to people.[181] Thus, if a law provided for cash benefits for the birth of a child, it would not be violative of the Equal Rights Amendment. It is important to note, however, that special maternity benefits laws are virtually non-existent.[182] If there were such laws, they of course would have to be reasonably related to the protection of pregnancy and childbirth and not designed to place women at a competitive disadvantage in the labor force.

The Citizens' Advisory Council on the Status of Women has adopted the following statement on "Job-Related Maternity Benefits:"

> Childbirth and complications of pregnancy are, for ALL JOB-RELATED PURPOSES, temporary disabilities and should be treated as such under any health insurance, temporary disability insurance, or sick leave plan of an employer, union, or fraternal society.[183]

The Council noted, however, that of the six jurisdictions which have government-sponsored temporary disability insurance programs, only New Jersey and Rhode Island require that the benefits under these laws be available for temporary absence from work for a normal delivery.[184]

The exclusion of childbirth from a state

temporary disability insurance program is in the nature of a "reverse benefit" or a detriment. If the special exclusion were reasonably related to DISCOURAGING pregnancy and childbirth (and if that were its true purpose which, of course, it is not), perhaps it would not be violative of the Equal Rights Amendment. The reason for the absence from work due to the worker's temporarily being disabled, whether due to childbirth, injury, surgery or other temporary physical incapacity, is of no concern to the employment. To single out absence for the particular reason of childbirth bears no employment purpose other than to discriminate against certain women workers. Though superficially neutral in that the law acts to exclude childbirth and not women, it results in treating some women workers differently than men workers who are absent from work due to temporary disability. In the guise of discouraging childbirth, the women are punished as workers.

Laws prohibiting women from working for certain periods before and after childbirth[185] discriminate against women because the true aim and effect is to regulate the women's employment and not to regulate or give "benefits" for pregnancy or childbirth. There is no comparable compelled period of absence from work for men who, for example, are temporarily disabled because of surgery.

In sum, singling out childbirth for special treatment does not discriminate on the basis of sex even though the law refers only to women because men cannot give birth. But if in referring to childbirth the law goes beyond to spheres other than the reproductive difference between men and women (e.g., employment), the law must treat women who give birth the same as men are treated in respect to the area of regulated employment (e.g., absence from work for temporary disability).

Similarly, women and girls could not be discriminated against in pursuing education because of childbirth. The expulsion or segregation of girls in public schools who have become mothers, but not boys who have become fathers, would be inconsistent with the Equal Rights Amendment. Just as laws prohibiting women from working for certain periods before (or after) childbirth regulate women's employment, not the childbirth, exclusion of pregnant girls from public schools regulates their education, not their pregnancy. The reproductive differences in the sexes are not relevant to employment and education and in these areas men and women must be treated the same.

A criminal abortion statute is an example of a law which is limited on its face to the reproductive function. As such, it does not involve a direct question of denial of equality but of denial of other human rights beyond the scope of this article. It may be noted, however, that the abortion issue is not unrelated to the equality issue because the same underlying bases for court decisions denying equality of the sexes (women as reproductive instruments of the state, as dangerous to morality, and properly under the control of men) are IMPLICIT in the abortion laws.

(b) HOMOSEXUALITY. It was suggested at the Senate Judiciary Committee hearings on the Equal Rights Amendment in September, 1970, that "[i]f the law must be as undiscriminating concerning sex as it is toward race, it would follow that laws outlawing wedlock between members of the same sex would be as invalid as laws forbidding miscegenation."[186] This is not the case. The amendment would affect only laws in which the difference in treatment is based on sex and not those where the difference is based on sexuality. It would not affect laws distinguishing as between homosexuality and heterosexuality. It would, however, require that male and female homosexuals be treated the same and that male and female heterosexuals be treated the same.

Although the issue is not relevant to the amendment, the interest of the state in recognizing heterosexual marriages is their capacity for reproduction and child raising. This element is not present in homosexual relationships. Any challenge to legal distinctions as between heterosexuals and homosexuals would have to be brought under the fourteenth amendment.

(c) RAPE. Forcible rape is sexual intercourse with a female not the wife of the assailant by force and without her consent. During 1969, there were approximately 36,470 reported forcible rapes, a rate of 35 for every 100,000 women in the United States.[187] The rate has almost doubled—up 93 per cent since 1960.[188] According to the Federal Bureau of Investigation, rape "is probably one of the most under reported crimes due primarily to fear and/or embarassment on the part of the victims."[189] The F.B.I. crime figures include only actual offenses established by police investigation.[190]

A reported study of 100 consecutive rape cases in Dade County, Florida, showed that 38 of the victims suffered physical injury (only gross injuries were counted).[191] In 18 of the cases, only one male assailant was involved; in 42 there were from two to ten assailants.[192] In 45 of the cases, the assailants were not apprehended. Nineteen were determined by the police after investigation to be "unfounded." Of the remaining 36, ten were found guilty of rape or a lesser crime.[193]

From 1930 to 1968 there were 455 executions for rape.[194] The Court of Appeals for the Fourth Circuit recently held that execution is a cruel and unusual punishment for all but the most aggravated types of rape and therefore violative of the eighth amendment.[195] No useful purpose is served in punishing rape more severely than other forms of assault that inflict comparable injury on the victim. The more severe penalties do not appear to add to the protection of women. The Model Penal Code treats both rape and aggravated assault as felonies in the second degree.[196]

It has been suggested that rape laws do not classify by sex because their application would not be any different if the prohibition applied to persons rather than to men and accordingly would not be constitutionally objectionable.[197] This assumes, however, that a woman or women could not force sexual intercourse on a man without his consent. If that is possible, then the Equal Rights Amendment would affect rape laws as follows: A man accused of rape could not be punished more severely than a woman who performed the same elements of the crime. She would be prosecuted under other applicable statutes, such as aggravated assault, kidnapping, maiming or burglary. Thus, in those states where the rape penalty is more severe than those criminal statutes that could be invoked to prosecute women who performed such acts upon men, the maximum rape penalty would be reduced to the level of that in the applicable non-rape criminal statute. This would accomplish equal treatment of men and women accused of the same elements of the crime. What the crime is called does not matter.

The elements in the crime of statutory rape, sexual intercourse with a girl under a certain age not the wife of the assailant, would be comparable to those involved in seduction by a woman of a boy under the same age. The law assumes that children do not have capacity to consent; absence of consent is not part of such crimes. Unlike forcible rape, where other criminal statutes would apply to both men and women and there is no statute applicable to women involving the same criminal elements,[198] the legislature would have to amend the law to apply to women or the state could punish the rape only if it were forcible. The net effect if the law were not amended, therefore,

would be to remove the presumption in the law that a girl under the specified age (the range is 14 to 21),[199] is incapable of consenting to intercourse.

(d) PROSTITUTION. As a matter of morality there probably should be no difference in treatment under the law as between a prostitute and her customer, but laws punishing prostitution generally punish only the woman.[200] The receipt of payment for sexual services, however, differs from giving payment; therefore, the prostitute and her customer are not comparable. The customer does not violate the same law as the prostitute because one element of the crime is not present, and accordingly, equal treatment of prostitute and customer would not be required by the Equal Rights Amendment. However, since it is possible for a man to sell his sexual services to a woman, as in the case of statutory rape, the appropriate legislative bodies would have to amend the law to apply to both sexes or women could no longer be punished for prostitution.[201]

3.2.17 5. Separation of the Sexes: Forbidden Except Where Necessary to Protect the Right to Privacy and Does Not Deny Individual Rights and Liberties

The Citizen's Advisory Council Memorandum on the Equal Rights Amendment[202] states that legally required separation of the sexes, to be consistent with the amendment, must meet two requirements: 1) the separation must not deny individual rights and liberties and 2) the government must show that the reason for the separation is to protect the right of privacy.[203]

Whether the generally unnatural and artificial condition of sex segregation is consistent with equal rights depends, in part, upon whether separate can be equal. In addition to the few remaining sex segregated systems of public higher education,[204] some public schools in the South have segregated by sex in connection with racial desegregation plans.[205] In BROWN v. BOARD OF EDUCATION, the Supreme Court held that "in the field of public education the doctrine of 'separate but equal' has no place."[206] The Court's reasoning in BROWN regarding the effect of separate educational facilities on Negro children is equally applicable with respect to the effect sex separation has upon girls:

To separate them from others of similar age and qualification solely because of their [sex] generates a feeling of inferiority as to their status in the community that may affect their hearts and minds in a way unlikely ever to be undone.[207]

In addition, sex separation reinforces artificial, exaggerated and meaningless distinctions between the sexes that further stereotype and limit both sexes.

It has been suggested that

> [the] constitutional right of privacy would prevail over other portions of the Constitution embodying the laws of the society in its collective capacity.
> . . . [T]he right of privacy would permit, perhaps require, separation of the sexes in public restrooms, segregation by sex in sleeping quarters of prisons or similar public institutions, and a certain segregation of living conditions in the Armed Forces.[208]

Presumably, individual privacy is affected more in these situations where the sexes are mixed than where all are of the same sex because of greater heterosexual interest and therefore greater invasion of the right to be left alone. While these particular examples do not appear to present problems, there is danger that the right of privacy, if used to justify segregation of the sexes, would be the new technique for discriminating against women.

Privacy in inherently INDIVIDUAL and not class oriented. Just as the right of an individual to be protected by government from harm may not be used to justify class discrimination,[209] the individual right of privacy should not justify governmentally enforced segregation where the separation affects the individual's right to equal treatment without differentiation by reason of sex. In other words, the rule should be that government has an obligation to construct its facilities so that integration of the sexes does not cause invasion of individual privacy, not that government can segregate the sexes if necessary to avoid invasion of privacy. Thus, in constructing university dormitories,

protecting privacy by segregating sleeping quarters and bathrooms does not warrant segregating students in facilities for eating, studying and social activities. The desired goal is to construct facilities to protect individual privacy from interference by anyone, regardless of sex.

CONCLUSION

3.2.18 The Equal Rights Amendment would not change the law. It would only require equality. Whether the amendment is literally added to the Constitution or read into existing provisions through interpretation, courts must no longer base approval of sex distinctions in the law on the "woman's place is in the home" or any variant of that assumption. Nor should the law make any distinction as between persons based on their class by birth.

Finally, who can speak for women, many of whom are too satisfied and/or oppressed to make their views known? Certainly not men, and certainly not the "authorities"—judges, legislators, lawyers, doctors, psychiatrists, writers, sociologists—regardless of their sex. This does not mean that every issue is "up for grabs" with the "degree" of equality decided by the loudest or most prestigious. The power of an individual to give up the right to equal treatment under the law is non-delegable.

Mary Eastwood, D.J.
Office of Legal Counsel,
Department of Justice

The views expressed in this article are those of the author. They are not presented as the views of the Dept. of Justice or any other government agency or official body.

REFERENCES

1. Sex distinctions in laws and official practices have been documented elsewhere. See L. KANOWITZ, WOMEN AND THE LAW (1969); PRESIDENT'S COMMISSION ON THE STATUS OF WOMEN, AMERICAN WOMEN (1963); U.S. DEP'T OF LABOR, WOMEN'S BUREAU, 1969 HANDBOOK ON WOMEN WORKERS (1969); CITIZEN'S ADVISORY COUNCIL ON THE STATUS OF WOMEN, REPORT OF THE TASK FORCE ON FAMILY LAW AND POLICY (1968); P. MURRAY, ENGLISH AND AMERICAN STATUTES ON QUALIFICATIONS, EXEMPTIONS, AND EXCUSES OF JURORS WITH SPECIAL REFERENCE TO WOMEN (1966).

2. One such example is the failure of the Federal Communications Commission to require station licensees to report their positive action programs for equal employment opportunity for women while requiring such reports of program with respect to Negroes, American Indians, Spanish-Surnamed Americans and Orientals. Nondiscrimination Broadcast Practices, 23 F.C.C.2d 430 (1970). See also 35 Fed. Reg. 8825 (1970) where the FCC announced that its major enforcement efforts would be with regard to employment of those groups (and not women). The National Organization for Women (NOW) has petitioned the Commission to amend its report forms so as to include positive action programs for women. F.C.C. No. RM-1722, filed December 4, 1970. Similarly, regulations of the Department of Labor issued under Executive Order No. 11246 of September 24, 1965, as amended, concerning nondiscrimination in employment under

government contracts require affirmative action programs to eliminate discrimination against minority groups. 35 Fed. Reg. 2568 (1970). In response to questions as to the applicability to affirmative programs for the employment of women, the Secretary of Labor stated he had "no intention of applying literally exactly the same approach to women in Order 4 [35 Fed. Reg. 2568 (1970)] which was designed for racial minorities." Washington Post, July 27, 1970, p.B, at 1, col. 1. The Labor Department's Washington Plan of affirmative action programs for federally involved construction contracts also excludes women. 35 Fed. Reg. 19352 (1970). See also PRESIDENT'S TASK FORCE ON WOMEN'S RIGHTS AND RESPONSIBILITIES, A MATTER OF SIMPLE JUSTICE, 18-26 (1970).

Early interpretations of Title VII of the Civil Rights Act of 1964, 42 U.S.C. p. 2000e et seq. (1964), by the Equal Employment Opportunity Commission made clear that that agency did not at the time regard sex discrimination important. For example, the EEOC specifically allowed sex discrimination in job advertising. 30 Fed. Reg. 14928 (1965); 31 Fed. Reg. 6414 (1966). But see the current rule, 29 C.F.R. p. 1604.4 (1970), discussed in Fuentes, Federal Remedial Sanctions: Focus on Title VII, 5 Val. U.L. Rev. 374 (1971).

3. U.S. Const. amend. V prohibits the federal government from depriving any person of "life, liberty or property, without due process of law." U.S. Const. amend. XIV similarly prohibits the state governments from denying due process to any person and prohibits the denial "to any person within its jurisdiction the equal protection of the laws."

4. S.J.Res. 8, 92nd Cong., 1st Sess. (1971).

5. Murray & Eastwood, JANE CROW AND THE LAW: SEX DISCRIMINATION AND TITLE VII, 34 Geo. Wash. L. Rev. 232, 238 (1965).

6. H.J.Res. 264, 91st Cong., 2nd Sess. (1970), reported at 116 Cong. Rec. H7984-85 (daily ed. Aug. 10, 1970).

7. Id. at H7953.

8. PRESIDENT'S COMMISSION ON THE STATUS OF WOMEN, AMERICAN WOMEN 44 (1963).

9. Id. at 45.

10. The fifth amendment due process clause imposes restrictions on the federal government against discriminatory class legislation comparable to restrictions imposed on the states by the fourteenth amendment equal protection clause. Bolling v. Sharpe, 347 U.S. 497 (1954).

11. For an analysis of constitutional standards under the equal protection clause see DEVELOPMENTS IN THE LAW-EQUAL PROTECTION, 82 Harv. L. Rev. 1065 (1969).

12. Gulf, C&S. Ry. v. Ellis, 165 U.S. 150, 165-66 (1897). See also McGowan v. Maryland, 366 U.S. 420, 426 (1961); Hernandez v. Texas, 347 U.S. 475, 478 (1954); Royster Guano Co. v. Virginia, 253 U.S. 412, 415 (1920).

13. Korematsu v. United States, 323 U.S. 214, 216 (1944).

14. Loving v. Virginia, 388 U.S. 1, 11 (1967). See also McLaughlin v. Florida, 379 U.S. 184, 192 (1964).

15. Sherbert v. Verner, 374 U.S. 398, 406 (1963).

16. Bates v. City of Little Rock, 361 U.S. 516, 524 (1960).

17. Shapiro v. Thompson, 394 U.S. 618, 634 (1969).

18. Harper v. Virginia State Bd. of Elections, 383 U.S. 663, 670 (1966); Reynolds v. Sims, 377 U.S. 533, 561-62 (1964).

19. Skinner v. Oklahoma, 316 U.S. 535, 541 (1962).

20. Levy v. Louisiana, 391 U.S. 68, 71 (1968).

21. See note 7 supra and accompanying text.

22. 83 U.S. (16 Wall.) 130 (1872).

23. Id. at 141 (Bradley, J., concurring). See also In re Lockwood, 154 U.S. 116 (1894).

24. 88 U.S. (21 Wall.) 162 (1874).

25. Id. at 174.

26. Id. at 170.

27. See Muller v. Oregon, 208 U.S. 412, 419 n.1 (1908).

28. 198 U.S. 45 (1905).

29. 208 U.S. 412 (1908).

30. See also Miller v. Wilson, 236 U.S. 373 (1915); Bosley v. McLaughlin, 236 U.S. 385 (1915); Riley v. Massachusetts, 232 U.S. 671 (1914), cases upholding hours restrictions for women employees.

31. 208 U.S. at 422.

32. 243 U.S. 426 (1917).

33. For summaries of selected cases involving sex discrimination, see PRESIDENT'S COMMISSION ON THE STATUS OF WOMEN, REPORT OF THE CIVIL AND POLITICAL RIGHTS COMMITTEE, Appendix B (1963).

34. 208 U.S. at 421.

35. Radice v. New York, 264 U.S. 292 (1924.)

36. West Coast Hotel Co. v. Parrish, 300 U.S. 397 (1937).

37. 239 U.S. 33 (1915).

38. Id. at 41.

39. 118 U.S. 356 (1886).

40. 334 U.S. 410 (1948).

41. 335 U.S. 464 (1948).

42. Id. at 466.

43. Id.

44. Id. at 467.

45. 118 U.S. 356, 370 (1886).

46. McCrimmon v. Daley, 418 F. 2d 366 (7th Cir. 1966).

47. McCrimmon v. Daley, 2 F.E.P. Cas. 971 (N.D. Ill. 1970).

48. Paterson Tavern & Grill Owners Ass'n. Inc. v. Borough of Hawthorne, 57 N.J. 180, 270 A. 2d 628 (1970). See also Wilson v. Hacker, 200 Misc. 124, 101 N.Y.S. 2d 461 (Sup. Ct. 1950) where a New York court held that a bartenders union demand that women bartenders be excluded was unlawful.

49. Seidenberg v. McSorleys' Old Ale House, Inc., 308 F. Supp. 1253 (S.D.N.Y. 1969). For a discussion of discrimination against women in public accommodations, see Seidenberg, THE FEDERAL BAR v. THE ALE HOUSE BAR: WOMEN AND PUBLIC ACCOMMODATIONS, 5 Val. U.L. Rev. 318 Rev. 318 (1971).

50. 368 U.S. 57 (1961).

51. Id. at 62 (emphasis added).

52. Phillips v. Martin Marietta Corp., 91 S. Ct. 496 (1971). For an analysis of this case, see Berger, EQUAL PAY, EQUAL EMPYOYMENT OPPORTUNITY AND EQUAL ENFORCEMENT OF LAW FOR WOMEN, 5 Val. U.L. Rev. 326 (1971). See also Fuentes supra note 2: Note, THE MANDATE OF TITLE VII of the CIVIL RIGHTS ACT OF 1964: TO TREAT WOMEN AS INDIVIDUALS, 59 Geo. L.J. 221, 232-39 (1970).

53. 251 F. Supp. 401 (M.D. Ala. 1966).

54. Id. at 408.

55. Abbot v. Mines, 411 F. 2d 353, 355 (6th Cir. 1969).

56. State v. Hall, 187 So. 2d 861 (Miss.), appeal dismissed, 385 U.S. 98 (1966).
57. Id. at 863 (emphasis added).
58. MISS. CODE ANN. p. 1762 (Supp. 1968).
59. Longer prison terms for women than for men convicted of the same crimes have been declared unconstitutional. United States ex rel. Robinson v. York, 281 F. Supp. 8 (D. Conn. 1968); Commonwealth v. Daniel, 430 Pa. 642, 243 A. 2d 400 (1968). See also Morgan v. State, 179 Ind. 300, 101 N.E. 6 (1913); State v. Walker, 326 Mo. 1233, 34 S.W. 2d 124 (1930).
60. U.S. DEP'T OF JUSTICE, PRISONERS IN STATE AND FEDERAL INSTITUTIONS FOR ADULT FELONS 1967, at 10 (1969). On March 15, 1970, five percent of the adult prisoners confined in county and city jails were women. U.S. DEP'T OF JUSTICE, 1970 NATIONAL JAIL CENSUS 1 (1971).
61. 309 F. Supp. 184 (E.D. Va. 1970).
62. Id. at 189. But see Williams v. McNair, 316 F. Supp. 134 (D.S.C. 1970), aff'd mem., 91 S. Ct. 976 (1971); Allred v. Heaton 336 S.W. 2d 251 (Tex. Civ. App.), appeal dismissed & cert. denied, 364 U.S. 517 (1960), rehearing denied, 364 U.S. 944 (1961); Heaton v. Bristol, 317 S.W. 2d 86 (Tex. Civ. App. 1958), appeal dismissed & cert. denied, 359 U.S. 230, rehearing denied, 359 U.S. 999 (1959). For an analysis of sex separation in public schools as sex discrimination, see Barnett, THE CONSTITUTIONALITY OF SEX SEPARATION IN SCHOOL DESEGREGATION PLANS, 37 U. Chi. L. Rev. 296, 311-17 (1970).
63. Gruenwald v. Gardner, 390 F. 2d 591 (2nd Cir.), cert. denied, 393 U.S. 982 (1968).
64. 291 F. Supp. 122 (S.D. N.Y. 1968). See also United States v. Cook, 311 F. Supp. 618 (W.D. Pa. 1970).
65. 50 U.S.C. App. p. 451, 453 (1964).
66. 291 F. Supp. at 124-25.
67. United States v. Schwimmer, 279 U.S. 644 (1929). The case involved the exclusion of a 49 year old woman pacifist under the immigration laws because of her refusal to bear arms. The court noted that despite her own ineligibility for military service by reason of age and sex she might influence others.
68. 251 F. Supp. 401, 408 (M.D. Ala. 1966).
69. 291 F. Supp. 122, 125. Cf. Hoyt v. Florida, 368 U.S. 57 (1961).
70. 284 F. Supp. 950, 956 (C.D. Cal.), vacated, 393 U.S. 83, rehearing denied, 393 U.S. 993 (1968), rev'd & remanded, 437 F. 2d 563 (9th Cir. 1971).
71. 42 U.S.C. p. 2000e (1964).
72. Cal. Labor Code p. 1350 (West Supp. 1971).
73. 208 U.S. 412 (1908).
74. 236 U.S. 373 (1915).
75. 162 Cal. 687, 127 P. 427 (1912).
76. A case challenging the constitutionality of Louisiana's hours laws was similarly dismissed by the district court but was not appealed. Ward v. Luttrell, 292 F. Supp. 162, 165 (E.D. La. 1968).
77. 42 U.S.C. p. 2000e-5(f) (1964).
78. 393 U.S. 83, rehearing denied, 393 U.S. 993 (1968).
79. Jurisdictional Statement at 2, Menkelkoch v. Industrial Welfare Comm'n, 393 U.S. 83 (1968).
80. 28 U.S.C. p. 1253 provides for a direct appeal to the Supreme Court "from an order granting or denying, after notice and hearing, an interlocutory or permanent injunction in any civil action, suit or proceeding required by any Act of Congress to be heard and determined by a district court of three judges."
81. See Currie, The Three-Judge District Court in Constitutional Litigation, 32 U. Chi. L. REV. 1 (1964), for a discussion of the three-judge statute.
82. 437 F. 2d 563 (9th Cir. 1971).
83. Id. at 566-67.
84. Id. at 567.
85. Id.
86. Id.
87. See notes 27-45 supra and accompanying text.
88. 437 F. 2d at 569.
89. 42 U.S.C. p. 2000e (1964).
90. See Berger, Equal Pay, Equal Employment Opportunity and Equal Enforcement of the Law for Women, 5 Val. U.L. Rev. 326 (1971); Ross, Sex Discrimination and 'Protective' Legislation, published in Hearings on S.J. Res. 61 Before the Subcomm. on Constitutional Amendments of the Senate Comm. on the Judiciary, 91st Cong., 2d Sess., at 392 (1970).
91. Brief for Appellant at 14-15, Mengelkoch v. Industrial Welfare Comm'n, 437 F. 2d 563 (9th Cir. 1971); Brief for Human Rights for Women as Amicus Curiae at 18-20, Rosenfeld v. Southern Pacific Co., 3 F.E.P. Cas. 130 (9th Cir. 1971); Brief for Plaintiffs at 24-25, Kirstein v. Rector & Visitors of the University of Virginia, 309 F. Supp. 184 (E.D. Va. 1970).
92. 281 F. Supp. 8 (D. Conn. 1968).
93. Id. at 14.
94. Id. at 13. The court relied upon Hoyt v. Florida, 386 U.S. 57 (1961); Goesaert vs. Cleary, 335 U.S. 464 (1948); and Muller v. Oregon, 208 U.S. 412 (1908).
95. Kanowitz, Constitutional Aspects of Sex-Based Discrimination in American Law, 48 Neb. L. Rev. 131, 142 (1968). See also Berg, Title VII: A Three-Year's View, 44 NOTRE DAME LAW. 311, 344 (1969). The concept of "benign" discrimination to make up for past damage to a class of course would be fraught with danger if applied to women. Recent Developments-Equal Protection, 82 Harv. L. Rev. 1065, 1104-20 1969). Any permitted difference in treatment as between men and women is likely to "protect" away women's liberties. It has even been suggested that discrimination against women in employment is benign if the purpose of restricting women is for their own "protection." Moewe, The Case for Benign Sex Discrimination, 44 Los Angeles Bar Bull., 337, 340-41 (1969).
96. 383 U.S. 663, 669 (1966) (emphasis in original).
97. DECLARATION OF INDEPENDENCE. The fact that the founding fathers did not have women or blacks in mind does not negate the applicability of the principle to those classes. It may be noted, however, that Abigail Adams had women in mind and is quoted as writing to her husband John:
    Remember: all men would be tyrants if they could. . . . If attention is not paid to the ladies, we shall foment a rebellion and will not hold ourselves bound by any laws in which we have no voice or representation.
    LENGYEL, FOUR DAYS IN JULY 123 (1958).
98. Compare Crozier, Constitutionality of Discrimination Based on Sex, 15 B.U.L., Rev. 723 (1935). The author states that "(o)nly permanent and natural classes are open to those deep, traditional implications which

become attached to classes regardless of the actual qualities of the members of the class." Id. at 727-28. Certain mental or physical defects may be permanent from birth, but these are conditions not classes. Therefore, special legislation to protect them would not be forbidden under this rule.

99. Shirley Hufstedler, Ninth Circuit Court of Appeals.
100. Sarah Hughes, Northern District of Texas; Constance Baker, Motley, Southern District of New York; June Green, District of the District of Columbia; Cornelia Kennedy, Eastern District of Michigan.
101. Senator Margaret Chase Smith of Maine.
102. Muller v. Oregon, 208 U.S. 412, 421 (1908).
103. State v. Hunter, 208 Ore. 282, 300 P. 2d 455 (1956). The reader should not be distracted by the subject matter of the case. It is the concept which might be applied in any sex discrimination case that is important.
104. Id. at 284, 300 P. 2d at 457.
105. S.J. Res. 21, 68th Cong., 1st Sess., 65 CONG. REC. 150 (1923).
106. S. Rep. No. 267, 78th Cong., 1st Sess. (1943).
107. H.J. Res. 208, S.J. Res. 8, 92d Cong., 1st Sess. (1971).
108. 116 CONG. REC. S18076 (daily ed. Oct. 14, 1970).
109. Id. A resolution simply expressing the sense of Congress that the right to equal treatment under the law without differentiation based on sex is protected by the fifth and fourteenth amendments might have been more appropriate.
110. Id.
111. See S. Rep. No. 267, supra note 106, at 2, for a history of congressional hearings on the Equal Rights Amendment. See also Hearings on S.J. Res. 61 & 231 Before the Senate Comm. on the Judiciary, 91st Cong., 2d Sess. (Sept. 1970); Hearings on S.J. Res. 61 Before the Subcomm. on Constitutional Amendments of the Senate Comm. on the Judiciary, 90th Cong., 2d Sess. (May 1970); Hearings Before the Subcomm. on Constitutional Amendments of the Senate Comm. on the Judiciary, 84th Cong., 2d Sess. (1956); Hearings on Proposing an Amendment to the Constitution Relative to Equal Rights for Men and Women Before Subcomm. No. I of the House Comm. on the Judiciary, 80th Cong., 2d Sess. (1948).
112. See, e.d., S. Rep. No. 1558, 88th Cong., 2d Sess. (1964); S. Rep. No. 2192, 87th Cong., 2d. Sess. (1962); S. Rep. No. 303, 86th Cong., 1st Sess. (1959); S. Rep. No. 1150, 85th Cong., 1st Sess. (1957).
113. 96 Cong. Rec. 972-73 (1950).
114. 99 Cong. Rec. 8954-55 (1953).
115. 116 Cong. Rec. H7985 (daily ed. Aug. 10, 1970).
116. This persistence is not surprising in view of the origin and history of the National Woman's Party. Its founder and honorary national chairman, Alice Paul, led the suffrage campaign which culminated in adoption of the nineteenth amendment. The suffragists' tactics included peaceful demonstrations and picketing. Some of the women who were arrested in the summer of 1917 "for obstructing traffic" were tried and sentenced to prison. When they went on a hunger strike to protest their brutal treatment in prison, they were painfully and forcibly fed. In an effort to break the spirit of their leader, Miss Paul was held incommunicado in a psychopathic ward for a week. For a history of the suffragists' experiences

as political prisoners, see IRWIN, UP HILL WITH BANNERS FLYING: THE STORY OF THE WOMAN'S PARTY 269-99 (1964). In 1971, Alice Paul continues as the spearhead in the drive for passage of the Equal Rights Amendment.
117. Established by Executive Order No. 11126 of November 1, 1963, 3 C.F.R. 791 (Supp. 1963), the Council consists of 20 members appointed by the president.
118. The Task Force is an ad hoc group set up in October, 1969 to review the status of women and make recommendations to the President. See PRESIDENT'S TASK FORCE ON WOMEN'S RIGHTS AND RESPONSIBILITIES, A MATTER OF SIMPLE JUSTICE (1970).
119. Reprinted at Hearings on S.J. Res. 61 Before the Subcomm. on Constitutional Amendments of the Senate Comm. on the Judiciary, 91st Cong., 2d Sess., at 369-90 (1970). Representative Griffiths also had the Memorandum reprinted at 116 Cong. Rec. E2588 (daily ed. March 26, 1970).
120. Hearings on S.J. Res. 61, supra note 119, at 384-86.
121. Remarks of Representative Celler, 116 Cong. Rec. H7961 (daily ed. Aug. 10, 1970).
122. Neal v. Delaware, 103 U.S. 370, 389 (1880): Graves v. Eubank, 205 Ala. 174, 87 So. 587, 588 (1921).
123. Proportional representation in government might be initiated by adoption of the following constitutional amendment:
    Section 1. One Senator from each state shall be a woman and the other shall be a man. As near as may be, one half the Senators elected at each election shall be female and the other half shall be male. The three Classes of Senators shall be further divided into six Classes, to effectuate this Article.
    Section 2. The Supreme Court of the United States shall consist of not less than one half women Judges.
    Secton 3. The Congress shall have power to enforce the provisions of this Article by appropriate legislation.
124. The extreme view that women are a subspecies is expressed by the National Socialist White People's Party (formerly the American Nazi Party) as follows:
    The halls of Congress are actually ringing with the serious debate on legislation designed to make women equal. And perhaps we shouldn't be surprised at this foolishness, because it is simply a logical extrapolation of the liberal fantasy that all featherless bipeds are, or should be "equal," and that racial sexual, and other differences are nature's mistakes which can be legislated away.
    Pierce, Weekly Telephone Recording, Arlington, Va. (1970).
125. U.S. Dep't of Labor, Women's Bureau, supra note 1, 26, 265, 274-75.
126. Id. at 265.
127. 42 U.S.C.A. pp. 402(b)(1) (C) (1970).
128. In at least 12 states, courts may award alimony to either husband or wife. U.S. Dep't of Labor, Women's Bureau, supra note 1, at 287.
129. Int. Rev. Code of 1954, pp. 61, 71, 215.
130. See COUNCIL OF STATE GOV'TS, RECIPROCAL STATE LEGISLATION TO ENFORCE THE SUPPORT OF DEPENDENTS 20 (1964).

131. The Women's Bureau states that at least 8 states give the mother preference if the child is of tender years and the father preference ''if the child is of an age to require education or preparation for labor or business.'' U.S. Dep't of Labor, Women's Bureau, supra note 1, at 287.

132. The Supreme Court has agreed to review a case challenging an Illinois law allowing the natural mother to have custody of an illegitimate child but requiring the natural father to either adopt or seek permission to become legal guardian of the child. In re Stanley, 45 Ill. 2d 132, 256 N.E. 2d 814 (1970), cert. granted, 91 S. Ct. 584 (1971).

133. Arkansas and North Dakota allow a husband to obtain a divorce on grounds of the wife's failure to support in certain circumstances. Ark. Stat. Ann. p. 34-1202 (1962); N.D. Cent. Code pp. 14-05-03, 14-05-07 (1960).

134. For a listing of grounds for divorce by state as of December 1, 1969, see Steele, The Legal Status of Women in The Book of the States 309, 404-05 (Council of State Gov'ts ed. 1970).

135. For an enlightened view of divorce grounds, see Goldstein & Gitter, On Abolition of Grounds for Divorce: A Model Statute and Commentary, 3 FAMILY L.Q. 75 (1969). See also CITIZEN'S ADVISORY COUNCIL ON THE STATUS OF WOMEN, REPORT OF THE TASK FORCE ON FAMILY LAW AND POLICY 34-38 (1968).

136. Property acquired by either spouse during the marriage is jointly owned, i.e., ''community property'' of the spouses in Arizona, California, Idaho, Louisiana, New Mexico, Nevada, Texas and Washington.

137. U.S. DEP'T OF LABOR, WOMEN'S BUREAU, Supra note 1, at 290.

138. Ch. 888, p. 1 (1969) Texas Laws (effective 1970).

139. See U.S. DEP'T OF LABOR, WOMEN'S BUREAU, supra note 125, at 290-92.

140. IDAHO CODE ANN. p. 15-314 (1948).

141. Reed v. Reed, 93 Idaho 511, 465 P. 2d 635 (1970), prob. juris. noted, 91 S. Ct. 917 (1971).

142. For an analysis of the law pertaining to consortium see Kanowitz (Sex-Based Discrimination in American Law: Law and the Married Woman, 12 St. Louis U.L.J. 3, 49-50 (1967); Kanowitz, Constitutional Aspects of Sex-Based Discrimination in American Law, 48 Neb. L. Rev. 131, 143-51 (1968).

143. A property interest in another person entitling one to sue for its loss seems repugnant to concepts of individual liberty and perhaps should be abolished altogether.

144. U.S. DEP'T OF LABOR, WOMEN'S BUREAU, supra note 125, at 284, A District of Columbia law allowing women to be excused because of sex was repealed in 1967. Pub. L. No. 90-274, p. 103, 82 Stat. 62. See 28 U.S.C.A. p. 1862 (Supp. 1970)

145 White v. Crook, 251 F. Supp. 401 (M.D. Ala. 1966).

146. This discussion relates to state juries; federal law prohibits discrimination based on sex in federal jury service. 28 U.S.C.A. p. 1862 (Supp. 1970).

147. 50 U.S.C. App. pp. 451, 453 (1964). The present induction authority terminates July 1, 1971. 50 U.S.C. App. p. 467 (1964). Whether or not the authority is continued, the draft issue cannot be avoided.

148. 116 Cong. Rec. H7953 (daily ed. Aug. 10, 1970). See also S. Ref. No. 5158, 88th Cong., 2d Sess. 2-3

149. Holm, Women and Future Manpower Needs, DEFENCE MANAGEMENT J., Winter, 1970, at 6, 10.

150. Turner, Women in Military Services, DEFENCE MANAGEMENT J. Winter, 1970, at 12.

151. Pub. L. No. 90-130, 81 Stat. 374.

152. Gen. Elizabeth Hoisington, Director of the Women's Army Corps and General Anna Mae Hays, Chief of the Army Nurse Corps. Col. Jeanne M. Holm, Director of Women in the Air Force, is on the list of nominees for promotion to general.

153. Holm, supra note 149, at 10. It may be noted that ''KP'' and latrine duty, the traditional army punishments, are also traditional ''women's work.''

154. Id.

155. See 10 U.S.C.A. p. 3215 (Supp. 1970); 32 C.F.R. p. 580.4 (1970).

156. REPORT OF THE PRESIDENT'S NATIONAL ADVISORY COMMISSION ON SELECTIVE SERVICE 11, 16 (1967).

157. H. Rep. No. 194, 79th Cong., 1st Sess. (1945).

158. 311 F. Supp. 618, 622 (W.D. Pa. 1970).

159. 42 U.S.C. p. 2000e (1964).

160. Bowe v. Colgate-Palmolive Co., 416 F. 2d 711 (7th Cir. 1969); Weeks v. Southern Bell Tel. & Tel. Co., 408 F. 2d 224 (5th Cir. 1969).

161. 116 Cong. Rec. S17895 (daily ed. Oct. 13, 1970).

162. Statement on Bayh Substitute and Ervin Amendment to the Equal Right Amendment, Citizens' Advisory Council Release, October 29, 1970. No amount of private karate lessons, currently in vogue in the women's movement, can match the training provided by the military at taxpayers' expense.

163. G. W. (George Washington University) Women's Liberation, The Equal Rights Amendment and the Draft, November 13, 1970.

164. U.S. DEP'T OF LABOR, WOMEN'S BUREAU, supra note 1, at 277-78.

165. Id.

166. See notes 159-60 supra and accompanying text.

167. U.S. DEP'T OF LABOR, WOMEN'S BUREAU, supra note 1, at 277-78.

168. See Murray & Eastwood, supra note 5, at 248-53.

169. U.S. DEP'T OF LABOR, WOMEN'S BUREAU, supra note 1, at 271.

170. Alaska, Arkansas, Delaware, Hawaii and Wisconsin. CITIZENS' ADVISORY COUNCIL OF THE STATUS OF WOMEN, supra note 135, at 44-59; U.S. DEP'T OF LABOR, WOMEN'S BUREAU, supra note 1, at 284-85.

171. U.S. DEP'T OF LABOR, WOMEN'S BUREAU, supra note 1, at 284-85.

172. Georgia, Idaho, Kentucky. Id. at 292.

173. Id.

174. See notes 125-63 supra and accompanying text.

175. See notes 163-73 supra and accompanying text.

176. The Council of State Governments lists Arkansas, Idaho, Nevada, North Dakota, Oklahoma, South Dakota, and Utah as having such laws. COUNCIL OF STATE GOV'TS, supra note 130, at 21-25.

177. Such a law in Oklahoma was recently upheld as not violative of boys' rights to equal protection of the laws under the fourteenth amendment. Johnson v. State, 476 P. 2d 397 (Okla. Crim. App. 1970).

178. Steele, supra, note 134, at 403.

179. Loving v. Virginia, 388 U.S. 1 (1967).

180. Truax v. Raich, 239 U.S. 33 (1915).

181. See Murray & Eastwood, supra note 5, at 240.
182. See CITIZENS' ADVISORY COUNCIL ON THE STATUS OF WOMEN, REPORT OF THE TASK FORCE ON SOCIAL INSURANCE AND TAXES 44-46 (1968).
183. Citizens' Advisory Council on the Status of Women, Statement of Principles, Oct. 29, 1970.
184. Id. at 3. See also CITIZENS' ADVISORY COUNCIL ON THE STATUS OF WOMEN, supra note 182.
185. CITIZEN'S ADVISORY COUNCIL ON THE STATUS OF WOMEN, supra note 182, at 32.
186. Statement of Paul A. Freund, Hearings on S.J. Res. 61 & 231 Before the Senate Commitee on the Judiciary, 91st Cong., 2d Sess., at 74-75 (1970).
187. FEDERAL BUREAU OF INVESTIGATION, U.S. DEP'T OF JUSTICE, UNIFORM CRIME REPORTS—1969, at 11 (1970).
188. Id. at 12.
189. Id. at 11.
190. Id. at 12.
191. Schiff, Statistical Features of Rape, 14 J. For. Sci. 102, 106-07 (1960).
192. Id. at 105.
193. Id. at 109.
194. 405 of those convicted were black (398 in the South and 7 in Missouri). U.S. DEP'T OF JUSTICE, CAPITAL PUNISHMENT 1940-1968, at 10-11 (1969).
195. Ralph v. Warden, 8 Crim. L. Rptr. 2193 (4th Cir. 1970).
196. MODEL PENAL CODE pp. 211.1, 213.1 (Proposed Official Draft, 1962).
197. Murray & Eastwood, supra note 5, at 240. It was thought that the specification of a female victim in the law would make it impossible for a woman to commit rape. However, the essence of the statute is to prohibit forcible heterosexual attack (unless the particular law also applies to homosexual attacks). Focusing attention on the victim's gender seems too easy an out, and equal justice would seem to prohibit such a narrow and literal disposition of the question.
198. Kanowitz states that only a few states provide penalties for a woman who engages in sexual intercourse with a young boy. Kanowitz, Law and the Single Girl, 11 St. Louis U.L.J. 293, 312 (1967).
199. Id.
200. Id. at 310.
201. The propriety of punishing prostitution perhaps needs to be reassessed.
202. CITIZENS' ADVISORY COUNCIL ON THE STATUS OF WOMEN, THE PROPOSED EQUAL RIGHTS AMENDMENT TO THE UNITED STATES CONSTITUTION: A MEMORANDUM 14 (1970).
203. Although the Council Memorandum does not state that the right to privacy is the exclusive potentially acceptable reason for separation, no other is mentioned nor has any other been suggested by women who support the amendment.
204. For example, Virginia and South Carolina. See note 62 supra and accompanying text.
205. See Barnett, The Constitutionality of Sex Separation in School Desegregation Plans, 37 U. Chi. L. Rev. 296, 297 (1970).
206. 347 U.S. 483, 495 (1954).
207. Id. at 494.
208. Statement of Thomas I. Emerson, Hearings on S.J. Res. 61 & 231, supra note 186, at 298.
209. "(I)mportant as is the preservation of the public peace, this aim cannot be accomplished by laws or ordinances which deny rights created or protected by the Federal Constitution." Buchanan v. Warley, 245 U.S. 60, 81 (1917). See also Cooper v. Aaron, 358 U.S. 1, 16 (1958).

Chapter 4

Women in Education

Women have played the primary role in education in all English speaking countries since the end of the last century. However the administrative roles have usually been filled by men. Two arguments drawn from past assumptions about women have been used to justify this state of affairs: first that the school teacher should be in the place of the substitute mother, an argument which was enshrined in law in the notion of *in loco parentis,* "in the place of the parent," and second, that the natural sympathy of women would be less harsh than the stern ecclesiastical school masters of the early modern period. Female educators and students are challenging both suppositions.

The American university and college system grew from an entirely different source than American public primary and secondary school. The university originated from the Medieval cathedral school and adapted the ancient latin seven liberal arts to a Christian purpose. The Jews of Spain and the North African cities brought the learning of the Arab and the classical world together in Spain and Italy and so by 1400 medicine and architecture had joined the curriculum. In the late Renaissance the great universities of Paris, Oxford, Mainz, Cracow, Edinburgh and so on were established. Since the leaders of the Puritans were university men the whole idea came to the new world with the organization of Harvard in 1639. Throughout Europe and the New World the pattern of organization left the operation of the university and later the college up to boards of students and faculty. However in the U.S. a new entity came into being, the administration. While women have frequently served on faculties very few have held executive positions in administration. With increased funding and enrollments guided by the state and federal governments, administration has gradually become of increasing importance. In the matter of salaries alone, professors of various ranks are paid from $8,500 to $24,000 per year in American institutions while administration salaries often run from $16,000 to well over $75,000 per year. The very wide discrepancy is a continual source of concern to the women who hold faculty positions and the students and their families who have to pay the bills.

In public education there has been less pressure by women as a group and more unified action by teacher's organizations the majority of which are always women. Here again the distribution of pay and position between men and women is widely disparate. What part the acceptance of women's studies into the curriculum at all levels will play is very unsure until the third or fourth year of such programs.

EDUCATION AND SOCIALIZATION OF THE AMERICAN FEMALE

4.1 In the same fashion that colonialism and racial segregation were supported by false appeals to biologic factors, the suppression of women in society has also been based on equally fallacious grounds. The biggest single offender in this latter case has been the process by which children are separated and educated for roles that society has deemed proper for their sex. Dr. Osofsky, one of the pioneer professors of women's studies, demonstrates the extent to which much sexual differentiation is mythological. It has frequently been alleged that the public school is the chief instigator and enforcer of the secondary role of women. The author discloses the pseudo-scientific basis upon which this has been done and the subtle mechanisms by which it is carried on still. The large number of basic shifts in the organization and delivery of education to the student in American society have so far assumed the correctness of the sex differentiations. However if McLuhan and others are correct that individuals must be continually educated throughout life and that workers in an electronic environment must learn their jobs, rather than merely work at them, then a new definition of sexual difference must come about. The largest single innovation in that direction has been the movement for the inclusion of women's studies in the curriculum at all levels of education. Even if such a change met with limited success the ramifications in society in the decades thereafter would be noticeable.

In the case of women's studies its popularity and importance has arisen at a phenomenal rate and its impact is nowhere near its zenith.

4.1.1 At the present time, in mid-1972, a number of women's studies programs and approximately 650 courses on women are being offered at about 500 colleges and universities in the United States. These programs and courses have a variety of objectives including: establishing a portion of the curriculum specifically concerned with the past and present position of women in society; allowing both female and male students the opportunity to obtain a greater understanding of the role of women; initiating research concerning such topics as women's position in the labor force, sex role development and stereotypes, the history of antifeminism, and other topics; providing services to women in the community, allowing them to participate in activites on campus, and informing them of possibilities for personal change; developing educational programs for women who have left education or the work force; establishing speakers bureaus to better disseminate available information and ideas; and in some cases raising consciousness and sharing personal experiences. Student interest and general acceptance have been high on most campuses. The long-range future of women's studies programs and courses on women still remains an unknown. However, the possibilities for additional growth appear great, and the opportunities for contributing to increases in knowledge, the development of female potential, and the creation of opportunities for women are exciting. The material and thoughts for the topic of this article were developed and presented in an interdisciplinary course offered by the author as part of the women's studies program at Cornell University.

Society never remains static, but, rather, continually undergoes change stimulated by diverse sources. Present day society is experiencing even greater disruption and change than that of earlier periods due to a combination of unusual and rapidly moving factors interacting at once. In this erratic world, one turns to institutional aspects of the society for stability and comfort.

The family has traditionally been such a stable refuge. Roles of individuals within the family have been clearly defined and accepted, and it has been assumed that one can depend upon such continuities for reassurance. However, in the 1970's, even the traditional notions about the family and sex roles are being questioned. Along with other previously accepted definitions, such as the role of war in a democratic society and racial prejudice in an egalitarian country, the role of the family is changing. It is no longer possible to define the family as a unit in which the father works outside of the home to provide financial support, and in which the mother works within the home, primarily to be a helpmate to her husband and to provide emotional support for her children. Within the family, more women are working. Some are employed to gain income for family support; however, others—and the numbers in this category are increasing rapidly—are working for personal satisfaction. Further, overpopulation is becoming a serious concern in this country, and in the world at large. With greater emphasis upon the need for serious population control, many individuals find themselves questioning the validity and morality of having one-half of the population devote their lives solely to family life, with their primary function being directed to the rearing of children. In fact, the emphasis upon having children, for both women and men, is changing, perhaps in part related to the conclusions of demographers that limitation of procreation is necessary for the very survival of our society.

With such changes, it is necessary to give serious consideration to individuals, and their new roles within society. Life styles of individuals must be thought through, and roles must be redefined. Old answers must be questioned; where they cannot withstand the test of time, new answers must supplant them. The present paper will analyze some of the traditional practices of socialization and education of females in our society and will consider some of the necessary and inevitable changes which must be accomplished in this changing world.

4.1.2 *Socialization of Sex Roles: Learning, Abilities, and Achievement.* Children in our society are taught behaviors, which have been defined as appropriate for individuals of their sex, by parents, teachers, and other authoritative figures in their environment. The processes through which children incorporate these behaviors, attitudes, and values are reinforcement, modeling (adults displaying sex-typed behaviors), and identification. Reinforcing or encouraging the occurrence of sex-typed behaviors is important early in development, while identification and modeling become increasingly important later in development. Children imitate sex-appropriate behaviors of their parents and other authority figures in their environment.

While reinforcement, modeling, and identification are important processes through which children learn sex-appropriate behaviors, certain events or practices comprise the medium through which these general processes occur. Parents usually dress their sons and daughters in different ways, give them different toys, encourage certain behaviors for a child of one sex which are discouraged for a child of the opposite sex, and participate in sex-specified activities themselves. Therefore, an important question which should be considered, and which is related to differential socialization and treatment of females and males in our society, is whether there are innate differences in ability which would warrant differential treatment, or whether differences in ability and resulting behavior are learned through the acculturation processes within our society.

Psychology has provided an abundance of literature concerning sex differences in abilities. Much of the literature has been interpreted to indicate sex differences in abilities. However, it would seem worthwhile to look at the over-all findings, since it is possible to draw different conclusions. The interested reader is referred to Terman and Tyler[2] and to Maccoby[3] for further information in this area. Few differences in abilities and behaviors are present when children are young; however, differentiation by sex increases after acculturation has occurred with age. One important specific intellectual sex difference related to age is that of language proficiency. School achievement tests and reading tests show that young girls generally do better than young boys; at a later point, the males tend to gradually catch up with the females. Also, more young boys than girls are stutterers.

In postulating reasons for these sex and age differences in language ability, several plausible explanations are possible. The most likely is that sex differences in abilities and behaviors are not innate, but, rather, that they are learned through the socialization processes within the society. Identification with the same-sex parent or with a same-sex adult is important for the child's sex role development. In our present family and school structure, most of the models for children in the home and in school are female. For boys, there are no appropriate males with whom to identify; therefore, language learning may have a female or "sissy" connotation. Further, in elementary school, male children are not yet strongly encouraged to

concentrate on achievement for career goals. For young females, school performance and achievement is encouraged at this time. The increase with age in male children's verbal proficiency would logically be expected with increased reinforcement for educational success as future career expectations are emphasized. Females show a leveling-off and thereafter a decline in the earlier verbal competence; this decrease is understandable with relatively less reinforcement given for educational success. The presence of more male models for boys to emulate in the higher grades, and proportionately fewer female models for girls to identify with in other than wife and mother roles, may contribute to the reversal in language proficiency. However, precise data in this area are not yet available.

As for achievement in science and related areas, studies show that in the preschool and primary years, there is little difference in science achievement among girls and boys. However, during junior high school years, boys do better in science and related subjects than do girls, and in high school, when the children are older, this sex difference markedly increases. In attempting to explain these discrepancies, it can be hypothesized that they may be due to differences in interests and encouraged interests, rather than in basic abilities. The reason for this explanation is that the differences do not appear early in life, but rather occur at an age when science is becoming socially more appropriate for males, and less so for females.

Sex differences in arithmetic achievement are similar to those reported for science achievement. Among preschool children, there are few differences in arithmetic achievement. In grade school, tests show slight superiority among boys in arithmetic reasoning, and either no differences, or superiority, for girls in simple computation. In higher grades, boys begin to out-distance girls; the skills required at this time tend to include more complex levels of arithmetic reasoning. Again, interests and encouraged interests may have a role. However, no systematic investigations have been done to clarify these issues.

Kagan[4] has offered some explanations and interpretations for sex differences in children's general and age-related abilities. He notes that girls have lower motivation to do well in science and mathematics; they are taught to believe that they are less competent in these areas. Cultural definitions of the female sex role places more emphasis upon the ability to attract and maintain a love relationship than upon academic skills. For males, however, academic excellence is a necessary antecedent to vocational success, and vocational success is essential for the culturally appropriate sex role identity.

Although slower maturational processes may conceivably play a role in males' slower development, the primary reason for boys' early difficulty and later success would seem to relate to the thinking that intellectual achievement, at an early age, is considered "feminine," and, at a later age, is considered "masculine." Conversely, for girls, motivation toward mastery decreases with age. Anxiety is experienced over feeling and behaving more competent than boys intellectually; conflicts arise over being competitive with boys. Girls, at puberty, may unconsciously or consciously inhibit intellectual performance; this inhibition increases during adolescence and adulthood, except where females overcome strong cultural pressures.

Thus, data on sex differences in abilities and behaviors, with the possible explanations which were offered, lend support to the suggestion that sex differences in these areas are learned through the socialization process. It is possible to make the further assumption that changes in the traditional sex role learning of females and males, which could be accomplished through altering the socialization practices of parents, schools, and other institutions in our society, would result in definitions of femininity and masculinity vary at

4.1.3 *Femininity and Masculinity.* Although definitions of femininity and masculinity vary at different ages, certain traits seem to emerge as culturally appropriate. The definitions mentioned in the following section are culture-bound, and they may be changing. Their usefulness may certainly be questioned; however, at present they exist, and have influence. In the domain of physical attributes, males, in order to be masculine, must be tall, have a muscular physique, and have facial and body hair. Females, in order to be feminine, must have an attractive face and body, be pretty and small, and have little extraneous facial and body hair. Of course, as is ironically apparent, these physical attributes are racially-specific to Anglo-Saxons. However, they remain as standard norms on dimensions of masculinity and femininity (Terman and Tyler,[2]).

Turning to behavioral characteristics, research evidence supports culturally defined conceptions of masculinity and femininity. Males are encouraged to be verbally and physically aggressive, whereas

females are discouraged and sometimes even prohibited from showing these traits. In fact, the same behaviors which are encouraged among males, are often labeled as aggressive among females, and are condemned and prohibited for them. By our cultural standards, females are not supposed to manifest the competency required of males. At the same time, males must inhibit passivity, dependency, and conformity, all of which are encouraged among females. Males must also show interpersonal dominance with men and women, initiation of sexual behavior and conquests, and concern with acquisition of money and power. Females must be submissive with males, inhibit overt signs of sexual desire, and cultivate domestic skills. As is apparent in these definitions, a double standard in sexual behavior is present. With the recent availability of contraceptives, and the apparent loosening of moral standards among younger people, there may be beginning a change in the double standard in sex. However, it is also possible that this kind of change will occur only when there is less male-female role differentiation.

When an individual deviates from these societally specified norms, problems arise both in his self-perceptions and in societal conscriptions and judgments. Thus, men are not supposed to demonstrate warm, nurturant behaviors and must not be dependent upon others, particularly females, for support. Women must be nurturant toward children and submissive toward other people; they must be dependent upon males—rather than independent as individuals—in order to be considered feminine and "real women" by societal standards. Interestingly, college men score high in femininity on the masculinity-femininity scale, and college women score high in masculinity. Clearly there are contradictions between societal definitions of masculinity and femininity and those of more educated people. Even "professional" games show girls in subordinate relationships to men as for example, being a nurse to the male doctor, or secretary to the male executive. When asked to judge whether toys are masculine or feminine, school children clearly consider knives, boats, planes, trucks, and cement mixers to be masculine, and dolls, cribs, dishes, and nurses' equipment to be feminine. Of importance in light of previous comments, there is also evidence to show that children, at least at any early age, consider books and other things associated with school to be feminine (Maccoby,[3]; Kellogg,[5]).

4.1.4 Masculinity-femininity tests measure the degree to which children have incorporated these culturally defined standards of masculinity and femininity. The "IT" test (Brown,[6]) presents children with a figure, which is ambiguous with respect to sex, and a variety of toys and objects. The child is asked to select the object or activity that the IT figure prefers. It is assumed that the child's choices will reflect his personal preferences. The findings tend to reveal the following information. Boys show an increasing preference for sex appropriate games with age. As early as age 3, boys are aware of and tend to favor activities and objects which our culture regards as masculine. Although awareness of female role is present, with behavior reflecting this comprehension, preferences of girls are more variable up to 9 or 10 years of age. Girls between 3 and 10 show a strong preference for masculine games, activities, and objects, whereas it is unusual to find many boys who prefer feminine activities during this period (Brown,[6] Hartup, et al,[7]; Reed and Asbjornsen,[8]). It may be that masculine activities and toys are considered more desirable by both boys and girls, suggesting reality factors as well as societal preferences. In addition to the differences in game preferences, girls frequently state a desire to be a boy or a wish to be a daddy, rather than a mommy, when they grow up (Brown,[6]). Boys do not demonstrate a similarly great cross sex preference.

Of some note, because of the incorporation of these arbitrary, societally proscribed definitions of femininity and masculinity, women who work face a difficult double dilemma. Not only may male peers and employers present difficulties, but also strong internal conflict seriously effects working females. Erik Erikson[9] has summarized the problem in a symposium devoted to women in the scientific professions. He describes the ambivalence, which exists in women who attempt to achieve in the outside world, while fulfilling traditionally defined female functions as well:

". . . If, as has often been said, the lack of available women in some areas constitutes more of a problem than the lack of available jobs, I think that one reason is to be found in whatever the prejudices of men are against an expansion of women's role in these fields, prejudices, as I have said, that only reinforce what the women themselves feel. The fact is that there is always a historical lag between any emancipation and the inner adjustment of the emancipated. It takes a much longer time to emancipate what goes on deep down inside us—that is, whatever prejudices and inequalities have

managed to become part of our impulse life and our identity formation—than the time it takes to redefine professed values and to change legalities. And any part of mankind that has had to accept its self-definition from a more dominant group is apt to define itself by what it is *not* supposed to be. Thus, it is easy to impress on the working women of some classes and pursuits the proposition that they should not be unfeminine, or unmaternal, or unladylike, all of which may well come in conflict with that identity element in many successfully intellectual women whose background decreed that, above all, they should not be unintelligent. It is, then, not enough, as has been said, to be 'changing with the changing forces.' One must become part of a force that guides change, and this with a reasonably good conscience."

Similarly, a recent study performed by Horner[10] demonstrates and points up some of these difficulties empirically. Horner investigated achievement motivation in females and males. She became interested in this area because many of the traditional studies concerning achievement motivation had not included women in the sample, stating that to include women would confuse the results. She administered the Thematic Apperception Test (TAT) to measure achievement motivation to 99 college females and 88 college males, and also asked her subjects to tell stories, which she later rated for achievement orientation or achievement avoidance. Her results indicated that female achievement incurs anxiety; this result had been demonstrated previously by other experimenters (Maccoby,[3] Sarason,[11]). Horner reasoned that most women equate intellectual achievement with loss of femininity. Therefore, in achievement-oriented situations, women will worry not only about failure, but also about success. According to Horner, "If she fails, she is not living up to her own standards of performance; if she succeeds, she is not living up to societal expectations about the female role." Horner's major hypothesis was that, for women, the desire to achieve is often very much in conflict with what she labeled the "motive to avoid success." She found that 65 per cent of the girls in her study demonstrated attitudes which could be classified as desiring to avoid success; fewer than 10 per cent of the boys showed evidence of such conflicts. In a second part of the experiment, she investigated the effect of competition upon the performance of males and females. She found that men tended to do much better when they were in competition than when they worked alone. However, the reverse was true for the women; fewer than one-third of the women, as compared to two-thirds of the men, did significantly better in competition. Horner concluded that most women attempt to realize their intellectual potential only when they do not need to compete, and that they do worst when they are competing with men. In addition, she concluded that achievement motivation in women is a much more complex drive than it is in men, and that it is complicated by many factors which may inhibit both the motivation and the performance. Horner's study illustrates that the socialization process, through which a female learns appropriate sex-typed behavior, influences her achievement motivation and abilities.

Some Thoughts Concerning the Future

4.1.5   What are the changes that are currently taking place, and what are the prospects for future change in the socialization and education of females in American society? Alterations in the usual patterns of female and male behavior are occurring. They are undoubtedly altering definitions of sex role development; in the future, their effects will be even more profound. Although traditional sex roles still represent the accepted norm, many variations are evident. Different patterns of behavior seem to be functional and acceptable to many individuals. At present, changes are occurring in societally accepted roles for women. There is greater acceptance of, and in some quarters encouragement of, women's participating in meaningful work. Especially among the young, there is more sharing of traditional household responsibilities by husbands and wives. Alternative marital and child rearing patterns are becoming more common. Some of the changes will certainly affect accepted definitions of sex-appropriate behavior and concepts concerning masculinity and femininity. The socialization process itself which influences female and male development will of necessity also change. Both women and men will be encouraged to foresee and experience greater opportunities in role choice than are presently available. Hopefully, such an increase in opportunities will allow all individuals to find satisfaction in many more ways.

Appropriate "adjustment" should depend upon both individual inclinations and the good of society. It should not, however, be arbitrarily determined, as has unfortunately frequently been the case, by one group of individuals for others. Definitions of "adjustment" must allow for much variation and freedom; the needs of society neither benefit from, nor require, arbitrary conformity. A well-adjusted male may enjoy being a responsible executive. He may also—or instead—like being nurturant and catering, doing the cooking and taking care of the children. A well-adjusted female may similarly enjoy working full time in a responsible executive position; she may wish to share household responsibilities with her husband or allocate most of them to him. On the contrary, she, too, may prefer household responsibilities and child rearing. Options which include assertive, competitive, and independent behaviors should not be closed to women. Options which include dependent, passive, and nurturant behaviors should not be closed to men. Changing role definitions for women in society should occur concurrently with changes for men. Socialization patterns should be determined by individual inclinations and abilities, rather than by the supposedly biological grounds of sex.

4.1.6   In order to achieve these goals, many changes need to be made. Obviously, because of the need for brevity, not all can be included. However, a few necessary alterations in our present system of socialization and education of American females will be described. The interested reader is also referred to the 1964 paper of Alice Rossi[12] which has explored this subject. Beginning when the child is very young, patterns of socialization and education should be changed. For example, at birth, the clear differentiation in treatment of infants by sex can be eliminated. Female babies need not be dressed only in pink, feminine clothes and male babies in blue, more masculine outfits. Patterns of dressing infants spread to treatment of them, with expectations for males including aggressive behavior, and those for females including passive behavior. As demonstrated in an unpublished study by Sloan,[13] adults react to infants in ways that encourage these expectations.

At present, the mother has primary responsibility and involvement in the care of the young child. It has been traditionally assumed that she, because of her sex, is better able to care for children. Further, in most families in our culture, mothers are home and fathers are not. This situation deserves reconsideration. Both parents should take an active role in child rearing. Not only would this change allow the father more of the rewards which exist, but it would expose the child more fully to its father, a male figure, who is nurturant and concerned about child rearing. Some critics suggest that the father is not important for the early development of the child. Yet, in homes where no father is present, if the child becomes delinquent, these same critics may question whether father-absence has been deleterious for the child, or whether or not good one-parent families are sufficient. There is no clear empirical evidence to support hypotheses negating the importance of the father's role; rather, logic and available data suggest the contrary.

When the child enters school, major changes in existing patterns should be made. First, children at this age still should be raised with full involvement of both parents. This is not to suggest that mother and father need to be home at all times, but, rather, that they each make an active commitment to the child. Second, it is desirable that children be exposed to male and female teachers at all levels in school. Third, children should be taught through the use of textbooks which depict females and males participating in many positions in society, and not only in traditionally prescribed roles which are currently depicted in textbooks. For example, at present, women are depicted almost solely as housewives, nurses, and secretaries, and men are shown as blue and white collar workers, professionals, and executives. Both women and men should be shown participating in work, homemaking, and child rearing activities.

4.1.7 A fourth area related to education which needs to be changed concerns the covert and overt counseling which currently is offered to females and males. On almost all levels, as school progresses, females are encouraged to be passive and, sometimes, achieving. Males are encouraged to be independent and constantly achieving. It has been shown that many teachers prefer and differentially reinforce such behavior, since active achievement is viewed as more important for males than females. Most guidance counselors and teachers encourage girls to get married and to be good wives and mothers; careers are usually presented as an alternative if marriage is not achieved, or if families need the money. Guidance counselors traditionally have not encouraged girls to take their careers seriously and to pursue both family and career lines simultaneously. Rather, they suggest that a choice must be made between marriage and career, with the assumption being that the latter is a less fortunate outcome. Although this description sounds harsh, it is unfortunately borne out by numerous reports and communications. The same counselors encourage males to compete, behave aggressively, and pursue careers in order to gain

esteem and support a family. Males are rarely provided with alternative options to such achieving behaviors. In other words, males are encouraged to have a career and to marry, and are neither required, nor usually allowed, to make a choice between these options. Females are encouraged to marry, and possibly work, but if they want a career, it is usually presented as an alternative. A clear differential is made for females between a *job* and a *career*. A job brings in needed money and is consistent with the role of helpmate; a career connotes dedication and, thus, is seen as excluding, or at least being devisive to, the appropriate full-time roles of wife and mother.

As a result of these proposals, there would inevitably be changes within the students before high school graduation and possible college entry. During their formative years, females will have identified with adults with more diverse life styles. Parents will have presented different images. Teachers and counselors will have encouraged more varied behaviors and achievements. Growing children will have been exposed to women who are doctors, lawyers, and executives—and who are simultaneously wives and mothers; similarly, they will have seen men in comparable positions who are truly also husbands and fathers. Colleges, as a result, will inevitably have to become different in order to accommodate to this new group of students. In addition, colleges, of their own volition, should change in order to further aid the process. Just as more males are needed in elementary and secondary schools, more females should be in meaningful positions on university faculties. Females should be adequately represented as presidents and other major administrators of colleges. Courses should present academically fair views of females and males and the opportunity should exist, formally and informally, to experience and further learn about relations between women and men which are based upon mutual respect and interdependence. Thus, the college could serve in providing both unbiased academic knowledge and preparation for more meaningful adult life styles.

It can be anticipated that the proposed changes in patterns of socialization and education of females and males will lead to increased alternatives and benefits for individuals of both sexes. Young boys may no longer regard either school, or household and child rearing activities as feminine. This may well lead both to boys having a diminished incidence of early learning problems in school, and to their achieving more fulfilled and relaxed lives as adults. Females will come to develop skills in accordance with their abilities, and not to see achievement as excluding homemaking and child rearing. This may lead both to females achieving greater self-development during education and having less conflict and resentment related to marriage and children at a later point. Thus, there will be increased development of talents of all individuals, regardless of sex, and

at the same time, more satisfaction in the many meaningful aspects of life. Our society and the individuals within it are changing. Hopefully, we, in our varied roles, can contribute to a healthful orientation and progressive growth. There is a great challenge before us, but if it can be successfully met, the results, in terms of human satisfaction and fulfillment, will be most exciting.

REFERENCES

1. Mussen, P. H., "Early sex-role development," D. A. Goslin ed. *Handbook of Socialization Theory and Research,* Chicago 707-731 (1969).
2. Terman, L. M. & L. E. Tyler, "Psychological sex differences," L. Carmichael ed. *Manual of Child Psychology,* N.Y. 1064-1114 (1946).
3. Macooby, E., ed. *The Development of Sex Differences,* Stanford, Calif. Stanford University Press (1966).
4. Kagan, J., "Acquisition and significance of sex typing and sex role identity." M. L. & L. W. Hoffman eds. *Review of Child Development Research,* N.Y. Russell Sage 137-168 (1964).
5. Kellogg, R. L., "A direct approach to sex-role identification of school-related objects," *Psychological Reports* 24:839-841 (1969).
6. Brown, D. G., "Masculinity-femininity development in children," *Journal of Consulting Psychology* 21:197-202 (1957).
7. Hartup, W. W., & E. A. Zook, "Sex role preference in three- and four-year old children," *Journal of Consulting Psychology* 24:420-426 (1960).
8. Reed, M. R., & W. Asbjornsen, "Experimental alteration of the IT scale in the study of sex-role preference,"

Perceptual and Motor Skills 26:15-24 (1968).
9. Erickson, E. H., "Concluding remarks," J. Mattfield &C. Van Aken eds. *Women and the Scientific Professions,* Cambridge, Mass. M.I.T. Press 232-245 (1965).
10. Horner, M., "Women's motive to avoid success," *Psychology Today* 62:36-39 (1969).
11. Sarason, S. B., & K. S. Davidson, F. F. Lighthaas, R. R. Waite, B. K. Ruebush, *Anxiety in Elementary School Children,* N.Y. (1960).
12. Rossi, A., "Equality between the sexes: An immodest proposal," R. J. Lifton ed. *The Woman in America,* Boston 98-143 (1964).
13. Sloan, D., an unpublished manuscript (1969).
The body of this paper has been published in the article, "The Socialization and Education of American Females," in *What is Happening to American Women,* edited by A. Scott, published by the Southern Newspaper Publishers Association, (1970).

Prof. Joy D. Osofsky, Ph.D.
Temple University,
Philadelphia, Pennsylvania

DISCRIMINATION AGAINST WOMEN IN HIGHER EDUCATION

4.2 With the rise of science and technology as the strongest motivators for the growth of the American economy, less and less attention was paid to the academic subjects which smacked of contemplation and value-judgement. Thus in the last twenty-five years, classical studies, history and philosophy, once the main-stays of a liberal education, have all but failed on many campuses. Since women were not expected to achieve in the sciences and the practical world of business, positions teaching these subjects were left open for them. In the last few years the relaxation of massive technological input has brought many students back to these forgotten disciplines. At the same time interpersonal conflicts between people have never been more serious and a broad understanding of the workings of racism, sexism, colonialism and other prejudices is considered by many to be a national priority. The social and behavioral sciences at the large majority of smaller colleges and a large minority of large ones, have fallen by default to women faculty members. The result however has been quite to the good as it is in these areas where the best work on the place of women in society has been done. Sooner or later the women who were equipped with the tools of the modern social sciences were bound to turn their critical inquiries upon the system itself. A study of that analysis of the place of women in the academic world by women of the academic world is presented by Dr. Sandler. It yields a picture of two-fold disgrace, a portrait of suppression by design and neglect.

4.2.1 During the women's rights movement of the 19th century, one of the major centers of activity was focused on higher education as women fought for the right to obtain a college education on a par with men. In the current rebirth of feminism, once again the world of education has

become a major focus of criticism, discontent and action. Of all the areas in American society that have come under fire for inequitable treatment of women, the academic world has been one of the most frequent targets of women's anger.

In the late 1960's the grumbling of women on

the campus began to be heard as women started to examine and review their status in the academic world. At Columbia University, for example, a Women's Liberation group (which included Kate Millet) gathered data on the status of women faculty. At the University of Chicago, a student sit-in included demands concerning women, and Jo Freeman, a graduate student, analyzed women on the social science faculties, and unearthed the startling fact that the percentage of women on the faculty was *less* in 1969 than it had been in 1899. At both the University of California at Berkeley and the University of Chicago, faculty committees were set up in May 1969 to inquire into the status and opportunities for women as students and as faculty.

In more than 25 professional associations, women began asking for committees to investigate the status of women in their profession and to correct discriminatory practices (such as "help wanted: male" advertisements in professional journals) and to increase the number of women in decision-making posts.

On campus after campus, women began to examine their status and discovered that it was indeed bad. They found that there was little comfort in the current situation. Despite the myth that things had been getting better for women, they discovered in fact that that situation had worsened: in 1870, women held more than a third of all the faculty positions in colleges and universities. By 1970, women barely accounted for 19% of the faculty. In the more prestigious institutions women are barely 10% of the faculty or less. Women are more likely to be found in the lower paying, lesser-known institutions, where they account for 40% of the faculty.

Women, when hired, are likely to be promoted far more slowly than men. The general pattern is: the higher the rank, the fewer the women. Women are 32% of the instructors, 19% of the assistant professors, 15% of the associate professors, 8% of the full professors, and very few of the department chairman. Numerous studies document the fact that women with the same qualifications are hired less frequently, promoted more slowly and receive less pay. Ninety per cent of the men with doctorates and 20 years of experience are full professors; for women with the identical qualifications, barely half will be at that rank.

At one university, a statistician of the Women's Faculty Rights Committee estimated that by keeping women in low level teaching and staff positions, the institution saved between 2 and 4 million dollars annually. At a southwestern state

university, women earned 15–20% less than their male colleagues. At another well known midwestern state university the differences averaged 32%, and in some instances it ranged up to 50%.

4.2.2 In administration women are conspicuous only by their absence. It is almost impossible for a woman to become a President or a Chancellor of an institution, unless she is a Catholic sister heading up a small women's college. Almost all of the non-sectarian women's colleges have men presidents. Less than 1% of all college presidents are women. Few women head departments, other than the strictly "female fields" such as nursing and home economics. Of the 50 largest academic libraries, not one is headed by a woman. The number of women in administrative positions in colleges and universities is less now than it was 21 or even 10 years ago. The landmark study of the American Association of University Women revealed that 21% of the institutions they surveyed had no women on their Board of trustees; 25% had one token woman.

As women confirmed their poor status in the academic world, they began to examine legal remedies, and were quickly disappointed to find that legal remedies were sadly lacking. Women in education, whether as students or as faculty are not covered by existing legislation.

For example, Title VI of the Civil Rights Act of 1964 forbids discrimination against beneficiaries of federally assisted programs and activities, but it only applies to discrimination based on race, color, and national origin. It does not forbid sex discrimination.

Title VII of the same Civil Rights Act forbids discrimination in employment based on race, color, religion, national origin and *sex*. However, Section 702 exempts every "educational institution with respect to the employment of individuals connected with the educational activities of such institution." Thus, faculty and professional staff are excluded from coverage under Title VII.

The Equal Pay Act of 1963 requires that men and women receive equal pay for equal work. It specifically excludes from coverage administrative, executive and professional workers. Therefore it does not apply to faculty and other professional staff within the educational community.

The 14th Amendment of the U.S. Constitution is of *potential* use in combatting sex discrimination in state supported institutions. However, no case concerning discrimination against women in education has ever been decided in favor of women by the Supreme Court. Several cases testing out the applicability of the 14th Amendment are now in process but the eventual outcome is far from clear. Even the U.S. Commission on Civil Rights has no jurisdiction whatsoever concerning sex discrimination; it is limited by law to matters pertaining to race, color, religion and national origin.

4.2.3 Late in 1969, the Women's Equity Action League (WEAL), a women's civil rights group, discovered a new legal route that was to prove of enormous help. WEAL noted that President Johnson had issued Executive Order 11246 in 1965 forbidding discrimination by *all* federal contractors on the basis of race, religion and national origin. Executive Order 11375, effective October 13, 1968, amended the original order to include discrimination based on sex. Unlike Title VII, there is no exemption for educational institutions. Universities and colleges receive over 3 billion dollars annually, much of it in federal contract money. Most universities and colleges (other than very small institutions) have federal contracts and are therefore covered by the Executive Order.

On January 31, 1970, WEAL launched a national campaign to end discrimination against women in education by filing an historic class action complaint against all universities and colleges in the country. The charges were filed with the U.S. Department of Labor under the Executive Order. The order had been used almost exclusively with blue collar workers in the construction industry, most notably in the "Philadelphia Plan." Although the Executive Order had covered sex discrimination since October 1968, there was virtually no enforcement by the government until WEAL began its campaign. Government compliance agencies simply ignored the sex discrimination provisions of the order.

In its initial complaint in January 1970, WEAL charged an "industry-wide pattern" of discrimination against women in the academic community. Dr. Nancy E. Dowding, then President of WEAL, asked that the Department of Labor investigate the following areas: admission quotas to undergraduate and graduate schools, discrimination in financial assistance, hiring practices, promotions and salary differentials. More than 80 pages of materials documenting the charges were submitted to the Secretary of Labor with the complaint.

WEAL requested an immediate "class action" and compliance review of all institutions holding federal contracts. Specific charges were simultaneously filed against the University of Maryland, soon to be followed by more than 260

others as word went out to women in the academic community. (This represents about 10% of the nation's institutions of higher learning.) Among the institutions charged by WEAL were the University of Wisconsin, the University of Minnesota, Columbia University, University of Chicago, Yale University, and the entire state university and college systems of California, Florida and New Jersey. In October 1970, a class action was filed against all the medical schools in the country. The National Organization for Women (NOW) also charged Harvard University and the entire state university system of New York. Additional complaints by individual women and other women's campus groups have brought the number of formal charges to over 360 colleges and universities, with no end in sight. A similar class action against the nation's law schools was also filed by the Professional Women's Caucus in April 1971.

None of these charges have yet been refuted in any of the subsequent investigation conducted by the Department of Health, Education and Welfare, which has the responsibility for enforcing the Executive Order in universities and colleges.

As word went out that institutional pocketbooks could be endangered, and that there was recourse for campus sex discrimination, women on campus after campus began to organize, often in groups that cut across traditional lines, with women faculty, staff and students often working together. The WEAL filings and the investigation of campus sex discrimination by HEW accelerated a trend that had already begun: the documentation of discriminatory practices, and the pressure by women on colleges and universities to end discrimination.

What women discovered was that the myths of academia concerning women were just that— myths. Supposedly, doctoral training is wasted on women, yet Helen Astin's research, *The Woman Doctorate*, demonstrated that 91% of women doctorates were working, 81% of them full-time; 79% had not interrupted their career in the 10 years after they got the doctorate. (Only 81% of all men work, and of men with doctorates, only 69% work full-time in their original field of study.)

Women examined the myth that they were somehow less qualified academically than men and the myth that this explained why women are paid less on the campus. They found that in study after study which examined factors such as the number of publications, years of teaching, papers read at meetings, honors and the like, women still earned less than equally qualified men. At one midwestern university, a sophisticated statistical analysis indicated that all other things being equal, a woman's sex cost her $845 per year, even though identically qualified.

Other studies examined the myth that women do not publish as much as men. The differences between the sexes are slight; married women, however, published somewhat more than men, although unmarried women published slightly less.

4.2.4 The myth of a shortage of qualified women was also demolished when women began to use the percentage of doctorates awarded nationally to women as a base with which to compare the percentage of women in a particular department. For example, nationally, women receive 23% of the doctorates awarded in psychology; that is about the same per cent of women listed as psychologists in the National Register of Scientific and Technological Personnel. In 1970–71, the per cent of women in the psychology department at Rutgers was 9%; at the University of Maryland, 6%; at the University of Wisconsin, 3%; at Columbia University, *zero* per cent despite the fact that Columbia awarded about 36% of its doctorates to women. Until 1971, when two women were finally hired, the psychology department at the University of California at Berkeley, had not hired a woman for its faculty since 1924. These figures can be duplicated in virtually every institution and in department after department. Numerous institutions have a lower percentage of women on their faculty now than they did 30 or 40 years ago.

The myth that women are poor risks because of supposedly greater absenteeism and a higher rate of turnover has also been contradicted. Forty-five per cent of women doctorates had the same job in the first ten years after they received their degrees; 30% had changed their job only once in the ten years. The Women's Bureau of the Dept. of Labor has analyzed absenteeism and concluded that it is the level of the job, rather than the sex of the individual that affects the rate of absenteeism: the unskilled jobs have the highest rate of absenteeism; at the professional level absenteeism is less for both sexes.

Academic policies are often discriminatory in their effect. Nepotism rules, either written or unwritten, almost always limit the wife's ability to hold a comparable position at the same institution as her husband. Often the rules are circumvented so that she can be hired, but at a lower rate of pay, with no possibility of tenure and often no fringe benefits. At the University of Arizona, in 1970, five faculty wives sued, claiming that the nepotism rules violated several of their constitutional rights. The University, realizing that it might well lose its case in court, rescinded the rules rather quickly instead of going to court.

Fringe benefits also penalize women. On some campuses, wives of faculty members can obtain maternity coverage on their health insurance, but women faculty members cannot get the same benefit. In other places, women cannot use sick leave for childbirth, nor do they retain their job if they leave, even for a short period for childbirth or childrearing. The rationale is that childbirth is not an illness and therefore should not be covered in the same was as other temporary disabilities. Women are quick to point out that such "normal" activity involves hospitalization and a risk, although small, of death itself. Women who leave their jobs for a year or two of child rearing are viewed very differently from their male colleagues or fellow students who spend two years away from the university because of the draft and military service.

Similarly, TIAA and other retirement benefits, based on actuarial tables, pay women less when they retire, even though they will have contributed the same amount as the men they have worked along side. The rationale for this is that women live longer. However, women point out that the mortality gap between whites and blacks is greater than that of men and women, yet there is no retirement benefit differential between the races.

Some campuses still bar women from their all male faculty clubs, depriving the women of access to the informal contacts that are so necessary in the professional and academic worlds. At Yale, many departments still hold meetings and other functions and job interviews at Mory's, where women faculty and women students are still barred.

4.2.5 Discrimination against students is equally widespread. Girls need higher grades and test scores to get into many colleges. The percentage of women undergraduates is about 41%; although this figure has been increasing in the last 20 years, it is still below what it was in 1920, when girls were 47% of the undergraduates, or in 1899, when 53% of all undergraduate degrees were awarded to women. Similarly the percentage of women graduate students is less now than it was in the 1930's. About 75–90% of the well qualified students who do not go on to college are women. The proportion of boys who make it to college despite high school grades of C or lower, is double that for girls, 40% to 20%. Girls are not sought after as students because they do not earn as much money as males, and are therefore poor alumni donors. By not admitting them, institutions insure that women indeed will earn less money, thus perpetuating a self-fulfilling prophecy. Women point out that men students who are preparing for social work, the ministry, teaching and other low paying fields are never turned away as potentially poor alumni donors.

Many institutions maintain artificial quotas and restrict the number of girls that will be admitted. Pennsylvania State University is not unusual with its quota of 2½ men to every woman under-graduate; Harvard maintains a 4 to 1 ratio, etc. In one study by University of Wisconsin researchers, bogus applications were sent to 240 institutions, with the sex of applicant varying, so that in some instances the applicant was listed as male, and in others, female. Males were preferred over females, particularly at the low ability level. At the high ability level there was little difference; at the undergraduate level the exceptionally gifted woman will not face very much discrimination in admission. However, since most students—male or female—are not exceptionally gifted, and indeed more students are in the "low ability" or "average" group, it is clear that many women will be discriminated against when they apply for admission. One woman bitterly phrased it this way: "Admission to college is not based on ability only, but also on the particular set of reproductive organs that one possesses. Such artificial quotas based on sex hurt women just as much as artificial quotas based on race hurt minorities."

One way in which education is denied to girls is through the excuse of dormitories or the lack of dormitories: "We'd love to have more girls but we just don't have the room for them." Yet dormitories, like hotels, apartments and houses are not built differently for one sex or the other. When Yale converted some of its previously all-male dormitories for women students, it only added new locks and full-length mirrors. Even the presence of urinals previously all male dormitories has posed no problems for inventive women students at other institutions: the urinals make marvelous planters and the university is spared the expense of removal. Women's groups have been quick to point out that dormitories can be changed from one sex to the other merely by administrative fiat, unless one wants to arbitrarily limit the number of women students. Women have

also pointed out that some institutions which claim a shortage of dormitories for women often refuse to let their women students live off-campus, although men students have that privilege.

On many campuses, women students are treated differently, with far more restriction in terms of hours and the freedom to live off-campus. Gynecological services are often not available for women students, although urological services are available to male students. On some campuses women students clean their own dormitories, while men's dormitories are provided with cleaning services. Many students are denied leave for pregnancy and childbirth. Honorary society are often segregated by sex, with the men's honoraries being far more prestigious than the women's. On at least one campus, the women need to be better qualified for admission to the women's honorary than the men need to be for admission to the men's honorary.

4.2.6 Women students, like women faculty, are enveloped in a blanket of myths. They are believed to have a higher attrition rate than men. Yet the percentage of women undergraduates who graduate in four years is 15% higher than for men. At the graduate level, attrition for all students is usually higher in the humanities where there are more women concentrated. When data on attrition are collected by departments, the differences between men and women are much smaller, and in some instances are higher for men than for women. The lower amount of financial support given to women as well as the lack of encouragement given to women students undoubtedly affect the attrition rate.

At the graduate level, mobility may play havoc with the statistics, since many women may take graduate work at more than one institution as their family changes location; they will be listed as "drop-outs" from these institutions other than the one in which they received their degree.

Another myth is that men students do better in school than women. The contrary is true, since women students represent a more highly selected group of students because of the discriminatory restriction in admission policies. For example, at the University of Michigan, girls had higher grade point averages than male students, as well as a higher success rate in completing the degree with four years.

Women's groups accuse faculty of not encouraging young women students. Many women students have lower aspirations when they leave college than when they entered as freshmen: girls who wanted to become doctors decide to become medical technicians instead; a prospective biologist decides to become a high school science teacher, and an aspiring writer becomes an editorial secretary.

Professors are not exempt from believing erroneous notions about women students. Sometimes women students are denied admission to graduate school because of logic like this: "If she's not married, she'll get married." "If she is married, then she'll probably have children." "If she has children, she can't possibly be committed to study." "If her children are older, then she's too old to begin training, and what a pity it is that she didn't start her training earlier."

Supposedly education is wasted on undergraduate women because they marry and do not work. Yet the more education a woman has, the more likely she is to work. The average working woman today is married. More than half of the mothers of school age children work. Women are nearly half of the labor force, about 40%. At age 35, women with husbands can expect to work fully 24 years. At the same age, 35, women who are widowed, separated or divorced have a worklife expectancy of 28 years, only a half year less than a man of the same age.

4.2.7 Women graduate students face serious discrimination and discouragement. Professional schools often have quotas. The University of Michigan had 25% women in its medical school in 1900; in 1971, the figure is less than 10 per cent. In all the professions women have lost ground over the past forty years and discrimination in graduate school cannot be written off as an insignificant factor. The Committee on Senate Policy at the University of California at Berkeley reported to the Academic Senate in May 1970:

"There are departments which train large numbers of women undergraduates and graduate students and yet appoint no women to regular faculty positions. . . . There are departments which apparently discourage women faculty from seeking promotion, and few actively push them forward. There are departments where women applicants for graduate admission are told that the preferred candidate is "the highly intelligent young man" or that the women stand little chance of admission because they are not expected to complete the degree. . . . There are departments where women graduate students report difficulties in receiving support while men are regularly provided with assistance. There are departments where women students are told in seminars that women are unable to think objectively or analytically. There are departments where suggestions that women might be dissatisfied with the present state of affairs are met with wit and jibes or with scornful comments about aggressive women."

Discrimination against women on the campus has gone virtually unchecked and unchallenged for years. Sex discrimination is the last socially acceptable prejudice. Much of it is unconscious and not deliberate. The Chairman of a department sees nothing wrong in paying a woman less because she is married and therefore doesn't need as much, or paying her less because she is not married and therefore doesn't need as much.

Our educational institutions have generally not been very concerned with the problems of women as students and as members of the faculty until very recently when women themselves began to press for change. To some degree, the academic community could be described as a vast "men's club" where women are at best tolerated as foreign visitors but never admitted as equals. Education is designed as though the only people who ever attended school were young, single and male.

Women are a new advocacy group on campus. Women students, staff and faculty are banding together, asking for fair treatment, and will be satisfied with nothing short of that. In the years to come women on the campus will very likely be more militant than previously. In response to the criticisms of women, and under threat of the loss of government contract funds, many universities and colleges have begun to move in the direction of greater equality. Affirmative action plans to remedy the effects of past discrimination are required by the Executive Order, and these plans are being developed on a number of campuses, sometimes even before charges have been filed. Some have begun to actively recruit women in earnest. The University of Oregon, for example, will try to fill half of its new openings with qualified women and minorities. Many institutions have hired an Equal Employment Opportunity Officer whose job it is to look after the rights of women and minorities, including minority women.

Pressure from the government is undoubtedly a major factor in causing universities and colleges to re-examine their treatment of women, although women's groups have consistently criticized the government for not adequately enforcing its non-discrimination regulations. Nevertheless, there is a new hope on the campus as women work together to end discrimination in the academic community.

4.2.8 Legislation has been introduced in the 91st and 92nd Congress that would forbid such discrimination. Representative Edith Green conducted hearings in June and July 1970 that were the first to ever examine the problems of discrimination against women in education. These hearings documented in voluminous detail the second class status of academic women, and described the discriminatory patterns that exist on virtually all campuses.

One woman activist summed it up: "We've taken the first long steps on the hard and rocky road of equal opportunity. The anger and discontent among women on the campus is increasingly widespread. We have learned that we can rock the boat and effect change, and the campus will never be the same again."

The documents listed under Institutional Data

Sources provided the information on colleges which was used both in the text and the statistical summaries. Many of these documents appeared in the first review on academic women (Robinson, 1971) with both an annotation of their contents and detailed information about their accessibility. Many of the sources have been entered into the Educational Resources Information Center's (ERIC) system, and therefore may be purchased from the ERIC Document Reproduction Service. ERIC Research in Education, available in the reference section of many libraries, should be consulted for an abstract of the particular document of interest along with ordering instructions. The ERIC Clearinghouse on Higher Education, The George Washington University, Washington, D.C. 20006, also houses all of the documents listed in this section. The author thanks the Clearinghouse for the use of its facilities in the preparation of this chapter.

4.2.9 Institution Data Sources

University of Akron
Van Fleet, David D., December 1970. Salaries of males and females: a sample of conditions at the University of Akron. 9 pp.

Amherst College
Achbar and Bishop, 1970.

University of Arizona
Sigworth, Heather, July 1970. Supplemental letter on the University of Arizona. 5 pp.

Assumption College
Achbar and Bishop, 1970.

Baldwin-Wallace College
Institutional Analysis Committee, June 1971. Status of women at Baldwin-Wallace. 8 pp.

Boston College
Achbar and Bishop, 1970.

Boston University
Achbar and Bishop, 1970.

Brandeis University
(1) Achbar and Bishop, 1970.
(2) Murray, Pauli, June 1970. Statement of Dr. Pauli Murray, Professor of American Studies, Brandeis University. *Discrimination against Women: Hearings before the Special Subcommittee on Education of the Committee on Education and Labor.* Washington, D.C.: House of Representatives, pp. 328–341.

University of Bridgeport
Anon. (1971). (Salary data). 5 pp.

Brooklyn College, City University of New York
Babey-Brooke, Anna M.; Amber, R. B., July 1970. Discrimination against women in higher education. A 15-year survey. Promotional practices at Brooklyn College CUNY: 1955–1970, all ranks—tenured and untenured. 26 pp.

Brown University
Brown University Chapter of the American Association of University Professors. October 1970. Report of the AAUP Committee on the Employment and Status of Women Faculty and Women Graduate Students at Brown. 22 pp.

California State Colleges
(Dominquez Hills, Fullerton, Hayward, Kern Co., Long Beach, Los Angeles, San Bernadino, Cal. Poly-Pomona and San Luis Obispo, Chico State, Fresno State, Humboldt State, Sacramento State, San Diego State, San Fernando State, San Francisco State, San Jose State, Sonoma State and Stanislaus State)
Anon. (1970). Employment status of women in the California State Colleges. 4 pp.

California State College at Fullerton
The National Organization for Women and Woman's Liberation, California State College at Fullerton June 1970. A report on the status of women at the California State College at Fullerton. 18 pp.

University of California.
(Berkeley, Davis, Irvine, Los Angeles, Riverside, San Diego, Santa Cruz, San Francisco and Santa Barbara)
(1) Anon. (1969). Representation of women among the high level administrative posts within the University of California, all campuses. 1 p.
(2) Card, Emily, July 22, 1970. Women faculty at the University of California—summary of testimony before Senate Education Committee California State Senate. 2 pp.

University of California, Berkeley
Academic Senate Subcommittee on the Status of Women, May 1970. Report of the subcommittee on the status of academic women on the Berkeley campus. 79 pp.

University of California, Irvine
Task Force on the Status of Women, Fall 1970. Task force on the status of women at University of California, Irvine. 31 pp.

University of California, Los Angeles
Harris, 1970.

Carnegie-Mellon University
Anon. (1970). Survey broken down
by sex of Carnegie-Mellon
University appointments at an
academic level higher than
graduate student. Taken from the
official published directory for
1969–70. 1 p.

East Carolina University
Faculty Affairs Committee, (1970).
Faculty affairs committee report:
analysis of faculty salaries
(1969–70). 9 pp.

Case Western Reserve University
Ruben, Alan Miles; Willis, Betty J.
1971. Discrimination against
women in employment in higher
education. *Cleveland State Law
Review* 20 (3): pp. 472–491.

University of Chicago
(1) The Committee on University
Women, May 1970. Women in the
University of Chicago—report of
the Committee on University
Women. Chicago: The University
Senate. 125 pp.
(2) Freeman, Jo, 1969. Women on the
social science faculties since
1892. 14 pp.

Clark University
Achbar and Bishop, 1970.

University of Colorado, Boulder
Minturn, Leigh, May 1970.
Inequities in salary payments to
faculty women. 6 pp.

Columbia University
Columbia Women's Liberation,
Spring 1970. Report from the
Committee on Discrimination
against Women Faculty. *Barnard
Alumnae* 59: pp. 12–18.

Connecticut College
Committee W, (1970). Report to
AAUP by Committee W on the
status of women at Connecticut
College. 3 pp.

Cornell College
Committee on the Status of
Women, (1970). A report of the
Cornell College chapter of the
AAUP: Committee on the Status
of Women. 3 pp.

Cornell University
Francis, Barbara, (1970). The
status of women at Cornell. 6 pp.

University of Detroit
Action Committee for Federal
Contract Compliance in Education,
April 1971. (Formal charge of sex
discrimination lodged by Women's
Equity Action League.) 1 p.

Fisk University
Action Committee for Federal
Contract Compliance in Education,
June 1971. (Formal charge of sex
discrimination lodged by Women's
Equity Action League.) 2 pp.

State University System of Florida
(Florida A & M University, Florida
Atlantic University, Florida International
University, Florida State University,
Florida Technological University,
University of Florida, University of
Northern Florida, University of South
Florida and University of West Florida)
Anon, April 1970. State University
system of Florida. 1 p.

University of South Florida
(1) AAUP Committee on Employment
Status of Academic Women,
April 1971. Employment status of
academic women committee:
faculty report. 64 pp.
(2) AAUP Committee on the
Employment Status of Women,
November 1970. Status of women
committee: faculty report. 31 pp.
(3) MacKay, E. M., February 1971.
Portions of current study of T and
R faculty women. 6 pp.

University of Delaware
Dahl, K. H., 1971. Report on
women at the University of
Delaware. 35 pp.

Georgetown University
Anon. July 1971. The pattern in
Georgetown University faculty
employment for the year 1970–
1971. 1 p.

Harvard University
(1) Anon. (1969). Harvard statistics.
7 pp.
(2) Bynum, Caroline W.; Martin, Janet
M. June 1970. The sad status of
women teaching at Harvard or
"From what you said I would never
have known you were a woman."
Radcliffe Quarterly 54: pp. 12–14.
(3) Committee on the Status of
Women, April 1971. Report of the
Committee on the Status of
Women in the faculty of arts and
sciences. Cambridge: Faculty of
Arts and Sciences, 96 pp.
(4) The Women's Faculty Group,
March 1970. Preliminary report
on the status of women at Harvard.
16 pp.

Holy Cross College
Achbar and Bishop, 1970.

Eastern Illinois University
Anon. (1970). Discrimination
against women teachers at
Eastern Illinois University. 2 pp.

Southern Illinois University, Carbondale
Klaus, Michelle S., July 30, 1971.
HEW team coming to investigate:
faculty women to file complaints.
Southern Illinoisan: p. 2.

**Southern Illinois University,
Edwardsville**
Committee on Female Concerns,
(1971). Report of Committee on
Female Concerns. 3 pp.

**University of Illinois, Champaign-
Urbana**
Ferber, Marianne; Loeb, Jane,
November 1970. Rank, pay, and
representation of women on the
faculty of the Champaign-Urbana
campus of the University of Illinois.
28 pp.

Western Illinois University
Anon, May 1970. Sexual equality
at W.I.U.? 2 pp.

Indiana State University
(1) Anon. (1970). Evidence of
discrimination against women at
Indiana State University. 13 pp.
(2) Hardaway, Charles W., (1970).
The status of women on the faculty
of Indiana State University. 29 pp.

University of Indiana, Bloomington
(1) AAUP Committee on the Status of
Women, January 1971. Study of the
status of women faculty at Indiana
University, Bloomington Campus.
55 pp.
(2) Berry, Sara; Erenburg, Mark,
(1969). Earnings of professional
women at Indiana University. 21
pp.

Johns Hopkins University
Alexander, Anne, 1970. Who's
come a long way, baby? *The
Johns Hopkins Magazine* 21 (2):
pp. 11–15.

Kansas State Teachers College
Committee on the Status of
Women, (1970). K.S.T.C. Chapter
of American Association of
University Professors, Report 1 of
Committee on the Status of
Women. 16 pp.

University of Kansas, Lawrence
(1) Associated Women Students
Commission on the Status of

Women, (1970). Reports of Associated Women Students Commission on the Status of Women: 1967–1970. 30 pp.
(2) Committee W, (1970). Report of Committee W (Status of Women). 3 pp.
(3) The Office of Academic Affairs, (1970). The University of Kansas faculty salary study—1970–1971. 15 pp.

Eastern Kentucky University
Riffe, Nancy L., April 1971. Committee W—AAUP, EKU Chapter. 5 pp.

University of Kentucky
Anon. (1970). The status of women at the University of Kentucky. 31 pp.

Louisiana State University.
Action Committee for Federal Contract Compliance in Education, December 1970. (Formal charge of sex discrimination lodged by Women's Equality Action League). 1 p.

Loyola University
Action Committee for Federal Contract Compliance in Education, December 1970. (Formal charge of sex discrimination lodged by Women's Equity Action League.) 1 p.

University of Maryland, Baltimore
The New University Conference, April 1970. The Status of women at the University of Maryland, Baltimore County. 9 pp.

University of Maryland, College Park
Sandler, Bernice, Fall 1969. Sex discrimination at the University of Maryland. 12 pp.

Massachusetts Institute of Technology
Achbar and Bishop, 1970.

University of Massachusetts, Amherst and Boston
Achbar and Bishop, 1970.

University of Miami
Anon. April 12, 1970. UM faculty dominated by males. *The Miami Herald.*

Michigan State University
Office of Institutional Research, July 1970. A compilation of data on faculty women and women enrolled at Michigan State University. 55 pp.

University of Michigan
(1) Shortridge, Kathy, May 1970. Women as university nigger: how the 'U' keeps females in their place. Pittsburgh: KNOW, Inc.
(2) Shortridge, Kathy, May 1970. Women at the University of Michigan. 5 pp.

University of Minnesota, Twin-Cities
(1) Council for University Women's Progress, December 1970. Academic women at the University of Minnesota (Minneapolis-St. Paul): their number and departmental affiliation. 11 pp.
(2) Minnesota Planning and Counseling Center for Women, May 1970. Research on the status of faculty women—University of Minnesota. 15 pp.
(3) Subcommittee on Equal Opportunities for Faculty and Student Women, April 1971. Report of Subcommittee on Equal Opportunities for Faculty and Student Women. 18 pp.

University of Missouri, Kansas City
Anon. (1971). University of Missouri at Kansas City— information taken from UMKC Bulletin, 1971–72. 1 p.

Mount Holyoke College
Achbar and Bishop, 1970.

University of New Hampshire
Achbar and Bishop, 1970.

State University of New York at Buffalo
Scott, Ann, May 14, 1970. The half-eaten apple: a look at sex discrimination in the university. *Reporter:* 8 pp.

Northeastern University
Achbar and Bishop, 1970.

Northwestern University
Houston, Susan, (1970). Faculty women at Northwestern University College of Arts and Sciences. 2 pp.

Notre Dame University
Stidham, Greg, April 2, 1971. Less than three percent. *The Scholastic:* pp. 12–13.

Ohio State University
Ruben, Alan Miles; Willis, Betty J., 1971. Discrimination against women in employment in higher education. *Cleveland State Law Review* 20 (3): pp. 472–491.

University of Oregon
Ad Hoc Committee, (1970). The status of women at the University of Oregon. Report of an Ad Hoc Committee. 20 pp.

Pace College
Anon. (1970). (Pace College faculty.) 14 pp.

Pennsylvania State University
Action Committee for Federal Contract Compliance in Education, February 1971. (Formal charges of sex discrimination lodged by Women's Equity Action League.) 3 pp.

University of Pennsylvania
Committee on the Status of Women, March 1971. Women faculty in the University of Pennsylvania. 36 pp.

University of Pittsburgh
(1) Advisory Council of Women's Opportunities, November 1970. Progress report to the Chancellor. 14 pp.
(2) Anon. Spring 1969. Number of women holding top level administrative positions at the University of Pittsburgh. 1 p.
(3) The University Committee for Women's Rights, November 1970. Discrimination against women at the University of Pittsburgh. 70 pp.

Princeton University
The Task Force on Equal Academic Opportunities, April 1971. A preliminary report on the status of women at Princeton University. 22 pp.

Purdue University
Metzler, Cindy, (1970). The status of women at Purdue University. 9 pp.

University of Rhode Island
Achbar and Bishop, 1970.

Rockefeller University
Rockefeller University Committee of Women, (1970). Status of academic women at the Rockefeller University. 1 p.

Rutgers University
(The State University of New Jersey System: Rutgers, Douglass and Livingston Colleges in New Brunswick, the College of South Jersey (Rutgers-

Camden) and Rutgers-Newark)
(1) Anon. (1970). Statistics of Rutgers College. 7 pp.

(2) Boring, Phyllis Z., 1971. Distribution of women faculty at Rutgers University. *American Association of University Professors Council of Rutgers Newsletter* 2 (6): pp. 1–3.

(3) Boring, Phyllis Z., 1971. Salary differential and the women faculty members at Rutgers University. *American Association of University Professors Council of Rutgers Chapters Newsletter* 2 (5): pp. 1–3.

(4) Selick, Barbara, 1971. Women want Rutgers men to lib a little. *The Home News* 93 (199): pp. 1, 49. *Chapters Newsletter* 2 (6): pp. 1–3. Dinnerstein, Dorothy, 1971. Some discrepancies between the situations of male and female faculty members Newark College of Arts and Sciences of Rutgers University: a preliminary analysis. 19 pp.

(5) Smith, Georgina, (1971). Summary—survey of faculty career patterns. 7 pp.

(6) Staff writer, May 9, 1971. Rutgers women charge bias. *Newark Sunday News:* sec. 1, p. 12.

Sacramento State College
Anon. (1970). Statistics on women at Sacramento State College. 2 pp.

Salem State College
Achbar and Bishop, 1970.

San Diego State College
Jancek, Camilla, (1969). Women in teaching at San Diego State College, 1968–1969. 2 pp.

Simmons College
(1) Achbar and Bishop, 1970.

(2) American Association of University Professors' Salary Committee, March 1971. Sex discrimination at Simmons College—AAUP report. 6 pp.

Smith College
(1) Anon. (1970). A report important to the future of Smith College: the status of women faculty in academic departments in Smith College in 1969–1970. 4 pp.

(2) Personal correspondence to Dr. Florence Howe, Goucher College, Towson, Maryland 21204, March 1970. 4 pp.

University of South Carolina
Action Committee for Federal Contract Compliance in Education, November 1970. (Formal charges of sex discrimination lodged by Women's Equity Action League.) 1 p.

Southern Methodist University
Action Committee for Federal Contract Compliance in Education, December 1970. (Formal charges of sex discrimination lodged by Women's Equity Action League.) p. 1.

Stanford University
Siegel, Alberta E.; Carr, Ronald G., March 1969. Education of women at Stanford University. In *The Study of Education at Stanford: A Report to the University* 7: pp. 81–100. Stanford: Stanford University.

Middle Tennessee State University
American Association of University Professors' Chapter, (1970). An internal salary study of Middle Tennessee State University for the academic year 1970–1971. 10 pp.

University of Tennessee, Knoxville
Anon. (1970). The University of Tennessee, Knoxville, academic staff. 4 pp.

University of Texas, Austin
(1) Office for Institutional Studies, December 1970. (Tables of salary rates.) pp. 55–62.

(2) Rogoff, Regina et al., July 1971. (Formal charge of sex discrimination against the University of Texas at Austin.) 30 pp.

Tufts University
Achbar and Bishop, 1970.

Virginia Public Colleges
(Longwood, Madison, Old Dominion and Radford College, Richmond Professional Institute (now part of Virginia Commonwealth University), University of Virginia—Clinch Valley, Eastern Shore, Lynchburg and Patrick Henry, Virginia Military Institute, Virginia Polytechnic Institute, Virginia State—Norfolk and Petersburg, College of William and Mary—Christopher Newport and Richard Bland, Community Colleges—Blue Ridge, Central Valley, Dabney Lancaster, Danville, John Tyler, Northern Virginia, Virginia Western and Wytheville)
Peninsular Chapter of the New University Conference, 1971. Women in Virginia higher education. 35 pp.

Virginia Polytechnic Institute
Anon. (1971). Status of women at Virgina Polytechnic Institute and State University. 11 pp.

University of Washington
The Associated Students of the University of Washington Women's Commission, October 1970. Report on the status of women at the University of Washington: Part 1, faculty and staff. 48 pp.

Wayne State University
Anon. (1970). Fact sheet. 5 pp.

Wellesley College
Achbar and Bishop, 1970.

College of William and Mary
Action Committee for Federal Contract Compliance in Education, November 1970. (Formal charges of sex discrimination lodged by Women's Equity Action League.) 1 p.

Williamette University
Action Committee for Federal Contract Compliance in Education, May 1971. (Formal charges on sex discrimination lodged by Women's Equity Action League.) 6 pp.

University of Wisconsin, Madison
(1) Anon. (1970). University of Wisconsin, Madison Campus 1969–70. 2 pp.

(2) Central University Office of Planning and Analysis, 1971. Final report on the status of academic women. 492 pp.

(3) Women's Research Group, (1969). Women at Wisconsin. Beaver Dam, Wisconsin: National Organization for Women. 20 pp.

Yale University
(1) Anon. (1970). Yale faculty. 1 p.

(2) Yale Faculty and Professional Women's Forum, March 1971. Women on the Yale faculty. 33 pp.

(3) The Yale Faculty and Professional Women's Forum, Yale Non-faculty Action Committee, Yale Law Women's Alliance, Yale Medical Women's Association, Yale Graduate Women's Alliance, Yale Public Health Women, and the Yale Sisterhood, May 1971. Sex discrimination at Yale: a document of indictment. 77 pp.

Dr. Bernice Sandler
Executive Associate
Association of American Colleges
Washington, D.C.

Women's
Viewpoint

The eighteenth century saw many strong and independent women culminating in the feminine citizens of the French Revolutionary committees. The pomp and ceremony of chivalry gave way to the breath of pure reason. To the rational man or woman the worst of all human characteristics was "enthusiasm," which smacked of unbridled passion and madness. In the literature of the time, the differentiation of social class was more important than that of sex and it is impossible to tell from the documents which essays are written by men and which by women. A women's viewpoint if it existed was valid only in regard to women's roles as mothers and wives.

The nineteenth century lost its first decade in wars against Napoleon. The soulish, romantic society which developed after his defeat was largely dependent upon two intellectual forces, the "critical philosophy" of Kant, and the politics of nationalism. The sensibilities and emotions were respected and writers and poets never ceased in their praise of The Difference, between man and woman. Unfortunately however, the middle and lower classes were little able to appreciate these refinements of romance, they were too busy fueling the fires of the industrial revolution. In the writings of Hugo and Dickens we can shudder at the quality of life on the lower end of the economic scale. In the same era the American manifest destiny to reach the Pacific was allowing a new, self-reliant woman to develop her potential. It is from this period of time that the modern acceptance of the inherent, experiential difference in male and female viewpoints dates.

The dialetic between male and female was canonized by Freud in his revolutionary views of human sexuality and special attention has been paid to female variables ever since. The assumption that this sexuality renders the woman in some way less rational, less objective, or even less able than the male, although inherent in the views of Freud and his disciples, is flatly rejected by almost all supporters of the women's movement. Although the orthodoxy of Freud soon failed, the place of psychological investigation and psychological theory was assured. Is there a basically feminine viewpoint aside from the experience of sex, conception and birth? The answer is a definite yes. This may be societal or sociological but a difference there most certainly is.

Ultimately the women's liberation movement is simply the statement of the women's viewpoint on the social and economic situation of women in our time. It is widely believed that whenever there is a new social force at work in human affairs, the artist is the first to sense it and the theoretician the last. In the essays that follow both will be represented as they see the movement and themselves.

WHAT DO WOMEN WANT?

5.1 The liberation of women is a very personal and individual movement. Not only does it draw forth weighty studies from the brilliant minds of women scholars and female attorneys, it also strikes certain responses from women and girls in much more commonplace situations. In the eyes of the movement activists, one of the most pitied of all women's roles is that of the housewife and mother. From an all time high of romantic approval at the turn of the century, housewifemanship has sunk to the level of being the despised state. The actual truth probably lies somewhere in the middle of the two historical extremes.

Karen De Vos is a school-teacher and free-lance writer as well as a housewife and mother. She lives in the benign heartland of white, anglo-saxon, culture, the protestant bastion of Mid-America. Her views are interesting because they indicate the degree of empathy that many women from the solid middle class feel for the women's movement. Few of the other social upheavals of the Twentieth Century have been able to penetrate the hard shell of affluence and security felt by the American housewife-consumer. This has been the greatest challenge for the movement and there is no doubt that it is making headway. However the unassailable status of romantic "momism" has been criticised by antagonistic male authors as widely diverse as Philip Wylie and Eldridge Cleaver. Mrs. De Vos states the position of the middle class white women in America in the perspective of women's liberation. She demonstrates at how many points there is an amazing unity of concern and sense of common interest.

5.1.1 Women who write in favor of "women's liberation," whom I shall call feminists vary, immensely in their beliefs and programs. The most moderate of the larger groups, the National Organization of Women (NOW), concentrates its efforts on changing laws that discriminate against women and agitating for day-care centers, job training, equal job opportunity, and other such services that can be provided by government or business. Other groups concentrate on "consciousness raising," getting women to see the extent of their oppression and to develop the self-images and techniques necessary to fight that oppression. Very radical groups talk of "revolution," of restructuring our whole society, sometimes on a Marxist model, sometimes on an almost anarchic model. Hence, any reference to "women's liberation," without specifying which groups or women are being considered is somewhat misleading. One can, however, see some demands and tendencies that run through nearly all the literature, surely through enough of it to make them qualify as answers to the question "what do those women want?" In this essay, I will attempt to show what concerns and attitudes can legitimately be said to typify the women's liberation movement, broad though that term is, to indicate some of the variations within the movement, and to indicate what I consider to be the valuable insights offered by the feminists or, at times, ignored by them.

Perhaps the most obvious and least controversial of the goals set by the feminists is that of equal job training and job opportunity, equal pay for equal work, freedom for women to pursue careers, even when they are married and have children. NOW concentrates almost exclusively on this aspect of liberation. Even though the equal rights laws have been passed, much remains to be done before genuine equal opportunity exists. Genuine freedom to pursue careers cannot be achieved by mothers until there is some better provision for child-care than now exists, and some way of arranging to have babies without losing one's seniority or chance of advancement. Hence, feminists work toward the establishment of day-care centers, the right of maternity leave, and the elimination of discriminatory tax laws such as the one that has

permitted a widow or widower to deduct child-care expenses on his income tax, but has not granted the same benefit to working mothers with husbands, and the social security laws that require married women to pay into the fund without receiving the same benefits that their husbands do.

Equal job opportunity demands some change in sex roles as they relate to care of home and children; we shall take up these at greater length in the discussion of the family. Along with, or perhaps prior to, that change in roles, is needed a change in the legal definitions of marriage. The current situation, though it varies from state to state, generally assumes that marriage is an agreement of support from the male in return for housekeeping, child-rearing, and sexual relations from the female. A change in law that would make fathers and mothers equally responsible for the support of children would do a great deal to stimulate girls to think seriously about the need for job training and would eliminate, much faster than consciousness raising groups will do it, the traditional economic dependence of women.

5.1.2 A 1968 report to the United Nations describing the position of women in Sweden, made it very clear that Swedish opinion, both popular and governmental, is concerned to seek changes in three vital areas: 1. the economic independence of the individual; 2. the amount and quality of contact a father has with his children; and 3. the social well-being of the home-bound parent. In these areas, Sweden affords a model for the kind of laws and programs that feminists are encouraging in the United States.

A more subtle need, if women are to be given equal opportunity to develop careers, is to change the self-image of women and girls. The consciousness raising groups that have proliferated among feminists are engaged in precisely this work. Little girls are bombarded from the time they are old enough to recognize images with the idea that girls and women stay home and take care of babies, houses, and husbands. From their pre-school television watching and their first reading primers, to their high-school counselors and the women's magazines, they are taught that a "normal" woman loves children, cares whether her kitchen floor is yellowing, is more concerned with recipes and beauty hints than with political and social issues, and thinks that being unmarried is the worst of all possible worlds. A conscious effort should be made to change this image, say the feminists, by insisting that boys and girls be treated exactly alike in school, by deliberately changing the image in the textbooks and mass media, and, of course, by changing the laws about marriage and child support. Until such measures are taken, girls will always have a harder time committing themselves to careers than boys will.

Another aspect of the feminine image that all feminists want to get rid of is woman as sex symbol. Two different points about this matter are important to feminists. First, they want to destroy the ideal of beauty created by American society. The excessive concern with youth, slimness, hair color, wrinkles, soft skin, make-up, odor—all of the attempts to make women spend vast amounts of time and money making themselves look better than they by nature look. Feminists want to return to a really natural look, instead of the "natural" look promoted by the cosmetic manufacturers. They want women to be able to show their age, and their natural defects without being made to feel unfeminine or ugly or guilty because they "ought to do something" about themselves. Secondly, feminists want to destroy the use of women as sex objects. They want manufacturers to stop selling their products by relating them to some "sexy" model, they want men to stop being proud of a beautiful but dumb woman and embarrassed by a homely but intelligent one, they want to be liked or disliked on the basis of their character and personality, not their appearance.

5.1.3 If one had to pick a topic for a conflict-free women's liberation convention, the safest would be abortion. Feminists agree absolutely on the need to repeal all abortion laws. They want repeal, not reform. They will not settle for laws permitting abortion in cases of rape, mental or physical deformity of the child, or any other such listing of instances. They want the state to keep hands off abortion, to consider it just another medical procedure to be done at the request of the patient and the discretion of her physician. The argumentation for this position generally begins with some assumption concerning the individual rights of women to control both their bodies and their methods of birth control. Nowhere in the literature is there a reasoned argument for this position that takes into account

the question of the fetus' humanity, that even considers the possibility that the fetus might be human at some time in its intra-uterine life. The general view of the feminists seems to be that the fetus is merely a collection of cells, certainly not another human being.

If one accepts their assumption, there is, of course, no reason why abortion laws should not be repealed. An abortion, on that assumption, is precisely the same thing as the removal of a tumor or mole. But the humanity of the fetus is precisely the point at issue in the abortion debate, and to ignore the necessity of dealing with that issue is almost to guarantee that those with the most serious objections to abortion law repeal will remain unconvinced. All of the heart-rending stories of misery and physical abuse (and they are genuinely moving) suffered by women who were unwillingly pregnant are irrelevant to the issue as long as the question of the fetus' humanity remains unresolved. For if it should be the case that the fetus is at some point a human being, then he has, at that point, rights which the state must protect just as any other human being of any age whatsoever has rights that the state must protect. Then abortion must be decided on the basis of whose rights are to take precedence, of when, if ever, one human life may be sacrificed for the good or benefit of another human life, not on the spurious talk of the mother's right to control her body or her reproductive functions.

Total abortion law repeal would permit abortion right up to the moment of birth, if mother and doctor were willing. Under that condition, one can easily foresee the possibility that at some time a doctor will be required to deliberately kill a fetus that could live on its own, even without the aid of an incubator; yet somehow that fetus is not to be considered a human being until it makes a "natural" appearance a few weeks later. Such problems as this are what the abortion debate is about; the possibility that the fetus is human at some point in its development cannot simply be ignored.

In a society as interdependent as ours, nobody has the right to total control of his own body. Many things may be demanded of any citizen's body if the welfare of another citizen or group of citizens or of the entire society depends upon it. One may cite the draft, the requirement to have certain immunizations, the demand that children attend school, as beginning examples. One could argue, of course, that the state has no right to *any* of these powers, as some of the more radical feminists no doubt would, but that issue must then be clarified before the abortion issue can be settled.

5.1.4 The stories told by the women who have suffered unwanted pregnancies do argue forcefully for another point, if they do not settle the abortion issue. They make very clear that we have far too little concern for the unwed mother or the woman who, though married, does not wish to be a mother. Certainly better facilities and care should be available for these people. If the state requires that a woman, once pregnant, must bear a child, it should also surely provide the services necessary to make that birth as physically and emotionally painless as possible, and should do everything to make sure the child finds a home where it can be loved.

Another point at which the feminists have struck squarely is the relative unconcern with finding an entirely safe contraceptive that does not also produce uncomfortable or dangerous side effects in many women. Finding one would surely contribute at least as much to the national welfare as finding a cure for cancer; yet it is not considered nearly as important a goal by either the government or the medical profession.

As I mentioned above, genuine job opportunity for mothers requires some system of day-care centers that would relieve parents, at least partially, of babysitting chores. Except for the most radical, all feminists agree that some kind of day-care is an immediate necessity. Plans vary from those that would incorporate day-care into the public schools to those that would provide day-care controlled by the parents and based on cooperative arrangements. Again on this issue, a basic assumption goes almost unquestioned among the feminists: that day-care would not be harmful for children of any age.

I could find no studies on the effects of group day-care on infants. Since such group care is practically non-existent in the United States, the dearth of information is no surprise. What evidence there is from communes and the Israeli kibbutziym is not entirely relevant to the typical American situation because both of those group settings involve relatively small groups of people who live and work together far more intimately than would be likely among any group of parents in an American city. The effects of day-care on children certainly demands more study.

Even if good day-care should prove to be beneficial or harmless to children and infants, some of the proposals made by the feminists are frightening in their assumption that they can get good day-care from programs instituted by governments, either local or national. We have yet to develop good public school systems in most of our large cities; the likelihood of our getting good day-care, which would demand a much lower child-adult ratio than school, seems slight. The impersonality of our public institutions, whether schools, universities, hospitals, mental institutions, or homes for delinquents is too well documented to need repetition here. To demand, as many of the feminist groups do, a broad program of child care facilities for children from infancy to adolescence is to invite for infants the same kind of custodial care common to our public schools. All of this is not to deny the validity of the demand for day-care, nor even the validity of the demand that it be publicly financed. What is of concern to those who feel that American children are already too homogenized, too standardized, is the demand for creating by law a system that will almost surely reflect all the faults of our existing systems. Such people would encourage a more innovative approach to this problem, such as tax vouchers that would permit parents to create and choose day-care centers or tax incentives to businesses that provide day-care for employees' children.

5.1.5 Feminists are not enthusiastic about the family, at least as it is presently constructed. Some find it positively reprehensible while others feel there is some hope for it, if it is changed considerably. The Marxist feminists argue that the only real function of the family is economic and that it serves the capitalistic system rather than the family members. With extremes such as the replacement of families with various communal arrangements being advocated by many, the most moderate position seems to be that which seeks to find specific ways in which the marriage partners can change their habits and mind sets, thus making the relationship more tolerable.

The nuclear family has many faults, without a doubt. Its tendency to isolation, to unnecessary demands, to emotional pressures, to over-consumption are all adequately documented in the literature by feminists. But the chief function of the nuclear family, its main contribution to the well-being of our society is largely ignored or unrecognized. That function is its provision of emotional development and support to its members. Granted it frequently does this inadequately and some families do not do it at all, nevertheless the family is almost the only institution in our society where one can get individual attention, love, the feeling of being important and needed, the feeling of belonging. An adult may receive some feeling of belonging and being needed in his work, but a child is excluded from these rewards by the fact that his society considers him to be non-productive. Another basic deterent to the proper functioning of the family is the impersonality of the schools. The desperate desire that people have for this emotional support, and the failure of so many homes to provide it, is attested to by the rash of psychologically based groups such as "sensitivity sessions" which seek to implement if not construct an ersatz family. Not all such groups try to provide this support, but many of them aim at precisely the acceptance, individual attention, and physical contact that families should provide. Whatever is wrong with the family and however much some might like to destroy it, replace it, or transform it, realistic feminists face the fact that Americans and Canadians will resist the deliberate destruction of the family with a vengence that only God, home, and motherhood can muster.

5.1.6 Our society is becoming steadily more depersonalized. The extended family has almost disappeared as a social unit; the neighborhood that functions as a community is gone in the city and often in the suburb as well; the school or church or club where everyone knew everyone else has disappeared. In place of a comparatively small group of friends, most Americans now have a vast number of passing acquaintants. The one place where people could experience genuine intimacy, love, and concern on a continuing, long-range basis is the nuclear family. Instead of trying to destroy the family, or accepting it as a necessary evil, feminists should be working to strengthen that aspect of family life that is not being provided anywhere else in our society— emotional support.

The group that gives such support need not be a biological family, of course. Theoretically, any group of people who were committed to each other and determined to live together could provide this intimacy and love. But as a practical matter, destruction of the biological family in our society will not produce a better grouping of individuals into committed groups functioning as the family should; it will produce an even greater sense of separateness and aloneness, and even greater emphasis on individuality and mobility than we now have. Besides the kind of intimacy and sense of belonging that should be an outgrowth of the nuclear family, the family permits

individuals to commit themselves whole-heartedly and unreservedly to other people. "Commitment" is not a word that appears often in the feminist literature; when it does appear it is usually in the context of commitment to the cause of liberation or to "the sisterhood." But commitment to something beyond oneself is a human need as surely as the need to be loved is. In fact, it is precisely the tendency of men to commit themselves to their work that causes the problems in many marriages, and precisely the need for a commitment like it that brings many women into feminist groups.

But the commitment to job or career is not the kind of commitment that develops people as people. It develops great businessmen, lawyers, and so on—even great wives sometimes—but it does not make people more loving, more able to be themselves, more accepting of others, in short, more human. What does make a person more human is a commitment to another person or to other people. Until one feels that another person's (or other persons') needs are just as important as his own, he has not really understood what love is. Within the family one learns what it is to be so committed and the value that the commitment has in making life meaningful and valuable. To claim that this can be learned only within the family would no doubt be an exaggeration, but if we grant that it is worth learning and teaching, surely the family is the most viable and available place to teach it. The feminists are understandably wary of such talk, for what they are perceiving and reporting very accurately is that frequently such a commitment is demanded only of the woman and not of the man; of the children only in their relationship to their father, not to their mother; and that too often that commitment is, and it is thought, ought to be, the only commitment in the woman's life.

The woman's commitment in marriage differs from her husband's in that her commitment is to his and the children's welfare, while his is usually as much to his career, to "success," whatever that means to him, as to the welfare of his family. Thus, executives may uproot children regularly, whether children can tolerate it or not, in order to move on to the next rung of the ladder; thus the dedicated doctor seldom sees his own children; thus every other demand, whether of business, church, education, community group, is more important to the man than the fact that his wife needs some companionship. The wife, meanwhile, is expected to adjust; to find "interests," meaning flower-arranging or macrame, or ceramics; to do whatever entertaining and visiting her husband's career demands, regardless of her interest in the matter. If both were as concerned about the children's welfare as she is, if he were as concerned about her welfare as she is about his, many of the problems of married women would disappear.

5.1.7 Men do not admit that they are less committed to their marriages and families than their wives, of course. They claim their interest in their careers is really a concern to "provide" for their families. And many a woman feeds this feeling by demanding more and more things from him so that he can continue to believe that it is really money for her that motivates his climb toward greater recognition and importance. The moment a woman realizes this and says "If it's us you're concerned about, forget the promotion and spend your evenings with the kids," the facade comes tumbling down. When a couple begin to see her needs as being just as important as the demands of his career, then a genuine and equal commitment of each to the other can be developed. Feminists generally fail to see the value of such commitment because they are seeing far too much of the commitment by only the wife, a commitment that results in her being stifled, repressed, and only half of the human being she could be.

The second problem with commitment as it is currently practiced in American families is that women are expected to commit themselves, seriously at least, to only their families. Nothing must interfere with husband and children, not even her own needs. And 'interfere' here refers not to serious harm to husband or children, but to mere inconvenience. Any job or education she can work around the family's schedule is fine, but anything that might irritate husband or children is out. The woman is not supposed to have any commitments to herself, to her own growth or needs. If she is desperately unhappy at home but going to work will "not be good for the children," she must give way, as if her needs were not just as important as the children's. The result of this exclusiveness, besides its destruction of women's talents and mental health, is a smothering of the children, a fostering of their dependence, and an overly heavy reliance on her husband for all of her needs.

5.1.8 In sum, the feminists, in their realization of the damage that commitment to husband and children alone does to many women, and in their anger at the one-sidedness of the commitment in marriage, have failed to see the important role that commitment to other people must play in a fully developed life. As a result, they are far too willing to junk the family, forgetting that the very important tasks of providing intimacy and love and of teaching commitment are done almost nowhere else in our society.

In their antagonisms toward the family, feminists have pointed out some of the problems that could be solved if we were only aware of them and willing to work at them. The father's lack of time with his family, the mother's unnecessary isolation from other adults, the inequality in sharing of the work that all admit is dull, repetitive, and boring— the feminists have seen these problems and have provided specific solutions.

They suggest that busineseses and other organizations be prepared to accept half-time work from each of the marriage partners and this could be implemented very easily at some levels of business and in some kinds of careers; yet nobody appears willing to do it. Schools and colleges could accomplish this division of labor with almost no adjustment at all, if they were only willing, as could many social welfare agencies and retail businesses. Even such a simple arrangement as an agreement between husband and wife that he will keep the children and house one whole week each year would go far toward making husbands more aware of how dull housework is and how little of child-care is creative.

Popular mythology suggests that feminists are man-haters, frustrated women, who are taking out their anger at the world by attacking men. Such a view is held by only a tiny fringe of feminists. Most are very much aware that the enemy they are fighting is not men but sexism. They are fighting a system of education and a cultural milieu that oppresses both men and women by forcing them into stereotyped roles dependent on sex, regardless of how well the individuals fit into those roles. Leaders such as Betty Friedan have expressed publically, on several occasions, an awareness of the pressures on the male to "be a man," of the anxiety of being totally responsible for supporting a family, of the inability to express emotion or gentleness without being scorned. While the radicals may grant only grudgingly that men, too, are oppressed, the moderates are very clear about the need for liberation of both sexes.

5.1.9 Feminists almost invariably take a negative view of Christianity in general and the church institution in particular. Much of their ire is aimed at the Roman Catholic Church, particularly for its stand on birth control and abortion, but more generally for its attitude toward women, the bi-polar view that woman is either Eve, responsible for drawing men into sin; or Mary, the virgin mother. They are fond of quoting the writings of the Apostle Paul to indicate the oppression of women that Christianity has brought, particularly the passage in the New Testament, "It was not Adam who was deceived, it was the woman who yielding to deception, fell into sin, yet she will be saved through motherhood." (I Timothy 2:14-15) With texts like this and the refusal of the churches, both Roman Catholic and Protestant to allow women full participation in all aspects of church life, it is understandable that feminists should dislike the church. Unfortunately their dislike is not limited to the organized church but spills over into a distrust of Christianity itself. As a matter of historical fact, however, Christianity was a liberating force for women in the later Roman Empire. With its belief, stated again by the Apostle Paul that "There is no such thing as Jew and Greek, slave and freeman, male and female; for you are all one person in Christ Jesus, (Galatians 3:28) Christianity proclaimed the notion that women were equal to men before God. Distortion of this teaching has much to do with the warping of structures that has taken place in the Christian church.

Nearly all societies that we know of have assigned roles to their members at least partially on the basis of sex. In western culture that assignment has generally put women at home with the children and servants and men out in the world earning money (or food), and protecting the home and country. Feminists are saying that they do not like their role. They do not want to stay home with the children and servants any more; they want to get out and do what the men have been doing. People have been discontended with their lot since the beginning of time and those who see the feminists as protesting only their assigned role tend to dismiss them as malcontents. But feminists are saying something a good deal more radical than that they want the right to play the men's role; they are saying that the whole assignment of roles on the basis of sex is foolish, that sex does not determine character or attitude or aptitude for certain kinds of work. They are suggesting that people be allowed to develop their abilities and personalities without regard for whether activities and attitudes are "masculine" or "feminine." They are demanding that each individual be permitted, as much as society possibly can tolerate it, to develop his individual talents, abilities, and characteristics, without letting stereotyped sex roles get in the way.

Mrs. Karen DeVos
Grand Rapids, Michigan

MY VIEWS ON WOMEN IN AMERICA: DISCRIMINATION AGAINST WOMEN

5.2 Shirley Chisholm is the first Black woman ever elected to the U.S. House of Representatives. She is also the first to mount a campaign for the presidency. Irrespective of how her campaign for the highest elective office in the land may fare or what one thinks of her presumption to run, her point of view is very important. She like Representative Bella Abzug, has had a strong relationship with the liberation movement. Her view of the movement is influenced by the doubly difficult situation of the Black woman in America. She is a vocal spokeswoman for both the black and women's communities. The way in which she intermingles both concerns is interesting but shows the severe difficulty that faces women's liberation advocates in recruiting black women.

The approach of Ms. Chisholm is neither completely subjective nor totally detached and it is coherently in line with much of the civil rights thinking of our time. She like Rep. Abzug, accepts the principle of government financed social programs to solve social problems. She seems to assume the rightness and practicability of the rule of law and seek to work within that rule. Whether a new round of social programs will soon appear in the congress of the United States is not clear. But congress woman Chisholm's dedication to them is clear enough. She appeals to all classes and groups within female society to find a personal freedom for themselves. It is on the basis of this freedom that she then calls for legal restructering of the social priorities.

5.2.1 Most men, and not a few women, do not understand the campaign for equal rights for women. They may know that women are a majority of the population, 51 percent, and that they are supposed to control a majority of the nation's wealth. How, then, could it be that women are discriminated against? At first glance, the idea may seem silly. The Department of Labor found that in 1966, white men had an average income of $7,179. Black men made $4,508, and white women $4,142. Black women, who are almost universally confined to menial service jobs, averaged only $2,934. My main point in quoting these figures is to show you, in dollars and cents, that white women are more discriminated against than black men in the labor market. This has some very serious and costly consequences for our society, to which I will return in a moment.

In my own experience, I have suffered from two handicaps—being born black and being born female. I remember vividly one incident at Brooklyn College. One of my favorite professors, a blind political scientist named Louis Warsoff, was impressed by the way I handled myself in a debate. He told me, "Shirley, you ought to go into politics." I told him, "Proffy, (that was a pet name we had for him), you forget two things. I am a woman, and I am black." During my entire political life, my sex has been a far greater handicap than my skin pigmentation. From my earliest experience in ward political activity, my chief obstacle was that I had to break through the role men assign women. A young woman, in a newspaper story I read somewhere, defined that role beautifully. She was talking about her experiences in the Civil Rights Movement. "We found that the men made the policy and the women made the peanut butter sandwiches."

5.2.2 Every man in Congress is there because of the efforts of the women who form the backbone, the effective troops, of a political organization. Without its thousands of women volunteers, the American Party System would not work. It would break down in a confusion of unanswered letters, unmade phone calls, unkept appointments, unwritten speeches and unheld meetings. Men are not aware of the incredible extent to which they rely on women or to be more precise in my choice of words, the extent to which they exploit women—to handle the details while the men take the credit.

This brings me to one of the mainpoints I want to make. The prejudice against women has gone unnoticed by most persons precisely because it is so pervasive and thorough-going that it seems to us to be normal. For most of our history, the very closely analogous prejudice against blacks was invisible to most white Americans because it was so normal to them. It was a deeply ingrained, basic part of their personalities. Discovering that fast has been a great shock for many whites. Many others have not yet come that far, unfortunately.

When they have, if they ever do, the race problem will vanish. But if we ever succeed, as we must succeed if we are to survive, in rooting out the racism that is such a prominent part of our American heritage, we will still be very far from being a just society if we are not also ready to accord full human dignity to women. After all, half of the blacks and every other minority group in this country are women. When we talk about women's rights we are talking about the rights of the majority of the population. Sex cuts across all geographical, religious, class and racial lines. Every sector of the American population has a stake in eliminating anti-feminist discrimination. To quote a brilliant black woman lawyer, Dr. Pauli Murray, "Discrimination because of one's sex is just as degrading, dehumanizing, immoral, unjust, indefensible, infuriating and capable of producing societal turmoil as discrimination because of one's race." In both cases, please note this, exclusion implies inferiority. The stereotypes are closely parallel. The happy little homemaker, the dumb blonde, the bubble-brained secretary, are the kind of distorted pictures, drawn by prejudice, as that of the contented "old darky" and black mammy and little pickaninnies, down on the old plantation.

5.2.3 Blacks and women have both been taught from childhood because our society is run by and for white males, that they are inherently inferior. To keep them in their place, the same, the very same characteristics are imputed to women—as to blacks—that they are more childish, emotional and irresponsible than men, that they are of lower intelligence, that they need protection, that they are happiest in routine, undemanding jobs, that they lack ambition and executive ability. The parallels are striking and almost frightening, aren't they? Stereotypes are no more credible where they are applied to women than they are when they are applied to blacks. As far as the argument that the woman's place is in the home goes, I would like to borrow a campaign slogan from Congresswoman Bella Abzug. I believe "A woman's place is in the house, and the Senate and the AFL-CIO Executive Board and the Gridiron Club." The important thing that must be understood is that women are first and foremost people.

A woman who aspires to be Chairman of the Board or a member of the House does so for exactly the same reasons as any man. Basically, she feels and knows that she possesses the talents, the attributes and the requisite skills for the job. That and that alone should be the criteria in the business world, the professional world and the political world! The most articulate and active members of the Women's Rights Movement have, of course, been the professional women.

5.2.4 I would like to devote some of my remarks to the problems of the working class and poor women of this country. Our society's attitudes toward women are closely bound up with one of its major problems, that of social welfare. The staggering costs of social services are straining the national budget and threatening to bankrupt most of our cities. One of the commonest characteristics of welfare families is that they are headed by women. In many cases, the problem began with a man who rejected or evaded the role we assign him, of protector and breadwinner, but that is another question with which I cannot deal here. The result, obviously, is that some women are forced to assume the breadwinner's role in addition to that of mother and homemaker.

Three million, eight hundred and sixty thousand (3,860,000) white families are headed by women, and 30 percent are poor, earning less than $3,000 a year. One quarter of all black families are headed by women and 62 percent of them are poor. In toto, women head 1,920,000 impoverished families. Let me recall the income figures I quoted earlier— white women averaged $4,142 in 1966 and black women $2,934. No one can support a family today on such pitiful incomes. One cannot really be blamed for giving up even trying to do so. But although the problem is most grave when it concerns women who are heads of households, it is not confined to them. Other women who work do not do so because of the personal fulfillment, but one-third of the United States' families where both parents work, the husband's income is less than $5,000.

It is almost universally true that women are paid less than men for doing the same work. In college teaching, as has been stated by Virginia R. Allan, women are paid median salaries $400 to $2,000 less than men of the same academic rank. Women, like blacks, Puerto Ricans, and other groups that are the targets of discrimination, are clustered in the low-level, dead end jobs and are rare in more responsible ones. Although 38 per cent of the women in the United States work, only 2 per cent of them make more than $10,000 a year.

5.2.5 Women are also discriminated against in manpower training programs. First, because they are frequently channeled in to training programs for low-entry level jobs with no opportunities for advancement and second, because the "quota"

for women enrollees is much smaller than for men. In 1968 only 31.7% of the on-the-job training (OJT) enrollees were women; the job opportunities in the business sector (jobs) program had only 24% female enrollees and the now defunct job corps had 29% female enrollees. If we are sincerely interested in solving our welfare problem and helping our poor and working class families, we must recognize the correlation between their problems and the battle to provide equal opportunities for women. For these women, their income is not a supplement, it is essential for the survival and well being of the family unit. They must have more and better job training opportunities, equal pay and a fair opportunity for advancement. Finally they must also have adequate day-care facilities. Right now, we have five million pre-school children whose mothers have to work, but day care facilities are available for only 2% of our women. Without adequate day-care we have seriously handicapped, and in some cases doomed our women to failure in the job market.

Sex is not, any more than religion or race, a valid basis for discrimination. Women are individuals, just like men, or blacks, or Polish-Americans. To consider them as a homogeneous group is manifestly unjust and it is pre-judging each individual woman, which as you know is the origin of the word prejudice.

Economic Justice For Women

5.2.6 At one time or another we have all used the phrase "Economic Justice." I would like to turn your attention to economic justice for women. Of course this is only an illusory phrase, as it is an undeniable fact that economic justice for American women does not exist. As I look back over the years of my own lifetime, the transformation in the economic, social and political role we women play in American life has been almost incredible. But we are still quite a long way from anything like equality of opportunity. We are still in a highly disadvantaged position relative to men. This is revealed by our earnings. On the average, women who are full-time, year-round workers receive only about 60% of what men who are similarly employed earn. The median income for fulltime, year-round women workers was $3,973, compared to $6,848 for men. This is somewhat below the official poverty level decreed for a family of four. This reflects the fact we are all too often paid less for doing the same work;

even more it reflects our concentration in the lower-paid, lesser-skilled occupations, and we are steadily losing ground.

Columnist Clayton Fritchy, in *Women In Office,* noted that, "Although more women are working, their salaries keep falling behind men's. Some occupations are still closed, by law, to women. In 1940 women held 45% of all professional and technical positions as against 37% today." Among all employed women, not college women alone, 82% are clerical, sales, factory and farm workers in service occupations. 6% of us are teachers in the grammar and high schools and only 7% of us are medical and health workers, college teachers or other professional and technical workers. Just 5% of us are managers, officials or proprietors.

The factors which have narrowed our opportunities are multiple and complex. There are restrictive hiring practices. There is discrimination in promotions. Many myths, which run entirely counter to the facts, maintain that women make poor supervisors, or that they have substantially higher rates or absenteeism and labor turnover. A recent department of labor survey revealed that women are more reliable and are absent less frequently than the male population of our labor force. The myth about the unreliability of women is somewhat like the one about women being bad drivers. That one has been disproven lately also by the insurance companies; women pay lower rates.

5.2.7 The claim is often made, and without the slightest justification, that even women with more than adequate training and knowledge lack the ability to assume higher level positions in industry. As the late President Kennedy declared in December 1961, in the opening words of his executive order establishing a commission on the status of women, "these continuing prejudices and outmoded customs act as barriers to the full realization of women's basic rights, which should be respected and fostered as part of our nation's commitment to human dignity, freedom and democracy." When President Nixon's first nomination for the Supreme Court was rejected, it appalled and disturbed me greatly that he did not even consider nominating a woman. Our women have too long been overlooked for positions of importance in policy-making and decision areas. The underutilization of American women is one of the most senseless wastes of this century. It is a waste our country can no longer afford. David Deith, a financial reporter, wrote that the Swedish national income could

be 25% higher if women's labor potential were fully utilized. The standard of living in France would rise 35% if women were as professionally active as men. To my knowledge no comparable studies have been made in the U.S. on women, but Federal Reserve Board member Andrew Brimmer once estimated that racial bias costs our nation 20 billion dollars a year and there are five times more women in America than there are blacks.

Meeting the challenge presented by a dynamic, expanding economy in the 70's and beyond, will require that American businesses employ all the financial, material and human resources at its command. We are expected to maintain and improve a high standard of living for a rapidly growing population. We are called upon to meet greater demands for American goods abroad.

5.2.8 The greatest domestic problems of today —poverty in our urban ghettos, inadequate housing, substandard housing, the lack of meaningful, rewarding jobs for many thousands of our citizens—are all challenges that the business sector is being asked to take up. At the same time, we must maintain a growing economy in which all can participate. In mobilizing our resources for the task, we must make sure that none are overlooked, particularly we must train, develop, and use effectively the knowledge and skills of all our people. It is not enough that we talk of the nation's manpower needs; we are going to need "womanpower" as well. Statistically, the simple inevitable fact is that America will have to draw upon the whole of her human resources and offer vastly wider opportunities, without discrimination in race or sex, if we are to accomplish these objectives. The male prejudice against female achievement is usually in a subtle, often unconscious form. Men who would recoil in horror at the thought of being called anti-feminist, who view themselves as impartial feel no inconsistency in saying the "little woman's" place is in the kitchen, with the kids, etc., etc. When these men are accused of prejudice, they reply that they are being sensitive to the "female character."

When I decided to run for Congress, I knew I would encounter both anti-black and anti-feminist sentiments. What surprised me was the much greater virulence of the sex discrimination. It seems that while many, many Americans still harbor racist emotions, they are no longer based on so-called racial characteristics. Paternalism has to a great extent disappeared from racial bias. But I was constantly bombarded by both men and women exclaiming that I should return to teaching, a woman's vocation, and leave politics to the men.

5.2.9 Like every other form of discrimination, anti-feminism is destructive both to those who perpetuate it and to its victims. Male school teachers, for example, are well aware of this. They have had to fight against both men and women who cast aspersions on their maleness because of their vocation. No one knows how many men have declined careers in teaching jobs they would have enjoyed because of the "female" character of that profession. When one group of society is as oppressed as American women are, no one can be free. Males, with their anti-feminism, maim both themselves and their women. Like black people, women have had it with this bias. We are no longer content to trade off our minds and abilities in exchange for having doors opened for us by gallant men. While most men laugh jeeringly at the fledgling "Women's Liberation Groups" springing up across the nation, they should know that countless women—including their cohorts, their wives, and their daughters—silently applaud such group's existence. We—American women—are beginning to respond to our oppression. While most of us are not yet revolutionaries, we are getting in tune with the cry of the liberation groups. Women are not inherently passive or peaceful; we're not inherently anything, but human. And like every other oppressed people rising today, we're out for freedom by any means necessary.

Such is the predicament of all American women; the problem is multiplied for those of us who operate also under racial prejudice. So far most of the feminine revolution has been directed at the problems of professional women whose skills are not recognized or rewarded. However, this very fact that professional ladies have spokesmen who will protest their condition gives them hope of alleviating their suffering. I turn now to the specific dilemma of the black woman.

5.2.10 The feminine revolution has been headed mostly by middle class white professional women aimed toward the higher level jobs. More of our attention should be directed toward those women who comprise the menial working force of our country. Particularly, the black woman, who usually has to find employment as a maid, housekeeper, day worker, cafeteria helper, etc. These women are in dead-end jobs, jobs inherently degrading and humiliating, jobs which barely provide a subsistence existence. Today young women are revolting against this kind of subservient employment. They refuse to take a job which robs them of their self-respect and dignity in exchange for a few dollars. They want the opportunity to prove their worth, to show, both whites and black men that they are women, black women and they are proud. Most of these black women lack the academic training to compete for professional and white collar jobs. Our society must begin to give them training. But in the meantime, there are definite steps which can be taken now to utilize the talents of black women and to provide them with an income above the poverty line, steps which will eliminate the discrimination on the basis of race and sex. Some of you may be thinking, "How can she say that this discrimination is so virulent? Isn't she the first black female member of Congress? That proves that the bias isn't really so great." On the contrary, my battle was long, incredibly hard and continual. Because I pushed, I encountered the strongest prejudice of less competent males, both black and white. That I won is a tribute to the women in my neighborhood who are finally saying "No" to the system. They are fed up. And as each day goes by and the awareness of women to our plight grows, there will be more and more who will say "No."

We live in revolutionary times. The shackles that various groups have worn for centuries are being cast off. This is evidenced by the "developing" nations of the world, which we consider, for the most part, underdeveloped. Countries, such as India, Ceylon and Israel, have women for Presidents, Prime Ministers and in other decision-making positions. American women must stand and fight, be militant even for rights which are ours. Not necessarily on soapboxes should we voice our sentiments, but in the community and at the polls. We must demand and get day-care centers, better job training, more opportunities to enter fields and professions of our choosing and stop accepting what is handed to us.

Race, Revolution and Women

5.2.11 Everywhere we turn today we are confronted with a revolution of some kind. Slogans that range from "You've come a long, way, baby" to "All power to the people," have become jaded cants that drizzle from the mouths of jaded TV announcers. There is an almost paranoid fear eating at the guts of all Americans. Black-White,

Male-Female, Young-Old represent schisms between us. Racial Polarization, the Generation Gap and Virginia Slims are all brand names for products that may become lethal. The Doomsday Criers are amongst us chanting their wares and bemoaning their fate. Vietnam and the Middle East are no longer powder kegs; they are instead the sputtering fuses. The campuses and the ghettoes are eruptions of revolutionary acne. The President circles the globe seemingly handing out carte-blanche military commitment credit cards and scientists in Houston dissect dusty rocks in search of other life-forms while humans starve to death—physically, mentally and spiritually—at home and abroad. The author of *Soul On Ice* has become a soul on the run—an unwilling refugee from his heritage and his mission—a latterday man without a country.

The King is dead and so are the Kennedy Princes of Politics, victims all of hot lead spit out by paranoia, collective guilt and their destructive handmaidens, hate and fear. Deaths purchased, some say, by modern-day robber barons immersed in the cement coffin of the status quo. And here gather we, in this quiet reading, to debate the possibility that there may be *no* future. In a few minutes we leave for our homes and our separate battlefields. What is it that we must find here that will sustain and strengthen us in the days, weeks and years ahead. Communion, understanding, and agape certainly are on the list but there is one other that I might point out, Commitment.

Most women in America have never had the opportunity to fully measure the extent of their own—their personal commitment—to ending poverty—to ending racial discrimination—and to ending social and political injustice. Many of us are old enough to remember the Second World War. In that war, women in many foreign countries learned first-hand what was necessary to maintain life under the most adverse of conditions. While they were begging, stealing, fighting and even killing for bits and morsels of food to feed themselves and their families we continued to enjoy a high standard of living, good jobs and a night's sleep uninterrupted by rifle and artillery fire. I am not saying that anyone of us escaped unscathed by the war and its surrounding horror but I am saying that the flames in which our steel was forged was not hot enough, cruel enough, or close enough to produce an exceptionally high quality steel. Today we are perched on the precipice of internal holocaust—a holocaust that may well be only the trigger for the world-wide one.

And perched there many of us continue to give the easiest things to give—the most detachable extensions of ourselves—money and sympathy.

5.2.12   For those of you who may have forgotten —there are revolutions going on. It is true that some of them are false—designed to build the ego—cleverly camouflaged in order to sell a product that in the final analysis is harmful to the purchasers health.

Some of them are revolts by people who are refusing to accept age-worn patterns of doing things and who are therefore carving new ways that are more satisfactory to their needs. And finally some of them are revolutions in deadly earnest—designed to strike off the shackles of oppressed people throughout the world. Both the so-called black revolution and the Women's Liberation Movements fall into the last two categories. Black people are in deadly earnest about freedom from oppression and women are refusing to accept traditional and stereotyped roles. Because I am both black and a woman I would like to make some comments and observations about both. First, the Black Revolution is not solely black. I say that what black people in America are doing, is participating, in a world-wide rebellion that encompasses *all* aspects of human life. When we talk about the black revolution therefore we immediately attempt to limit the goals of the black man, attempt to strip black revolutionaries of the right to be idealistic, attempt to strip the black man of the right to feel that what he wants is not just freedom for himself but wants a totally new totally free world.

When we separate the so-called black revolution in America from the other revolutions; in literature, in the Church, in the arts, in education and throughout the world we attempt to maintain our own peculiar form of slavery. One of the most noted and most quoted black revolutionaries in this country was Malcolm X. While Malcolm was on a trip through the Holy Land he sent back a letter that read in part:

"You may be shocked by these words coming from me, but I have always been a man who tries to face facts and to accept the reality of life as new experiences and knowledge unfold it. The experiences of this might have taught me much and each hour in the Holy Land opens my eyes even more . . . I have eaten from the same plate with people whose eyes are the bluest of blue, whose hair was the blondest of blond, and whose skin was the whitest of white . . . and I felt the same sincerity in the words and the deeds of these "white" Muslims that I felt among the African Muslims of Nigeria, Sudan, and Ghana."

As Eldridge Cleaver so aptly pointed out there were many blacks who were outraged and felt that Malcolm had betrayed them with that statement. It may very well have been Malcolm's signature on his own death warrant but the point that I want you to bear in mind is that it is exactly that type of personal courage and integrity that marks the true revolutionary. Malcolm X was certainly aware that as an established black leader who had consistently, constantly and continually assailed the "white devil" here at home he was jeopardizing his position. But I think that Malcolm also knew, instinctively, what a Roman slave, Epictetus, had in mind when he said: "No man is free until he is master of his own mind."

5.2.13 What white women, must realize is that black people in America are not yet free and know that they are not yet free. This is true also for a great number of dark-skinned people throughout the world. But I do not find it astonishing that there are so many people who are aware that they are not yet free. What I do find astonishing is that so many of the non-homogeneous grouping that we call white western think of themselves as free. The master does not escape slavery simply because he thinks of himself as free—as the master. Neither do the brother and sister of the master escape slavery when they stand idly by and watch while their brother enslaves their brother. The master is inseparably bound to the slave and so is white America inseparably bound to black America.

A while back while testifying before the Office of Federal Contract Compliance, I noted that anti-feminism, like every form of discrimination, is destructive both to those who perpetrate it and its victims; that males, with their anti-feminism, maim both themselves and their women. Bear in mind that that is also true in terms of black and white race relations. No one in America has escaped the wounds imposed by racism and anti-feminism. In *Soul On Ice* Eldridge Cleaver pointed out in great detail how the stereotypes were supposed to work. Whether his insight is correct or not it bears closer examination. Speaking of the white woman in the passage "The Primeval Mitosis" he describes her stereotype thusly, ". . . she is required to possess and project and image that is in sharp contrast to his (the white man), so that the effeminate image of her

man can still, by virtue of the sharp contrast in the degrees of femininity, be perceived as masculine. Therefore she comes "Ultra-feminine." Isn't this an essential part of what the Women's Liberation Movements are all about? Women, especially in the upper classes, have been expected to be nothing more than dangling, decorative ornaments—non-thinking and virtually non-functional. In other places in the passage, Cleaver describes the other stereotypes that white western society has accepted in the place of reality. He states that the black male is expected to supply the society with its source of brute power through his role as the "Supermasculine Menial"—all body and no brain. The white male assigned himself the role of the "Ominipotent Administrator" all brain and no body, because that could be seen as the clearly superior role. The black female was assigned the role of "Subfeminine" or Amazon. What the roles and the strange interplay between them have meant to America, Cleaver goes on to point out quite well. There is only one thing that I want to point out. Because of the bizarre aspects of the roles and the strange influence that non-traditional contact between them has on the general society blacks and whites—males and females must operate almost independently on each other to escape from the quicksands of psychological slavery. Each—black male and black female—white female and white male must escape first from their own historical traps before they can be truly effective in helping others to free themselves.

5.2.14 The goal must clearly be freedom—integration is not yet feasible as a goal. It is not feasible because integration depends on mutual concepts of freedom and equality. Cleaver stripped from some of our eyes for all time the wool that we tried so desperately to hold over them. Black women and white women have been for the most part the opposite sides of the same coin as have been black men and white men. Our society has always required that those coins come up head and head or tails and tails for all kinds of spurious reasoning. But no matter what the reasoning it is part of the reason why white women are not now and never have been truly accepted working in the ghetto. One of the questions that I am most often asked by white women these days is "What can we do?" In many ways it is a strange question—strange because the phrase: "to help you people" is only implied. It is strange because of the implied assumption that they are free to help and strange because of the implied assumption that they are in a position to help.

I have responded to that question in many ways—pointing out the political arena—education and many other things. But I have always left only the implication of the real—the true answer—the one thing that they not only might do—the only thing that they must do. Today I must state it. Free yourselves! And in order to do that you must first free yourselves of the assumption that you are now free. I have pointed out time and time again that the harshest discrimination that I have encountered in the political arena is anti-feminism—from both males and brainwashed "Uncle Tom" females. When I first announced for the United States Congress last year, both males and females advised me, as they had when I ran for the New York Assembly, to go back to teaching, a woman's vocation, and leave politics to men. I did not go back then and I will not go back as long as there exists a need to change the politics of this country. Like the colleagues that I had in Albany, many of my fellow Members in the House treat me with a deference that is patronizing. On May 20 of this year I introduced legislation concerning the equal employment opportunities of women. At that time I pointed out that there were three and one-half million more women than men in America but that women held only two per cent of the managerial positions; that no women sit on the AFL-CIO Council or the Supreme Court; that only two women had ever held Cabinet rank and that there were at that time only two women of ambassadorial rank in the diplomatic corps. In the Congress there were only ten Representatives and only one Senator. I stated then as I do now that this situation is outrageous.

5.2.15 I would like to quote an excerpt from the speech that I made on the Floor that day: "It is true that part of the problem has been that women have not been aggressive in demanding their rights. This was also true of the black population for many years. They submitted to oppression and even cooperated with it. Women have done the same thing. But now there is an awareness of this situation, particularly among the younger segment of the population. As in the field of equal rights for blacks, Spanish-Americans, and Indians and other groups, laws will not change such deep-seated problems overnight. But they can be used to provide protection for those who are most abused, and begin the process of evolutionary

change by compelling the insensitive majority to reexamine its unconscious attitudes." Women in this country must become revolutionaries. We must refuse to accept the old—the traditional—roles and stereotypes. Because of the present situation the tactics for black women must be slightly different than the tactics for white women but the goals can be the same. The tactics of revolution used by the white liberal community must be, as they will be, slightly different than the tactics used by the black ghetto community but the goal can be the same. The goal, though, must be more than political freedom. It must be more than economic freedom. It must be total freedom to build a world-wide society that is predicated on the positive values of all human life. It must be freedom from the waste and ravages of all natural resources including human resources. Women must do more than sacrifice husbands and sons in the present Social Revolution. They must also sacrifice themselves. And for many women, black and white, those who will call first for that sacrifice will be their own sons—their own husbands. You must start in your own homes, your own schools and your own churches.

Listen to me well and get me straight. I don't want you to go home and talk about integrated schools, churches or marriage when the kind of integration you are talking about is black with white. I want you to go home and work for—fight for—the integration of male and female—human and human. Franz Fanon pointed out in "Black Skins—White Masks" that the Anti-Semitic was eventually the Anti-Negro. I want to point out that both are eventually the Anti-Feminist. And even further I want to point out that all discrimination is eventually the same thing—Anti-humanism. Our task will not be easy—it will be hard but it must be done. Perhaps the greatest power for social change—for a successful Social Revolution lies in our Hands.

But it is not an unlimited power nor is it an invincible power. Further the use of power will always cause a reaction therefore we must use our power well and we must use it wisely.

Representative Shirley Chisholm
Democrat, New York

SEXISM

5.3 The third wave of feminism has produced a number of able writers who research and write primarily in the books and news media of the movement. One of the best is Ann Forfreedom, whose work in and about the history of women has appeared in a number of publications. She represents one of the major positions of the newest wave of feminism, namely that all aspects of American society and all of its social institutions are based on a class structure which places women in a secondary and demeaning role.

The authoress is not only defining the concept of "sexism" as understood by the movement, she is making demands upon the society which she perceives practicing it on every hand. She is far from being alone in either her viewpoint or her goals. The general media of the movement state and restate instances of subordination and insult as outlined in detail in the public press.

A large number of assumptions about the foundations and developments of modern society are included in all contemporary feminist literature. Whether these assumptions are true or false partially depends upon the individual's conception of history and whether in the final analysis the movement succeeds in achieving its goals. The third wave literature is controversial and inflammatory, it is trying to encourage the followers of the movement and win new followers. It is a development of the long tradition of polemical political writing which has bloomed over and over again in the free atmosphere of the United States. Both Rep. Chisholm and Ms. Forfreedom equate the aspects of exploitation involved sexism with those of racism and this is a valuable insight into the use of the former term. Although many of the movement authors draw conclusions from psychology and sociology, the underlying motive or ground-motivation is economic. It is at this point that many of their writings confuse American capitalist materialism with Marxian dialectic materialism. The phrases of the New Left-economics run through the women's liberation literature and take many new forms with the replacement of sexual qualities for the racistic or class distinctions found elsewhere.

Although the quotations and citations used by the polemicists are usually taken from the popular press, the all-important interpretations are based on the academic writings of the women social scientists who are ultimately the backbone of the movement. While apparently shunning theory, these writers are dependent upon the theoretical analysis of women who hold positions in the academic institutions and who follow the tradition of contemplative scholarship.

5.3.1 Charlotte Bronte wrote in 1850, "Men begin to regard the position of woman in another light than they used to . . . They say, however—and to an extent truly—that the amelioration of our condition depends on ourselves. Certainly there are evils which our own efforts will best reach; but as certainly as there are other evils— deep-rooted in the foundations of the social system—which no efforts of ours can touch, of which we cannot complain, of which it is advisable not too often to think."[1]

Today, women and men again are reexamining the social position of woman and, again, women are being told that their problems as women are due to their own feelings. But a woman's life today, as in Bronte's time, is governed more by the rules and expectations of society than by her own personal feelings. What kind of rules and expectations do American women face in 1972? A closer look at the problems faced by women of all colors and classes in the U.S. provides insight into the nature of these "evils" Bronte mentions.

American women are nearly 106 million strong. Most are married, most have had some schooling beyond high school, and many have become the sole support of their households due to divorce, death, or desertion. American women are more than one-third of the national wage-earning work force, and they have been active in government, writing and art circles, theater and acting professions. The American woman has better education and job opportunities, better contraceptive and abortion methods, easier divorce, and more "labor-saving" devices available to her than ever before in U.S. history.[2]

But almost from the moment of birth, an American girl's life is circumscribed by certain expectations about her sex, about females: she will be secondary to any males in the family, her education will be considered less vital, her future more entwined with being a good wife and mother than with being a good and strong *person*. If forced by poverty or ethnic-minority background, or if encouraged by her parents, she will be expected to work for wages most of her life (wifehood and motherhood not being paid jobs) and so will be encouraged to learn a trade or profession. But whatever job she holds will be expected to be less important to her than the man or men she will care for, the children she will raise. In an information-rich society, she will be expected to keep up with the news, but not to make the news. As a woman, her horizons will be limited, though as an American she will participate in a far-flung empire. She may live a long life during which she will rarely have been encouraged to seek to change her world, to define herself not by the people she serves but by her own goals and needs.

More specifically, whatever area the American woman looks at today, she is considered secondary, unimportant, and exploitable there. In jobs, she may be a large part of the labor force, but she usually can get jobs only in the lesser-skilled, lower-paying, less-prestigious areas. Also, most jobs or careers available to her pay her less than a man doing the same work, and she is, like men of ethnic minorities, the last hired and first fired, except in "women's jobs," open only to women. In a reversal of the school-job ratio for men, American women generally do not gain higher-paying jobs in response to greater amounts of schooling. Of women who have completed 3 years of college, 70% are employed in the less-skilled occupations (service workers, operatives, sales clerks, clerical workers). About 20% of women with 4 years of college also work in these less-skilled occupations, as do 7% of women with 5 or more years of college.[3] Women pay taxes at the same rates as men, but are not allowed large deductions for child care, maternity, and other financial difficulties Congressmen don't consider legitimate. Even the civil service jobs show a pattern of sex discrimination: women hold 1.5% of the top grade jobs at salary levels beginning at $28,000 a year, though they abound in the lower ranks. In all major U.S. institutions, including foundations, labor unions, universities, hospitals, newspapers, and churches, women are paid little, worked hard, listened to not at all, and expected to accept this bitter situation with a smile.[4]

5.3.2 The U.S. educational system also discriminates against women in its internal hiring policies (women are the secretaries, men are the principals); its separation of boys and girls for arbitrary reasons in the first through the twelfth grades (for example, why do boys and girls have to be in separate lines to board a school bus or to get a drink of water?); in admissions policies, through quota systems; in its curricula (didn't women ever write novels good enough to be on the reading list in literature courses, didn't women do more in U.S. history than cross the frontier and have a suffrage movement?); and in its general attitude toward females.

That attitude can best be summarized by an incident that occurred in March, 1971. A Paintsville, Kentucky high school suspended 15 women until they would agree to submit to paddling because they showed up for classes in pantsuits during the near-zero weather at the end of January. The high school principal, indicting them for a "deliberate rules violation," told them to go home until they were willing to be spanked. This incident might not have become public at all if the underground High School Independent Press Service (itself outlawed in many schools, violating students' rights) had not printed an account, which was later reprinted by Liberation News Service.[5] The school, through its highest officials, was telling these women that (a) women don't wear pants, men do; (b) even though pants are logical attire in cold weather, the need to distinguish men from women overrides common sense, so no pants are allowed—ever; (c) even though its rule is illogical, man-made, and arbitrarily enforced (are male students forbidden to wear ruffles or jewelry?), it is the law, and you must always obey a law, even one you didn't make, agree to, or consider justifiable; (d) lawbreakers must be punished, and since your crime really lies in denying male control over your behavior, you must be forced to submit to humiliation and physical violence at the hands of men, especially those men here to teach you the tenets of your society. The issue differs from school to school, the meaning, does not.

In the doctor's office, women face the same lesson: submit to male control over your life, even in the tiniest or most intimate details, and you will be helped; resist or question, and you will be humiliated or hurt by insensitive doctors, particularly gynecologists, who will tell you your pain is all in your head. In the everyday encounters in a woman's life, the same lesson is taught. On the street, where any male passerby making an obscene or suggestive remark is shocked if met with a response of anger—or even just a response, because women are presumed to be "naturally" passive. On the highways, where even bad male drivers are cursed as "woman driver." In casual conversations, where remarks disparaging of women or openly hostile towards women are left unchallenged: when did anyone last call a high-powered executive *male* a "bitch," or assume that a prostitute or coed or hurricane was *masculine*, or admire a man who gushed "But my real duties are as a good husband and father!"?

5.3.4   American religions are fond of the American woman: she works hard at raising funds for religious establishments, doesn't complain about being relegated to auxiliary groups within the main bodies, and, until recently, hasn't minded being in organizations always headed by men (even nuns' councils have been headed by men), espousing belief in a male Deity with a male-dominated priesthood and giving pronouncements that either ignore or denigrate females.

American courts, too, don't mind relying on underpaid female labor, such as stenographers and clerks, as well as male-dominated judgeships and juries to dispense justice. Though such overwhelming male presence may not affect most court business, it certainly affects the trials of women and any trials focusing on an issue intertwined with myths and fears about women (e.g. trials about rape, intercourse with a female minor, prostitution, abortion, divorce, child custody, alimony, or "passion crimes"). Can American women receive justice in courts run by men raised in a country in which women are not the legislators, interpreters, implementors, or redressors of the laws? And from the Republican Party to the Peace and Freedom Party, political leadership has excluded women from all but token positions.

American art and architecture don't include many women, either. Art galleries don't exhibit many shows by women. For example, in Manhattan's art marketplace, the 100 principal art galleries represent about 1,000 artists, of whom only 20% are women. And a recent survey of commercial galleries showed only 18% displaying works by women, though women are 75% of art school students. And of 52 shows at the Los Angeles County Art Museum, none was by a woman, while the New York Museum of Modern Art, which has exhibited 1,000 one-artist shows, has shown works by 5 women.[6] Women's art is, of course, judged by men: male critics, male artists, male gallery owners, male buyers, male art historians, male art teachers. Many of these men denigrate art by women for being too sentimental or too passive or overly detailed. Women are barely present in architecture; 6% of the students in architecture schools are women, while 1% of members of the American Institute of Architects are women (so guess who designs the little boxes women live in, with a kitchen and bathroom but no get-away-from-it-all room for a woman).

In literature and drama, the most familiar women are stereotypes such as the temptress, the devourer, the tough broad with a heart of gold, the clown, the waif, the housewife, the maid. This correlates with the lack of women in the higher levels of the writing, publishing, and entertainment industries. Only 2 out of 7 members of the Writers Guild of America are women.[7] And women are readers or editors but not publishers or agents in the publishing industry. In addition to critical disparagement of writing done by women, males sometimes use psychological harassment to discourage potential writers; a classmate of mine at UCLA in 1969 was in a writing class in which the teacher consistently criticized her work as not "phallic" enough, because "writers write with their balls." As a result of such discouraging male-orientedness, she dropped out of the class and decided not to become a writer.

5.3.5   Women are practically invisible off-screen at TV studios, and on-screen roles for women tend to be stereotypic. TV journalist, Sheila Hobson notes that "the general level of all women on television is low. And I really think it is meant to be that way (by the industry). Smart, personable women turn people off. . . ."[8] The three major TV networks have 1 female video tape technician between them. There is only 1 union film camera-woman in the country. In 26 new TV shows for the fall 1972 season, men outnumber women cast members by 283 to 81.[9]

Women are visible in the management of large magazines, but most of their work goes into magazines aimed at exploiting women. *Seventeen*, for example, carries nearly 43 ads for engagement rings in each issue, impressing upon its readers the importance of catching a man, getting a man, spending lots of money on the wedding, and then dropping out of sight. Movie fan magazines attract readers with lurid but misleading headlines, exploiting women's sexual anxieties and romantic fears. In American music, rock lyrics ("under my thumb," "I like boobs a lot," "stand by your man") denigrate women, while classical music ignores women. The classical music of Pauline Viardot-Garcia or Frieda Mary Swain remains unheard in this country; not since 1903 has Ethel Mary Smyth's *The Forest* been performed in the U.S. But then, conductors, concert managers, and tour arrangers are usually men, many of whom have no interest in or knowledge of women's works.[10]

Is a pattern emerging? Is this denigration of women, this placing of females at the bottom of whatever is involved, is this just an American phenomenon? Is this just part of our time and era?

In England and Mexico today, women are protesting the lack of equal pay and the lack of child care centers, as well as the overreliance on mothers staying at home all day to care for their husbands and children. In France, Germany, and Canada, women are protesting man-made anti-abortion laws, and fighting for the right to get effective contraceptives publicly and cheaply. In Scandinavia, Italy, and Switzerland, women are fighting their lack of political presence in government and their lack of adequate child care centers. In India, Egypt, and Tanzania, women are disputing man-made laws favoring males in marriage, divorce, and property inheritance.

And every day newspapers carry items about facets of anti-womanism that are appearing across the world. In 1972, 12-year-old Jackie Fuller, described as "real championship class" by boxing coach Bill Green, was disqualified from belonging to any boxing club or fighting future boxing matches in South Oxhey, England—because Jackie is a girl;[11] thus, Jackie is learning that because people, especially men, have certain preconceived ideas about what boys can do and girls can't, and because these ideas group all girls together without allowing exceptions, she must now stay away from a form of exercise that could have taught her endurance, strength, self-defense, and self-reliance. Also in 1972, the official Communist Party newspaper in Prague blamed the 1968 reform movement on women;[12] so Czech women, who are underpaid and overworked in factories and at home, and who received practically no representation during the popular movement, must now feel guilty for causing that "counter-revolutionary" economic and political movement by stepping out of their role as mothers. And in 1972, the BBC in London revealed that Saudi Arabia is not the only place in the world in which women are still bought and sold; a Catholic priest in southern India apparently has been "nun-running," sending untrained and scared young girls from India to Italy for a travel fee of $350 per girl, so that these girls can enter convents in which the shortage of nuns and novices has become so acute that the housekeeping in the convents is falling behind.[13] And back in the U.S., not too long ago a Long Island, New York man narrowly failed to stop his estranged wife from having a legal abortion she wanted.[14] In many countries, a woman is still considered the chattel or property of her father or husband, so that she has no rights in the society except to clean house, and bear babies, and service men's sexual needs.

The *L.A. Times* has carried a major article studying American attitudes toward rape[15] and a later article about Bangladesh attitudes toward the nearly 25,000 Bangladesh women and girls raped and impregnated by West Pakistani soldiers during the 9-month war.[16] Almost 15,000 of these victims have been hiding in rural areas, ashamed and afraid to come to clinics for abortions and aid.

In 1971, a Tucson, Arizona high school teacher was fired for "teaching about witchcraft . . . in such a way that it affects students psychologically . . .";[17] a year later she was reinstated on a technicality. And recently, protests by Christians and Jews over the display and sale of "grotesquely fashioned dolls labelled 'Jew'" forced supermarkets to withdraw these dolls from the French provinces, but no such protests were heard regarding the display and sale of grotesque dolls labelled "Witch" in the same French supermarkets.[18] These two widely separate incidents reveal some overlapping fears and myths about women. Witchcraft and women are related in the minds of most people, and male fears about sexual potency and political power are intertwined with myths about witches (for more details see H. R. Hays' *The Dangerous Sex* and Margaret Murray's *The Witch-Cult in Western Europe*).

American educators saw nothing ridiculous about immediately accepting a charge of witchcraft against a female colleague, and French humanists who were able to connect disfigured "Jew" dolls with the strains of anti-Semitism and religious intolerance woven into the fabric of popular psychology were totally unable to recognize the harmful effects of anti-womanism and sexual bigotry. On a deeper level, as men make the positions in society to which women are confined, men write, publish, and teach from the history books that ignore or demean woman and the female past. The accusation of witchcraft has cost women more than jobs or reputations. From the witchhunts of medieval Europe until the trials in the American colonies, millions of women (some estimates run as high as 9 million) were hanged, tortured, or burned to death as witches. Many thousands were crippled and raped in prisons from Wurtzburg (900 witches, including only 18 men, executed in a 3-month period)[19] and Toulouse (400 witches burned in a single day, including 346 women and girls, and 14 males)[20] to Salem (20 killed in Salem, perhaps 300 in all the Colonies in this period).[21] But this we are not taught in school or in movies. Nor are we taught that many of these women, our foremothers, were killed not for adherence to some male Devil, but for defying male-created laws and male-dominated society by proclaiming their rights to social independence and sexual freedom. Today the term "witch" is used to frighten women so they won't be too independent, won't look more closely at society than at their own fading beauty.

5.3.6 On still another level, this easy acceptance of women as scapegoat serves to hide the history of women's struggles in the areas of education, economics, and culture. In the United States, women can go to high school or college today mainly because other women fought long and hard for that privilege. High schools were not open to girls until after the Civil War, and the first coed college, Oberlin (founded in 1833, admitted a few women in 1837), saw its task as preparing girls for wifehood and motherhood. Oberlin's attitudes were that women needed better education to become better mothers, not better citizens, so it followed that: "Washing the men's clothes, caring for their rooms, serving them at table, listening to their orations, but themselves remaining respectfully silent in public assemblages, the Oberlin co-eds were being prepared for intelligent motherhood and a properly subservient wifehood."[22] As shown in a recent series of reports by the National Organization for Women (especially the New York chapter report *Sex Bias in the Public Schools, 1971,* and their 1968 report written partly by Kate Millett, *Token Learning: A Study of Women's Higher Education in America*), most schools today still have that bias. The texts used in the schools (with titles like *Representative Men: Heroes of Our Time,* or a U.S. history book that mentions no more than 5 or 6 women), the class attitudes (girls can't do higher math or complex science, boys don't like English or drama), their unit requirements (home economics or cooking for girls, woodshop or metalshop for boys), their greater interest in the funding of boys' sports rather than girls' sports (and keeping girls barred from even non-contact sports with boys) all combine to create walls of misunderstanding and ignorance between males and females, and among females about their own past. And that fear of the past has led to the resurrection of a 400-year-old accusation against a teacher who did nothing more than talk about witches to her high school class.

We can parallel the effects of this schooling on the sexes by remembering the effects of similar training on blacks and whites in the U.S.: both learn myths rather than facts, both are taught the inferiority of blacks to whites and the superiority of white culture, and the physical and educational development of blacks are subordinated to the needs and desires of whites. Sexual bigotry, like racial bigotry, goes deep into the fabric of American society; Gunnar Myrdal notes that "When a legal status had to be found for the imported Negro servants in the 17th century, the nearest and most natural analogy was the status of women and children."[23] But male children can outgrow that status.

However, sexual bigotry is not a solely American dilemma. The attitude of the French humanists shows an ignorance, or avoidance, of the French past. Frenchwomen have been protesting the French male's lack of concern about sexual chauvinism for a long time. Christine de Pisan, a late-14th century philosopher and astronomer at the French court, wrote books like *Cite des Dames (The City of Women)* defending the right of woman to think freely and learn about her heritage. The 16th century French queen Marguerite of Navarre is reputed to have headed a nascent feminist movement. And during the French Revolution (1789–1793) the French feminist movement produced a large number of pamphlets and writings about the lives Frenchwomen were forced to lead, bereft of education, skills, or a future. A group of them wrote: "Man is a born egotist . . . he reduces us to managing his household affairs and to partaking of his rare favors when he feels so inclined."[24] And women in the Commune governments of 1848 and 1871 tried to change educational and economic systems so that men and women could work together as equals.[25] Yet in France today, these humanitarians can ignore the insult to women's history, the insult to those who died for their sex's freedom; and while anti-Semitism is combatted as an affront to all humankind, anti-womanism goes unnoticed. Further, many Western and Asian cultures have certain common fears and ideas about women that have become institutionalized through religion and the social sciences, particularly psychology, sociology, and history.

Most religions preach that, as the Hindu Laws of Manu proclaim, "In childhood a female must be dependent on her father; in youth, on her husband; her lord being dead, on her sons; a woman must never seek independence."[26] And the secondary nature of *femina sapiens* is taught in the illogical *Genesis* formula: "She shall be called woman because she was taken out of Man."

5.3.7 Psychology assumes that these assertions are biological commands, and then proceeds to help women follow them. The majority of psychologists are men who went to male-dominated university psychology departments. The major psychological theoreticians, like Freud, Jung, or Adler, grew up in male-dominated societies and each eventually assumed that the "female" is merely a substandard "male." Even modern popularizers of psychology take male dominance and female passivity for granted. Erik Erikson explains that "Much of a young woman's identity is already defined in her kind of attractiveness and in the selectivity of her search for the man (or men) by whom she wishes to be sought. . . ." As Dr. Naomi Weisstein notes, "It is an interesting but limited exercise to show that psychologists' ideas of women's nature fit so well with the common prejudice and serve industry and commerce so well. . . ."[27]

Religion and psychology often rely on the theme of biology or "anatomy is destiny" to explain woman's nature and social status. But the Jackie Fullers show that some women are not born obviously inferior to males, some women are not born interested only in sexual fulfillment. With such notable exceptions, why do psychologists keep asserting that all women are *by nature* interested only in marrying and mothering men?

Sociology goes forward to examine the actual lives women and men lead. Actually, sociology departments discriminate heavily against women faculty members, so most sociologists are men used to seeing and dealing with women in lower positions. Recently, Dr. Alice Rossi found that while women are 43% of the college seniors planning graduate work in sociology, they are 30% of the Ph.D. candidates, 27% of the full-time lecturers and instructors, 14% of the full-time assistant professors, 9% of the full-time associate professors, 4% of the full professors, and 1% heads of graduate sociology departments in the U.S.[28]

Not surprisingly, sociologists have declared that woman's "role" is in the home, where it has "always" been, and in keeping the family together. That term "the family" is used to justify economic discrimination against women, since women have some place to be besides the job. Further, "the family" is generally defined as "the nuclear family" of husband, wife, and children, or as an institution based on the continual presence of the mother or female member. So, by sociological definition, a woman engaged in raising a family violates her "role" if she leads another life in the public area. Sociologists rarely emphasize the existence and feasibility of other family forms that do not rely heavily on the 24-hour presence of the mother. And the family forms of the past—the nuclear family is a recent form—are mentioned even less often.

Finally, history is used to buttress any flaws in the anti-woman assertions of other social sciences. Historians include almost no women as makers, or even subjects, of history. In a recent survey, Dolores Barracano and E. R. Schmidt found that in the leading 27 colleges U.S. history texts used in survey courses, the percentage of words devoted to women ranges from a high of 2% to a low of 5/100 of 1%. Women are portrayed more often in illustrations, though, with a high of 6% of pictures showing women.[29] History departments do not hire many women, and the history of women is not included in most schoolbooks. In addition, the usual portrait of women in history books emphasizes the sexual or maternal roles women have played, but does not present women fighting for causes, changing their world, living lifestyles different than the prescribed patterns of their times. And history is used to justify the rise of, and continuation of, the interlocking economic, political, psychological, and biological (rape, anti-abortion laws, etc.) restrictions against women. History is cited as tracing the social inferiority of women back to some mythical cave or hut in which the hunting male is somehow considered more socially important than the food-gathering female; actually, women have hunted, fished, herded cattle and sheep, raised crops all over the world, in different cultures at different times. But the myth of caveman dominance is convenient for excusing an anti-woman status quo in the modern world.

Most of these fears about the restrictions on women are in effect in any specific culture today, this intertwining system, this sexism, not only exists, but is costing women's lives every day. How did it arise? We don't know for certain. Feminists are starting to analyze sexism and produce theories on its rise,[30] but essentially we are only beginning to realize the extensive effects of sexism, the "evils" that Charlotte Bronte could not think of too often. Today we face the same battles, and we are speaking out, fighting on.

REFERENCES

1. In a letter to Elizabeth Gaskell, quoted in *Aphra,* Vol. 2, No. 3, (summer 1971), in *"Aphra*-isms" pp. 57-58.
2. Figures from *Time* magazine, special issue on The American Woman, March 20, 1972, pp. 27-28.
3. Reported in *Underutilization of Women Workers, 1971* (Women's Bureau, Dept. of Labor), cited by Wendy Martyna, "Women: Equality in Education?", a Fact Sheet, Los Angeles Women's Center (1972).
4. *Time,* March 20, 1972, *op. cit.,* p. 28 and throughout the issue.
5. Reprinted in *Everywoman,* March 26, (1971) p. 7.
6. *Time, op. cit.,* p. 77.
7. *Ibid.,* p. 94.
8. Sheila Smith Hobson, "Women in Television", in *Sisterhood is Powerful,* edited by Robin Morgan (Random House, 1970), pp. 70-76, quote on p. 75.
9. *Time, op. cit.,* p. 94. For more on women in film, see *Take One* (magazine—P.O. Box 1778, Station B, Montreal 110, Canada), special issue on Women in Film, Vol. 3, No. 2. Also see *Women & Film* (2802 Arizona Ave., Santa Monica, Ca. 90404, or 2022 Delaware St., Berkeley, Ca. 94709).
10. From "Have You Heard Of . . ." in *Goodbye to All That* (newspaper—P.O. Box 3092, San Diego, Ca. 92103), Issue 27, March 17-April 7, 1972, p. 6.
11. Los Angeles *Times,* March 26, 1972, Sec. C, p. 2.
12. *Ibid.,* March 9, 1972, Part 1, p. 7.
13. *Ibid.,* March 24, 1972, Part 1, p. 25.
14. *Ibid.,* March 19, 1972.
15. *Ibid.,* March 12, 1972, Section E, p. 1.
16. *Ibid.,* March 31, 1972, *View* Section, p. 1.
17. Reprinted from the *New York Times* in *Everywoman,* February, 1972, p. 6.
18. No. 16 *Ibid.,* March 9, 1972.
19. Caroline Hennessey, *The Strategy of Sexual Struggle* (Lancer paperback, 1971), p. 97.
20. *Ibid.*
21. *Ibid.,* p. 98.
22. Quoted from Robert Fletcher's *History of Oberlin College to the Civil War,* cited by Eleanor Flexner, *Century of Struggle* (Harvard Univ. Press, 1959), p. 31. Also see *The American Woman, Who Was She?,* edited by Anne Firor Scott (Prentice-Hall paperback, 1971), pp. 60-64 on Oberlin.
23. Gunnar Myrdal, *An American Dilemma* (McGraw-Hill, 1944, 1962), Vol. 2, Appendix 5, pp. 1073-1078.
24. *Request of Women to be Admitted to the Estates-General,* quoted in "Women in the French Revolution: The Thirteenth Brumaire of Olympe de Gouges, With Notes on French Amazon Battalions", by Smache de Jacques, available from *Female Liberation Newsletter,* P.O. Box 14061, Univ. Station, Minneapolis, Minn. 55414. Reprinted in *Women Out of History; A Herstory Anthology,* edited by Ann Forfreedom, published by Ann Forfreedom, P.O. Box 25514, Los Angeles, Ca. 90025. Quoted on p. 132.
25. See Edith Thomas' *The Women Incendiaries.*
26. Quoted in David and Vera Mace's *Marriage East and West* (Doubleday, 1960), p. 69.
27. Quoted from Dr. Naomi Weisstein's " 'Kinder, Kuche, Kirche' As Scientific Law: Psychology Constructs the Female." Reprinted in *Sisterhood is Powerful, op. cit.,* pp. 205-220. Quotes on pp. 206, 207.
28. Alice Rossi, "Status of Women in Graduate Departments of Sociology," in *American Sociologist,* Fall, 1969. Cited by Carol Andreas, *Sex and Caste in America* (Prentice-Hall, N.J., 1971).
29. Dolores Barracano Schmidt, "The Invisible Woman, The Historian as Professional Magician," in *Women Out of History: A Herstory Anthology, op. cit.,* pp. 91-101. Also see Kathryn Taylor's pamphlet *Generations of Denial* (times Change Press, 1023 Sixth Ave., N.Y., N.Y. 10018, 1971) 75 short biographies of women generally not in history texts.
30. For recent feminist theories on the rise and growth mechanisms of sexism: See "The Rise of Man: The Origins of Woman's Oppression: One View" by Barbara Mehrhof and Shelia Cronan, available from The Feminists, 120 Liberty St., N.Y., N.Y. 10006. Also excerpted and reprinted in *Women Out of History; A Herstory Anthology, op. cit.*
    Also see "The Male Power Hierarchy" by Helen Victry, available from *Female Liberation Newsletter, op. cit.* Reprinted in *Women Out of History; A Herstory Anthology, op. cit.* and the following references: "Secrets of Genesis (Patriarchy Overcomes the Matriarchy)" by Bernice Mitchell, excerpted and reprinted in *Women Out of History; A Herstory Anthology, op. cit.;* the "Manifesto of the New York Radical Feminists," excerpted and reprinted in *Women Out of History; A Herstory Anthology, op. cit.;* Karen Sacks' "Social Bases for Sexual Equality: A Comparative View," reprinted in *Sisterhood is Powerful, op. cit.;* Roxane Dunbar's "Female Liberation As the Basis for Social Revolution," reprinted in *Sisterhood is Powerful, op. cit.;* all 5 issues of the *Journal of Female Liberation,* available from Cell 16, 16 Lexington Ave., Cambridge, Mass. 02138. Contains theories that have been and are the foundation for many contemporary new theories; Cellestine Ware's eloquent *Womanpower: The Movement for Women's Liberation* Tower paperback, (1970); Lucy Komisar's *The New Feminism* Franklin Watts, N.Y., (1971), particularly chapters 1, 10, 11-13, 15-20. "Women in American Society, An Historical Contribution," by Ann D. Gordon, Mari Jo Buhle, and Nancy E. Schrom, in *Radical America* magazine—Cambridge, Mass., Vol. 4, No. 4, pp. 3-66.

Ann Forfreedom
Venice, California

A VIEW FROM INSIDE THE MOVEMENT

5.4 In the final analysis it is not the national figures and women scholars alone who will make the movement work and carry through programs to their goals, but the success of the local groups. The California cities have been the scene of much of the protest and group action of the 60's and 70's.

They have been the first to experience government by elected representatives of radical action groups. There is no doubt that a part of the fervor for the women's liberation movement in the Bay Area has come from the long tradition of political liberalism and the repetition of protest in the area. Ms. Barnett is a photographer/writer and activist in the movement. She sees the movement and its members sympathetically and expects even greater accomplishments for them in the future. There is no denying that her speech and possibly her formulations of the problems to which the movement speaks have been influenced by the jargon and the theses of the New Left. The philosophical mainspring of that segment of the protest movement in America has been structured by possibly three men of influence, the physician Benjamin Spock, the philosopher Herbert Marcuse, and the theoretician Herbert Apetheker. Interestingly enough, all three are men, but there are able women thinkers and spokeswomen now appearing upon the scene. These women will be the new architects of the movement. Some of them are introduced by Ms. Barnett.

The statements of purpose of each of the organizations mentioned here are important because they detail clearly and succinctly what the ladies are about. Their concerns are not only on the national scale but also on the immediate and local scale. Their actions are not only directed towards federal and state abortion law reform, but they are doing something physical and present about the problems in their immediate surroundings.

One of the most controversial aspects of the movement is mentioned by Sherry Ryan Barnett, the position of the lesbian, the female homosexual, in the movement. Due to their psychological independence of all aspects of masculinity, they have been very strong movers and shakers in the movement. However there is a slight difference of emphasis in their arguments which indicates the wide divergence of their situation from that of the oppressed housewife and mother. The lesbian literature of the movement continually insists upon the acceptance by law and custom of their life style as merely an alternate form of human behavior, fully legitimate and responsible as any other. This argument is derived from that used with telling force by Blacks, Chicanos, and other racial and ethnic minorities in the court battles of the last two decades. As yet the point of view of the lesbians has not been widely accepted outside of the more radical activist groups in the movement. On the basis of the inflexibility of middle class standards it is doubtful whether this strategy will meet with success. The author shows the elaborate but very informal organization of women's liberation and the personal emotional communication that exists among its members. Such devotion to the mutual benefit and the sisterhood is not easily broken and makes real social action possible.

5.4.1 The Women's Liberation movement is local and communal as well as national and individualized. Few local groups have been as successful and dynamic as the Los Angeles, Bay Area activities. A high degree of participation by members, a good sized group of sisters with special and outstanding talents, and the general liberal environment have all combined to motivate the Bay Area movement. I have gathered together a sampling of some of the sisters who contribute so much to the local organization. A little glimpse at them as individuals is reinforced with a look at some of the local activities and purposes and some of the national groups with which we are associated. In the months ahead the same spirit and drive will be awakened in many locations around the United States and ultimately in many countries as women see the potential and accomplishment of the movement.

It is necessary for you to meet some of the sisters in the movement first of all. They are representative of every status and stratum of society and they have gained invaluable experience in almost every facet of American life.

Jeanette Rankin—born in 1892, has been a life-long pacifist. Her first major achievement was accomplished in 1916 when she ended male monopoly in Congress by her victorious entry into the House of Representatives. While in office, she pioneered the movement by introducing the first bill to grant women citizenship independent of their husbands and authored the first bill for government-sponsored instruction in hygiene, maternity, and infancy. Early in her career, she voiced anti-war sentiments by voting in the House against American entry into World War I. Some years later she was the sole dissenting vote against entry into World War II. Still living a totally independent existence, Ms. Rankin resides, unmarried, on a simple ranch with a dirt floor—devoid of material "comforts". She wishes that "women wouldn't waste their time and energy talking about money, as it needn't be an important factor." She does see great hope for the movement however, and is thrilled by the recent steps taken. In looking back on her own life and imagining a life reincarnate, she says, "I'd live it the same way, but this time I'd be nastier."

Gloria Steinem—spokeswoman author/editor, and media personality, recently elevated to celebrity status by the press, following much publicized acclaim for her various accomplishments. She has been awarded a standing ovation by the National Press Club in Washington and also at the Harvard Law Review dinner. Ms. Steinem was chosen to write Time Magazine's essay on women's liberation, and was the first woman to guest-host the David Frost television show. In January 1972, she and co-editor and writer Betty Harris published the first issue of *MS.* magazine. During the same period of time, these two women jointly organized the Women's Action Alliance. In reference to her personal hopes regarding the struggle for liberation, she remarks, "The human animal will stop dividing itself because of visible difference and begin to act according to the potential inside."

5.4.2 *Carly Simon*—First female rock superstar to write lyrics from a standpoint of women's liberation, her million-selling recording of "That's the Way I've Always Heard It Should Be" expresses a theme of a common woman's struggle, "I'll never learn to be just me first, by myself." Ms. Simon's success marks the emergence also, of the female in rock music and is a manifestation of the changing attitudes within the music industry. On this subject, Carly has commented, "In the past, they said that unless I used my sexuality, I wouldn't be in a position to get a break. . . . If women fight for what they want to do, only then do they have a chance to be heard. That's my general position on it."

Marge Buckley—practicing attorney since 1958, whose experience includes practice before the U.S. Supreme Court. After the first years of practice in her home state of Michigan, she became involved with the National Lawyers Guild in Mississippi investigating civil rights matters. Her next move brought her to California (where she has since taken up residence) with the purpose of aiding victims of the Watts Rebellion, in conjunction with the American Civil Liberties Union. The following year, she became the first woman counsel for a commercial bank, a position she held for five years. The job terminated with her filing an employment discrimination complaint

on behalf of all women bank employees. While continuing general practice in southern California, she ran for the office of Attorney General in 1970 on the Peace & Freedom party platform. She is presently a candidate for Los Angeles District Attorney, as a leading proponent of the ideas behind the women's liberation movement. She has stated throughout her campaign that the freedom of women will be possible only in a radically transformed society.

Marta Asevido—instrumental in introducing the goals of women's liberation to the Mexican population. She is recognized as being the instigator behind the 1970 demonstration against the myth of Mother's Day in Mexico City. More recently, she has been effective in securing directive positions for women in South American governments, that have been previously held only by men.

Alma Cremonisi—in her own words, "vagabond of the women's movement." She became politically active during the 1960's by forming anti-war discussion groups with G.I.'s in Colorado. While still in that state, she participated in the Denver Anti-Bridal Conference, to protest the ways in which women's bodies are used. She has been most productive in the Bay Area (San Francisco and Berkeley) area of California in recent years by contributing in the publishing field. Functioning in positions involving production and distribution she has been associated with the San Francisco Women's Press Collective, Free Women's Press, and the Shameless Hussy Press. Her work at the SF Women's Library, and as distributor of the magazine, "It Ain't Me, Babe" led her to publish the Bay Area's "Women's Liberation Newsletter."

5.4.3 *Judy Chicago*—32-year-old painter, sculptor, photographer, and feminist movement organizer. Ms. Chicago has been the guiding force behind many radical advancements by women. Her more recent accomplishments include instituting the existing feminist art programs at Fresno State and the California Institute of the Arts at Valencia. From the latter program sprang the Womanhouse art project in Los Angeles. She believes art to have gender, and states, "Feminist art often has a central image, repeated forms, concern with a state of emotional reality and focuses on the nature of a female identity."

Joan Hoffman (Robins)—author of the *Handbook of Women's Liberation*. After moving from Albuquerque to her home in Southern California, she co-founded the Los Angeles Women's Liberation Center. She has been most effective in her work with the Anti-Rape Squad and in the "Shirly Chisholm for President" campaign this year. An experienced educator and researcher, she devotes much time to her numerous speaking engagements that have been offered her since the tremendous success of her book.

Helen Emmerich—reporter and free-lance writer, most active in the anti-war movement. Ms. Emmerich, a widow with a 23-year-old son, became involved in 1967 by way of an assignment that took her to Vietnam. After going on roughly 100 missions, she returned thoroughly disillusioned and proceeded to commit herself to the anti-Vietnam movement. Independently she began to give speeches before both men's service organizations and women's clubs. Another trip to Indochina reiterated and intensified her hostility toward the war. As a consequence, she prodded the Army into an investigation of certain war atrocities that she'd witnessed in Cambodia. She has since made over 300 get-out-now speeches and is running for Congress in the California Democratic Primary.

Judy Parker—feminist writer, singer and musician. Ms. Parker is the composer of numerous songs and articles as well as being the founder of the Women's Theatre & Media Center. She is currently in the process of revising a radio script concerning sexist attitudes in rock music. It has already been recorded by Jane Fonda, and will eventually be expanded into book form. The tape itself provided the subject matter for a workshop discussion that was held at the Women's Festival at Ash Grove in 1971, where Ms. Parker served as music co-ordinator.

Nancy Robinson—co-founder of the Los Angeles Women's Liberation Center. Her activities there range from representing the Lesbian Feminists to co-ordinating the LAWLC newsletter. As a writer, she is a frequent contributor to the publication, *Born A Woman.*

5.4.4 *Lupe Anguiano*—catalyst for the involvement of the Chicana in political, cultural, and business affairs. Though born in La Junta, Colorado, her father moved the family to California to work with the migrant fruit pickers. Ms. Anguiano quickly understood the plight of these exploited, oppressed workers. Less than two decades later, at Cesar Chavez's request, she successfully organized the state-wide boycott of grapes in Michigan. The action was a turning point in her life, bringing to attention her qualities of leadership. She soon became aware of another aspect of her people's oppression, other than the blatantly racial one. She recognized the secondary role that the Chicana has been brought up to accept, and began research to launch the Chicana Liberation Movement. The study found the Chicana a minority woman and a victim of sex stereotyping within her own culture. Such women are raised under great pressure to marry young, stand behind the man, and stay home to support the family unit. An advantage Ms. Anguiano has had in reaching the Chicana who has never realized herself as a capably strong, talented being, is her bilingual and bicultural background. Although the east coast is beginning to feel the emergence of bilingual women, the majority reside in the southwestern sections of the U.S., where Ms. Anguiano is most active. Subsequently, groups of these women are forming to study their heritage and to make themselves aware of the sexist teachings that they've been subjected to. Ms. Anguiano's list of credentials includes much responsibility for the creation of Spanish Women's Coalitions, organizing the National Spanish Speaking Women's Caucus, serving as president of the Council of Mexican-American Women, and working in HEW's Women's Action Program. She has hopes of establishing a Spanish Women's Center in Washington, D.C.

Lee Hansen Sisson—humanist aspiring to the liberation of people. A lady of diverse knowledge, she devotes much energy to the women's struggle, as well as applying fundamental theories of liberation to her domestic lifestyle as a wife and mother. She is an active member of the Women's Study Center currently in operation on the UCLA campus, where she is a frequent lecturer. In the fall of 1971, she conceived and conducted the well-attended Workshop on Non-Sexist Child Rearing—which has recently been revised for radio broadcast (Feb. 23, 1972—KPFK). Ms. Sisson is in the process of writing her dissertation on that subject while studying for her Ph.D. in educational psychology and child development. She has just been elected president of U.C.L.A.'s student body. As the first woman applicant, she is now awaiting acceptance to Phi Delta Kappa after having met the necessary qualifications with an additional recommendation from the dean. Her off-campus activities include working with the LA Women's Liberation Center and attending to her position of Chairman of the Board of the Gay Community Services Center. She is also busy producing radio shows in conjunction with the Los Angeles Women's Theatre Media Center.

Linda Jeness—born in 1940 in Oklahoma, she has been a life-long political activist, particularly in the anti-war and feminist movements across the U.S. Her educational background includes attendance at the University of Mexico City, Antioch, and Emory—where she organized the university's women's liberation movement. The majority of her years have been spent in the arena of Georgian politics. Ms. Jeness spearheaded the Atlanta Mobilization Committee to end the Vietnam war during the mid-1960's. In 1969, she ran for mayor of Atlanta, and in 1970 for governor of Georgia. She is currently the Socialist Workers' Party candidate for President of the United States in the 1972 election.

Deena Metzger—native California poet/educator. Gained reputation as subject of controversy when the California Institute of the Arts tried to remove her from her teaching post there. Her contemporaries and students claimed the cause to be her more radical poetry readings. She has recently written a new book of poetry entitled, *Rape*.

Marge Piercy—writer "from the movement, for the movement." Originally from Detroit, Michigan, she writes of the American condition from the slums of Chicago to this country's great universities, Michigan State and Northwestern, and Manhattan's west side. Her poems appear in numerous periodicals such as *Born A Woman*, besides two volumes of her own works *Breaking Camp* and *Hard Loving*. Her first novel *Going Down Fast* has been released.

5.4.5 *Women's Liberation Center of LA,* 1027 South Crenshaw Blvd.—was formed in 1969 by a collective of women from UCLA and other community groups. It provides a central place of communication to answer the needs of women of all ages. All work at the center is done on a volunteer basis and its budget relies solely on individual contributions. Its functions range from acting as a referral of counseling service (giving legal aid and child care), anti-rape squad (to raise public consciousness as to the dangers of rape), speaker's bureau (travelling panel to extend awareness and bring distant sisters together)—to being a self-help clinic (to teach women to examine and care for their own bodies). All women are invited to share in its activities and to use the center as a springboard from which to explore other women's liberation groups. Ideas formulated at the center have led to the existence of—

Women's Liberation School—offering two types of classes—I. practical—to help women develop skills to function autonomously. II. theoretical—to help women to understand the nature of their oppression. Women's Shelter (Liberation House)—project jointly planned by the Lesbian Feminists and other sisters form the center to serve as a temporary home for transient or misguided women. It is distinguishable as the only female-oriented shelter in a city possessing more than adequate facilities for men in similar situations. To maintain a degree of order, a certain few sisters have been given the authority to direct their guests either to jobs or welfare aid.

Everywoman Bookstore—carries the largest supply of women's literature (books, periodicals, pamphlets, etc.) in Southern California. Their catalog is revised every two months to keep up with the most recent releases. The bookstore is completely independent of any organization. All monies beyond expenses go into improving *Everywoman* or other women's liberation projects. The Bookstore was created with two purposes in mind—I. to provide women dignified jobs for women, II. to provide materials about women's liberation.

Everywoman—monthly radical feminist magazine containing reports of current news items pertaining to the constantly changing status of women in contemporary society. In addition to gathering information relating to what's happening in the movement, its staff of proficient writers, along with other contributors publish poetry and fiction by, for, and about women. *Everywoman* is a member of the Liberation News Service and the Underground Press Syndicate.

Feminist Book Club—offering a catalog of hardbound and paperback literature as well as prints and posters by women artists. Membership dues are set at $1.00 per year to make possible discounts up to 40% on their vast selection of biographies, autobiographies, poetry, novels, herstories, survival handbooks, etc.

Women's Exchange of LA—aimed at having a representative of each women's group in the greater LA area meet at certain intervals to learn about their purposes and recent programs. It is meant to be just what the word implies, an exchange—not a policy-making action group. The first such meeting was attended by Gloria Steinem, who helped to formulate its goals. She articulated on the various tactics and strategies that must be employed in order to successfully organize new structures without aggressive leadership. The general consensus at past gatherings has been that the Exchange can successfully fill the gap growing because of a lack of awareness. In the future kindred groups will be finding it advantageous and will join together in campaigns and actions.

5.4.6 *Los Angeles Council of Women Artists*—Structure of approximately 120 artists film-makers, collectors, and teachers joined together to challenge women's 1% representation at the County Museum of Art. Organized by painter Joyce Kozloff in the summer of 1971, they are constantly having to battle antiquated cultural attitudes. Their continual struggle is aimed at eliminating sexual discrimination at museums, galleries, and art school locations.

The First Women's Multi-Media Festival—a two-week program presented at the Ash Grove (west LA folk club) during October 1971. A staff of several women having extensive backgrounds rooted in the arts was responsible for staging the event. Among the various mediums of expression to be experienced were music, mime, dance, theatre, film, handcraft, art and photography. An entirely different program of performers was presented every night to enable both known and unknown sisters to contribute their talents.

Womanhouse—pioneer project of the Feminist Art Program at the California Institute of the Arts. The program's 24 members transformed a deserted mansion for the purpose of presenting it as a symbolic art exhibition. To follow through their idea of building an environment, definitely creative, but not necessarily functional, they completely redecorated the house in a style representative of their feminist beliefs. What resulted was a tribute to all those women who have thrown all their energies into decorating a home. The materials they employed were those that are exclusively associated with the typical American woman who is cast into the role of a housewife. Exhibits included a fur-lined bathtub, a crocheted room environment, and other displays utilizing silks, satins, and plastics to emphatically satirize the image of femininity perpetrated by society. Artists represented included Faith Wilding, Kathy Huberland, Miriam Schapiro, and Judy Chicago.

Women's Theatre & Media Center of LA—organized in 1971 to produce a series of radio programs of KPFK (Pacifica Radio). It now consists of a core group of approximately 10 women—including several charter members who previously staffed the Women's Multi-Media Festival. They are currently involved in projects not only involving the medium of radio, but of documentation of the movement through means of film and music. Tapes, recordings, films, and slide shows will be made accessible for television syndication, college campuses, and various other public organizations. The movement in the Bay area is not separate or divided from the women's organizations of national scope but works together with them.

5.4.7 *National Organization for Women*—a civil rights organization pledged to work actively to bring women into full participation in the mainstream of American society. This includes exercising all the privileges and responsibilities thereof in truly equal partnership with men. NOW is a group of both women and men dedicated to actions to change the conditions which prevent the female sex from developing to its full human potential. Convinced that women's problems are linked to many broader questions of social justice and that human rights for all are indivisible, they give support to the common cause of equal rights for all those who suffer discrimination and deprivation. NOW describes itself as an action organization working for basic changes in the life style of America and breaking through curtains of prejudice that have given its citizens such a limited view of their capacities to contribute to social progress. In line with these concepts, NOW is working towards the following primary goals: the full participation in Political Activities—by eliminating separate women's divisions within the political parties; urging the crossing of party lines to support candidates in favor of NOW's goals; encouraging women to refrain from taking on traditional menial headquarters' tasks—Instead NOW attempts to demand meaningful roles; working for equitable representation on all policy-making bodies which have bearing on the over-all well-being of people. The revision of the Educational System—working to eliminate the idea of restrictive quotas (written or unwritten) based on sex, perpetrated by universities, graduate, and professional schools; supporting changes in the system to enable more women to combine the education with their child-rearing and family duties. NOW seeks public accommodations—taking various tactical measures to eliminate sex discrimination in restaurants; ban "executive" airline flights; initiating federal legislation to make such practices unlawful. It supports passage of the Equal Rights Amendment—calling upon NOW's members to work for Congressional approval and subsequent submission for state ratification of the impending Constitutional amendment. ("Equality of Rights under the law shall not be denied or abridged by the U.S. on account of sex.") NOW fights for the abolition of laws penalizing abortion—endorsing the principle that it is a basic right of every woman to control her reproductive life; pressing for widespread sex education, provision of birth control information and contraceptives. It insists on the revision of state protective laws for women—pledging to repeal those laws which raise barriers to employment based on sex, in the guise of offering protection to workers. NOW seeks enforcement of the Civil Rights Act of 1964, Title 7—supporting the decision of the Equal Employment Opportunity Commission which—1. calls for the elimination of help wanted advertising columns segregated by sex. 2. declares that sex is not a bona fide occupational qualification for the position of airline flight attendant. 3. states that retirement ages which are different for each sex violate Title 7.

NOW's intent is to help resist any Congressional efforts to undermine its decisions by restrictive legislation. NOW has initiated a campaign to change mass media's portrayal of women—working in communities to present models of women that do not merely reflect the image of a homemaker; and set up speakers' bureaus to direct their campaigning at the level of mass media—radio, television, commercial advertising, newspapers, magazines, textbooks. NOW insists on the expansion of child-care services—developing child-care facilities on an all-day, all-tear basis, adequate to the needs of children from the pre-school years to early adolescence; believing that such centers should be community resources; opposing efforts to force welfare mothers to place children in child-care centers and work. Since formation in 1966, membership has been open to all persons in favor of NOW's purposes. Chapters exist in nearly every state of the union.

5.4.8 *Redstockings*—New York City based group that dedicated itself to building unity amongst women to achieve final liberation from male supremacy. The Redstockings Manifesto comprises of seven articles which go into much detail on the subjects of: I. A theory of unity to win necessary freedoms. II. Recognizing women as an oppressed class, exploited (as sex objects, domestic servants, cheap labor) to enhance men's lives. Personal suffering becomes a political condition with conflicts that must be solved collectively by women. III. Men are identified as agents of oppression. History has shown male

supremacy (i.e, powerful structures controlled by men and backed by physical force) to be the most basic form of domination. IV. Rejecting the idea that women consent to their own oppression. Submission on the part of women is the result of daily pressure from men. V. Regarding personal experience, not existing ideologies, as the basis for an analysis of our common situation. The method which enables a program for liberation (based on concrete realities of our lives) to work, is consciousness raising—an honest group sharing of experience. VI. Identifying with all women. Redstockings repudiate all economic, racial, educational, or status privileges that can act as divisive factors between women. VII. Calling on all sisters to join in the struggle. Redstockings will not ask what is solely revolutionary but simply what is good for women.

National Women's Political Caucus—guided by a primary goal of supporting women to hold positions in public office and to give active support to those candidates who support women's issues. To activate their political ideas on a nation-wide scale the Issues & Guidelines Task Force has been formed within the Caucus itself. It believes that the core of a female politic is: I. the challenging and altering of institutions, including existing political party structures, which limit women to a subordinate position in society. II. the creation of new institutions to meet the emerging needs of women. To accomplish these goals, it is necessary that the nation's priorities be reordered. This position is the only basis upon which the NWPC will encourage women to seek office and upon which it will support candidates. Other subordinate divisions created by the NWPC structural plan are:

Policy Council—made up of elected representatives of the Task Forces.

Local Caucuses—having limited geographic boundaries; is concerned with elective and appointive offices in local government.

Steering Committee—members elected from the Policy Council conducting routine work but retaining no policy-making power.

5.4.9 *Women's Action Alliance*—Headquartered in New York City to dispense information and advice concerning funds for local programs dealing with women's issues. On hand are consultants offering research and technical assistance to action groups in areas left uncovered by existing organizations (e.g., elimination of sex stereotyping in child-care; integration of male teachers in early childhood training). Also in production is an annotated directory of organizations that are helping women in all fields who are facing instances of discrimination, including a list of sympathetic professional women (i.e., lawyers, doctors, psychiatrists). The printing of a national newsletter to enable geographically separated women to benefit from the knowledge of each other's experiences is underway. Charter staff members are Brenda Fasteau (feminist activist) acting as co-ordinating director, along with Cathie Samuels (organizer of the Manhattan Women's Political Caucus), and Carol Shapiro (field representative for the National Council on Hunger and Malnutrition)—both project directors.

International Women's Day—celebrated on March 8 to commemorate the struggles of herstory. The first festivities occurred in Berkeley in 1969 and is reaching an international level with each succeeding year. When considering the fact that male supremacy is world-wide, it is easy to understand the nature of rebellion by women everywhere.

Women's Abortion Project of New York City— provides women throughout the country with inexpensive abortions by experienced gynecologists. The doctors have been carefully evaluated by the Project women according to both their medical competence and psychological attitudes. A re-evaluation occurs during the procedure of each abortion, since a Project woman is always present. In order to have the suction method (simplest, quickest, safest) performed, women should be in touch with the Project before their 12th week of pregnancy. Those in need of assistance can receive counseling to help diminish their fears and get answers to questions regarding body functions. Another advantage to the care provided by the Project is that women who are the sole supporters of themselves and/or their children can obtain an abortion for less than $100 (the usual fee), and sometimes free of charge.

West-East Bag—international information network, begun by Judy Chicago and Miriam Schapiro to synchronize actions by women artists.

Its first major success of 1972 was the Western Conference of over 100 women artists at the California Institute of the Arts. The WEB is giving women a chance to become aware of the ways in which they can bring attention to their art through group action. Their efforts are aimed at making their work understood by the public.

Feminist Press—producers of feminist educational materials dealing with the reconstruction of "herstory" and changing the character of children's books. Their biography series pamphlets (50-75 pages in length) have made available a number of herstorical accounts for use in the classroom and by the general reading public. Operating as a non-profit educational corporation allows the Feminist Press to offer other women financial aid to support further writing, designing, and editing of pamphlets. The encourage the submission of manuscripts and artwork for possible publication. Any interested women should contact this group.

Feminists on Children's Media—collective designed to evaluate children's books by a standard based on the incorporation of positive and non-stereotyped portrayal of girls by authors. With sponsorship by the New York chapter of NOW, a bibliography entitled "Little Miss Muffet Strikes Back" has been printed. With hundreds of interested parties (librarians, publishers, editors, reviewers) suggesting titles for inclusion, the bibliography recommends non-sexist books for young readers. Primary ideas associated with the acceptance of a particular listing usually involve: girls and boys participating equally in both physical and intellectual activities; female characters leading active and independent lives; girls having a variety of choices and aspiring to a variety of goals; male characters respecting female ones and responding to them as equals. In hope of continuing to upgrade the choice of children's literature, updated versions of this listing are being considered.

Ms. Sherry Ryan Barnett
Hollywood, California

NOTES ON THE PHILOSOPHICAL PROBLEMS OF WOMEN

5.5 It is extremely difficult to classify and codify the manifold variations of opinion and shades of meaning put forth by a movement like women's liberation. There are many, many sides to the issue and they represent all sorts of discrete and mutually exclusive points of view. Bonnie Greene examines the basic philosophical structures of a large number of the key writers who have contributed to the movement. Her analysis is based on certain insights which are more European than American and this offers a chance to understand the movement from an external stance.

The author is a writer, graduate student, mother and housewife in the Seattle area. She utilizes an historical perspective on the movement but with a stern and rigorous philosophical study of the ideas and opinions presented. She comes to grip with many of the fundamental problems which the movement itself tends to avoid. There is no doubt that this kind of analysis is difficult to follow from the vantage point of American pragmatic utilitarianism, however the effort is very rewarding in increased awareness of the roots of the sexual crisis.

5.5.1 With his sandwich safely hidden under the bed, the three-year old assures his parents that he has finished his lunch and is now ready for ice cream. In some families a discussion on truth and lies follows while the parents retrieve the sandwich, set the child back on his chair, and proceed with their own lunch. Suddenly the child asks, "But what's the truth?" The parents take turns trying to answer his question, only to discover that answering it for a child becomes more complex the longer they talk. Eventually they come to a point where they make a commitment to what they believe to be true. Unfortunately for the parents, the three-year old confronted them with a "religious" question, the type children ask all the time, but which modern Americans find increasingly difficult to answer for themselves, let alone for their less sophisticated children.

Feminism, in whatever form it has taken over the years, has also plagued us with "religious" questions, a fact which undoubtedly accounts for some of the antagonism which many champions of women's rights have met among both men and women, private citizens and public officials. For instance, the early American feminists consistently raised the question of justice in taxing women without allowing them to vote on the uses to which their taxes were put. Others raised the question, "How can men assume the authority to *give* women the vote; who gave them this authority?" Many who talk of the human race in terms of two classes—men and women—assume an autonomy for human beings which forms the basis of an anthropology that a pre-Renaissance man would have found totally foreign. While the modern Women's Liberation Movement is not really characterized by theoreticians and philosophers, the questions which women within the movement are raising are "religious" questions. Similarly, the solutions which have been suggested are basically "religious" solutions. A religious question demands a religious answer, not in the sense of orthodox Christian, Islamic, or Judaic dogma and doctrine, but in the sense that a question about "truth," "justice," "freedom," "authority," or the "nature of man" involves us in an examination of the foundations from which we interpret the world

and our place in it. A religious question ultimately leads to a religious commitment, that is, one which is comprehensive, taking in a variety of aspects of human life. Out of religious questions and commitments grows a religious view of life which deals with (or chooses *not* to deal with) those basic questions raised in Philosophy I classes: Where did man come from? What is he really like? What will become of him? An individual's religious world view is very seldom articulated, and he might very well pass his entire life without ever consciously spelling out what he believes, but on a non-theoretical level he lives out his particular religious commitment in everything he does. For example, during the sixties when the pressure was on foreign language teachers to make a radical shift to the aural-oral method of learning language, some observers were surprised to discover that the resistance to the new approach was not limited to older teachers. In fact, friends and enemies of the method were scattered throughout all age groups; more important than age was a teacher's view of knowledge and the nature of the "knower." For some teachers, the new method created a wrenching conflict between two basic, if only vaguely formulated, religious commitments. Or take another example: most American textbooks contain some sort of introduction in which the authors suggest their general approach to the subject. They might make statements like, "Everything is matter and energy," or "Man is a grammar-producing machine." It would be a very unusual author who would encourage the students to think about what they are assuming about the universe when they accept or reject such statements. Americans are not known for their systematic or analytical approach to life. If we're typical middle Americans, we take an eclectic approach, and if we make our living by "thinking," we might call our approach positivistic. By whatever name we choose to characterize ourselves, our very eclecticism or positivism is a religious commitment in the sense of which I am speaking, for it implies that we prefer the problem-solving approach of modern scientism to a philosophical system which ultimately cannot be proved by means of empirical science.

5.5.2 Historians have given us countless paperback accounts of radical changes which men made in their religious world views between the time of the late Middle Ages and the Renaissance. In a general and limited way, the men who held the traditional world view during the Middle Ages believed in a universe which was the orderly creation of God who held it together according to his laws and who brought order into the personal lives of men through his moral law. When men gradually gave up their religious commitment to a supreme being who ruled the universe, they committed themselves to a new concept of the universe, one in which the cornerstone of the world was autonomous man himself. Without God to provide order from without, man faced the problem of producing his own order and control. Historically, the Christian West has vacillated between two secularized versions of the principles of authority and freedom found in Anselm, Augustine and writers in the tradition of the Protestant Reformation. For these men authority and freedom found their perfect balance in commitment to Jesus Christ. Once man freed himself from the rule of God, he secularized the orthodox Christian position and thereafter vacillated between two general approaches to the problem of controlling the universe: at times he relied on reason, appealing to man's logical function as the source of true freedom; at other times he asserted himself as a totally free personality, appealing to man's will as the source of true freedom. Ordering the world through reason, science, or an empirical method, I'm calling the NATURE ideal; ordering the world through the free personality, emphasizing intuition and feeling, I'm calling the FREEDOM ideal.

Naturally, a life which is totally dominated by the nature ideal can become something of a nightmare, à la Elmer Rice or Barry Commoner; therefore, the individual at least has to touch base at the freedom ideal to maintain some kind of balance in his life. Yurii Zhivago, the physician in Pasternak's famous novel, is a relatively modern example of a character who attempted to bring order into his life by balancing himself somewhere between the nature and freedom poles. As a famed diagnostician, he attempted to achieve control over the threats of disease and age to the body through his medical knowledge. But Zhivago also sought freedom in his flight to eastern Russia, his relationship with Lara and other women, and in his poetry. Numerous other examples will come to mind, none of which is likely to be entirely

consistent in a commitment to one ideal or the other. When technology edges too close to the individual, he flees to the freedom pole; when freedom threatens him with anarchy and disintegration, he leaps back from the edge and clings to the nature pole.

5.5.3 Historically, the commitment to the nature and freedom ideals has shaped the work of people like Pope and Wordsworth or the gardeners at Versailles and the contemplatives such as Thoreau at Walden. In more recent terms, we might confront such opposites as B. F. Skinner and Neil Summerhill, John Cage and Bessie Smith, Stanislavsky and the La Mama players, T. S. Eliot and Apollinaire, Nijinsky and Merce Cunningham, or Hitchcock and Andy Warhol. Wherever we turn, we face the cultural formation which has resulted from a commitment to one ideal or the other.

The same vacillating polarization has characterized the feminist movement from the days of Mary Wollstonecraft to the present. Even since the rise of the new feminism of the sixties and seventies so many approaches to the problems of men and women have arisen that the general public latches onto labels and catch-phrases to characterize a movement so diverse that thinking about it comprehensively is a mammoth task. Still, nearly all proposals for the rights and liberation of women have been a somewhat tardy appeal for the freedom of the other half of the human race—the freedom which men took for themselves when the self-proclaimed autonomous man came out from under the authority which had formerly been attributed as of the God who had structured western life for so many centuries. In that search for freedom, women have proposed various ways of solving the problems which face them, some of them oriented to the nature ideal and some oriented to the freedom ideal.

The Freedom Ideal And The Feminist Movement

5.5.4 Feminists who have leaned toward the freedom ideal as a means of achieving the free, independent personality have appealed to the will, virtually challenging the rest of society to pull itself together and determine to change the situation for women. The course of action which individuals must set themselves to has varied with the feminist, for the possibilities are as varied as the aspects of the human personality. Usually feminists have abstracted one or another of the elements which make up man and have attempted to bring change and a sense of order through it; for example, they may approach man as an ethical being, or as a logical creature. Other possibilities might include man's juridical, economic, social, or biotic aspects. Throughout the history of American feminism, appeals to all of man's functions have arisen as women have attempted to achieve freedom. For some the achievement of freedom could only come through following a moral and ethical system. Such an approach is highly unusual in modern America, but it was not quite as unusual in the days of the Grimké sisters. Sarah Grimké, a devout Quaker, called for a return to the Scriptures rather than the interpretations which men had given to the Scriptures in their efforts to assert power over women. She based her claims to the equality of the sexes on the ethical system which Jesus taught and which was given to man in her view in the direct revelation of the Scriptures. In a letter dated July 17, 1937, Sarah Grimké wrote:

"The Lord Jesus defines the duties of his followers in his Sermon on the Mount. He lays down grand principles by which they should be governed, without any reference to sex or condition. . . . I follow him through all his precepts, and find him giving the same directions to women as to men, never even referring to the distinction now so strenuously insisted upon between masculine and feminine virtues: this is one of the antichristian "traditions of men" which are taught instead of the "commandments of God." Men and women were CREATED EQUAL; they are both moral and accountable beings and whatever is *right* for man to do, is *right* for woman."[1]

In another letter written in September of the same year, Sarah Grimké spoke of the enslavement which women suffered because they did not follow the Scriptures and the teachings of Jesus:

"In the wealthy classes of society, and those who are in comfortable circumstances, women are exempt from great corporeal exertion, and are protected by public opinion, and by the genial influence of Christianity, from much physical ill treatment. Still, there is a vast amount of secret suffering endured, from the forced submission of women to the opinions and whims of their husbands. Hence they are frequently driven to use deception, to compass their ends. They are taught that to appear to yield is the only way to govern. Miserable sophism! I deprecate such sentiments, as being peculiarly hostile to the dignity of woman. If she submits, let her do it openly, honorably, not to gain her point, but as a matter of Christian duty. But let her beware how she permits her husband to be her conscience-keeper. On all moral and religious subjects, she is bound to think and act for herself. . . ."[2]

For Sarah Grimké, duplicity led to a far worse slavery than submission under which women have chafed for centuries; even at that, submission in this passage is a matter of a voluntary obedience to a principle of the wife's Christian faith and therefore rises above the category of a sign of slavery.

5.5.5 Although the search for freedom for women through moral and ethical systems, particularly those associated with Christianity in our country, are relatively rare, appeals to at least parts of moral systems have characterized both the feminists and the anti-feminists from the early rumblings of the movement in western culture. Aileen Kraditor points out that the rise of the social gospel saw a parallel rise in people's concern for "the public good." Women then began to argue that giving them the vote would allow them to do more to ameliorate the lives of the oppressed. Furthermore, towards the end of the nineteenth century, women turned the anti-suffragist argument to their own advantage when they began to declare that if women, as the bastions of morality and justice in a world corrupted by the secular pursuits of men, were allowed to vote, they should help to clean up the immoral situations which men had created for the world. The freedom to vote, then, rested for some on an assumed tendency in women to follow Christian morality more steadfastly.

At least since the rise of the suffrage movement in the United States, women have expressed their commitment to the freedom ideal through appeals to justice and attempts to convince the public that the existing situation was unjust according to the criteria of the Constitution. Such appeals assumed that man was a just being and would correct injustice if it were only pointed out to him. Elizabeth Cady Stanton, for example, appeared at a congressional committee hearing to appeal to the legislators to allow the women to vote. Although the form of Mrs. Stanton's argument was coldly logical and might therefore seem to be a reliance on the nature ideal, the fact that she appealed to legislators instead of to the general public, which was relatively powerless, indicates that she saw legal and constitutional changes as the most expedient way to do something for women. Her paper, called "The Solitude of Self," argued from the grounds that men and women shared a common humanity which necessitated the right of the individual conscience and judgment. Mrs. Stanton went on to argue that if women were not only individuals, but also citizens, they must have the rights which all other citizens enjoy, particularly the right to individual happiness and development. As Aileen Kraditor observes:

"Mrs. Stanton was demanding for woman not the right to manifest her equality but the right to become equal. For this she needed education and the vote. Hence the claim to equality for women could not rest upon an abstract assertion of equality; it required concrete demands for specific social and political rights."[3]

5.5.6 Probably the most notorious members of the feminist movements which have appeared periodically in America are those who seek freedom for women through the biological function. Victoria Woodhull and others who have followed in her less and less shocking footsteps have optimistically declared that equality of sexual opportunity, rights, freedom, and pleasure would liberate women. In the days of Woodhull, the free love advocates found their most concrete programs in the utopian societies ilke those of John Humphrey Noyes. In the sixties free love advocates tried similar experiments in which women had intercourse whenever and with whomever they liked, but as someone put it in *Sisterhood is Powerful*, "Woman is . . . *not* getting married, just living together in 'free love,' and finding out it's just the same as marriage anyway, and you're the one who pays for the 'free.' "[4]
Running throughout much of the women's movement literature is the common complaint that even when women carry out their demands for sexual equality and freedom, they suffer because their partners don't really care about satisfying them sexually. Countless articles have been written explaining the reasons for women's inability to find sexual fulfillment during intercourse as marriage manuals have been advising people to practice it for decades. Such writers as Anne Koedt and Germaine Greer latched onto the Masters and Johnson findings to denounce the long-held theory of the vaginal orgasm. Anne Koedt's widely-published article, "The Myth of the Vaginal Orgasm," concluded with a statement which may in part explain the growing interest in lesbianism as a means of sexual fulfillment. She said that men perpetuated the myth of vaginal orgasm because accepting clitoral orgasm would free women from attempting to find sexual satisfaction with men. If

orgasm is actually clitoral, another woman makes just as good a sexual partner as a man, according to some women. Although it would be very difficult to document the reasons for turning to lesbianism, it is certain that dissatisfaction with traditional sexual relationships and a different approach to female orgasm had something to do with it.

For some groups within Women's Liberation the rise of Gay Liberation has been slightly embarrassing. However, with the heavy emphasis on sisterhood and empathy for the problems of all oppressed minorities, movement women can't really turn their backs on those within their midst whose primary concern is making society stop its repression of lesbians. Unfortunately, such a demand claims a lot of time and space in the media who rely on whatever they can dredge up to titillate the public into buying magazines and newspapers or tuning in to a particular network. Therefore, while the actual number of lesbians within Women's Liberation may be a very small proportion, to the general public it often appears that anyone who has anything at all to do with Women's Liberation must be a lesbian. (When my very liberated pediatrician came to visit me in the hospital after the birth of my last child, he noticed my feminist books on the bedside table and asked if I were committed to Women's Liberation and to sexual fulfillment through other women. Under the circumstances, the question seemed slightly ludicrous, but he was only expressing a very common misconception held by people outside the movement, as many women who have participated in demonstrations can testify.) The real problem faced by women who seek liberation through their biological functions is that an over-sexed American society looks on such an approach as so sensational that it can't hear anything else for the sheer shock of hearing about free love, autoeroticism, and lesbianism. Under such circumstances the bigger claims of Women's Liberation which should reach millions of women across the country are overshadowed by the sensational and are very largely lost to the general public.

5.5.7 A closely related approach to the problems of liberating women is the increasingly frequent proposal to divorce sexuality from the ethical and legal commitments of monogamous marriage. Mary Wollstonecraft's suggestion that sexual love which was consummated in marriage was transitory and risky was taken up and expanded by the Claflin sisters in the last century. According to Tennessee Claflin, the ethical commitment involved in marriage was impossible to maintain because men and women were only sexual partners instead of true companions. Page Smith quotes Claflin and says of the men and women who shocked nineteenth-century Americans with their ideas of free sexual associations:

> It was on this specific issue that "the main part of the Woman Question" rested. The resistance of men to woman's suffrage had little to do with the vote as such, but much to do with masculine prerogatives in general. "Men under the new *regime* will become the companions of women instead, and will receive it as a special favor if so permitted to be."[5]

Tennessee's sister Victoria Woodhull declared by both theory and practical living that freedom from monogamous marriage would provide "the only cure for the immorality, lewdness, and licentiousness which may corrode the holy institution of the Sexual Relation."[6]

Although such ideas seemed shocking in the nineteenth century, particularly when they were put into practice, they are heard with more and more frequency in the most recent feminist efforts to achieve the free personality. A modified extended family is probably the most frequently heard proposal as women seek to combat the isolation which they feel in a mobile society which sequesters its women in housing developments or in apartments where neighbors don't dare to talk to one another. The call for community is a call for a kind of truth or ethical commitment which many have failed to find in monogamous marriage. Some, like Germaine Greer, endorse a kind of extended family, while at the same time they are willing to tolerate others who choose to maintain monogamous marriages out of free choice. Others, find an ethical commitment more appropriate among women as a sisterhood. For them, the oppression of one woman is the concern of all women, and therefore, monogamous marriages must be abolished under all circumstances. In extreme cases, women deal with their sexuality through lesbian "marriages," but others say they are able to satisfy their emotional and social needs through their careers and the associations they make at work. For Shulamith Firestone, another possibility is "the household" in which people who are not biologically related (as the extended family implies) live together in a situation which is like the community living of

the present family; the household, however, does not involve the division of labor and the power hierarchy which frequently result when marriage and family roles are confused and the wife assumes the emotional role of a child. Firestone's system actually attempts to strengthen the ethical or troth relationships between human beings by easing the tensions and pressures which destroy so many modern marriages.

5.5.8 Still another route to the liberation of women is the advice to exercise their own wills and do what pleases them instead of remaining the slaves of their husbands and children. Germaine Greer is probably the most widely known writer in this particular approach because her comparatively tolerant attitude toward the choices other women make renders her somewhat more palatable to wary American housewives. Greer has the further advantage of being appealing to the media and of following a long-established tradition in American life: the do-it-yourself approach to problems. Greer's approach is almost confusing in its eclecticism; she tolerates individual approaches and even actively encourages women to do what they like, yet she speaks of the need for revolution rather than reformation. She argues that women must seek revolution by stopping their admiration for the victor in violent confrontations, by refusing to marry (or by facing the realities of a poor marriage and doing something about it), and by rejecting their role as principal consumers in the capitalist state. Such tactics are piecemeal at best, but they are appropriate to Greer's view of the means of liberating women:

> The chief means of liberating women is replacing compulsiveness and compulsion by the pleasure principle. Cooking, clothes, beauty, and housekeeping are all compulsive activities in which the anxiety quotient has long since replaced the pleasure or achievement quotient. . . . The essence of pleasure is spontaneity. In these cases spontaneity means rejecting the norm, the standard that one must live up to, and establishing a self-regulating principle.[7]

Greer accepts the products of technology insofar as they free women from drudgery and boring routine, but she is careful to keep them at bay, for the free personality is of supreme importance to her. The astounding popularity of *The Female Eunuch,* despite the lack of the easy journalistic style to which most Americans have become accustomed, and Germaine Greer's overnight rise to celebrity status on the American talk-show circuit indicate that she has hit the American public where it is most vulnerable. The real clincher for her, however, is the fact that her piecemeal, non-philosophical approach to the problems of women is perfectly in tune with the American religious commitment to an eclectic and pragmatic approach to problem-solving.

5.5.9 Within the Women's Liberation Movement itself this highly subjective approach to personal problems finds expression in small, loosely-organized groups of women who attempt to overcome their difficulties as females through whatever means are currently available to them. For a large number of women, consciousness-raising groups provide the opportunity to share common problems and to discuss possible solutions. For some, just knowing that others feel as they do is enough to give them the courage to refuse to bear another child, to apply for a better job, or to reject the wife-mother way of life altogether. For others, consciousness-raising groups offer radical re-education and the opportunity to learn more about themselves. It is in these groups that the supreme confrontation takes place between the victim of too much technology with its isolation and dehumanization and the about-to-be-liberated woman. Consciousness-raising groups, with their lack of organization, their informality, their theoretical concern for the needs of every individual, no matter how small her problem, represent a desperate effort to escape the tyranny of too much organization at the hands of technology. In some instances the reaction to technology and over-organization is so strong that women give up contraceptives until better and safer methods are found, in spite of the risk of an unwanted pregnancy. In still other cases, lack of control and organization are so important that leaders and representatives are chosen by lot to prevent the formation of an elite.

In whatever way women have sought to achieve the free, independent personality, they have usually appealed to an abstracted element of the human personality as a means through which women could exercise their wills to free themselves. Since such appeals inevitably suffer from a crippling reductionism, it is not really surprising that within the feminist movement, and in particular within the most recent manifestation of the movement, there are almost as many proposed solutions to the difficulties of liberating women as there are feminists to propose them.

The Nature Ideal And The Feminist Movement

5.5.10 Those who have sought to bring order into human life without sacrificing freedom by committing themselves to the nature ideal have produced just as great a variety of approaches as those who have leaned toward the freedom ideal. In general, however, they saw the source of freedom, not in man's will, but in his reason and his ability to achieve control through an empirical approach to the "woman question" and through the achievements of modern science and technology. Charlotte Perkins Gilman, for example, offered one approach to the problems of women when she suggested that labor-saving devices would produce freedom or women. Essentially, she was relying on technology to control the nature which was oppressing women with unending household cares. In more modern times, Premier Khrushchev suggested the use of whatever technological means could be found, as well as cooperative housekeeping and day-care services, to free Soviet women from the unjust burdens of maintaining a job which benefited the state while they carried out full-time jobs in the home during the evenings.

During the nineteenth century Tennessee Claflin advocated a scientific approach to improving the population. She suggested that only the best specimens in the population should mate for reproductive purposes; the other sexual encounters between men and women would not demand careful matching of partners for the purpose would be mutual fulfillment rather than the production of children. Clearly, those who would control such a program would have to be experts in genetics. Similarly, the emphasis on a scientific approach to child care during the twenties encouraged large numbers of Americans to gain greater control over nature by taking up the techniques and under-standings of the experts.

The work of Margaret Sanger and her associates stands as another monument to man's attempt to liberate himself through technical means. Sanger was not content to instruct women in the use of relatively unsafe diaphragms and pessaries, but she actively encouraged such advanced technological achievements as the pill and an anti-toxin which would make women incapable of pregnancy for brief periods of time. Modern feminists carry on Sanger's tradition in their efforts to supply birth-control information to women of all ages and economic situations. At the same time, such groups as the Boston Women's Health

Course Collective, which published *Our Bodies, Our Selves,* are particularly concerned with overcoming the fears and suspicions which long years of exposure to myth and superstition have produced in many women. Such educational efforts often place the feminists in the peculiar position of fighting against the scientist-technician (doctor) with one hand, while they attempt to educate women in scientific "truth" with the other hand.

The demands for the repeal of abortion laws also attempt to free the individual through the best means available, not the back-alley butcher whose scientific knowledge was acquired as a medic in the military. Nancy Williamson clarifies the argument in her article in *The Second Wave:*

> We know that abortion law repeal is only the first step in the total process of freeing women from sexist oppression. We know that women's liberation means a total restructuring of patriarchal society. We know that the winning of one of our demands—the repeal of all abortion laws—is just the beginning. But it is an important beginning, for once we control our reproductive organs, we are on the way to controlling our lives.[8]

As radical as such a demand seems to some Americans, it is only the logical consequence of man's great leap into autonomy during the Renaissance. How can women be expected to forego the advantages which self-declared autonomy apparently brought to men? As long as human beings really believe that the universe can be reduced to a small enough size to accommodate an autonomous man, women are right in demanding that same autonomy for themselves.

5.5.11 A completely different use of the nature ideal to resolve the "woman question" is found in the writings of academic and professional people who have attempted to bring about change by applying the techniques and insights of their disciplines to problems at hand. There are good examples elsewhere in this book. Most of them could hardly be called part of the new wave of Women's Liberation because much of their work has gone on for decades and now their findings fill the bibliographies of Women's Studies courses and the most recent books on feminism. The common bond linking such people as Lee Rainwater, Mirra Komarovsky, Margaret Mead, Jessie Bernard, Alice Rossi and others like them is a commitment to freeing women through problem-solving by means of their respective scientific skills. As Betty Friedan has pointed out, if women had taken Margaret Mead's life as a pattern rather than her more detached and conservative

anthropological observations, she would have done a great deal more for the Women's Movement than she has done. This could be said for some of the other social scientists, too, of course. However, it cannot be denied that studies of educated women such as those done by Eli Ginzburg, Jessie Bernard and Alice Astin have done much to make at least the more privileged parts of the public conscious of the discrimination which had previously remained invisible to most observers. Similarly, such studies as Rainwater's work on the workingman's wife, have informed the privileged college women who read such works in their sociology courses that the lives of non-college women are not particularly free of discrimination either. Thus a sense of women facing different problems in different parts of society is developed through the educational efforts of the academics and professionals who possess scientific skills and techniques far beyond those of the average layman.

The academic, problem-solving approach to the quest for freedom for women has its natural outgrowth in the proliferation of Women's Studies courses which have cropped up in universities and colleges around the country. The courses represent more of an ideological victory than a practical victory because they indicate that some administrators recognize that women have been ignored in many departments. (Unfortunately, it is more than likely that other administrators are the kind who simply wish to avoid trouble and give in to pressure when the voices are loud enough and persistent enough.) The best courses are those sponsored by history, political science, and sociology departments because in these areas the historical, political, and sociological roles of women can be studied within the norms and philosophical frameworks of each discipline without having to stray too far into another field in which both instructor and students are untrained for the astute analysis the problems require. However, many of the courses have been shunted into English departments, the traditional dumping ground for courses which other departments do not want. Since the leading function of English study is aesthetic, courses offered by English departments on the status of American women in history must either distort or totally ignore aesthetic norms in order to accommodate the norms of studies which could be studied with more intellectual integrity in other departments. To turn literature study into politics or sociology is to deny the validity of the aesthetic function of human life. Such a denial arises from a vision of life which interprets the whole by means of only one of the parts. On the other hand, some contend that the proliferation of Women's Studies courses will form the wedge which will open the way for existentialist theories and methods to enter the American school system which is now dominated by pragmatic theories. Existentialist educators advocate meeting the student "where he is," helping him to confront the realities of his situation, and encouraging him to commit himself to one course of action or another. Learning is gained by "discovery" rather than absorbing standard data from a superior source. In an existentialist approach, then, it is entirely appropriate for English classes to become women's consciousness-raising sessions.

5.5.12   One of the writers most frequently studied in Women's Studies courses is Mary Wollstonecraft whose *Vindication of the Rights of Women* is sometimes credited with being the document which started the entire feminist movement. Wollstonecraft's efforts to free women appealed to man's reasonable and logical faculties. Such appeals are quite uncommon today because they demand a logical system with a broad enough base that a large number of people will be likely to subscribe to it; furthermore, modern thinkers seldom believe that men can act on the basis of reason alone because so many of the factors which influence them are subconscious. In Mary Wollstonecraft's day, however, men were not as uncertain of the validity of human reason; therefore, she was able to argue that the use of reason was the key to achieving dominance over "brute creation" and that,

> "Perfection of our nature and capability of happiness, must be estimated by the degree of reason, virtue, and knowledge, that distinguish the individual and direct the laws which bind society: and that from the exercise of reason, knowledge and virtue naturally flow, is equally undeniable, if mankind be viewed collectively."[9]

Thus Wollstonecraft sought to achieve personal freedom for women by appealing on logical grounds to reasonable men to acknowledge that women are also rational and must be treated as such. She carried her argument ever farther when she declared,

> "But I still insist that not only the virtue but the KNOWLEDGE of the two sexes should be the same in nature, if not in degree, and that women, considered not only as moral but rational creatures ought to endeavour to acquire virtues (or perfections) by the *same* means as men, instead of being educated like a fanciful kind of *half*being . . ."[10]

Feminists still argue on rational grounds, of course, but there is less certainty today that enough people subscribe to a particular system of thought to rely on the use of cold logic to change the social order. Today, we are more likely to try to achieve change through political action, educating the public, restructuring of the economic system, or a highly individualistic problem-solving approach.

5.5.13   Instead of talking about man's reason, modern feminists sometimes talk about the reasonable system which will work if women will approach it through the proper channels. For instance, the perennial proposal of an Equal Rights Amendment has only recently been given any chance of ratification; even if the Amendment should be ratified, consistent enforcement of the law would be an entirely different question. Therefore, the more moderate branches of the Women's Liberation Movement are not taking any chances on a possible legal solution. Instead, a number of groups have chosen to work consistently to get around the legislative obstacles through court appeals and efforts to make the general public aware of the rights which have already been guaranteed to women by the inclusion of the word "sex" in Title VII of the 1964 Civil Rights Act. The National Organization of Women declared the general purpose of such legal appeals in its statement of purpose:

> "We believe that the power of American law, and the protection guaranteed by the U.S. Constitution to the civil rights of all individuals, must be effectively applied and enforced to isolate and remove patterns of sex discrimination, to ensure equality of opportunity in employment and education, and equality of civil and political rights and responsibilities on behalf of women, as well as for Negroes and other deprived groups."

Although the inclusion of women among those against whom it was illegal to practice discrimination was originally a joke at best and an effort to kill the Civil Rights Act at worst, women who believe that freedom can come about through the legal system have carried the Act farther than the legislators who passed it imagined. Groups like NOW and the Women's Equity Action League (WEAL) have filed charges of discrimination against women against three hundred fifty colleges and universities in the United States since 1970. Charges include the use of discriminatory salary scales, enforcing anti-nepotism rules to the disadvantage of women, and discrimination against women in the granting of stipends and fellowships. Employers are being challenged in the courts for discriminatory hiring practices which make women the last workers to be hired, but the first to be fired on the arbitrary grounds that they may marry or become pregnant and drop out of the labor force. The so-called protective laws are also being challenged because women feel they prevent them from working at better paying jobs for unrealistic reasons. While the approach of NOW and others who seek justice through the existing system is not very appealing to many feminists, these groups have managed to keep the public's attention more consistently and to arouse more widespread sympathy for their work than have the smaller groups who espouse more radical programs. Using established techniques borrowed from other civil rights groups, women who wish to work within the system have successfully lobbied to encourage legislators to make the kinds of legal changes which they feel are desirable for women. The unflagging energy and persistence of these women is indicated by the fact that governmental protection agencies, such as the Office of Equal Opportunity, have received over half of their complaints from women who felt they were discriminated against on the basis of sex. When the Civil Rights Act was enacted, few would have guessed that discrimination against women would ever become a serious governmental concern.

5.5.14　Two very serious problems face women's groups which work through the system they feel they can trust. First, many wonder whether more can be accomplished through the courts or whether women could reach their goals more economically and more quickly through constitutional changes. Second, there is some doubt as to whether or not women are able to bring about the changes they desire by withholding their votes from candidates who do not seek justice for women. Although the threat is clearly and frequently articulated, at this stage in the Women's Liberation Movement, the concentration of votes which might actually be withheld is not very large. Until a large enough number of middle-class housewives can be brought out from behind their split-level doors, the efforts of such groups are likely to be diffused and difficult to evaluate in terms of concrete results. These two questions are extremely important to women within NOW, WEAL, and similar groups for they raise a third question: is the system worthy of the religious commitment they have made to it?

Some of the sharpest criticism of Women's

Liberation efforts to organize women into groups to achieve power comes from women who have achieved great success in a world which is almost totally in the hands of men. As the example of former member of Congress Jeannette Rankin well illustrates, even in the worst of times there will always be a few women who will make it on their own. Therefore, the question which movement women ask of the successful women is how can justice be provided for those who are not Jeannette Rankins or Margaret Meads or Indira Gandhis? A few highly competent women have recognized the validity of such an argument and have lent their support to the movement. Such women can do a great deal to educate the public because they possess great personal charisma and have proven that they also possess the expertise to reach the top of their field in a very competitive man's world. In politics, Shirley Chisholm and Bella Abzug come immediately to mind. In the highly competitive field of journalism Gloria Steinem stands out as the best-known example of a woman whose charisma and skills have won public attention for Women's Liberation. Besides the highly developed skills with which Steinem attacks the problems of women, she also makes use of technology to spread her ideas through *Ms* magazine and the television networks. Without her charisma and her expertise she would be very unlikely to receive any mention at all. However, Steinem appeals to the media and to the general public more than many others associated with the movement do; she is highly photogenic, she associates with the people the media like to photograph, and she is careful to push for the liberation of women in the unstructured, non-philosophical way that Americans like.

Whether feminists have leaned toward the nature ideal or the freedom ideal in their efforts to free women, the thread of secular humanism runs throughout the movement. Free from the God whom people formerly believed to rule the world, women have appealed to the reason or to the will in their attempts to achieve the kind of autonomy men seemed to have.

Two Structured Uses of the Ideals: The American Suffrage Movement And The Socialist Marxist Women's Rights Movement

5.5.15　While humanism is the basic foundation of feminist efforts, the confusion which many people feel when reading about the movement is frequently justified. Few of the feminists who have arisen in American history have attempted to deal self-consciously with their religious or philosophic commitments. Most have chosen to work on the problems at hand and have cranked out article after article on current issues. The modern woman, isolated from the centers of Women's Liberation activities, has little chance to sort out the diverging opinions which she meets in the anthologies and books published in the last few years. She has a right to ask just who is in favor and who is in disgrace as far as Women's Liberation is concerned. The answer isn't likely to be very satisfactory though, because so few theorists are working within the movement. Furthermore, developed ideologies, when they do exist, rarely get the attention they should because most Americans, members of Women's Liberation included, fail to see the importance of a systematic philosophical analysis of grave social issues. Probably the most structured approaches to freeing women have arisen in the American Suffrage Movement and in the development of a socialist/Marxist dialectic.

The early feminists have often been compared to the founders of Women's Liberation in this century because both groups of women found their self-awareness and their philosophical direction in their efforts to achieve civil rights for blacks. The women who worked for the abolition of slavery formed a sort of idealistic first phase of the American Suffrage Movement. Their arguments were based on appeals to natural rights for all human beings, black and white, male and female. The arguments which men had used a century earlier to free themselves from British sovereignty were turned to apply to women as well. Those who fought for freedom for the colonies argued that it was unjust to tax people who had no voice in the use of the taxes; nor was it just to govern without first getting the consent of those who were governed. The idealistic suffragists saw that the constitution had extended civil and political rights to all men; the principle was universal and, in the view of the suffragists, must therefore apply universally to women as well. In an address before the New York State Legislature in 1854, Elizabeth Cady Stanton summarized a view which many of the idealistic suffragists held, but believed to be too shocking to express openly:

"Look at the position of woman as woman. It is not enough for us that by your laws we are permitted to live and breathe, to claim the necessaries of life from our legal protectors—to pay the penalty of our crimes; we demand the full recognition of all our rights as citizens of the Empire State. We are persons; native, free-born citizens; property-holders, tax-payers; yet are we denied the exercise of our right to the elective franchise. We support ourselves, and, in part, your schools, colleges, churches, your poorhouses, jails, prisons, the army, the navy, the whole machinery of government, and yet we have no voice in your councils. We have every qualification required by the Constitution, necessary to the legal voter, but the one of sex. . . ."[11]

Part of the confusion which arose in the arguments of the suffragists and in those of the more progressive men who supported them lay in the mixing of authority structures. In the *Seneca Falls Declaration of Sentiments and Resolutions,* the women declared that men had held them down in a variety of social institutions: marriage, family, state, church, school, labor, the professions. Furthermore, the Declaration stated, man had attempted to destroy woman's sense of moral responsibility and conscience before God. As for the men, it seems abundantly clear that they had, indeed, usurped power over women in every social area; however, the women were demanding the right to make a similar error by attempting to free themselves from authority in every social institution without ever discussing the sources and legitimate uses of that authority. Furthermore, neither the men who victimized women nor the women who sought to be free from men concerned themselves with the relationships between the different social institutions and their sources of authority. Men assumed that if the Bible had called them to be head of the house, they were also the only ones who could be heads of schools, churches, governments, labor unions, and so forth. In earlier centuries when men believed that authority structures were established by God, the question of where authority comes from was hardly as complex or as open to hot debate. However, once men decided that authority to manage a group arose from the will of the members of the group, serious problems and conflicts grew up. As long as women were content to keep quiet and be governed by the men who had pushed themselves into positions of blanket power, the "woman question" was the concern of only a few eccentrics. But once women accepted democracy's idea of rule by the consent of the governed, the "woman question" became a source of great social upheaval. To the most progressive men the claims of the suffragists were only right. If there were no authority governing the structures of society outside of man himself, it was only just that women must be allowed to share in the structuring which would develop.

5.5.16 If the problem had been resolved at the admission of abstract equality for women, the early suffragist movement might have remained an idealistic effort to establish justice under the terms of democracy. However, with the influx of immigrants, the rapidly growing threat of the working class, and the obvious corruption which arose when the new industrialists fell to the temptation to misuse capitalism and the free enterprise system, the question of equality shifted ground. Yes, men and women might be theoretically equal before the constitution, but were *all* men and *all* women equal before the constitution?

Once the question of equality for everyone was out in the open, the idealistic phase of the American Suffrage Movement suffered a rapid demise. The idealistic argument based on equal rights was replaced by a typically American pragmatic approach. Women began to argue that the votes of sober, white middle-class wives of sober, middle-class white men could outweigh the votes of such undesirable males as immigrants, enfranchised blacks, and lower-class whites who were swelling the voting rolls. With their strong background in reform movements, it was only natural that American suffragists would also point out that their votes added to those of the liberal white men of the progressive era would do much to control the frightening power of big business, hold down the liquor interests long enough to pass prohibition, and help to deliver the nation from the grip of party machines. Women optimistically hoped that the vote would also make them better wives and mothers who would build more solid marriages based on equality with their husbands and would train superior citizens for the country.

The shift from the idealistic approach to obtaining the vote to a blatantly racist, pragmatic approach is only puzzling when we ignore the question of authority and liberty in the various institutions or spheres of the society. As we saw before, around the time of the Renaissance, men shrank their universe to a small enough size that they felt competent to declare themselves its autonomous rulers. However, the male half of the human race kept almost all of the autonomy for itself. When the female half began to demand the same autonomy, as was only right in the new conception of a world freed from the authority structures formerly believed to have been handed down by God, the men with the power could not

deny the logic of their wives' arguments; they were essentially the same arguments they had used in achieving their own freedom. However, the confusing and disturbing circumstances of late nineteenth century America made it almost impossible to retain even a token theoretical approach to the question. Changes were much too rapid to allow Americans the time to assess the situation calmly from a consistently worked-out philosophical stance. The only alternatives were to be swallowed up in a welter of social problems and decay or to attack the problems via the eclectic approach of the layman's pragmatism. Being unwilling to go down at the hands of the undesirables, Americans chose the pragmatic route, and the idealistic women of the early suffrage movement became the conniving racists of the movement's second wave. The women themselves could hardly be said to have degenerated or lost their ideals. Instead, they simply saw that ideals would not work in a country where autonomous men had to handle overwhelming problems at much too rapid a pace.

5.5.17 There are some who go to great lengths to try to prove that the roots of the modern Women's Liberation Movement lie in the seventy-year struggle to get the right to vote for women. In a very limited sense this is probably true. The first phase of the suffrage movement with its theoretically-inclined women has its modern counterparts in the smallest and most radical parts of the modern movement. And even admitting that the feminist movements of both centuries grew out of civil rights work and showed a great interest in social reform, such connections seem quite superficial, particularly in view of the many steps backward which women have taken since the time of their enfranchisement. Undoubtedly, the most basic connection between the early and modern feminist movements is the general abandonment of any systematic analysis of society and the problems facing women, coupled with an embracing of a totally eclectic pragmatism which is most characteristic of the large majority of Women's Liberation people today.

A few modern feminists, however, reject the customary piecemeal approach and actively seek to order the world through a fairly thorough ideology. Outside of the movement literature, they are seldom mentioned. In the first rash of publicity, SCUM and WITCH received attention, but it was primarily media exploitation to get a story that would sell. The silence arises in part from an American distaste for analytical approaches to social problems and from a pervasive belief that a theoretical system or a developed world view is not possible. Even within the movement itself, many groups do not realize the significance of the growing socialist interpretations of Women's Liberation. In fact, many of the recently developed women's studies courses do not even include the writings of Reed, Firestone, Ware and other radical theorists. Yet the theoretical work done by the socialist or Marxist and by the Radical Feminists is of such far-reaching consequences that it suggests the Women's revolution may very well be key to world-wide revolution of an unforeseen scope. Some of the radical women still maintain membership within radical organizations whose goals include the liberation of women, but who see world revolution as a more basic concern. Females within the Black Panthers or the Weathermen are concerned for the problems faced by the Left, such as the war issue and draft resistance; to them the liberation of women is part of a larger revolutionary program. In a major editorial in *Triple Jeopardy*, published by the Third World Women's Alliance, someone wrote:

> "As women, it is important for us to study in order to understand how the role of Third World women in the home and in society fits into the general picture of Third World people in this country and to fully understand how our struggle as Third World women fits into the struggle against exploitation and oppression of the peoples of our various communities. . . . As Third World women we must be engaged in the mass struggles going on in this country against war, racism, and repression. At the same time, we must study revolutionary theory and tactics to provide ourselves with a tool which will be a guide to our actions for changing the conditions of our lives, our children and our loved ones."[12]

Although this was written after the Third World Women's Alliance was formed as an organization separate from SNCC, the sense of engagement in a global revolution of which the liberation of women is a key part is clearly present. The theoretical work of such women as Evelyn Reed and others who follow a Marxist analysis of society relies heavily on the anthropological and historical work of J. J. Bachoven and Robert Briffault, as well as the writings of Marx, Engels, and Lenin on the oppression of women. In general, however, these writings suffer from a sort of defensiveness which arises from trying to prove that women were the developers of culture and industry, but were victimized by men who seized power through private property and thus developed a class society. The result is a kind of female chauvinism which centers around analyses done during the nineteenth century and thus short-changes a really comprehensive program for a modern women's revolution. Still, the Marxist women have a theoretical basis for their approach to revolution which is lacking in every other Women's Liberation group with the exception of the Radical Feminists.

5.5.18 Shulamith Firestone, one of the founders of Radical Feminists, wrote a book called *The Dialectic of Sex* which is probably the most revolutionary, comprehensively analytical, and hence one of the most important books to come out of the modern feminist movement. Yet in its typically facile way, *Time* (March, 1972) missed the theoretical basis of the book and summarized it as if it were another Ray Bradbury novel. Since missing the point is an American pastime, Firestone's book runs the risk of being only cursorily read even with some parts of the Women's Liberation Movement. This is unfortunate because ignorance of such a book allows the rest of the movement women to continue their eclectic attacks on generalized and personal problems without ever developing any kind of comprehensive alternative analysis which would give the movement the base that would prevent splintering, fragmentation, and efforts wasted on comparatively tangential issues such as whether or not women can "rape" men, as one writer has suggested. Without some sort of theoretical base, women's groups will swing back and forth between the nature and freedom ideals as the political and social currents shift beneath their feet. Worse still, the women's movement runs the risk of becoming a liberal fad rather than the key to widespread social change.

Firestone's book takes what she finds acceptable in Marx and Freud and then goes beyond their work to create what she calls a new dialectic, a dialectic of sex. Firestone, who leans closer to the nature ideal than most other feminists, is most appreciative of Marx and Engels' analytical method. Using a dialectical, materialist method, she says, "Marx and Engels . . . attempted a scientific approach to history."[13] But Firestone later points out that "the class analysis is a beautiful piece of work but limited; although correct in a linear sense, it does not go deep enough. There is a whole sexual substratum of the historical dialectic . . ."[14] According to Firestone, Engels made his error in reducing to "the economic filter." Therefore, while she values the insights and particularly the method of Marx and Engels, she sets for herself the task of doing a kind of vertical analysis which will carry the economic analysis of class society to its biological roots.

5.5.19 Firestone's respect for Freud is unique among movement women who have castigated him for the "penis envy" and "vaginal orgasm" theories until many think of Freud as one of the arch enemies of women. Firestone, however, feels that Freud's basic insight was correct and must be considered in forming a feminist critique of culture: "Freudianism is so charged, so impossible to repudiate because Freud grasped the crucial problem of modern life: Sexuality." She goes on to interpret Freud in feminist terms. For example, the Oedipal Complex makes sense to her as a shorthand way of describing the "power/dependency" relationships which are set up within the patriarchal nuclear family. The child growing up in this kind of family recognizes that he is dependent on his parents, but his mother is also dependent upon his father; because of early conditioning and because of his identification with her in her oppression, the child prefers his mother to his father even though he eventually comes to recognize her essential helplessness. The conflict for the child comes in repressing his attachment to the underdog in the family and in overcoming his desires to wrest the power from his father's hands. In the same way Firestone goes on to reinterpret in feminist terms Freud's concepts of the Electra Complex and the results of the incest taboo. She concludes:

> "The separation of sex from emotion is at the very foundations of Western culture and civilization. If early sexual repression is the basic mechanism by which character struc-tures supporting political, ideological, and economic serfdom are produced, an end to the incest taboo, through abolition of the family, could have profound effects. Sexu-ality would be released from its straitjacket to eroticize our whole culture, changing its very definition."[15]

Firestone, of course, could hardly be called a Freudian; she points out that Freudianism pre-empted Feminism and that the bankruptcy of psychoanalytic therapy is only too obvious. What she actually does is to take from Freud some essential insights and place them within the political terms of the feminist movement where they can be used as arguments for the abolition of the patriarchal nuclear family. Thus, she concludes that the caste system or the social organization of society is based on the dialectic between the two sexes.

The sexual dialectic in social organization may seem obvious, but Firestone points out that it exists in even more subtle ways in the division of the human race into classes. Because of the limitations of biology, women have been relegated to a lower status and thus to a lower class, while men have been free to carry out the society's productive activities and have thus gained status as a class. Going beyond Engels' observation that within the family "the husband is the owner, the wife the means of production, the children the labor," Firestone rephrases and amplifies his definition of history by applying her feminist understanding of the "psychosexual" basis of economic class:

> "Historical materialism is that view of the course of history which seeks the ultimate cause and the great moving power of all historic events in the dialectic of sex: the division of society into two distinct biological classes for procreative reproduction, and the struggles of these classes with one another in the changes in the modes of marriage, reproduction and childcare created by these struggles; in the connected development of other physically-differentiated classes (castes); and in the first division of labor based on sex which developed into the (economic-cultural) class system."[16]

5.5.20 In Firestone's analysis of society, the basic division between men and women also applies to culture which she defines as "the realization of the conceivable in the possible." The "technological mode," which currently enjoys the greater status, is dominated by men, and the more lowly "aesthetic mode" is dominated by women because of the psychological traits which are assumed to characterize each sex. For instance, a masculine approach is likely to be "objective, logical, extroverted, realistic, concerned with the conscious mind (the ego), rational, mechanical, pragmatic and down-to-earth, stable." A feminine approach, on the other hand, is thought of as "subjective, intuitive, introverted, wishful, dreamy or fantastic, concerned with the subconscious (the id), emotional, even tempera-mental (hysterical)."[17]

A major element which distinguishes Firestone's work from all other feminist writings is her unwillingness to separate careful analysis from a carefully planned program for revolution; most other feminists are content to supply one or the other. Before her utopian world can emerge, Firestone says that the tyranny of the biological family will be broken down by a revolution of those whom it oppresses: women, children, young people, and exploited minority races. The goal of such a revolution is "full sexual freedom" which Firestone says can be realized by using the best technological means available to man: artificial means of reproduction and scientific breakthroughs to eliminate childhood, aging, and death.

A proletarian revolt will end the economic exploitation of the owners of the means of production, with the ultimate goal being the disappearance of classes and the state. On the cultural level, science will bring about a merging of the aesthetic and the technological modes through the use of cybernetics which will level class barriers and family power structures by eliminating both the economic necessity to work and the prestige which results from controlling the sources of money. Firestone continually emphasizes that women must seize control of the means of reproduction and of production in order that the power of the patriarchal biological family can be broken down. The possibility of producing children outside the human body and the full use of cybernetics are important keys to Firestone's future society of which she says, "The revolt against the biological family could bring on the first successful revolution, or what was thought of by the ancients as the Messianic Age." For Firestone man's salvation lies not in the eradication of sin through orthodox religion, or in the individual and piecemeal efforts of committed women, but rather in the most comprehensive use of science and technology possible.

Whether or not we call Firestone's proposal utopian, she is not really as far as she may seem from classic responses to the problems of balancing the nature and freedom ideals. Hendrik Van Riessen points out in *The Society of the Future* that the balance between the authority of the employer and the freedom of the worker was destroyed by automation, the industrial revolution, and industry's unceasing efforts to increase worker efficiency; the result was enervated workers who no longer saw the meaning of their work and soon came to think of themselves as no more significant than a number on a plant ID badge. Eventually they became "mass" men, isolated in their work from the finished product and directed by the management as part of a machine. (The parallels in the individual's relationship to other social spheres like government, labor, school, and the church are obvious.) The worker was forced to band together with other mass men to achieve the sense of control and security that he felt he needed. However, security and control were only possible when scientific organization brought order to his group. Instead of liberating himself from the tyranny of overorganization, he became an even more oppressed victim. The pattern has emerged in utopian writings from the time of Plato to B. F. Skinner.

5.5.21   That Firestone is fully aware of the plight of the worker is clear in her assertion that the workers must seize the means of production and liberate themselves. However, her solution to the problem of balancing authority and freedom (and it seems that she is particularly interested in achieving freedom for the individual since she says that eventually authority structures will become unnecessary) is based on her belief that through science and technology man can fully understand and completely control reality. The society which emerges under the rule of science becomes more and more collectivistic as scientific organization attempts to eliminate the burdens of modern life for the individual. Furthermore, the use of cybernetics to improve human life demands considerable organization since the variables must be as tightly controlled as possible to insure the accuracy of the machine's work. Firestone emerges, then, as another modern thinker whose religious commitment is to the creative use of science and a certain optimism which convinces her that the very small elite which will control the organization of society will be good individuals who will not misuse their gargantuan powers.

What is genuinely unique about Firestone's analysis of the human situation is her belief that the division between the sexes lies at the root of class society with its exploitation. She very astutely points out that Marx and Engels erred in reducing everything to economics. In much the same way, however, Firestone is forced into a reductionist position herself, though admittedly she gets to a much more basic level—the biotic. Although she anticipates a world of restored, whole personalities, for the present her analysis is still basically reductionist.

Feminism in America is not really the radical or unique movement which some claim it is. Rather, feminism is only another manifestation of the humanist drive for freedom which has spurred artists, politicians, poets, social organizers, and educators into attempting to create a new and better world in which men can enjoy full autonomy. The movement only seems radical because at last women are demanding a share in creating that world where they hope to achieve autonomy also. Any movement which has a potential membership of half of the human race is certain to bring sweeping changes in the social order. However those changes are brought about, by reference on the nature ideal or by reliance on the freedom ideal, women have yet to discover whether the autonomy which they envy in men is as satisfying as it appears to be in the midst of the struggle.

REFERENCES

1. Schneir, Miriam, *Feminism: the Essential Historical Writings,* N.Y. *Random House* (1972) p. 40.
2. *Ibid.,* pp. 47, 48.
3. Kraditor, Aileen S., *The Ideas of the Woman Suffrage Movement,* Garden City, N.Y. Doubleday (1971) p. 41.
4. Morgan, Robin, ed. *Sisterhood is Powerful,* N.Y. Random House (1970) p. 167.
5. Smith, Page, *Daughters of the Promised Land,* Boston Little, Brown, and Co. (1970) p. 49.
6. *Ibid.,* 147
7. Greer, Germaine, *The Female Eunuch,* London Paladin (1971) p. 326.
8. *The Second Wave,* Vol 1, #3 (1971) p. 14.
9. Wollstonecraft, Mary, *Vindication of the Rights of Women* (1972), p. 3.
10. *Ibid.,* p. 43.
11. (#1, p. 111.)
12. *Triple Jeopardy,* Vol. 1. #1, p. 16.
13. Firestone, Shulamith, *The Dialectic of Sex,* N.Y. Bantam (1970) p. 3.
14. *Ibid.,* p. 4.
15. *Ibid.,* p. 60.
16. *Ibid.,* p. 12.
17. *Ibid.,* p. 175.

Bonnie Greene
Snohomish, Washington

Chapter 6

What Men Think About the Movement

The masculine reaction to the movement ranges very widely and moves as much as the feminine viewpoint on two fulcrums, the individual's philosophical-political assumptions and his previous experience with women. This latter aspect has run the gambits from President Lincoln's relationship with his mother to that of Portnoy in Roth's popular novel. At least four distinct attitudes have been expressed, the extremely masculine, originating in Nietzsche's ideal superman with touches of Napoleon and the playboy philosophy; The partner-ship concept that the roles of male/female are complementary; the liberal-tolerant view; and the outright revolutionary based upon Marx, Che, or Mao. All of these have been aired in the public press.

The real problems will arise when the demands of women's liberation meet with success in the labor field and quotas for employment are established by sex as has already happened in regard to race. The result is either outright social planning by percentage or objective merit employment. Neither one will sit well with the breadwinner whose wife and family accept the traditional role of the wife and mother as homemaker. Already the signs of strain are beginning to show in the two professional environments where liberation has made its greatest gains, education and the law. The legal and financial structure of the United States has assumed for two centuries the legitimacy of the family unit with a working head, the census, social security and taxation systems all assume this hierarchical organization. A change away from this practice is loaded with such incredible complexity and filled with so many momentous outcomes that it should be very carefully weighed before a pattern of lower court decisions brings it about without regard to its total meaning. The innovation of electronic data processing has made possible government at one level and record keeping of all individual citizens at another level. Can the traditional family structure resist the erosion of its relationship by unilateral government dealing one to one with its members? This may well be the greatest single social problem of the 70's and 80's before which all other problems of race, education, and drugs will shrink to nothing.

Men's reactions to women's liberation have for the most part been uninformed about the movement and based on popular myth. Mr. Tuten attempts to solve both deficiencies. The very fact that very few men have taken the first two waves of feminism seriously, as indicated by the astonishingly few authors who have written on them, has given impetus to the third wave.

ANOTHER VIEWPOINT ON WOMEN'S LIBERATION

6.1 Another viewpoint is that of a male author. Mr. Robert Tuten, a free-lance editor and writer specializing on small business, examines the recent writings of male authors concerned with the status and movements of women. These vary from bemused, liberal agreement, to outright seething hostility. He then traces some of the longer term historical aspects of the movement. It is clear that giant corporations and big advertising budgets have long established sophisticated sociological models for selling and reselling the American housewife. In time the middle class woman begins to feel some way inferior if she does not fulfill the dreams portrayed in both print and electronic media. But these dreams have been spun by males, the women can see through them, criticise, and comfortably reject them, and so the battle is joined.

The reaction of the organizations and institutions of society are particularly important. Among these, business, government media, and the church are probably the most deeply rooted and influential. All are under the pressure of having to make meaningful reforms in their structures and functions. The author examines what is being done and said by the leaders of these institutions and brings the movement to the facts which may order its future.

6.1.1 The contemporary success of women involved with the liberation movement in getting strong publicity for their cause has left many men dazed and wondering about the future and their place in it. Women's Liberation is a topic on which very few men are able to keep silent. From the coverage given the movement by the public media, it seems to tantalize the male ego in such a way that wisdom and common sense are abandoned. Masculine writers and celebrities of every type and age have found it necessary to pontificate on the subject. Comments have been publicized from both political parties and from every political philosophy from radical liberal to ultraconservative. Hugh Hefner, Benjamin Spock, Bob Hope, Spiro T. Agnew, and even the popular entertainer, Tiny Tim have said their piece about the female revolution.

The only full literary work devoted to the combat has been Norman Mailer's *The Prisoner of Sex.* In it the author says that he is clashing horns with, "a squadron of enraged Amazons, an honor guard of revolutionary vaginas." He records in a fictional but critical format his thoughts and suspicions about the Women's movement. His arch enemy and alter ego is Kate Millet, the authoress of *Sexual Politics.* Although Mailer makes the usual minor concessions about occupational equal rights, he feels threatened by the women's demands. In the major section of the book he unrelentingly attacks the feminists and what he considers to be their many myths. Here we encounter an interesting situation where both the champions and detractors of feminism assume the veracity and necessity of finding psychological explanations of the other's actions.

They assume in some strange almost Maoist way that "right thinking and right understanding," will cleanse the evil bigotry from their detractors' minds. Mailer follows this tack implicitly as he challenges what he believes to be the myths of the movement, such notions as male "pussy envy," and the male being an incomplete female, which sounds strangely like Freud in reverse. He attacks Millet's book and its treatment of many subjects, but nowhere is he more intense than in his defense of Henry Miller's writings. He asserts that Millet has misrepresented both Miller and the time in which he lived (1920's). For strange reasons Mailer and his viewpoint have been both embraced and rejected by Women's liberation spokeswomen. Germaine Greer in a magazine interview expressed a remarkably passive opinion of Mailer.[1]

A survey of some of the comments made by men about the feminist enthusiasm bears out several interesting things. For one, many males just do not like the fact of change for any reason or for any goal. For another, the common but unexamined suppositions which many men had about women, the stereotyped opinions, are being blown to the winds and ventilated with scorn. For a good many masculine writers raised on the dual notions of women's place on the pedestal and the incontrovertible excellence of American society, the spectre of angry American women is a nightmare. This is not to say that from some points of view and in some situations women have not received benefits over their male counterparts, or that for a large number of human beings American society does not proffer good things. However, the depth and breadth of the discontent was more than many men realized. The real crux of the matter is whether this discontent is the general one felt by all in a technocentric, mass society, or whether it is particularly feminine and due to some specific acts of male arrogance.

Despite the outlandish stage appearance that he invokes, Tiny Tim's opinions are very conservative and very commonplace. Writing in *Esquire,* he argues that the mother's place is in the home and not in competition with men. He appeals to the laws of nature and the Bible to justify his assertion that woman is God's second choice and that it is natural for women to take care of children and husbands. Tiny Tim fears that society will suffer from the total emancipation of women. He concedes that today women are free, have "free will" to go contrary to nature, but that harm will come if women take this option. In such views Tiny Tim stands foursquare for the middle class conservative virtues and classic American fundamentalism.

6.1.2 Among the men who have made careers and millions writing for women's publications, Drs. Spock and Ruben have been forced to backpedal not knowing just how their readers would be influenced by the movement and wanting above everything else to maintain rapport with the winning side. Both of these men and many lesser names have made a mark on contemporary society by producing pseudo-scientific avuncular advice to the middle class lady of the house. Their medical credentials evoked an atmosphere of plausibility and authority in the magazines in which they wrote. Magazines which were often purveyors of what some analysts have labeled "soft-sell" pornography, the type of personal sex-directed medical experience which purports to guide the readers who are also facing the honeymoons, hysterectomies, or menopauses which many middle class women fear. The male authors and advisers have had to do some journalistic tightrope walking fearful of the scissors of economic and personal rejection on the part of their readers. They have adopted the stance of suppliants for the mercy of their readers and have had recourse to such phrases as, "I was misunderstood," or "I was partially right," and in some instances their outright denial of past positions held. As more women write for women, a new façade will be constructed for the women's consumer magazines and their revenue-roots in luxury advertising.

An interesting apologetic for the Women's rights movement has come from the prolific pen of William Buckley who burst into the national limelight in the early 50's with a college-age McCarthyite credo on *God and Man at Yale*, which launched his career in journalism. Commenting on the writings of the two feminists, Freidan and Millet, in his *National Review*, he admits that much of their work is engrossing and brilliant, but that the stated ambition to make men and women equal breaks down. His reason is that one can not categorize emotions and to do so would rob one of his freedom. Perhaps the logic of this will escape many. Most have given up any attempt to capture it.

Traveling the same conservative path are the comments if not the mental footfalls of James J. Kilpatrick who recorded some "Random Thought on Women's Lib." The occasion for his random thoughts was the appearance of the first issue of the new women's magazine, *MS*, founded by Gloria Steinem. In a pitying, remorse filled tone, Mr. Kilpatrick opined that he was, "inexpressibly sad" about the magazine. Despite this pathos he went on to express himself and stated that it would invoke only pity from those indifferent or uninvolved with the movement. Kilpatrick lamented that the feminists exuded with self-pity as they equated the "meaning of high tragedy with the picking up of a husband's socks." Unfortunately he represented by this statement the very characteristic of a sock-dropping juvenile that the statement in *MS* meant to point out to its readers. When a woman must pick up the same grubby socks for the same thoughtless slob a million times off the same floor in the same room, they begin to take on the Grecian tragic proportions of Sisyphus' boulder. But Kilpatrick went on, he

concluded that if the movement were to be judged by the first issue of *MS* it would appear to be little more than a "threnody of complaint." He then suggested that the name be changed to one more descriptive of the movement, and possibly more akin to his estimate of the writers, his choice: *Barren.* The fact that all modern protest literature is undergirded by a common existential commitment is completely missed by both Buckley and Kilpatrick. For most members of the establishment, moneyed class in America, the constant anxiety and fear of the restive minorities is inconceivable. Obviously few of them have ever been in similar circumstances. As is rightly pointed out by many women authors the one great chasm across which the successful man can not leap is empathy with the oppressed, the outcast, and the rejected.

6.1.3   The opinions of Lionel Tiger are especially repulsive to those women who resent being considered as less than human by their male oppressors. His findings are based upon his extensive studies with primates. Tiger feels that the very effort of the female to equal the male has contributed to the basic inequality of the relationship which the female experiences. He feels that the only freedom for the women is for the social, business, and legislative processes to take into consideration the limitations inherent in the female of the species. He really enrages his audience when he begins to enumerate those features which render the women inherently limited. He places the menstrual cycle high on the list of those factors that have some "appreciable and predictable effect on the female social, psychological, and technical behavior." He frequently utilizes the noun or qualifying adjective, "sexist." This is unfortunate because it seriously detracts from his positive insistence on day care centers, and leaves for pregnancy. Like all too many combatants in the male versus female dialogue, he appears to have little real consideration for his opponents' position.

Possibly of greatest interest of all are the views of women's movements expressed by Hugh Hefner. Few men have made as much money or won as many followers and emulators by exploiting women as have Hefner and his empire of publishing and dinner club ventures. By his lights he sees himself as a liberator of womankind, redressing the grievances wrought by Victorian morality and sequestration upon active, earthy, and eager women. In an interview conducted by Gloria Steinem for *McCall's*, Hefner displayed a well studied annoyance. He feels that there are many more important things for women to do today than to waste their time on this "women's lib foolishness." Commenting on the position of women in today's world, Hefner said, "I don't think that in the generation or two immediately ahead women have any major beefs. They have all the opportunities that are really important to their human potential." Mind you, this is the buck-rabbit of the playboy hutches, whose laws of bunny-behavior *Life* likened to the *Code of Hammurabi.* Hefner offers the opinion that militant feminists "want to be men." And he vows that he would not want to live in a society "with no man-women difference." A credo that leaves something to be desired in the realm of potential. He labels the militants as "pathetic." Then professes amazement "why the feminists aren't grateful to us, to the playboy philosophy." He claims he is in favor of women being able to vote and own property. However he still wants "women to be attractive to men." He insisted here as in other interviews that the devotees of the playboy philosophy, first extolled in a long, episodic essay running over many issues of *Playboy*, should become the allies of the feminists. He reasons that both should turn their attack on the true enemy, the less than human role played by women caused by the Judeo-Christian religious tradition. This sort of reasoning has appealed to many hedonistic sophomores living in fraternity houses. Few if any advocates of a change in the situation of women have approved his ideas.

6.1.4. Politicians have been especially hard put to find a way out of the dilemma of favoring both the middle class suburbanite housewife and the radical woman. Strange as it may seem, otherwise liberal politicians have been very slow to adapt the views and definitions of women's liberation to their campaigns. Interestingly enough not one front-rank politician can boast a wife who is popular or even acceptable to the liberation advocates. In just the opposite situation, Mrs. Spiro T. Agnew and Mrs. Martha Mitchell have both made mock of the movement and its supporters. Some truth may be seen in this reaction, if one realizes that both women have around them a constant flurry of admirers and are fairly well insulated from the trials and tribulations of the working woman. Then it is not strange that they should not want to look at the milling mob of angry women at their doorstep.

The organization of the Women's Political Caucus has not found one single male politician to support but has rather found several women. Just how much pressure it can exert for the presidential candidacy of Representative Shirley Chisholm is hard to say, but given the cold facts of American politics, it will not be much. This brings up the reaction of males to specific women writers. However that is not usually indicative of their reaction to the movement as a whole. A case in point is the general acceptance of the witty and urbane, Germaine Greer, who became a literary lioness overnight and completed her P.R. tour of the U.S. with a smashing round of talk-show triumphs. On the opposite pole, the very carefully worked out theoretical analysis of Shulamith Firestone has received far less consideration by male writers than it deserves.

Undoubtedly the greatest gains for women's rights have been won in two areas: the one the tangible area of changes in the law, and the second in the intangible area of public recognition of their viewpoint. The first has been especially strong in the institutional environment where university and college employment practices have been radically altered by the decisions of the courts. The next step after the assumption of Black and Chicano demands on the campus, the submission to women's demands, is now coming to fruition. If the Black experience and the Chicano experience are valid objects of study and analysis, then the logic demands that women's opinions, the female experience, must be a curricular subject. In a nation which values the messianic mission of education to bring enlightenment and equality to men, why should it be denied to women? The push for incorporating Women's Studies courses and programs into American higher education is moving rapidly and some 700 such courses will be taught across the U.S. by 1973. The chief masculine objection to this trend in education has been twofold: primarily, that the program did not train students to do anything when they graduated. This is promulgated upon the widely held myth that higher education equips its products to be better producers and therefore higher consumers. The truth of the matter is that higher education equips a person to live, and to understand and function at whatever level he may choose to live in an ever more complex world. In such a world, women's studies are not only important but completely legitimate, as legitimate as the courses in "sex and the family," and "criminology" which dot America's campuses.

6.1.5. It is also important to consider the opinions of women's rights or the women's movement as seen in the corporate policy of the male-dominated institutions of American society. A good cross-section can be seen in four areas:

business, government, media, and the church. Business has been put against the wall by two pressures for increased hiring of special groups, the minorities and the poor. A further demand for increased female participation by women at corporate levels has run into severe difficulties. In the business realm women hold a different place than in either education or government. Many women, relative to the total number of owners, own stock. Many women hold important positions within companies. The problem has been that many of these positions are stereotyped to such a degree that while moving up in salary and responsibility, a secretary has still been a secretary. Some males have responded to this argument by statements that moving up in American business from one sector to another is virtually impossible anyway and that the best a woman without either professional license or inherited wealth can expect is "advancement in rank."

In all such dialogue, only a few have been able to look beyond the immediate situation to see more fundamental causes of the present business scene. Carl N. Degler, a professor of history at Vassar College, makes the point in *The Woman in America,* that the present immobility of women in business is as much the result of industrialization as it is a planned strategy on the part of the male hierarchy. The technology which produced our industrialization not only made female employment possible in formerly all male occupations, but it also created whole new areas of office skills to support the operations. Males were not able to meet this demand for new labor. Women were well suited for this type of job and represented a rich untapped source of labor. Consequently, women inherited sole possession of this "by-product" of industrialization. Over the years, they developed this inheritance into a self-contained almost self-sufficient community. In very large corporations, the clerical staffs exist as large sub-cultures complete with their own traditions, and mores. The responsibility of the male executive to this community has been the encouragement and strengthening of the community so that it might retain a certain amount of cultural identity. Having accomplished this, he then must ensure that the sub-culture is submissive to the larger culture of the corporation. This is usually accomplished through various bribes such as salary increases or "female" fringe benefits like pregnancy leaves or day care centers or luncheon "dates".

This is why the more militant feminists are correct in their contention that more substantive accommodations are needed if the basic sub-culture is going to be altered. There must be a breaking down of the "imperialistic" attitudes and practices of the male hierarchy. These tend to exploit the richness of a dominant sub-culture. In this case the clerical staff, and thus women, are little better than the "heathen" of the 19th century who were maintained to serve the interests of colonizing power. An attitude typical of this thinking appeared in a British business magazine.[3] The editor paternalistically granted the validity of some of the feminist demands and then proceeded to judge the movement as a whole as "unrealistic." Further, he suggested that "what the women still need most of all is to aspire higher," presumably to the heights of the men.

6.1.6   William Whyte, Jr., the *Fortune* magazine editor who was catapulted to national prominence with the publication of *The Organization Man,* seems to agree that the large corporation has become a master at manipulating its employees both on and off the job. In the essay, "The Wife Problem," he carefully shows how the corporation courts the wife of the executive so that more efficient service might be received from the husband. Playing on base emotions of greed, need for security, sexuality and social pressure, the executive wife is used as a pawn in the corporate chess game.

The area of business that has been the most responsible for the dehumanization of women according to the activists is that of advertising. Articles like the one by Midge Kovacs, "Women's Lib: Do's and Don'ts for Ad Men,"[4] have fallen on deaf ears. Little chance is there that the ad men are going to abandon their gold mine simply because it is destroying the employment environment.

In short, many businesses large and small have not responded very favorably to suggestions which would tamper with their mechanical android made in the image of dehumanized man. Even less will they welcome any alterations in the character of the sexy secretary. Any effort to replace the existing relationship between employer and employee, presently and all too often, I—it, to a more meaningful relationship of I—thou, will be handled with both distrust and suspicion. Advocates of women's rights should move very slowly before they laud any seemingly favorable concession on the part of big business. Several articles have appeared in leading business magazines making it clear that business was just a bit stunned by the recent waves of militant radicals. Many concessions appear to have been reached out of fear and a lack of strategy to deal with the circumstances. It would be a very grave mistake to interpret a concession on the part of business as a weakening of position. Quite the contrary, the leading men of business have been collecting resources and planning strategy for the next encounter at which there will be fewer concessions you can be sure. The simplest way for an employer to deal with the problem is so obvious as to be ridiculous: 1. tell the truth and 2. treat each employee with whom you come in contact as a person.

Since expansion and promotion within a company is closely tied to that firm's relative success on the market, and that in turn is involved with the general economic picture, demands for job betterment in a bear market are very unrealistic. Many of the feminists have recognized this and see the only way out as an economic restructuring of society. A few of the radicals advocate a Cuban type socialism but since none of the communist countries have broken any records in advancing women to top positions (see the article beginning 2.4.1) it is doubtful that it would really answer the problem. The pressure to equalize men's and women's wages for the same job has met token resistance on the surface although a deep dark current of discontent runs beneath. Federal law is moving in the equalizing direction and no real negative advocacy has arisen. But then the hard core of masculine labor, the craft unions, have not yet been threatened.

6.1.7 In government there are no women yet in top appointive positions in the executive branch. There may be few yet ready for the responsibility of such a position because of the fact that there are none at the next level of government either. The most likely path to change is still the ballot box and as yet only representatives Chisholm and Abzug have made the grade. With the exception of the irrepressible Jeannette Rankin, most of the women sent to congress or senate have been staunch conservatives. It is not clear just how much pressure more women in the government would have. Those in the Department of Justice are taking a slow but determined effect, which has not been supported by any recent administration. Public journalistic combats over these activities are rare and usually couched in legalese when they do appear. The likelihood is that the government, both federal and state, will acquiesce to the hiring of more women professionals, physicians, attorneys, technicians and the like. By virtue of their long years of education and more open

outlook, the majority of these women favor the movement and will continue to support its aims. Some masculine comment and premonition of this potential has been published and a few editorials and letters in *Science* and the journals of the various professional societies have demonstrated its existence.

It is in the media that the active feminist has made her biggest splash to date. It became very clear in the late 60's that if risque women made good copy, angry women made even better copy. This assumption was reinforced by the sales of the first few feminist books to hit the market. Strange as it may seem, *The Sensous Woman* and *The Female Eunuch* were competing with each other in sales at about the same time. One wonders if they both had some basic common appeal. In the name of spreading the word, many publishers vied with each other to snap up the latest marketable woman's viewpoint book. However the clang of the cash register was not totally drowned out in their ears. While the early women's newspapers were radical and decidedly underground, the later wave of new women's magazines are actively exploiting the feminist mood in the time-honored consumeristic fashion. This fact has been strangely missing from most reviews of the new glossy ladies' literature. The surprising thing is that so many sober male commentators took these female fulminations in the new slicks at face value and did not see through them as business ventures. While the print media has embraced the material and the profits from the women's movement, the electronic media have been much slower to deal with it. It may be that some fear of Mc Luhanesque mind-bending is involved but it is more likely that the T.V. imagery has not yet found a style and a livery which can be readily identified with the movement. The usual way that T.V. meets the challenge of minority viewpoints is to place the two standard stereotyped characters in opposition and then have them go through a quick dialectic interchange of responsibility. This technique was pioneered by such shows as "Gunsmoke," in which the hero and the villain would interchange roles, at first the one guilty and then the other until the real protagonist, fate, brought the show to an end just in time for the closing commercial. In Black/White and White/Black comedy and drama situations some of the same methodology has worked to alternate the expected Black aspects to the White character and the characteristics of the White to the Black, by this means confrontation can be solved in reconciliation. In many such film and T.V. situations a least common interest is found, usually sex or money, but in the women's liberation movement such goals simply will not work and this is what frustrates the Hugh Hefners and the television networks. After the violence of the 60's American T.V. fare slumped into an era of saccharin situation comedies, symbolized in the substitution of a canned *Lucy* episode for the Senate Foreign Relations Committee Hearings on the Viet Nam War. If the war, some 12,000 miles away was too hot to handle, the women's movement right here at home was a whole magnitude worse. The television newsmedia method for handling the problem has been to only publicize marches, demonstrations and political speeches. Only on an occasional talkshow has the basic claim of women's liberation come up for airing. The reaction of the hosts have been interesting. Most of them have taken a strictly two-valued orientation, they have agreed to economic demands within limits, but they have rejected the basic arguments on which those demands are based. Generally the interlocutors have attempted to see and portray the movement as another minority group seeking its day in the sun. With the quasi-liberal paternalism charac-teristic of network broadcasting, the movement is given its due. However this is not enough and does great violence to the principles of the movement. The result of this policy has been that a stable or harem of acceptable feminine spokeswomen have emerged, all of them are glamorous, highly photogenic, and capable of bantering about the popular phrases such as "sexual repression," "sexist society," and the like. Some heavy hands like Bob Hope and John Wayne have failed to play the game and actually lashed out at their feminist enemies as radicals. These antagonists portray the leaders of the movement as radical provocateurs only one step removed from the Weathermen and the Maoist revolu-tionaries. There is much evidence that the first wave of the new feminism did attract the disgruntled and largely unsuccessful cadres of radical women and girls from the fading new left of the 60's, however they make up a very small proportion of the movement. The outcome of the women's assault upon the electronic media is still in doubt, and much resolution of the fray is yet to come.

6.1.8 It is in the religious institutions that the real death struggle of the women's rights revolution will take place. Although both of the great religious traditions of Western man appeared in antiquity, both Judaism and Christianity as practiced in the world of today were formed in the high middle ages. The Judaism of Europe and America is slowly leaving behind its Rabbinic tradition and moving towards a modern interpretation which will be brought together in Israel. However this has not yet happened and so the character of Diaspora worship is still flourishing throughout the urban environments of the great democracies. The Judaism of the medieval period was learned, introverted, and imbued with sacerdotalism. This last quality is based upon the concept that some one individual or group of individuals has the right and authority to dispense God's grace to other members of the community. This can be in the form of a physical sign, as the anointment of the Torah, or it can be a decision of law or legal interpretation, as the Responsa of Spanish Jewry. In Jewish tradition, the priest, or *kohen,* the Rabbi, or the Talmudic scholar, were all men. Shulamith Firestone and other Jewish feminists have fled to Marxism to escape the consequences of this tradition. But like it or not, of all the world's religions, Judaism remains the most masculine. This has not prohibited women of great ability from becoming leaders of Jewish thought, and Israel is the only country with a women political head of world stature in Mrs. Golda Meir. However the sacerdotal character of the male in the Jewish family and in the Torah-study, the synagogue, did not prohibit private views in religion. Even though Moses Maimonides rationalized Judaism along the Neo-Aristotelian model, his system was not accepted by anywhere near a majority as dogma.

In the Roman and Greek catholic traditions of Christianity the same sacerdotal concept held sway. In the Latin church it took the form of the papal see with its view of the Bishop of Rome as the true vicar of Christ upon earth and the ulti-mate dispenser of God's grace through the means of the seven sacraments which only he could rightly enact. The possession of this power was to be the central point of conflict between the ecclesiastical and secular authorities throughout the long centuries from the Fall of Rome to the Renaissance, (400 to 1400 A.D.) Following the blue print of Augustine set down in his *City of God,* the church reinforced feudalism as the proper form of European society. In the feudal system three classes or estates of man were defined, at the top looking down benignly but watchfully was God. Each of the three classes or estates of mankind was predestined to their station and each had a divine right to its obligations and privileges, if there were any. The three classes thus blessed were: I. the royalty, the king and his kinsmen, and all those raised to royal rank. II. the clergy, the ordained priests who swore oaths of poverty, chastity, and obedience to mother church. III. the commoner who had a dual obligation to be pious toward the church and loyal to the royal establishment. One notes immediately that aside from wifedom and motherhood this is a completely masculine social order. The church left one ambivalent way out, a woman could renounce marriage and sexuality and the pains of childbirth and take orders as a nun in the church. This dual attitude toward the state of women plagued the church all the way up to its dogma. There Mary, the mother of Christ, was worshipped both as virgin and mother simultaneously. A woman could follow her in either but not both situations. This difficulty with the sacerdotal place of women is the root of the modern church's stand on two very controversial topics of prime importance to the liberation movement: birth control and abortion. Since in the medieval scheme of things paternity determined one's station in life and primogeniture (being the first born child) determined whether you would be king or pauper, servant or served, the legal preservation of sexual purity and the continuance of the inherited line were thought to be very important to civilization. Added to this was the Greek philosophical concept that the physical, the bodily, was somewhat less worthy than the mental and spiritual. For the Greek, knowledge was virtue and brute muscle was inherently evil and gross. The good body had to fulfill its functions but only at the disgust of the soul. In medieval Christian thought, the metaphysical sphere became the religious or realm of grace and the body became the natural sphere or realm of nature. This is what led to the denial of the body as seen in the severity and abstraction of medieval art. Of all the bodily functions, the most pernicious was sex. Since it was the women of the world who had the monthly cycle, conceived and bore the children, their lives were substantially more sexual than the male. And furthermore the Book of Genesis taught that it was through Eve, the first woman, that the knowledge of good and evil entered human experience, and the medieval church took that knowledge to be carnal, sexual knowledge. Johann Huizinga and other European scholars have masterfully examined the whole phenomenon of courtly love, chivalry, and unrequited affection which grew up in the society which was built on such ideas. In the rapid revolutionary changes which came about with the Protestant Reformation, the Enlightenment, and

the French Revolution the place of women rebounded violently from the ideal of Madam Pompadour on one hand to Charlotte Corday on the other. In literature, *Pamela* vied with *Moll Flanders*. The rationalism of the eighteenth century gave way to the romanticism of the nineteenth and overnight the Grecian respect for cool, calculating human relationships and common interest sexuality was out and the disparaged medieval chivalry was back in. One of the finest sources of the image of womanhood as dictated by popular culture in this period is seen in grand opera. The stage was filled with maudlin romances, and sinful, suffering Mimis, Gildas, and Margaretes were in the center of fashion. This ideal of womanhood was continued among the white upper-class of the American South. It is against this background that the religious tension at the heart of women versus the church was bound to come about.

6.1.9 The pressure of women's rage is beginning to take its toll on the churches and in Europe at least a whole generation raised on psychology and science has turned its back on the claims of the clergy. Very recently certain theologians have begun to see the hand writing on the wall, and noted that the hand was female. Father James A. O'Brien, motivated by the concessions of Vatican II, has tried to rewrite the formation of the Roman Catholic church's position on women. He sees it rooted in a paganism of Greek origin which was concocted together with Christian notions by the Thirteenth Century scholar, St. Thomas, author of the church's basic position paper, the *Summa Theologia*. Whether or not this kind of hindsight will save the day is doubtful and more changes are likely to come in the political maneuvers of church councils.

The protestant donominations which sprung up in the Sixteenth Century and have continued to fracture until the present are much more susceptible to any new minority viewpoint. They went through the rationalist period and managed to make their doctrines appeal to the rising industrial middle class which came to power in North America about the turn of the last century. However, protestantism has been slowly losing ground among the intellectual class and the poor and disadvantaged ever since the First World War. The backbone of the protestant churches is the middle class, white, anglo-saxon woman. The very woman despised or sought, depending upon the author, by the writers of the women's movement. The protestant denominations all defer to what are basically feminine viewpoints. The major thrust of protestantism was hammered out by the romantic thinkers and writers of the last century and the design of the church, the music and rituals, even the social organization of the churches dates from the mid-nineteenth century. The dynamic officialdom of almost all the stated protestant denominations is feminine. When the shift from preaching to teaching in the protestant environment came in the 1920's, the new office of teacher whether as trained religious education director or foreign missionary, was held by women by over 71%.

The theological fragmentation of protestantism which left it with a liberal hierarchy and a conservative following, brought down the kind of dogmatic statement of truth which had held the Roman church together for millennia. It was replaced with a general sense of humanitarianism which produced the "social gospel," the "red cross" and such organized philanthropies as the Girl Scouts and the Y.M.C.A. Unfortunately however the sense of duty and the need-goodness that these organizations embraced was largely defined by the establishment and its norms. The Black, Yellow, Indian and all other races and cultures were all treated as disadvantaged. The soft underbelly of protestantism was open to any attack and irresistible to politicization.

One could say that the women of the western world built the protestant church and that now some of them are unhappy with their handiwork. It is to be expected that before long a new strong wave will again take the protestant institutions by storm, this will be a feminist theology. Since almost all protestant sects ordain and elect women to the highest councils of their hierarchy the rise of a new women's view will be forthcoming, it is only a matter of when. The battle within these organizations and on the pages of their publications, *Presbyterian Life*, *Together*, *The Lutheran*, and the independent *Christian Century*, is already looming as the struggle between the old feminist control and the new.

The fundamentalist church groups, which often play a quieter role in American life are equally dominated by women of the middle class but not as obviously. Most of them still refuse to actually ordain women, but since they do not possess a sacerdotal clergy or priesthood this is a meaningless distinction. The fact that the overwhelming majority of readers of fundamentalist literature, members of fundamentalist organizations, and paid employees of fundamentalist groups are women is sufficiently eloquent to establish the point of where the power lies.

Among the educated classes in the U.S., the shift has been away from organized religion toward experiential religious expressions dominated not by theology but by psychology. It is at this point that the women's liberation movement encounters its most devastating critics, the professionally trained, women social or behavioral scientists who have made a successful entrance into the established male institutions and reject the movement. They are specially equipped to turn the weapons and grounds of psychology and sociology back upon their sisters in the movement. As the first onrush of the movement wanes, this viewpoint will grow rapidly and so the movement may well finish up feeding on its own momentum. If we understand religion as the basic presuppositional stance which each individual human being takes intuitively to explan his presence and position in time and space, then what we see here is a holy war as deep and deadly as any crusade. The weapons are not the Word of Jehovah against the Word of Allah, but the data and interpretations of Freud set against those of Horney and Adler and Maurer. In this combat a mere mortal man had best keep silent.

Mr. Robert Tuten
Sommers Point, N.J.

REFERENCES

1. *Playboy* (January 1972).
2. *Human Events* (January 8, 1972).

3. *The Economist* (April 3, 1971).
4. *Marketing/Communications* (January 1971).

Chapter 7

A Selected and Annotated Directory and Bibliography to Women's Liberation

The references below are in alphabetical order by key word, usually the last name of the principal author, the first name of the sponsoring agency, or the first word in the title of a journal, magazine, newsletter, or other periodical. All of the local groups and publishers listed do or did at one time publish and distribute papers of the movement on a regular sale or subscription basis. Some of the dates are speculative as not all shorter papers, books and the like are copyrighted. Slight inconsistencies in the style of the reference citations will be noted but the editors have tried to give all known information about a source rather than simply follow a particular format. In instances where an article has been reprinted many times by the movement press, the original author and the earliest citation has been included, in some few instances this material was not available. In the next few years a corpus of writings important to the history of the feminist movement of the nineteenth century as well as the twentieth will appear as more and more scholars and students research women's studies. The list of authors of literary works listed here are those found on the great preponderance of reading lists for the subject. For further or more precise information the reader is encouraged to check the author listings in the *Library of Congress Card Catalogue,* or to correspond with one of the research groups listed below.

Andrews, Charles McLean
Colonial Folkways; a Chronicle of American Life in the Reign of the Georges
New Haven: Yale University Press (1919)

Andrews, E. W.
Journal of a Lady of Quality
New Haven: Yale University Press (1923)

Andrews, John B. and W. D. P. Bliss
History of Women in Trade Unions
Senate Documents #645 X 61st Congress, 2nd Session
Washington, D.C.: U.S. Government Printing Office (1911)

The Annals of the American Academy of Political and Social Science
(entire issue devoted to women)
(May 1929)

Anthology of New Research, Analysis, and Thinking About Women,
6031 S. Kimbark, Chicago, Ill.

Anthology of Women's Oppression
Crescent
6278 Cates, 3E Union City, Mo. 63130

Anthony, Katherine
Louisa May Alcott
New York (1938)

Anthony, Katherine
Margaret Fuller: A Psychological Biography
New York (1920)

Anthony, Katherine
First Lady of the Revolution: a Life of Mercy Otis Warren
Garden City, New York (1958)

Anthony, Katherine
Mothers Who Must Earn
New York (1914)

Anthony, Katherine
Out of the Kitchen, Into the War
New York (1943)

Aonghusa, Proinsias Mac
"Ireland's Divorce Battle"
New Statesman
(December 27, 1967)

Aphra (literary magazine),
Formerly Box 355, Springtown, Pa. 18081, now P.O. Box 273, Village Station, N.Y., N.Y. 10014.
A very valuable source of creative writing from the movement.

Aries, Philippe
Centuries of Childhood: A Social History of Family Life
Widely cited study by a demographic historian-sociologist which concerns the treatment of children and the growth of the "concept of the family" during the development of western civilization. Drawing his conclusions from references in French historical documents and from works of art, Aries declares that a conjugal family existed but had no importance until the fifteenth or sixteenth centuries.

Armes, Ethel, ed.
Nancy Shippen: Her Journal Book; The International Romance of a Young Lady of Fashion of Colonial Philadelphia, with Letters To Her and About Her.
Philadelphia (1935)

ASC Newsletter
Abortion Counciling Service
P.O. Box 9199, San Diego, California 92109

ASSOCIATION FOR THE STUDY OF ABORTION, INC. (ASA)
120 W. 57th Street, New York, New York 10019 (212) CI-5-2360

Association of American Colleges
"Project on the Status & Education of Women"
1818 R Street N.W.
Washington, D.C. 20009

Astin, Helen S., Nancy Suniewick and Susan Dweck
Women: a Bibliography on their Education and Careers
Washington: Human Service Press (1971)

Astin, Helen S.
The Woman Doctorate in America
New York: Russell Sage Foundation (1969)
A sociological study of women who received the PhD during the years 1957 and 1958. The study was done after a seven to eight year time lapse to allow career patterns to develop. Of the women studied, admittedly privileged women, ninety-one percent were employed at the time of the study. They cited household duties and differential pay scales as their main obstacles in establishing satisfying life patterns. The author concludes the study with a set of "policy implications" similar to those offered by many other sociologically oriented writers in recent years.

Auchincloss, Louis
Pioneers and Caretakers: A Study of Nine American Woman Novelists
Minneapolis: University of Minnesota Press (1965)

Auerbach, Erich
Mimesis
Princeton: Princeton University Press (1953)

Auerbach, Stuart
"Women Disrupt Hearing on the Pill"
Washington Post
(January 24, 1970)

Austen, Jane
Emma
New York (1957)

Austen, Jane
Northanger Abbey
New York (1934)

Austen, Jane
Persuasion
New York (1965)

Austin, Mary
A Woman of Genius
Garden City, New York (1912)

The Autobiography of St. Therese of Lisieux: The Story of a Soul
trans. John Beevers
Garden City, N.Y. (1957)

Awake & Move
P.O. Box 19826, Philadelphia, Pa. 19143

Baistow, Tom
"Miss Keeler and the Establishment"
New Statesman
(October 10, 1969)

Baker, Elizabeth
Technology and Woman's Work
New York: Columbia University Press (1964)

Baker, Helen
Women in War Industries
Princeton, N.J.: Princeton University Press (1942)

Baker, Laura
Wanted: Women in War Industry
New York, (1943)

Balzac, Honore'
Le Lys dans La Valleé
Paris (1961)

Banks, Ann
"Present Company Excepted"
Brown Alumni Monthly
18-23 (1971)

Abbott, Edith
"Harriet Martineau and the Employment of Women in 1836"
Journal of Political Economy
XIV 614 (1906)

Abbott, Edith
Women in Industry: A Study in American Economic History
New York (1910)

"Abortion and the Changing Law"
Newsweek
(April 13, 1970)

Achebe, Chinua
Things Fall Apart
New York (1969), (c. 1959)

Ackerman, Louise M.
" 'Lady' as a synonym for 'woman' "
American Speech XXXVII 284 (1962)

Act Now
7460 N. Sheridan Road, Chicago, Ill. 60600

Acworth, Evelyn
The New Matriarchy
London (1965)

Adams, Charles F.
"Some Phases of Sexual Morality and Church Discipline in Colonial New England"
Proceeding of the Massachusetts Historical Society, 2nd series (1890)

Adams, Henry
Democracy, an American Novel
Greenwich, Connecticut (1961)

Adams, Henry
Esther
New York (1938)

Adams, Horace
"A Puritan Wife on the Frontier"
Mississippi Valley Historical Review XXVII 67-84 (1941)

Adams, Mildred
The Right to be People
Philadelphia (1967)

Addams, Jane
Democracy and Social Ethics
ed. Anne Firor Scott
Cambridge, Mass: Harvard University Press (1964)

Addams, Jane
Second Twenty Years at Hull House
New York (1930)

Addams, Jane
Twenty Years at Hull House
New York (1932), (c. 1912)

Ain't I A Woman Publications
Collective of the Iowa City Women's Liberation Front
301 Jefferson Building, Iowa City, Iowa 52240

Akamai Sister Hawaii Women's Liberation
Box 11042, Honolulu, Hawaii 96814

Akhmadulina, Bella Akhatanova
Fever and Other New Poems
(New York (1969)

Akhmatova, A.
Selected Poems
New York: Oxford University Press (1969)

Alcott, Louisa Mae
Little Men
New York (1963)

Alcott, Louisa Mae
Little Women
New York (1962)

Aldrich, D. G., Jr.
Research for the World Food Crisis
Washington, D.C. American Association for the Advancement of Science, publication #92 (1970)

Aldridge, John
In Search of Heresy; American Literature in an Age of Controversy
New York (1956)

Aldridge, Leslie
"7,000,000 American Women Take the Pill"
Esquire
(January 1969)

Alexander, Anne
"Who's Come a Long Way, Baby?"
The Johns Hopkins Magazine (1970)

Allen, David D.
The Price of Women
New York (1971)

Alliance Link
Equal Rights Alliance, 5256 Fairmount Ave., Downers Grove, Ill. 60515 or 1649 W. Touchy, Chicago, Ill. 60626

Alternatives (Now)
Olin Hall 809, 4550 Scott Ave., St. Louis, Mo. 63110

Alternative Press Index
Carelton College, Northfield, Minn.

Altshuler, Nathan
"Linguistic forms as symbols of people"
International Journal of American Linguistics, 22.2 106-112 (1936)

American Anthropology Association Commission on the Status of Women
Columbia University
Anthropology Department, Columbia University
New York, N.Y. 10027

American Friends Service Committee
Who Shall Live? Man's Control Over Birth and Death; a Report
New York (1970)

Amundsen, Kirsten
The Silenced Majority
Englewood Cliffs, New Jersey (1971)

Anderson, Mary
Woman at Work
Minneapolis: Univ. of Minnesota Press (1951)

Andre, le Chapelain (Capellanus, Andreas)
The Art of Courtly Love
ed. F. W. Lock
New York: Columbia University Press (1941)

Andreas, Carol
Sex and Caste in America
Englewood Cliffs, N.J. (1971)
A sociological study of the relations between the sexes in which the author shows that social class, historical events, the technological nature of a society, and the remnants of past cultural development affect the "power-dependence relationships" which exist between men and women. The result is a blurring of the relationships which might exist and a distortion of the nature of men and women. Therefore, the author concludes that a valid assessment of male-female roles and differences is impossible until both halves of the human race have real equality of opportunity. The author examines the caste system which has developed over the centuries as it is shaped by schools, the economic system, religious orders, business corporations, and the nuclear family.

Andrews and Bliss
History of Women in Trade Unions
New York (1938)

Banks, J. A. and Olive
Feminism and Family Planning in Victorian England
Liverpool: Liverpool University Press (1964)

Banks, James Ambrose
Prosperity and Parenthood: a Study of Family Planning Among the Victorian Middle Classes
London (1954)

Banning, Margaret Culkin
Women for Defense
New York (1942)

Bardwick, Judith M., Douvan, Horner, and Gutmann
Feminine Personality and Conflict
Belmont, Calif. (1970)

Barnes, Djuna
The Antiphon
New York (1958)

Barnes, Djuna
Nightwood
New York: New Directions (1949) (c. 1937)

Barth, John
The End of the Road
Garden City, N.Y. (1967)

Barthelme, D.
Snow White
New York (1967)

Battis, Emery
Saints and Secretaries
Chapel Hill: University of North Carolina Press (1962)

Battle Acts
YAWF Women, 58 W. 25th St., New York, N.Y. 10010

"The Battle of the Hemline"
Newsweek
(March 16, 1970)

Baudelaire, Charles
Les Fleurs du Mal 2 vols. New York (1961)

Bayer, Alan E., and Helen S. Astin
"Sex Differences in Academic Rank and Salary Among Science Doctorates in Teaching"
Journal of Human Resources, 3-191-200 (1968)

Bayer, Charles, K. Clouser, John Moore, John Pamperi
"Is Abortion a Right?"
Christian Century
(May 20, 1970)

Beach, Frank A., Ed.
Sex and Behavior
New York: Wiley (1965)

Beard, Mary R.
American Through Women's Eyes
New York: MacMillan Co. (1933)

Beard, Mary Ritter
A Changing Political Economy as it Affects Women
Washington, D.C.: American Association of University Women (1934)

Beard, Mary Ritter
On Understanding Women
New York (1931)

Beard, Mary R.
Woman as Force in History
New York (1946)

Bebel, August
Women Under Socialism
New York: New York Labor News Press (1904)

Becker, Gary S.
Human Capital
New York: Columbia University Press (1964)

Becker, Gary S.
The Economics of Discrimination
Chicago: University of Chicago Press (1964)

Becker, Gary
"A Theory of the Allocation of Time"
Economic Journal
(September, 1965)

Bedier, Joseph
The Romance of Tristan and Iseult
New York (1964)

Beecher, Catherine A.
Essay on Slavery and Abolitionism, with Reference to the Duty of American Females
Philadelphia: Henry Perkins (1837)

Beecher, Catherine A.
Treatise on Domestic Economy
New York: Harper (1846)

Beecher, Catherine and Harriet Beecher Stowe
The American Woman's Home: a guide to the formation and maintenance of economical, healthful, beautiful, and Christian homes
New York: J. B. Ford and Co. (1869)

Belden, Thomas and Marva Robins Belden
So Fell the Angels
Boston, (1956)

Bell, Mrs. Margaret Van Horn (Dwight)
A Journey to Ohio in 1810
New Haven: Yale University Press (1913)

Bell, Norman W. and Ezra F. Vogel
A Modern Introduction to the Family
New York (1968), (c. 1960)

Bell, Robert
Premarital Sex in a Changing Society
Englewood Cliffs, N.J. (1966)

Bender, Marilyn
"The Women Who'd Trade in Their Pedestal for Total Equality"
The New York Times
(February 4, 1970)

Benedek, Therese (Friedmann)
Psychosexual Functions in Women
New York (1952)

Bennett, John
Strictures on Female Education, Chiefly as it Relates to the Culture of the Heart
Philadelphia: W. Spotswood and H. P. Rice (1793)

Bennett, Margaret
Alice in Wonderland, or the Feminine Mistake
Englewood Cliffs, N.J. (1967)

Benston, Margaret
"Political Economy of Women's Liberation"
Monthly Review
(September, 1969)

Benson, Mary
Women in the 18th Century America
Port Washington, N.Y.: Kennikat Press (1966), (c.1935)

Benston, Margaret
"The Political Economy of Women's Liberation"
All We are Saying . . . : The Philosophy of the New Left
ed. Arthur Lothstein
New York (1971)

Berelson, Bernard
"Beyond Family Planning"
Science 533-543
(February 7, 1969)

Berkeley Women's Liberation Basement Press
P.O. Box 6323, Albany, Calif. 94706

Bernard, Jesse
Academic Women
University Park: Pennsylvania
State University Press (1964)

Bernard, Jesse
American Family Behavior
New York and London (1942)

Bernard, Jesse
The Future of Marriage
New York (1971)

Bernard, Jesse
*Marriage and Family Among
Negroes*
Englewood Cliffs, N.J. (1966)

Bernard, Jesse
Remarriage: A Study of Marriage
New York (1956)

Bernard, Jesse
The Sex Game
Englewood Cliffs, N.J. (1968)

Bernstein, Irving
*The Lean Years: a History of the
American Worker, 1920-1933*
Boston (1960)

Beroza, Morton (ed.)
*Chemicals Controlling Insect
Behavior*
New York (1970)

Berreman, Gerald
"Caste as Social Process"
*Southwestern Journal of
Anthropology* XXIII (1967)

Best, Mary Agnes
Rebel Saints
New York (1925)

Bettelheim, Bruno
Children of the Dream
New York (1969)

Bettelheim, Bruno
"Growing Up Female"
Harper's (October, 1962)

Beyond the Looking Glass
c/o Joanne Frankfurt, Associated
Students, UCSB
Santa Barbara, Calif. 93106

Bibliography of Women's Writers
Joyce Nower, Center for
Women's Studies, San Diego
State College, San Diego, Calif.

Bibliography on Abortion
Assoc. for the Study of Abortion
120 W. 57th St., New York, N.Y.
10019

Bibliography on Women's Movement
Sherry Fyman, 168-24 127th
Ave., Jamaica, N.Y. 11434

Bibliography on 20th Century Women

Writers who Write About Women
Bread and Roses, 1151 Mass.
Ave., Cambridge, Mass.

**Biddle, Bruce Jessee and
Edwin J. Thomas, Ed.**
*Role Teory: Concept and
Research*
New York (1966)

Bird, Carolina
*Born Female: High Cost of
Keeping Women Down*
New York (1968)

Birney, Catherine H.
The Grimke' Sisters
Boston: Lee and Shepard
Publishers (1885)

Blackburn, Helen
*Woman's Suffrage: A Record of
the Women's Suffrage Movement
in the British Isles*
London (1902)

Black Women's Alliance
c/o St. Peter's Church, 346 W.
20th St., New York, N.Y.

Blackwell, Alice Stone
*Lucy Stone, Pioneer of Women's
Rights*
Boston (1930)

Blackwell, Elizabeth
*Pioneer Work in Opening the
Medical Profession to Women*
New York: E. P. Dutton & Co.
(1895)

Blake, Judith
"Demographic Science and the
Redirection of Population
Policy"
Journal of Chronic Diseases,
XVIII, 1181-1200 (1965)

Blanchard, Phyllis
New Girls for Old
New York: Macaulay Co. (1930)

Blatch, Harriet and Alma Lutz
*Challenging Years; the Memoirs
of Harriet Stanton Blatch*
New York (1940)

**Blatch, Harriet, Stanton and
Theodore Stanton, Ed.**
*Elizabeth Cady Stanton as
Revealed in her Letters, Diary
and Reminiscences*
New York: Harpers and
Brothers (1922)

Blease, Walter Lyon
*The Emancipation of English
Women*
London: D. Nutt (1913)

**Blood, Robert O. and
Donald M. Wolfe**
*Husbands and Wives: the
Dynamics of Married Living*
Glencoe, Ill. (1960)

Blood, Robert O.
"Long-Range Causes and
Consequences of the
Employment of Married
Women"
*Journal of Marriage and the
Family*, XXVII, no. 1

Blumenthal, Walter Hart
*Brides from Bridewell: Female
Felons Sent to Colonial America*
Rutland, Vt. (1962)

Blumenthal, Walter Hart
*Women Campfollower of the
American Revolution*
Philadelphia (1952)

Boas, Louise Schutz
*Woman's Education Begins; the
Rise of the Women's Colleges*
Norton, Mass.: Wheaton College
Press (1935)

Bode, Carl
"Columbia's Carnal Bed"
American Quarterly (Spring, 1963)

Bodkin, Maud
*Archetypal Patterns in Poetry;
Psychological Studies of
Imagination*
London: Oxford University Press
(1934)

Bolitho, William
"The New Skirt Length"
Harper's (February, 1930)

Books for Women's Liberation
c/o Lenora Lloyd London
Socialist Woman Group
40 Inverness Rd., Southall,
Middx., London, England

Boone, Gladys
*The Woman's Trade Union League
in Great Britain and the United
States of America*
New York: Columbia University
Press (1942)

Borgese, Elizabeth Mann
Ascent of Women
New York (1963)

Boring, Edwin G.
"The Woman Problem"
American Psychologist, VI,
679-682 (December, 1961)

Boserup, Ester
*Woman's Role in Economic
Development*
London (1970)

Bott, Alan and Irene Clephane
Our Mothers
London (1932)

Bowen, Elizabeth
The Death of the Heart
New York (1939)

Bowen, Elizabeth
The House in Paris
New York (1936)

Bowen, Louise De Koven
Growing Up with a City
New York: MacMillan Co. (1926)

Bowen, William G. and T. Aldrich Finegan
The Economics of Labor Force Participation
Cambridge: Princeton University Press (1969)

Bowman, Garda
"Executive Attitudes Toward Female Executives"
Harvard Business Review
(July-August, 1965)

Bowman, G. W., Worthy, N. B., Greyser, S. A.
"Are Women Executives People?"
Harvard Business Review
(July-August, 1965)

Bowman, H. Woods
"More Working Wives, Fewer Children"
Business Conditions, 7-12
(August, 1970)

Boyle, Kay
Thirty Stories
New York: New Directions
(1957)

Bradford, Sarah
Harriet Tubman—The Moses of Her People
New York: Corinth Books, Inc.
(1961)

Brady, Anne Hazelwood
Unfinished Conversations
New York (1970)

Brady, Nyle C., Ed.
Agriculture and The Quality of Our Environment
Washington, D.C.: American Association for the Advancement of Science (1967)

Branch, Edward Douglas
Sentimental Years
New York (1965) (c.1962)

Bread and Roses
c/o Old Mole, 2 Brookline St., Cambridge, Mass.

Breasted, Mary
Oh! Sex Education
New York (1970)

Brecher, Ruth and Edward
An Analysis of Human Sexual Response
New York (1966)

Brecher, Ruth and Edward Brecher
An Analysis of Human Sexual Response
New York (1967)

Breckinridge, Sophonisba P.
Marriage and the Civic Rights of Women
Chicago; University of Chicago Press (1931)

Bremer, Fredrika
Homes of the New World; Impressions of America
trans. Mary Howitt
New York: Harper & Bros. (1853)

Brewster, Dorothy
Doris Lessing
New York (1965)

Bridenbaugh, Carl
Myth and Realities: Societies of the Colonial South
Baton Rouge: Louisiana State University Press (1952)

Bridges, William
"Family Patterns and Social Values in America, 1825-1875"
American Quarterly, XVII, 3-11
(n.d.)

Brien, Alan
"Anyone for Polygamy?"
New Statesman
(December 6, 1968)

Brien, Alan
"Drag Hunt"
New Statesman
(August 8, 1969)

Briffault, Robert
The Mothers; the Matriarchal Theory of Social Origins
New York: MacMillan Co.
(1931)

Brine, Ruth
"The New Feminists: Revolt Against Sexism"
Time (November 21, 1969)

Brittain, Vera
Lady into Woman: A History of Women from Victoria to Elizabeth II
New York (1953)

Brittain, Vera Mary
Women's Work in Modern England
London: N. Douglas (1928)

Brody, Sylvia
Patterns of Mothering
New York: International University Press (1970) (c.1956)

Bromley, Dorothy Dunbar
"Feminist, New Style"
Harper's (October, 1927)

Bronte, Charlotte
Jane Eyre
New York (1971)

Bronte, Charlotte
Shirley
London (1907)

Bronte, Charlotte
Villette
New York: Oxford University Press (1954)

Bronte, Emily
Wuthering Heights
New York (1956)

Brooks, Gwendolyn
Maud Martha
New York (1953)

Brooks, Gwendolyn
Selected Poems
New York (1963)

Brooks, Thomas
"New York's Finest"
Commentary (August, 1965)

Brown, Dee
Gentle Tamers: Women in the Old Wild West
New York (1958)

Brown, Donald R.
The Role and Status of Women in the Soviet Union
New York: Teachers College Press (1968)

Brown, Herbert
The Sentimental Novel in America, 1789-1860
Durham, N.C.: Duke University Press (1940)

Brown, Lester R.
Seeds of Change: The Green Revolution and Development in the 1970's
New York (1970)

Browne, Mattie (Griffith)
Autobiography of a Female Slave
New York: Redfield (1857)

Brown, Norman O.
Life Against Death
New York (1969)

Browning, Elizabeth Barrett
Aurora Leigh; a poem in Nine Books
London: Chapman and Hall (1857)

Browning, Elizabeth Barrett
Sonnets from the Portugese
Boston: Copeland and Day (1896)

Brownlee, Jean
"Where is the Professional Woman?"
Women Lawyers Journal, LIII, no. 1
(Winter, 1967)

Brownmiller, Susan
"Best Battles are Fought by Men and Women Together"
Village Voice

Brownmiller, Susan
"Everywoman's Abortions: The Oppressor is Man"
Village Voice (March 27, 1969)

Bryant, John
Health and the Developing World
Ithaca, N.Y.: Cornell University Press (1969)

Buckley, William R.
"On the Right: Women's Lib Watching"
National Review, p. 964-65 (Sept. 8, 1970)

Bullock, Edna Dean
Selected Articles on the Employment of Women
ed. J. E. Johnson
New York: Wilson (1920) (c.1911)

Bullough, Vern L.
The History of Prostitution
New Hyde Park, N.Y. (1964)

Burney, Fanny
Evelina
New York (1965)

Butcher, Margaret Just
The Negro in American Culture
New York (1957)

Byatt, A. S.
"Life-Lies", a review of *Les Belles Images* by Simone de Beauvoir
New Statesman (January 5, 1968)

Cadbury, Edward M., Cecile Matheson, and George Shann
Women's Work and Wages; a Phase of Life in an Industrial City
Chicago: University of Chicago Press (1907)

Cade, Toni, ed.
The Black Woman
New York (1970)

Cain, Glen
Married Women in the Labor Force: An Economic Analysis
Chicago: University of Chicago Press (1966)

Cairns, David
"Musgrave Ritual"
New Statesman
(December 22, 1967)

Caldwell, Lynton Keith
Environment: A Challenge to Modern Society
New York: The Natural History Press (1970)

Calhoun, Arthur
A Social History of the American Family from Colonial Times to the Present
New York (1945) (c.1917)

Callahan, Parnell Joseph Terence (pseud.: Philip Francis)
Legal Status of Women
Dobbs Ferry, N.Y.: Oceana Publications (1963)

Callahan, Sidney Cornelia
The Illusion of Eve: A Modern Woman's Quest for Identity
New York: Sheed and Ward (1965)

Campbell, Angus and others, ed.
The American Voter
New York (1960)

Campbell, Helen
Household Economics
New York: G. P. Putnam's (1897)

Campbell, Helen
Prisoners of Poverty
Westport, Conn. (1970)

Campbell, Joseph ed.
Myths, Dreams and Religions
New York: E. P. Dutton & Co. n.d.

Canary, Betty
Surviving as a Woman
New York: Regnery (1970)

Caplow, Theodore
The Sociology of Work
New York (1954)

Caprie, Frank S.
Female Homosexuality
New York: Citidel Press (1954)

Carr, Edward Hallet
The Romantic Exiles; a Nineteenth-Century Portrait Gallery
Boston: Beacon Press (1933)

Carroll, Paul
"What's a Warhol?"
Playboy (September, 1969)

Carson, Josephine
Silent Voices: the Southern Negro Woman Today
New York: Delacorte Press (1969)

Cassara, Beverly Benner, ed.
American Women: The Changing Image
New York: Beacon Press (1962)

Catalyst
6 East 82nd St., New York, N.Y. 10028

Cather, Willa
My Antonia
Boston: Houghton, Mifflin (1926)

Catt, Carrie Chapman and Nettie Rogers Shuler
Woman Suffrage and Politics: The Inner Story of the Suffrage Movement
New York: Scribner's and Sons (1923)

Chamberlain, Alexander F.
"Women's Languages"
American Anthropologist, XIV, 579-581 (1912)

Chambers, Peggy
Women and the World Today
London (1954)

Chasseguet-Smirgel, Janine and others
Female Sexuality: New Psychoanalytic Views
Ann Arbor: University of Michigan Press (1970)

Cheever, John
The Brigadier and the Golf Widow
New York (1964)

Chekhov, Anton
The Oxford Chekhov
London, N.Y.: Oxford University Press (1964)

Chesnutt, Mary B.
A Diary From Dixie
Boston (1949)

Child-Care Bibliography
Women's Union Child-care Collective
241 W. 108th St., New York, N.Y. 10025

Child, Lydia Maria
History and Condition of Women in Various Ages & Nations
Boston (1835)

Chisholm, Shirley
"A Visiting Feminine Eye"
McCall's (August, 1970)

Chopin, Kate (O'Flaherty)
The Awakening and Other Stories
ed. Lewis Leary
New York (1970)

"Church, Caste and Women"
Christian Century (January 21, 1970)

Cisler, Lucinda
"A Room of One's Own: The Architecture of Choice"
Vassar Alumnae Magazine (April, 1965)

Citizen's Advisory Council on the Status of Women
American Women 1968
Washington, D.C.: U.S. Dept. of Labor (1968)

Citizen's Advisory Council on Status of Women Newsletter
U.S. Dept. of Labor
Washington, D.C. 20210

Clark, Alice
Working Life of Women in the Seventeenth Century
New York: E. P. Dutton & Co. (1919)

Clark, Kenneth
The Nude: A Study of Ideal Form
New York (1956)

Clark, Sue Ainslie and Edith Wyatt
Making Both Ends Meet: the Income and Outlay of New York Working Girls
New York: Macmillan (1911)

Cleaver, Eldridge
Soul on Ice
New York (1968)

Cloward, Richard and Francis Fox Riven
"Starving by the Rule Book"
Nation (April 3, 1967)

Coburn, Judith
"A Pyrrhic Victory for the Military"
Village Voice (October 23, 1969)

Cohen, Rosalie
"Conceptual Styles, Culture Conflict and Nonverbal Tests of Intelligence"
American Anthropologist (October, 1969)

Cohen, Rose
Out of the Shadow
New York: George H. Doran Co. (1918)

Cohen, Yehudi, ed.
Social Structure and Personality
New York (1961)

Colebrook, Jean
The Cross of Lassitude; Portraits of Five Delinquents
New York (1967)

Coleman, Elizabeth Tyler
Priscilla Cooper Tyler
Alabama: University of Alabama Press (1955)

Coleman, John
"Where She Danced"
New Statesman (March 7, 1969)

Coleman, John
"Woman's Place"
New Statesman (May 17, 1968)

Coleman, Richard P., Gerald Handel and Lee Rainwater
Workingman's Wife: Her Personality, World, and Life Style
New York: Oceana (1959)

Colette
Cheri and the Last of Cheri
New York (1953)

Colette
Claudine and Annie
London (1962)

Colette
Claudine at School
New York (1957)

Colette
Earthly Paradise
New York (1966)

Colette
Earthly Paradise, an Autobiography Drawn from Her Lifetime Writings by Robert Phelps
New York (1966)

Colette
The Vagabond
New York (1955)

Collier, James Lincoln
Language in America
New York (1969)

Collins, Sheila D.
"Women and the Church: Poor Psychology, Worse Theology"
Christian Century (December 30, 1970)

Commoner, Barry
The Closing Circle
New York (1971)

Commoner, Barry
Science and Survival
New York (1966)

Common Woman
c/o Women's Center,
1126 Addison,
Berkeley, Calif. 94704

"Conference on Women's Rights"
Christian Century (March 11, 1970)

Congress to Unite Women
(Northeast Region)
P.O. Box 114, Cathedral Station,
New York, N.Y. 10025

Connecticut Feminists in the Arts
Women Connecticut (1971)

Connecticut Valley Newsletter
Women's Liberation
207 Hampshire House,
Amherst, Mass.

Connections (Prison Widows)
330 Ellis St.,
San Francisco, Calif. 94102

Connell, Evan
Mrs. Bridge
New York (1970)

Connel, Evan S.
Review of *The Woman Destroyed* by Simone de Beauvoir
New York Times Book Review (February 23, 1969)

Conrad, Earl
Harriet Tubman
New York (1969)

"Consensual Sterilization Declared Unlawful"
ACLU News San Francisco (August, 1969)

"Conversation with Masters and Johnson"
Psychology Today (July, 1969)

Conway, Jill
"Jane Addams: An American Heroine"
Daedalus (Spring, 1964)

Cook, Anna M.
The Journal of a Milledgeville Girl, 1861-1867
Athens: University of Georgia Press (1964)

Cook, Fred
"From the Warren Commission Report: Some Unanswered Questions"
Nation (June 13, 1966)

Cook, Joanne, Charlotte Bunch-Weeks, and Robin Morgan, eds.
The New Women
New York (1971)

Coolidge, Mary Roberts
Why Women are So
New York: H. Holt (1912)

Coppen and Keasel
"Menstruation and Personality"
British Journal of Psychiatry, 109,
711-721 (1963)

Coser, Rose L., ed.
The Family: its Structure and Functions
New York (1964)

Cowan, John
The Science of a New Life
New York: J. S. Ogilvie & Co.
(1913)

Cowell, Margaret
Women and Equality
New York: Worker's Library
(1942)

Cox, Harvey
The Secular City, ch. 9 "Sex and Secularization"
New York: MacMillan (1965)

Crable, Elizabeth C.
"Pros and Cons of the Equal Rights Amendment"
Women Lawyers Journals, XXX,
no. 3
(Summer, 1949)

Craik, Dinah Mulock
A Woman's Thoughts About Women
New York (1858)

Cremin, Laurence A.
American Education: The Colonial Experience, 1607-1783
New York (1970)

Croly, Jane Cunningham
The History of the Women's Club Movement in America
New York (1898)

Cromwell, Otelia
Lucretia Mott
Cambridge: Harvard University
Press (1958)

Crook, Margaret B.
Women and Religion
Boston, (1965) (c. 1964)

Crook, Margaret Brackenbury
Women and Religion
Boston (1965)

Cross, Barbara, ed.
The Educated Woman in America
New York: Teachers College
Press (1965)

Cross, Patricia K.
"College Women: A Research Description" Paper prepared for Annual Meeting of National Association of Women Deans and Counselors.
Washington, D.C.: Mimeo (1968)

**Cuber, John Frank
and Peggy B. Haroff**
The Significant Americans: a Study of Sexual Behavior Among the Affluent
New York (1965)

Cumming, Elaine and William E. Henry
Growing Old New York (1961)

Current Women's Liberation
Material Newsletter
c/o Laura X. 2325 Oak St.,
Berkeley, Calif.

Cussler, Margaret
The Woman Executive
New York (1958)

Cuthbert, Marion Vera
Education and Marginality; a Study of the Negro Woman College Graduate
New York: Columbia University
Press (1942)

Cutler, John Henry
What About Women?
New York (1961)

CWLU News
Chicago Women's Liberation
Union
2875 W. Cermak, Rm. 9,
Chicago, Ill. 60623

Cyrus, Della
"Why Mothers Fail"
Atlantic (March, 1947)
Daedalus, (Spring, 1964)
Entire issue devoted to Women.

Daggett, Mabel
Women Wanted: The Story Written in Bood. Red Letters on the Horizon of the Great World War
New York: George H. Doran Co.
(1918)

Dahlstrom, Edmund, ed.
The Changing Roles of Men and Women
Boston: Beacon Press (1967)

Daly, Maria (Lydig)
Diary of a Union Lady, 1861-1865
New York (1962)

Daly, Mary
The Church and the Second Sex
New York (1968)

Dangerfield, George
The Strange Death of Liberal England
New York: H. Smith
and R. Haas (1935)

Davidson, Sara
"An 'Oppressed Majority' Demands Its Rights"
Life (December 12, 1969)

Davis, Allen Freeman
Spearheads for Reform; the Social Settlements and the Progressive Movement
New York: Oxford University
Press (1967)

Davis, Anne
"Women as a Minority Group in Higher Academics"
American Sociologist (May, 1969)

Davis, Elizabeth Gould
The First Sex
New York (1871)

Davis, Paulina Wright
A History of the National Women's Rights Movement
New York (1971)

**Dawson, Richard E.
and Kenneth Prewitt**
Political Socialization; an Analytic Study
Boston: Little, Brown (1968)

de Beauvoir, Simone
The Long March
Cleveland: World Publishing Co.
(1958)

de Beauvoir, Simone
The Long March
Cleveland (1958)

de Beauvoir, Simone
The Mandarins
Cleveland (1956)

de Beauvoir, Simone
Memoirs of a Dutiful Daughter
Cleveland (1959)

de Beauvoir, Simone
The Prime of Life New York (1960)

de Beauvoir, Simone
The Second Sex (1953)

de Beauvoir, Simone
She Came to Stay
Cleveland (1954)

de Beauvoir, Simone
The Woman Destroyed
New York (1969)
"Decisions—Woman may not be Coddled"
Time (August 22, 1969)

DeCrow, Karen
"An Opinion: Karen DeCrow, women and Politics"
Mademoiselle (Fabruary, 1970)

Degler, Carl
Out of Our Past
New York (1970)

Degler, Carl N.
"Revolution without Ideology: The Changing Place of Women in America"
The Women in America
ed. Robert J. Lifton, Boston (1965)

Deiss, Joseph J.
The Roman Years of Margaret Fuller
New York (1969)

Dell, Floyd
Women as World Builders: Studies in Modern Feminism
Chicago: Forbes and Co. (1913)

DeMartino, Manfred F., ed.
Sexual Behavior and Personality Characteristics
New York (1963)

de Maupassant, Guy
A Woman's Life
London: Nonesuch Press (1942)

Deming, Barbara
Prison Notes
Boston (1970)

Demos, John
Little Commonwealth: Family Life in Plymouth Colony
New York: Oxford University Press (1970)

Demos, John
"Witchcraft"
American Historical Review (1970)

de Stael-Holstein, Anne Louise Germaine, baronne
Influence of Literature on Society
Boston: Wells (1813)

Deutsch, Helene
The Psychology of Women
New York: Grune and Stratton (1944)

Devlin, Bernadette
"A Lady from Ulster Jolts Commons"
Washington Post (April 27, 1969)

De Vos, Karen R.
"The Place of Women: a Look at the Biblical Evidence"
The Reformed Journal 22:3 (March, 1972)

De Vos, Karen R.
"Who Needs Women's Lib?"
The Reformed Journal 21:3 (March, 1971)

DeWolfe, Elsie
After All
New York: Harper (1935)

Dexter, Elisabeth Anthony
Career Women of America, 1776-1840
Francestown, N.H. (1950)

Dexter, Elisabeth Anthony
Colonial Women of Affairs; a Study of Women in Business and the Professions in America before 1776
Boston: Houghton (1924)

Diana Press: A Women's Poetry Magazine
c/o Regina Sigal,
1854 Wyoming Ave.
Washington, D.C. 20009

Dichter, Ernest
"Could You Be President"
Cosmopolitan (April, 1972)

Dickinson, Emily
Selected Poems and Letters
Garden City (1959)

Diderot, Denis
"On Women" (1772) in *Selected Writings*
ed. Lester Crocker
New York (1966)

Diner, Helen
Mothers and Amazons: The First Feminine History of Culture
New York (1965)

Dinesen, Isak (pseud. for Blixen, Karen)
Out of Africa
New York: Random House (1938)

Dinesen, Isak (pseud. for Blixen, Karen)
Winter's Tales
New York (1942)

Dingwall, Eric
Girdle of Chastity
London (1951)

Dingwall, Eric John
The American Women
New York (1957)

Directory of Liberated Churches
Free Church Publications,
P.O. Box 9177, Berkeley, Calif.

Discrimination Against Women
Hearings before the Special Subcommittee on Education of the Committee on Education and Labor, House of Rep.
91st Congress, 2nd Session
(June and July, 1970)

Ditzion, Sidney
Marriage, Morals, and Sex in America—A History of Ideas
New York: Bookman Association (1953)

Dizard, Jan
Social Change in the Family
Chicago: University of Chicago Press (1968)

Dodge, Mary Abigail
Woman's Worth and Worthlessness
New York: Harper and Brothers (1872)

Dodge, Norton D.
Women in the Soviet Economy; their role in Economic, Scientific, and Technical Development
Baltimore: Johns Hopkins Press (1966)

Doely, Sarah Bentley
Women's Liberation and the Church
New York (1970)

Dollard, John
Caste and Class in a Southern Town
Garden City, N.Y. (1957)

Donelson, Kenneth and Irene
Married Today, Single Tomorrow: Marriage Breakup and the Law
New York (1969)

Donoghue, Denis
"Musil" Review of *Five Women*, by Robert Musil
New York Review of Books (May 26, 1966)

Dooyeweevd, Herman
In the Twilight of Western Thought
Philadelphia (1960)

Dornbusch, Sanford, and David Herr
"The Evaluation of Work by Females"
American Journal of Sociology (July, 1957)

Dorr, Rheta
A Woman of Fifty
New York: Funk and Wagnalls (1924)

Dorr, Rheta
Susan B. Anthony, the Woman Who Changed the Mind of a Nation
New York: Frederick A. Stokes Co. (1928)

Douglas, Emily Taft
Margaret Sanger: Pioneer of the Future
New York (1969)

Douglas, Emily Taft
Remember the Ladies: the Story of the Great Women Who Helped Shape America
New York (1966)

Dow, Blanche
The Varying Attitudes Toward Women in French Literature of the 15th Century: the Opening Years
New York: Institute of French Studies (1936)

Dow, Blanche
The Varying Attitudes Toward Women in French Literature
New York: Institute of French Studies (1936)

Drabble, Margaret
The Garrick Year
New York (1965)

Drabble, Margaret
Jerusalem the Golden
New York (1967)

Drabble, Margaret
Thank You All Very Much
New York (1969)

Drabble, Margaret
The Waterfall
New York (1969)

Dreiser, Theodore
An American Tragedy
New York: Boni and Liveright (1925)

Dreiser, Theodore
Sister Carrie
New York (1970)

Duncan, Hugh Dalziel
The Rise of Chicago as a Literary Center from 1885 to 1920
Totowa, N.J. (1964)

Duncan, Irma
"Isadora: pioneer in the Art of Dance"
Dance Magazine (June, 1969)

Duncan, Isadora
My Life
Garden City, N.Y.: Garden City Publ. Co. (1927)

Duniway, Abilgail Scott
Path Breaking; An Autobiographical History of the Equal Suffrage Movement in Pacific Coast States
Portland, Ore.: James, Kerns, and Abbott Co. (1914)

Dunn, Nell
Talking to Women
New York (1968)

Duras, Marguerite
Four Novels: Ten-Thirty on a Summer Evening
New York (1960)

Duras, Marguerite
Hiroshima, Mon Amour
New York: Grove Press (1961)

Duras, Marguerite
Moderato Cantabile
New York (1960)

Durrell, Lawrence
Clea
New York (1969)

Durrell, Lawrence
Justine
New York (1969)

Duverger, Maurice
The Political Role of Women
Paris: U.N.E.S.C.O. (1955)

Earle, Alice Morse
Child-Life in Colonial Days
New York: MacMillan (1899) (1929)

Earle, Alice M.
Home and Child Life in the Colonial Days
ed. Shirley Glubok
New York (1969)

Earle, Alice Norse
Home Life in Colonial Days
New York: MacMillan (1910) (c. 1898)

East Bay Feminist Newsletter
c/o Leslee Corpier,
4901 Clarke St.,
Oakland, Calif.

Eastman, Max
Love and Resolution: My Journey Through an Epoch
New York (1964)

Earth's Daughters
eds. Judith Kerman, Mindy Sloff, Judith Treible
409 Richmond Ave.,
Buffalo, N.Y. 14222

Edgeworth, Maria
Belinda
London, F. C. & J. Rivington (1810)

Edwards, John N., ed.
The Family and Change
New York (1969)

Elder, Olen
"Appearance and Education in Marriage Mobility"
American Sociological Review 34:4 (August, 1969)

Eliot, George
Daniel Deronda
New York (1964)

Eliot, George
"Femina Sapiens"
Esquire, (March, 1970)

Eliot, George
Middlemarch
New York (1966)

Eliot, George (pseudonym of Mary Ann or Marian Evans)
The Mill on the Floss
New York (1961)

Ellet, Elizabeth
Women of the American Revolution, 2 vols.
New York: Baker and Scribner (1850)

Ellington, G.
The Women of New York or the Underworld of the Great City
New York (1869)

Ellis, Albert
"Rationality in Sexual Morality"
The Humanist (September/October, 1969)

Ellis, Havelock
Man and Woman: A Study of Human Secondary Sexual Characteristics
New York: Houghton, Mifflin (1929) (1904)

Ellman, Mary
"Academic Women"
Commentary (March, 1965)

Ellman, Mary
"A Most Uncommon Reader",
review of *Collected Essays* by Virginia Woolf
Nation (January 29, 1968)

Ellman, Mary
"The Dutiful Simone de Beauvoir"
Commentary (August, 1965)

Ellmann, Mary
Thinking About Women
New York (1968)

Engels, Frederich
The Origins of Family, Private Property, and the State
New York (1942)

Enough is Enough
Janet Parham, Bristol Militant Group, 8 Clifton Park, Bristol 8, England

Eoffin, Magdolen
"Contraception and the Church"
New York Review of Books
(July, 1966)

Epstein, Cynthia F.
"Encountering the male establishment: sex-status limits on women's careers in the professions"
American Journal of Sociology,
LXXV, 965-982 (1970)

Epstein, Cynthia
Women's Place: Options and Limits in Professional Careers
Berkeley: University of California Press (1970)

"Equal Rights NOW"
Newsweek (March 2, 1970)

Erikson, Erik H.
Youth, Identity and Crisis
New York (1968)

Escarpit, Robert
Sociology of Literature
trans. Ernest Pick
Painesville, Ohio: Lake Erie College Press (1965)

Essence
The Hollingsworth Group,
102 E. 30th St., New York, N.Y.

Evans-Pritchard, E. E.
The Position of Women in Primitive Society and Other Essays in Social Anthropology
London (1965)

Everywoman
6515 W. 83rd St.,
Los Angeles, Calif. 90045

Everywoman
1043B W. Washington Blvd.,
Venice, Calif. 90291

Expatriate Review
eds. Roger W. Gaest,
Wyatt E. F. James
P.O. Box D,
Staten Island, N.Y. 10301

Explode
c/o Lois Graessle,
27 Albany Mansions,
Albert Bridge Rd.,
London, S.W., 11 England

"Fact Sheet on the Earnings Gap"
U.S. Dept of Labor,
Washington, D.C. 20210

Fagen, Richard
The Transformation of Political Culture in Cuba
Stanford, Calif.: Stanford University Press (1969)

Fair, Ronald
Many Thousand Gone
New York (1965)

Fairchild, J. E.
Women, Society and Sex
New York (1956)

Fanon, Frantz
Black Skin, White Masks
trans. Charles L. Markmann
New York (1967)

Fanon, Frantz
Studies in a Dying Colonialism
trans. Haskon Chevalier
New York (1967)

Fanon, Franz
The Wretched of the Earth
trans. Constance Farrington
New York (1968)

Farber, Seymour M.
The Potential of Women
New York (1963)

Farber, Seymour and Roger H. L. Wilson, eds.
The Challenge of Women

Farina, Richard
Been Down So Long It Looks Like Up to Me
New York (1966)

Farson, R., and others
The Future of the Family
New York: Family Service Assoc. of America (1969)

"Fathers and Sons"
Newsweek (April 20, 1970)

Faulkner, William
Light in August
New York (1967)

Faulkner, William
The Sound and the Fury
New York (1966)

Fawcett, Millicent G.
The Women's Victory and After: personal reminiscences, 1911-1918
London, Sidgwick and Jackson, Ltd. (1920)

Fawcett, Millicent G.
What I Remember
New York: G. P. Putnam's Sons (1925)

Federally Employed Women
(FEW)
Ms. Daisy Fields, St. 487,
National Press Bldg.,
Washington, D.C.

Feelings
c/o Coleman, 243 Baltic St.,
Brooklyn, N.Y.

Female Liberation
P.O. Box 12333, Nashville, Tenn.

Female Liberation
Durham-Chapel Hill, N.C.

Female Liberation
371 Somerville Ave.,
Somerville, Mass. 02143

Female Liberation Movement
Nancy Hawley, 193 Hamilton St.,
Cambridge, Mass.

Female Liberation Newsletter
Box 14061, University Sta.,
Minneapolis, Minn. 55414

The Feminists
120 Liberty St., New York, N.Y.

Feminist Studies
c/o Ann Calderwood,
294 Riverside Dr.,
New York, N.Y. 10025

The Female State: A Journal of Female Liberation
Female Liberation,
371 Somerville Ave.,
Somerville, Mass.

Female Studies, Know, Inc.
P.O. Box 10197,
Pittsburgh, Pa. 15232

Fenelon, Francois de Salignac de la Mothe
Treatise on Education of Daughters
trans. Rev. T. F. Tibdin
Cheltenham: H. Ruff (1805)

Fernberger, S. W.
"Persistence of Stereotypes Concerning Sex Differences"
Journal of Abnormal Social Psychology, XLIII, 97-101 (1948)

F.E.W.: News and Views
Federally Employed Women,
Ste. 487, Natl. Press Bldg.,
Washington, D.C.

Fidell, Linda S.
Empirical Verification of Sex Discrimination in Hiring Practices in Psychology"
American Psychologist (1970)

Field, Vera Bernadette
Constantia; A Study of the Life and Works of Judith Sargent Murray (1751-1820)
Orono, Me.: University of Maine Press (1931)

Figes, Eva
Patriarchal Attitudes
New York (1970)
"Films/Robert Hatch"
Nation (November 14, 1966)

Finch, Edith
Carey Thomas of Bryn Mawr
New York: Harper (1947)

Finletter, Gretchen
From the Top of the Stairs
Boston: Little (1946)

Firestone, Shulmaith
The Dialectic of Sex: The Case for Feminist Revolution
New York: Bantam Books (1971)

Fischer, Ernst
"The Resurrection of Lenin"
New Statesman (March 27, 1970)

Fisher, Ann and Peggy Golde
"The Position of Women in Anthropology"
American Anthropologist, 25, 1094-98 (1970)

Fitzgerald, F. Scott
Tender is the Night
New York: Scribner (1934)

Fitzgerald, Frances
"A Nice Place to Visit", review of *Hanoi* by Mary McCarthy and *Trip to Hanoi* by Susan Sontag
New York Review of Books (March 13, 1969)

Fitzgerald, Zelda
Save Me the Waltz
New York (1968)

"Five Passionate Feminists"
interviews with Mrs. Malcolm Peabody, Judy Stein, Anne Keedt, James Clapp, and Ellen Willis
McCalls (July, 1970)

Flannery, Regina
"Men's and Women's Speech in Gros Ventre"
International Journal of American Linguistics 12, 3, 133-135 (1946)

Fleming, Sanford
Children and Puritanism
New Haven: Yale University Press (1933)

Flexner, Eleanor
A Century of Struggle
Cambridge, Harvard University Press (1959)

Flirt
Mrs. Samantha Potter,
2231 N.E. 35th Ct.,
Lighthouse Pt., Florida

Flynn, Elizabeth Gurley
I Speak My Own Piece; Autobiography of "The Rebel Girl"
New York: Masses and Mainstream (1955)

Foner, Philip
History of the Labor Movement in the U.S.
4 vols. New York: International Publishers (1947) (c. 1965)

Fontane, Theodor
Effi Briest
Berlin: S. Fischer (1923)

Foot, Paul
Review of *The Price of My Soul*
New Statesman (November 21, 1969)

Forbes, Thomas Rogers
The Midwife and the Witch
New Haven: Yale University Press (1966)

Forever Amber
1822 W. 4th St.,
Los Angeles, Calif. 90057

Forster, E. M.
Howards End
New York: Vintage (c. 1921)
also New York: Random House (1954)

Forster, E. M.
A Room with a View
New York: Knopf (1962) (c. 1922)

Forten, Charlotte L.
Journal of Charlotte L. Forten: A Free Negro in the Slave Era
New York (1961)

"The Fortune Survey: Women in America"
Fortune, 5-14, 5-6 (August and September, 1946)

Foster, Hannah
The Coquette; or the History of Eliza Wharton
Boston: S. Etheridge for E. Larkin (1797)

Four Lights
c/o Women's International League for Peace & Freedom
2006 Walnut St., Phila., Pa. 19103

Fowler, William Worthington
Woman on the Frontier
Hartford, S. S. Scranton & Co. (1877)

Fowles, John
The French Lieutenant's Woman
New York (1969)

Francis, David
" 'Yes, I do!' . . . 'No, you don't!' "
Christian Science Monitor (February 20, 1970)

Frankl, Viktor
Man's Search for Meaning
New York (1963)

Frazier, E. Franklin
The American Negro Family
Chicago: University of Chicago Press (1966)

Frazier, Franklin
Black Bourgeosie
New York (1962)

"An Opinion: George Frazier IV on Being a Bachelor"
Mademoiselle

Frederic, Harold
The Damnation of Theron Ware
ed. Donald Pizer
Cambridge, Mass.:
Harvard University Press (1960)

Free Kids
Newsletter on Radical Day Care,
c/o OOB, Box 4854,
Cleveland Park,
Washington, D.C. 20008

Freeman, Gillian
"Love for Love"
New Statesman (June 30, 1967)

Free & Proud
Tallahassee WL, Box U-6800,
Florida State Univ.,
Tallahassee, Fla. 32306

Freud, Sigmund
Civilization and Its Discontents
trans. Joan Riviere
London: Hogarth Press (1957) (c. 1930)

Freud, Sigmund
New Introductory Lectures on Psycho-Analysis
London: Hogarth Press (1946)

Friedan, Betty
The Feminine Mystique
New York (1963)

Friedan, Betty
"An Opinion: Betty Friedan on the Conventions"
Mademoiselle (October, 1968)

Friedan, Betty
The Feminine Mystique
New York (1963)

Fromm, Erich
The Art of Loving
New York (1956)

Furley, Paul Hanly
"Men's and Women's Language"
The American Catholic Sociological Review, V, 218-223

Furstenberg, Frank
"Industrialization and the American Family"
American Sociology Review, XXXI, 326-337 n.d.

Gagen, Jean
The New Woman; Her Emergence in English Drama 1600-1730
New York (1954)

Gans, Herbert
The Levitowners; Ways of Life and Politics in a New Suburban Community
New York (1967)

Gans, Herbert
The Urban Villagers; Group and Class in the Life of Italian-Americans
New York (1962)

Gantry, Michael
Black Woman, White Man
North Hollywood, Cal:
Dominion Pub (1968)

Gardner, D. Bruce
Development in Early Childhood: the Preschool Years
New York (1964)

Garland, Hamlin
Son of the Middle Border
New York (1962)

Gaskell, Elizabeth C.
Cranford
London: Oxford University Press (1934)

Gaskell, Elizabeth C.
Life of Charlotte Bronte
London: J. Lehmann (1947)

Gaskell, Elizabeth C.
Mary Barton
New York (1958)

Gaskell, Elizabeth C.
Wives and Daughters
Baltimore (1970)

Gaskell, Elizabeth C.
Wives and Daughters
New York (1970)

Gavron, Hannah
The Captive Wife: Conflicts of Housebound Mothers
London (1966)

Geilgud, John
"To Act a New Part"
New Statesman
(April 12, 1969)

Genet, Jean
The Balcony
New York (1958)

Genet, Jean
The Maids
New York (1956)

Geiger, H. Kent
The Family in Soviet Russia
Cambridge, Mass.:
Harvard University Press (1968)

George, Margaret
One Woman's Situation: A Study of Mary Wollstonecraft
Urbana: University of Illinois Press (1970)

Geyer, Georgie Anne
"Around the World with Pad and Pencil"
Northwestern Review
(Summer 1969)

Gibbard, Kathleen
"Coeducation for Girls"
New Statesman
(April 11, 1969)

Giedion, Siegfried
Mechanization Takes Command, a Contribution to Anonymous History
New York: Oxford University Press (1948)

Gilbert, Olive
Narrative of Sojourner Truth
New York: Arno Press (1968)

Gilchrist, B. B.
Life of Mary Lyon
Boston: Houghton (1910)

Gilman, Charlotte Perkins
The Home, Its Work and Influence
New York: McClure, Phillips and Co. (1903)

Gilman, Charlotte Perkins
The Living of Charlotte Gilman, an autobiography
New York:
D. Appleton-Century Co. (1935)

Gilman, Charlotte Perkins
The Man-Made World; or Our Androcentric Culture
New York: Charlton Co. (1911)

Gilman, Charlotte Perkins Stetson
Women and Economics
New York: Harper and Row (1966)
One of the most important theoretical works to arise out of the early feminist movement in America. A socialist and a follower of Darwin, Mrs. Gilman argued for both the priorities of the group and the need for equality of opportunity and rights for the members of the group. She abandoned the natural rights arguments used by earlier feminists in favor of an evolutionary view of women's emerging roles in the society as the natural development of the human species. Rejecting the views of earlier thinkers who believed in innate depravity,
Mrs. Gilman declared that the source of evil was the oppression of society itself. Still, she reflects great optimism because she sees hope for the liberation of women in progress, social and technological.

Ginzburg, Eli and A. M. Yohalem
Educated American Women
New York:
Columbia University Press (1966)
A summary of findings of a study done on women graduate students who worked at Columbia University shortly after World War II. Under the auspices of the Conservation of Human Resources program at Columbia, the authors questioned the women on their career aspirations during college, the encouragements which they received during their training, their attitudes toward their families and communities, their feelings on combining work or a career with marriage and family responsibilities, their occupational achievements and their life styles. The authors view the situation of women in America as full of options rather than problems; they are, therefore, quite optimistic that social changes will come about to allow society to use the potential of women now excluded from the work force for lack of such things as childcare facilities and public investment in female resources.

Giovanni, Nikki
Black Feeling, Black Talk, Black Judgement
New York (1970)

Giovanni, Nikki
Re:creation
Detroit: Broadside Press (1970)

Girson, Rochelle
"What did the 19th Amendment Amend?"
Saturday Review
(October 11, 1969)

Gisborne, Thomas
An Enquiry into the Duties of the Female Sex
London: Printed for T. Cadell and W. Davies in the Strand (1816)

Glasgow, Ellen
Barren Ground
New York (1959), (c. 1933)

Glasgow, Ellen
The Sheltered Life
Garden City, New York:
Doubleday, Doran (1932)

Glasgow, Ellen
Vein of Iron
New York: Harcourt, Brace (1935)

Glasgow, Ellen
The Woman Within
New York: Harcourt, Brace
(1954)

Glick, I. D.
"Mood and Behavioral Changes
Associated with the Use
of Oral Contraceptives:
a review of the literature"
Psychopharmacologia, X,
(1967) 363–374

Glover, Robert
Her Goes Kitten
New York (1964)

Glover, Robert
*One Hundred Dollar
Misunderstanding*
New York (1964)

Godden, Jon and Rumer
Two Under the Indian Sun
New York (1966)

Godey's Ladies' Book
63 vols.
ed. vol. 24–85, Sarah J. Hale
and others
Philadelphia: Louis A. Godey
(1831)

Goethe, Wolfgang
Torquato Tasso
Oxford (1962)

Goldbert, Philip
"Are Women Prejudiced
Against Women?"
Trans-Action, 5.5, (April 1968),
28-30

Goldman, Emma
Living My Life
New York: Knopf (1934)

Goldman, Eric F.
Rendezvous With Destiny
New York (1958)

**Goldman, George David
and Donald S. Milman, eds.**
*Modern Woman—Her Psychology
and Sexuality*
Springfield, Ill.: (1969)

Goldmark, Josephine
*Impatient Crusader: Florence
Kelley's Life Story*
Urbana: University of Illinois
Press (1953)

Goldwater, Ethel
"Women's Place"
Commentary, (December, 1947)

Gollin, Gillian Lindt
*Moravians in Two Worlds: A
Study of Changing Communities*
New York:
Columbia University Press (1967)

Goode, William Joseph
After Divorce
Glencoe, Illinois: Free Press
(1956)

Goodsell, Willystine
The Education of Women
New York (1923)

Goodsell, Willystine
*Pioneers of Women's Education
in the United States*
New York and London:
McGraw-Hill (1931)

Gordimer, Nadine
The Soft Voice of the Serpent
New York (1952)

Gordon, Milton
*Assimilation in American Life; the
Role of Race, Religion, and
National Origins.*
New York:
Oxford University Press (1964)

Gordon, Albert I.
Intermarriage
Boston (1964)

Gorky, Maxim
The Mother
tr. Margaret Wettlin
New York (1962)

Gornick, Vivian and Barbara Moran
Woman in Sexist Society
A Collection of essays by women
who are recognized in such fields
as sociology, psychology,
aesthetics, philosophy and so
forth, as well as a few essays
by militant feminists. The authors
consider such problems as the
woman executive, the lack of
female achievement in art, the
sexist character of the English
language, the development
of sex-role stereotypes in
children. Despite the cerebral
approach of most of the authors,
most of the solutions tend to
be middle-of-the-road American
approaches to sexism. An unusual
feature of the book is a
presentation of four views
of prostitution by women who
know the profession from
the inside.

Goslin, David A., ed.
*Handbook of Socialization Theory
and Research*
Chicago (1969)

Gould, Donald
"Abortion in Perspective"
New Statesman
(July, 1969)

Gould, Donald
"The Cervical Smear Mystery"
New Statesman
(September 13, 1968)

Gould, Donald
"A New Angle on Cancer"
New Statesman
(March 27, 1970)

Gould, Donald
"The Persona Pill"
New Statesman
(February 16, 1969)

Gould, Donald
"The Snags of Legal Abortion"
New Statesman
(April 26, 1968)

Goulden, Joseph
"The Indiscretions of Ma Bell"
Nation
(October 6, 1969)

Graham, Patricia Albjerg
"Women in Academe"
Science, 169, 1284-1290 (1970)

Grau, Shirley Ann
The Black Prince
New York (1955)

Graves, A. J.
Woman in America
New York: Harper (1858)

Graves, Robert
*The White Goddess, A Historical
Grammar of Poetic Myth.*
New York (1966)

Great Swamp Erie Dade Boom
Angry City Press
ed. Steve Serguson
14016 Orinoco Ave.
E. Cleveland, Ohio 64112

Greenburg, Dan
How to Be a Jewish Mother
Los Angeles (1964)

Greene, Bonnie M.
"How Come You're
Not Married Yet?"
Credo (June, 1971)

Greene, Bonnie M.
"Who is the One?"
Vanguard (December, 1970)

Greene, Bonnie M.
"You've Come a Long Way Baby"
Credo (July, 1970)

Greene, Felix
Awakened China; the Country Americans Don't Know
Garden City, N.Y. (1961)

Greene, Graham
May We Borrow Your Husband? and Other Comedies of the Sexual Life.
New York (1967)

Greene, Graham
Travels With My Aunt
New York (1969)

Greene, Lorenzo Johnston
The Negro in Colonial New England
New York (1968)

Greenstein, Fred I.
"Sex-Related Political Differences in Childhood"
Journal of Politics XXIII 353-371
(1961)

Greenwood Press Inc.
51 Riverside Ave.
Westport, Conn. 06880

Greer, Germaine
Playboy 19:1 p. 61 (Jan. 1972)

Greer, Germaine
The Female Eunuch
London (1971)
The widely publicized work by an Australian English professor which claims that women are castrated by the roles and expectations which are presently foisted upon them by the society. The book is erudite and carefully organized even though it suffers from the lack of a developed theoretical framework. The author discusses women in the context of body and soul, love and hate. Her chapter on the development of the middle-class myth of love and marriage as reflected in literature is particularly valuable and unique to her work. The author's plan for liberation relies on a belief in the pleasure principle and therefore, reflects much more tolerance of the choices other women make than is reflected in most modern feminist literature. She suggests a kind of extended family to take the place of the lost sense of community which plagues modern man, but her plan for liberation for both men and women is so individualistic that it offers few concrete suggestions for implementing the changes she envisions.

Gregory, John
"Legacy to His Daughters" in
The Lady's Pocket Library
Philadelphia: M. Carey (1809)

Greven, Philip
"Family Structure in Seventeenth Century Andover"
William and Mary Quarterly 234ff.
(1966)

Grier, William H. and Price M. Cobbs
Black Rage
New York (1968)

Grimes, Alan P.
Equality in America
New York:
Oxford University Press (1964)

Grimes, Alan
The Puritan Ethic and Woman Suffrage
New York:
Oxford University Press (1967)

Griffin, Clifford Stephen
Their Brothers' Keepers; Moral Stewardship in the U.S., 1800-1865
New Brunswick, N.J.:
Rutgers University Press (1960)

Grimke, Sarah M.
Letters on the Equality of the Sexes, and the Condition of Women.
New York: Source Book Press
(1970)

Grimm, Jakob Ludwig Karl
Grimm's Fairy Tales
Garden City, N.Y. (1954)

Gross, Amy
"Women's Lib Loves You"
Mademoiselle
(February 1970)

Gross, Edward
"Plus Ca Change . . .? The Sexual Structure of Occupations Over Time"
Social Problems (Fall 1968)

Gross, Irma Hannah, ed.
Potentialities of Women in the Middle Years
E. Lansing, Mich.:
State University Press (1956)

Grossman, Edward
"In Pursuit of the American Woman"
Harpers
(February 1970)

Group for the Advancement of Psychiatry
Sex and the College Student
New York (1966)

Gruberg, Martin
Women in American Politics
Oshkosh, Wisc. (1968)
A book which traces such elements in female political life as the role women have played in state and federal government, their voting patterns, their efforts to influence political leaders and their support of organized lobbies. The author's approach is documentary rather than polemical or prophetic. He gives extensive background on the political careers of women of national significance, but he also discusses briefly women who have played important roles on the state level.

Gruchow, Nancy
"Discrimination"
Science 559-61 (May 1, 1970)

Gruenberg, Sidonie M. and Hilda Sidney Krech
The Many Lives of Modern Woman
Garden City, N.Y.:
Doubleday (1952)

Gusfield, Joseph
Symbolic Crusade: Status Politics and the American Temperance Movement
Urbana: University of Illinois Press
(1963)

Hacker, Helen
"Women as a Minority Group"
Social Forces
(October 1951)

Hague, John A.
American Character and Culture; Some Twentieth Century Perspectives
DeLand, Fla.: (n.p.) (1964)

Haight, Gordon
George Eliot; a Biography
New York:
Oxford University Press (1968)

Hale, Sarah Josepha
Women's Record; or, Sketches of all Distinguished Women from the Creation to A.D. 1854
New York (1855)

Hall, G. Stanley
"Flapper Americana Novissima"
Atlantic Monthly (June 1922)

Hall, Radclyffe
Well of Loneliness
London: Hermes Press (1928)

Hamill, Pete
"The Neighborhood Girls"
New York Magazine
(February 16, 1970)

Hamilton, Alice
Exploring the Dangerous Trades
Boston: Little, Brown and Co.
(1943)

Hamilton, Mary Agnes
"Nothing Shocks Me"
Harper's (July 1927)

Hamell, Katharine
"Women as Bosses"
Fortune p. 104
(June 1956)

Han, Suyin
*Birdless Summer, China:
Autobiography, History*
New York (1968)

Hancock, Cecily Raysor
"Lady and Woman"
American Speech XXXVIII
234–235 (October 1963)

Hansberry, Lorraine
A Raisin in the Sun
New York (1959)

Hansberry, Lorraine
To Be Young, Gifted and Black
Englewood Cliffs (1969)

Harbeson, G.
*Choice and Challenge for the
American Woman*
Cambridge, Mass.: (1967)

Harding, Esther
Psychic Energy
Englewood Cliffs, N.J.:
Princeton University Press (1965)

Harding, Esther
The Way of All Women
New York: Longmans Green
(1933)

Harding, Esther
Women's Mysteries
New York (1955)

Hardwick, Elizabeth
"The Subjection of Women"
Partisan Review (May 1953)

Hardwick, Elizabeth
A View of One's Own
New York (1966)

Harmetz, Aljean
"To Be Young, Radical
and Movie Mad"

New York Times
(November 16, 1969)

Harmon, L. R.
*Careers of Ph.D.'s; Academic
versus Nonacademic*
Career Patters Report No. 2
Washington: National Academy
of Science (1968)

Harper, Ida Husted
*Life and Work of
Susan B. Anthony*
New York (1969)

Harris, Ann S.
"The second Sex in Academe"
*American Association of
University Professors Bulletin*
283-95 (1970)

Harrison, Evelyn
"The Working Woman: Barriers
in Employment"
Public Administration Review
XXIV no. 2, 78 (June 1964)

Hart, James
*The Popular Book: A History of
America's Literary Taste*
New York:
Oxford University Press (1950)

Hartman, Sylvia
"Should Wives Work?"
McCalls
(February 1969)

Harveston, Mae Elizabeth
*Catherine Esther Beecher: A
Pioneer Educator*
Philadelphia: n.p. (1932)

Hatcher, Orie
Occupations for Women
Richmond, Va.: Southern
Woman's Education Alliance
(1927)

Hatterer, Laurence
The Artist in Society
New York (1965)

Hauser, Arnold
The Social History of Art
New York (1951)

Hawkins, Ruth R.
"The Odds Against Women"
Change in Higher Education, 1,
34-36 (1969)

Hawthorne, Nathaniel
Blithedale Romance
New York (1958)

Hawthorne, Nathaniel
The Scarlet Letter
New York (1950)

Haynes, Muriel
"De Beauvoir: At the Deathbed,"
review of *A Very Easy Death* by
Simone de Beauvoir
Nation
(June 13, 1966)

Hays, Elinor
*Morningstar; a Biography of
Lucy Stone*
New York (1961)

Hays, H. R.
*The Dangerous Sex: The Myth
of Feminine Evil*
New York (1964)

Hecker, Eugene
A Short History of Women's Rights
New York:
Knickerbocker Press (1910)

Hedges, Janice Neipert
"Women Workers and Manpower
Demands in the 1970's"
Monthly Labor Review (June 1970)

Jeinstein, Martin
*Behavior Problems of Young
Children in California*
Sacramento: n.p. (1969)

Helfrich, Margaret L.
*Social Role of the
Executive's Wife*
Columbus: Ohio State University
(1965)

Heller, Celia
Structured Social Inequality
New York (1969)

Hellman, Lillian
An Unfinished Woman, A Memoir
Canada (1969)

Hellman, Lillian
An Unfinished Woman
New York: Random House (1939)

Hellman, Lillian
The Children's Hour
New York (1962)

Hellman, Lillian
Toys in the Attic
New York (1960)

Hemingway, Ernest
"The Short Happy Life of
Frances Macomber" in
*The Short Stories of
Ernest Hemingway*
New York: Modern Library (1938)

Henriques, Fernando
*Prostitution in Europe and the
Americas,* vol. 3 of *Prostitution
and Society, a Survey*
New York: Grove Press
(1963), (1969)

Henry, Alice
The Trade Union Woman
New York: Appleton and Co.
(1915)

Henry, Alice
Women and the Labor Movement
New York: Doran (1923)

Hensley, Jeannine, ed.
The Works of Anne Bradstreet
Cambridge:
Harvard University Press (1967)

Hentoff, Margot
"Aborting the Fetus, or Murder
as a Liberal Art"
Village Voice
(February 23, 1967)

Hentoff, Margot
"Notes From Above Ground"
New York Review of Books
(May 22, 1969)

Hentoff, Margot
"Wild Raspberries" (film review)
New York Review of Books
(March 27, 1969)

Her Own Right
c/o Women's Liberation Center,
Box 4026, New Orleans, La. 70118

Hernton, Calvin
Sex and Racism in America
New York (1966)

Herschberger, Ruth
Adam's Rib
New York: Harper and Row (1970)
One of the oldest of the new
feminist books. The author is
concerned primarily with the
biological elements of sexuality,
such as masturbation,
autoeroticism and guilt in young
children, menstruation,
pregnancy, miscarriage and
abortion, and women "raping"
men. Although the book seems
sketchy and a bit superficial
now, it occupies an important
place in the development of
the consciousness of women.
One of the authors greatest
concerns is the development
of sex roles and stereotyping
in the young child.

Hewitt, Margaret
*Wives and Mothers in Victorian
Industry*
London: Lockliff (1958)

Higgins, Frances C.
Life of Naomi Norsworthy
Boston and New York:
Houghton, Mifflin (1918)
High School Women's Coalition

711 Amsterdam Ave.
New York, N.Y.

Himes, Norman
*A Medical History of
Contraception*
Baltimore: Williams
and Wilkins Co. (1936)

Hinds, William
*American Communities and
Co-Operative Colonies*
New York: Corinth Books (1961)
also Chicago: C. H. Kerr and Co.
(1902)

Hill, Herbert
Sewing Machines and Union
Machines"
Nation
(July 3, 1967)

Himmelfarb, Gertrude
Victorian Minds
New York (1968)

Hirsch, A. H.
*The Love Elite (The Story of
Woman's Emancipation and Her
Drive for Sexual Fulfillment)*
New York (1963)

Hitchcock, James
"Women's Lib: Tending Toward
Idolatry"
Christian Century (Sept. 22, 1971)

Hobbs, Lisa
*Love and Liberation; Up Front
With the Feminists*
New York (1970)

Hobson, Harold
"The 'Surplus Tough' "
Christian Science Monitor
(January 7, 1970)

**Hoffman, M. L. and L. W. Hoffman,
eds.**
*Review of Child Development
Research,* vol. I
Russell Sage Foundation (1964)

Hoffman, Marilyn and Patricia Shelton
"Women's Liberation:
Where to Next?"
Christian Science Monitor
(April 24, 1970)

Hogtown Press
11 Olive Avenue
Toronto 174, Ontario, Canada

Hole, Judith and Ellen Levine
Rebirth of Feminism
New York: Quadrangle Books
(1971)

Holliday, Billie
Lady Sings the Blues
New York: Lancer Paperbacks,
n.d.

Hooks, Janet M.
*Women's Occupations Through
Seven Decades*
Washington, D.C.: U.S. Dept.
of Labor, Women's Bureau (1947)

Hope, Francis
"Girls Will Be Girls"
New Statesman
(August 15, 1969)

Hope, Francis
"Old Adam, New Eve," review of
Thinking About Women by
Mary Ellman
London Observer
(June 22, 1969)

Horner, Joyce Mary
*The English Women Novelists and
Their Connection with the
Feminist Movement*
Smith College Studies in Modern
Languages, vol. XI no. 1–3,
October 1929–April 1930
Northampton, Mass. (1930)

Horner, M.
"Fail: Bright Women"
Psychology Today, 3, 36-38, 62
(1969)

Horner, Matina
"Woman's Will to Fail"
Psychology Today
(November 1969)

Horney, Karen
ed. by Harold Kelman
Feminine Psychology
New York (1967)

Horowitz, Irving ed.
Power, Politics and People
New York:
Oxford University Press (1963)

Hottel, Althea K., ed.
*Women Around the World,
The Annals*
Philadelphia: American Academy
of Political and Social Science
(1968)

Houghton, Walter E.
The Victorian Frame of Mind
New Haven: Published for
Wellesley College by Yale
University Press (1957)

"How Women Are Doing in Politics"
U.S. News and World Report,
LXIX, 24–27
(September 7, 1970)

Howe, Julia Ward
Reminiscences, 1819-1899
Boston: Houghton (1899)

Howe, Florence
"A Talk with Doris Lessing"
Nation
(June 13, 1969)

Howe, Florence
*A Report from the Commission
on the Status of Women in the
Profession*
Modern Language Association
(1969)

Howe, Florence
Female Studies No. 2.
Pittsburgh, Penna. ???
(1971)

Howells, W. D.
Dr. Breen's Practice
Boston: J. R.
Osgood and Co. (1881)

HRW Newsletter
Human Rights for Women
P.O. Box 7402 Franklin Station,
Washington, D.C. 20044

Hudson, K.
*Men and Women, Feminism and
Anti-Feminism Today*
Devon, England: David
and Charles, Newton Abbot (1968)

Hughes, Douglas, ed.
Perspectives on Pornography
New York (1970)

Hughes, Gwendolyn
Mothers in Industry
New York: New Republic, Inc.
(1925)

Hunt, Harriet K.
*Glances and Glimpses; or, Fifty
Years Social, Including Twenty
Years Professional Life*
Boston: J. P. Jewett and Col.
New York: Sheldon, Lamport
and Blakeman (1856)

Hunt, Morton
"The Fiery Feminists"
Playboy (May 1970)

Hunt, Morton
*Her Infinite Variety: The
American Woman as Lover,
Rival and Mate*
New York (1962)
A sympathetic treatment of
the roles and the resulting
conflicts which women face as
they grow from infancy to old
age. Remarkably temperate,
the author discusses such myths
as the natural inferiority of
women, their weakness, their lack
of intelligence, their inclination
to hysteria, and their masochistic
tendencies. He also traces the

female's "progress" through
the seven stages of her life
as she takes up her roles of lover,
rival and mate.

Hunt, Morton
The Natural History of Love
New York (1959)

Hutchins, Grace
Women Who Work
New York:
International Publishers (1934)

Hutchinson, Emile
Women and the PhD
New York (n.d.)

Hyman, Herbert
*Political Socialization; a Study in
the Philosophy of Political
Behavior*
Glencoe, Ill.: (1959)

Hymes, Dell, ed.
*Language in Culture and Society;
a Reader in Linguistics and
Anthropology*
New York (1964)

Hysteria
Box 116, Cambridge, Mass. 02138

Irwin, Inez Hayes
*Angels and Amazons; a Hundred
Years of American Women*
Garden City, N.Y.: Doubleday,
Doran and Co. (1933)

Ishbell, Ross
Charmers and Cranks
New York (1965)

It Ain't Me, Babe
P.O. Box 6323
Albany, Ca. 94706

Ivey and Bardwick
"Patterns of Affective Fluctuations
in the Menstrual Cycle"
Psychosomatic Medicine, XXX,
336–345 (1968)

Jackson, Shirley
Hangsaman
New York (1951)

Jackson, Shirley
The Magic of Shirley Jackson
ed. Stanley Edgar Hyman
New York (1966)

Jacoby, Susan
"The True Working-Class Women
in Russia"
New Republic (April 4 and
11, 1970)

Jahoda, Marie and Joan Havel
"Psychological Problems of
Women in Different Social Roles"
Educational Record, XXXVI,
325-335 (October 1955)

James, Alice
The Diary of Alice James
ed. Leon Edel
New York (1964)

**James, Edward T., ed., Janet Wilson
James, assoc. ed. and Paul S. Boyer,
assis. ed.**
*Notable American Women,
1607-1950: A Biographical
Dictionary*
Cambridge, Mass.:
Harvard University Press (1971)

James, Henry
The Bostonians
New York (1956)

James, Henry
Portrait of a Lady
New York: Modern Library
(1936), (c. 1909)

James, Henry
What Maisie Knew
Garden City, N.Y.:
Doubleday (1936)

Janeway, Elizabeth
Man's World, Woman's Place
New York (1971)
Begins with the myth of its being
man's world, women merely
having a part of it, explaining
the mythic qualities of that
"idea," then traces it through
the results in society. She
doesn't, can't, explain how
to change the myth, which she
says can't be done logically, but
with answers "in reality to those
needs which the myth answers
in fantasy."

Jellicoe, A.
*The Knack and The Sport of My
Mad Mother: Two Plays*
New York (1964)

Jennings M. Kent and Norman Thomas
"Men and Women in Party
Elites: Social Roles and Political
Resources"
*Midwest Journal of Political
Science*, XII, No. 4 469-492
(November 1968)

Jensen, Oliver
The Revolt of American Women
New York (1952)

Jernegan, Marcus W.
*Laboring and Dependent Classes
in Colonial America, 1607-1783*
Chicago: University of Chicago
Press (1931)

Jespersen, Otto
*Language: Its Nature,
Development and Origin*

London: George A. Allen
and Unwin, Ltd. (1922)

Jespersen, Otto
The Philosophy of Grammar
London: George A. Allen
and Unwin, Ltd. (1958)
(c. 1924) see ch. 17

Jessup, Josephine L.
*The Faith of Our Feminists, a
Study in the Novels of Edith
Wharton, Ellen Glasgow, and
Willa Cather*
New York: R. R. Smith (1950)

Jesus, Carolina Maria de
*Child of the Dark: The Diary of
Carolina Maria de Jesus*
New York (1962)

Jewett, Sarah Orne
A Country Doctor
Boston: Houghton, Mifflin (1884)

Jex-Blake, Sophia
*Medical Women; A Thesis and a
History*
Edinburgh: Oliphant, Anderson
and Ferrier (1886)

**"Job Discrimination and What
Women Can Do About It"**
Atlantic (March 1970)

Joel, Lydia
"Finding Isadora"
Dance Magazine
(June 1969)

Jones, Claudia
"An End to the Neglect of the
Problems of the Negro Woman"
n.p. (n.d.)

Johnson, Guion
"Courtship and Marriage Customs
in Ante-bellun North Carolina"
North Carolina Historical Review,
VIII, 384-402 n.d.

Johnson, Paul
"The Faillible Pope"
New Statesman
(August 2, 1968)

Johnson, Paul
"Lovely War," review of
"Diaries 1915–1918" by Lady
Cynthia Asquith in Vain Glory,
Guy Chapman, ed.
New Statesman
(April 26, 1968)

Johnston, Johanna
*Mrs. Satan; the Incredible
Saga of Victoria C. Woodhull*
New York (1967)

Johnston, Mary
Hagar

Boston and New York:
Houghton, Mifflin Co. (1913)

Jones, Beverly
"Toward Women's Liberation"
Guardian
(January 25, 1969)

Jones, Beverly and Judith Brown
*Towards a Female Liberation
Movement*
Boston (1968)

Jones, LeRoi
*Dutchman and The Slave:
Two Plays*
New York (1964)

Jones, LeRoi
Home; Social Essays
New York (1966)

Jones, Mary Harris
Autobiography of Mother Jones
ed. Mary Field Parton
Chicago: C. H. Kerr and Co.
(1925)

Jordan, Joan
"The Place of American Women"
Revolutionary Age, I
(Summer 1964)

Josephson, Hannah
*The Golden Threads: New
England Mill Girls and Magnates*
New York: Duell, Sloan
and Pearce (1949)

Journal of Female Liberation (The),
Cell 16, 2 Brewer St.,
Cambridge, Mass. 02138

Joyce, James
Ulysses
New York (1961)

Just Like A Woman
Box 5432, Station E.,
Atlanta, Georgia 30307

Kaberry, Phyllis M.
Women of the Grasslands
London: Colonial Office Research
Pub. #14 (1942)

Kael, Pauline
"The Current Cinema"
New Yorker
(October 25, 1969)

**Kagan, Benjamin M.
and Sidney S. Gellis**
"Birth to Maturity"
Current Pediatric Theory
New York (1962)

Kanin, Garson
"Woman of the Year—
Katherine Hepburn"
McCalls
(February 1970)

Kanowitz, Leo
"Sex-Based Discrimination
in American Law: Law and the
Single Girl"
*St. Louis University Law
Journal,* XI, 293-330

Kanowitz, Leo
*Women and the Law: the
Unfinished Revolution*
Albuquerque: University of New
Mexico Press (1969)

Keezer, Dexter M.
"Watch Out Girls!"
New Republic
(September 13, 1969)
(Spring 1967)

Kelly, Benedict
"Ulster After the Bludgeons"
Nation
(May 19, 1969)

Kemble, Frances
*Journal of a Residence on a
Georgian Plantation in 1838-1839*
New York: Harper (1863)

Kempton, Sally
"Cutting Loose"
Esquire
(July 1970)

Kennedy, David M.
*Birth Control in America; the
Career of Margaret Sanger*
New Haven:
Yale University Press (1970)

Kenniston, E. and Kenneth
"An American Anachronism:
The Image of Women and Work"
American Scholar (Summer 1964)

Kerby, Phil
"Abortion—Laws and Attitudes"
Nation
(June 12, 1967)

Kermode, Frank
"Isadora" review of *Isadora
Duncan: Her Life, Her Art, Her
Legacy,* by Walter Terry
New York Review of Books
(March 5, 1964)

Key, Ellen Karolina Sofia
The Century of the Child
New York and London:
G. P. Putnam's (1910)

Key, Ellen
Love and Marriage
New York: G. P. Putnam's (1911)

Key, Ellen Karolina Sofia
Love and Marriage
trans. Arthur G. Chater
New York and London:
G. P. Putnam's (1911)

Key, Ellen Karolina Sofia
The Woman Movement
trans. Mamah Bouton Borthwick
New York and London:
G. P. Putnam's (1912)

Key, Ellen Karolina Sofia and others
The Woman Question
trans. and ed. T. R. Smith
New York: Boni and Liveright
(1918)

Kiefer, Monica M.
*American Children Through
Their Books, 1700-1835*
Philadelphia: University of
Pennsylvania Press (1948)

Kihss, Peter
"Miss Boudin Disillusioned
by Russia, Too"
New York Times
(March 18, 1970)

Kilpatrick, James J.
"Some Random Thoughts
on Women's Lib"
Human Events (Jan. 8, 1972)

King, Coretta
My Life With Martin Luther King
New York (1969)

Kinsey, Alfred
*Sexual Behavior in the
Human Female*
Philadelphia (1953)

Kirchwey, Freda, ed.
*Our Changing Morality; a
Symposium*
New York: A. & C. Boni (1924)

Kisselgoff, Anna
"What Happened to Isadora
in Russia"
New York Times
(August 31, 1969)

Klein, Viola
*The Feminine Character: History
of an Ideology*
New York: International
Universities Press (1946, 1948)

Klein, Viola
*Women Workers: Working Hours
and Services*
Paris: Organization for Economic
Co-Operation and Development
(1965)

Klemesrud, Judy
"When Liquor is the Most
Important Thing in a
Mother's Life"
New York Times
(November 26, 1969)

Know, Jo Ann Gardner
P.O. Box 10197
Pittsburgh, Pa.

Knudsen, Dean D.
"The Declining Status of Women:
Popular Myths and the Failure
of Functionalist Thought"
Social Forces, XLVIII
(December 1969)

Kluckhohn, Clyde
Mirror for Man
New York: Whittlesey House
(1949)

Koch, Stephen
"Sontag: Shaking the Tree of
Death" review of
Death Kit by Susan Sontag
Ramparts
(April 1969)

Kohn, Melvin
"Social Class and Parent-Child
Relationships: An Interpretation"
American Journal of Sociology,
LXVIII, 471-480
(January 1963)

Komarovsky, Mirra
"Cultural contradictions and
sex roles"
American Journal of Sociology,
LII (November 1946)

Komarovsky, Mirra
"Functional Analysis
of Sex Roles"
American Sociological Review,
XV, 508-516 (1950)

Komisar, Lucy
"The New Feminism"
Saturday Review
(February 21, 1970)

Konopka, Gisela
Adolescent Girl in Conflict
Englewood Cliffs, N.J.: (1966)

Kotlowitz, Robert
"Films: Aspects of Love, Stolen
Kisses, if . . . The Guru"
Harpers
(April 1969)

Kraditor, Aileen S.
*Ideas of the Woman Suffrage
Movement: 1890-1920*
New York:
Columbia University Press (1965)
A clear and concise account
of the theoretical bases of the
suffrage movement between
the years 1890 and 1920. The
book traces the genesis of the
"justice" and "expediency"
arguments of the suffragists and
carefully shows how women used
these arguments to gain the vote
as they grew more sophisticated
in their politics. The author also
shows how the broad aims of
the more idealistic first
generation of suffragists were
replaced by narrower aims when
the second generation took over.
The book is valuable for an
understanding of the strange
silence among women following
their success in getting the vote.

Kraditor, Aileen
*Means and Ends in American
Abolitionism, 1834-1850*
New York (1969)

Kraditor, Aileen S., ed.
Up From the Pedestal
Chicago (1968)
A collection of essays and
excerpts from the works of
people connected with the
American feminist movement.
In the interest of historical
perspective, the author includes
the writings of both supporters
and opponents of feminism,
among whom are such people
as Anne Bradstreet, Thomas
Dew, the Grimkes, Margaret
Fuller, Emma Willard, the Claflins,
Nette Blackwell, Ernestine Rose
and Carrie Chapman Catt. The
essays concern such questions
as the appropriate and natural
spheres of the two sexes, the
intellectual potential of women
and their need for education,
the relationship between fashion
and woman's status, marriage and
divorce, and the relationship
between religion and the women's
rights movement. The book also
includes a large section devoted
to the "justice" and "expediency"
arguments used by the first and
second generations of suffragists
in their efforts to secure the vote.

Kramer, Charles
"San Juan Abortion: Raising
the Ante"
Village Voice
(June 3, 1969)

Kramer, Hilton
"Politics Without Pain," review of
*Love and Revolution: My
Journey through an Epoch,* by
Max Eastman
Commentary
(July 1965)

Kreps, Juanita
*Sex in the Marketplace:
American Women at Work*
Baltimore: Johns Hopkins Press
(1971)

Kriesberg, Louis
Mothers in Poverty: a Study of Fatherless Families
Chicago (1970)

Kronhausen, Phyllis and Eberhard
The Sexually Responsive Woman
New York (1964)

L.A. Women's Liberation Newsletter
Women's Center,
1027 S. Grenshaw Blvd.,
Los Angeles, Calif.

Laclos
Les Liaisons Dangereuses
Garden City, N.Y. (1961)

Lacey, W. K.
The Family in Classical Greece
Ithaca, N.Y.:
Cornell University Press (1968)

Lader, Lawrence
Abortion
Boston (1967)

The Ladder
Box 5025, Washington Station,
Reno, Nevada 89503

Lander, E.
"Slave Labor in South Carolina Cotton Mills"
Journal of Negro History,
XXXVIII, 101-170 n.d.

Ladner, Joyce A.
Tomorrow's Tomorrow: The Black Woman
Garden City, N.Y. (1971)

Ladner, Joyce A.
Tomorrow's Tomorrow, The Black Woman
New York (1972)
Contains a good up-to-date bibliography.

Lamson, Peggy
Few Are Chosen: American Women in Political Life Today
New York (1968)

Langdon-Davis, John
A Short History of Woman
New York: Viking Press (1927)

Lantz, et al
"Pre-Industrial Patterns in the Colonial Family in America"
American Sociology Review,
XXXVII, 413-426 (1968)

LaFollette, Suzanne
Concerning Women
New York:
Albert and Charles Boni (1926)

Lagerlof, Selma
The Story of Gosta Berling

trans. Pauline Bancroft Flach
Garden City, N.Y.:
Doubleday (1934), (c. 1898)

Laing, Ronald Davis
The Divided Self
New York (1969)

Laing, R.D.
The Politics of Experience
New York (1967)

Laing, Ronald Davis and A. Esterson
Sanity, Madness, and the Family
New York: Basic Books
(1965), (c. 1964)

Larcom, Lucy
New England Girlhood, Outlined From Memory
Boston: Houghton (1890)

Larsen, Arthur J.
Crusader and Feminist, Letters of Jane Grey Swisshelm 1858-68
St. Paul: The Minnesota Historical Society (1934)

Larson, Roy
"Response to Coalition Encourages Nuns"
Chicago Sun-Times
(August 24, 1969)

Lasch, Christopher
The New Radicalism in America
New York (1965)
A book which is concerned with reform and women's movements as part of the development of an intellectual class. The book takes the form of a series of biographical essays in which the author portrays the intellectuals as a detached group which stands as commentator on society and therefore experiences extreme alienation from the rest of the society. He further sees the growing dissatisfaction of women as a sign of integration into the alienated intellectual class rather than merely a concern with sex rights. Jane Addams, Mabel Dodge Luhan, and other feminists are among the thinkers whom Lasch considers.

Lasch, Christopher, ed.
The Social Thought of Jane Addams
Indianapolis (1965)

Lasswell, Thomas E., ed.
Life in Society
Chicago (1965)

Lavender Vision
c/o Media Collective 2
Brookline, Cambridge, Mass.

Lawrence, D. H.
The Complete Short Stories of D. H. Lawrence
London (1955)

Lawrence, D. H.
Lady Chatterley's Lover
New York (1959)

Lawrence, D. H.
Sons and Lovers
New York: Modern Library (1922)

Lawrence, D. H.
Women in Love
London (1954)

Lawrenson, Helene
"The Feminine Mistake"
Esquire
(January 1971)

League for Women's Rights
Women's Liberation Center
of N.Y.
36 West 22nd St.
New York, N.Y. 10010

Leake, Albert H.
Vocational Education of Girls and Women
New York: Macmillan (1918)

Lederer, Wolfgang
The Fear of Women
New York (1968)

Leith-Ross, Sylvia
African Women: A Study of the Ibo of Nigeria
London: Faber and Faber (1939)

Lee, Dorothy
Freedom and Culture
Englewood Cliffs, N.J. (1959)

Lenin, V. I.
The Emancipation of Women
New York: International Publishers (1970)

Lenski, Gerhard
Power and Privilege
New York (1966)

Leonard, Eugenie Andruss, Sophie Hutchinson Drinker and Miriam Young Holden
The American Woman In Colonial and Revolutionary Times, 1565-1800: A Syllabus with a Bibliography
Philadelphia: University of Pennsylvania Press (1962)

Leonard, Eugenie A.
The Dear-Bought Heritage
Philadelphia: University of Pennsylvania Press (1965)

Lerner, Gerda
The Grimké Sisters from South Carolina
Boston (1967)

Lerner, Gerda
"The Lady and The Mill Girl: Changes in the Status of Women in the Age of Jackson
Mid-Continent American Studies Journal, X, 5-15 (Spring 1969)

Lerner, Max
America as a Civilization; Life and Thought in the U.S. Today
New York (1957)
The Lesbian in Literature
Box 5025
Washington Station
Reno, Nev. 98503

Lesley, Susan
Recollections of My Mother
Boston: Press of G. H. Ellis
(1886)

Lessing, Doris
African Stories
London (1964)

Lessing, Doris
Briefing for a Descent into Hell
New York (1971)

Lessing, Doris
Children of Violence
London (1965)

Lessing, Doris
The Four-Gated City
New York (1969)

Lessing, Doris
Going Home
New York (1968)

Lessing, Doris
The Golden Notebook
New York (1962)

Lessing, Doris
A Man and Two Women
London (1963)

Lessing, Doris
Retreat to Innocence
London (1959)

Leuchtenberg, William
The Perils of Prosperity, 1914-1932
Chicago: University of Chicago Press (1958)

Levertov, Denise
The Jacob's Ladder, Poems
New York (1961)

Levertov, Denise
O Taste and See, New Poems
New York (1964)

Levertov, Denise
The Sorrow Dance, Poems
New York (1967)

Levine, Steven
"The Girl I Love"
California Living
(January 25, 1970)

Levy, Richard G.
Why Women Should Rule the World
New York (1952)

Lewis, Edwin C.
Developing Woman's Potential
A psychological approach to women in the twentieth century. The author attempts to show the pressures, problems, opportunities which confront the typical woman in modern America, with the intent that counselors and others who work with women in shaping their futures will be adequately informed to counsel them wisely and with integrity. Lewis contends that woman's major dilemma is striving to become a person without knowing what kind of person she wants to be. He numbers among his concerns the tendency to treat women as stereotypes rather than as individuals, the conflict of role expectations resulting from society's ambiguous definitions of women's roles and the loss of productive years through faulty counseling and life planning.

Lewis, Helen Matthews
The Woman Movement and the Negro Movement: Parallel Struggles for Rights
Phelps-Stokes Fellowship Papers #19
Virginia: University of Virginia Press (1949)

Lewis, Janet
The Wife of Martin Guerre
Denver: A. Swallow (1950),
(c. 1941)

Lewis, Sinclair
Ann Vickers
Garden City, N.Y.: Doubleday, Doran and Co. (1933)

Lewis, Sinclair
Main Street
New York (1920)

"Liberation of Women Slated to be Crucial Issue"
Christian Science Monitor
(April 10, 1970)

Library on History of Women
Mrs. Herbert Haber, Librarian
Radcliffe College
3 James St.
Cambridge, Mass.

Liebow, Elliot
Tally's Corner; a Study of Negro Streetcorner Men
Boston (1967)

Lifton, Robert Jay
The Woman in America
Boston (1965)

Lileth
c/o Women's Majority Union
Box 1895
Seattle, Wash.

Limpus, Laurel
"Liberation of Women"
This Magazine is About Schools,
III, i (Winter 1969)

Limpus, Laurel
"Liberation of Women: Sexual Repression and the Family"
This Magazine is About Schools
(Spring 1969)

Linnér, Brigitta in collaboration with Richard J. Litell
Sex and Society in Sweden
New York (1967)

Livermore, Mary
My Story of the War: a woman's narrative of four years personal experience as nurse in the Union army, and in relief work at home, in hospitals, camps, and at the front, during the war of the rebellion.
Hartford, Conn.: A. D. Worthington & Co. (1890)

Locke, Alain, ed.
The New Negro: An Interpretation
New York (1968)

Lomas, Peter
"Family Democracy" Review of *Society Without the Father* by Alexander Mitscherlich
New Statesman
(April 11, 1969)

Lomas, Peter
Review of *The Hands of the Living God: An Account of a Psycho-analytic Treatment* by Marian Milner
New Statesman
(January 30, 1970)

Long, Clarence D.
The Labor Force Under Changing Income and Employment
Cambridge: Princeton University Press (1958)

Long, Priscilla, ed.
The New Left: A Collection of Essays
Boston (1969)

Lopate, Carol
Women in Medicine
Baltimore: Johns Hopkins Press
(1968)

Lopata, Helena Znaniecki
Occupation: Housewife
New York: Oxford University
Press (1971)
A Scholarly work by a
professional sociologist which
examines the attitudes of
housewives toward marriage,
the housewife's duties, the
mother's role, and the
neighbor's role. Although the
author strives for an objective
tone, she recognizes that the
"feminine mystique" does exist,
that women see their roles as
very limited and that they
realize their contributions to life
are minimal. The study provides
a great deal of sociological
evidence to support many of the
claims made by popular
journalists.

Lorca, García
*The House of Bernanda Alba,
in Three Tragedies*
trans. James Graham—Luján
and Richard L. O'Connell
New York: New Directions
(1955), (c. 1947)
Los Angeles Women's Center
1027 Crenshaw
Los Angeles, Calif.

Love, Cornelia Spencer
*Famous Women of Yesterday
and Today*
Chapel Hill, N.C.: University
of N. C. Press (1936)

Love/Woman Poetry Corp VII
Michael J. Phillips, Dept. of
English
University of Wisc.
Milwaukee, Wisc. 53201

Lowell, Amy
Selected Poems
ed. John Livingstone Lowes
Boston (1928)

Lowenthal, Leo
*Literature and the Image of Man;
Sociological Studies of the
European Drama and Novel
1600-1900*
Boston (1957)

Ludovici, Lawrence
The Final Inequality
New York (1965)

Luhan, Mabel Dodge
Intimate Memories
New York: Harcourt, Brace
and Co. (1933-1936)

**Lundberg, Ferdinand and
Marynia F. Farham**
Modern Woman, the Lost Sex
New York (1947)
One of the most important
contributors to the "feminine
mystique." Ranking with Freud
and Deutsch on the Women's
Liberation black list, the book
deplores woman's loss of
femininity and true womanhood
in her efforts to achieve
"liberation."

Lurie, Alison
Love and Friendship
New York (1962)

Lurie, Nancy, ed.
*Mountain Wolf Woman;
Autobiography of a Winnebago
Indian*
Ann Arbor: University of
Mich. Press (1961)

Lutz, Alma
*Created Equal; a Biography of
Elizabeth Cady Stanton, 1815-1902*
New York: The John Day Co.
(1940)

Lutz, Alma
*Crusade for Freedom: Women in
the Anti-Slavery Movement*
Boston (1968)

Lutz, Alma
*Emma Willard, Daughter of
Democracy*
Boston and New York:
Houghton, Mifflin (1929)

Lutz, Alma
*Susan B. Anthony: Rebel,
Crusader, Humanitarian*
Boston (1959)

Luxembourg, Rosa
*Prison Letters of
Rosa Luxembourg*
ed. Louise Kaitsky
tr. Louis P. Lochner
McBride (1925)

Lydon, Susan
"Understanding Orgasm"
Ramparts
(December 14-28, 1969)

Lynd, Staughton
*Intellectual Origins of
American Radicalism*
New York (1968)

Lynd, Staughton, ed.
Non-violence in America
Indianapolis (1966)

Lynns, Richard
"5 Women Named Aquanaut
Team"
New York Times
(March 3, 1970)

Lyon, Mary
Life and Labors of Mary Lyon
New York: American Tract
Society (1858)

Lysistrata
c/o Rony Howard, Dept. of
English
Slippery Rock State College
Slippery Rock, Pa. 16057

McCarthy, Mary
Memories of a Catholic Girlhood
New York (1957)

McClelland, Clarence
"The Education of Females
in Early Illinois"
*Journal of the Illinois State
Historical Society*
XXXVI, 318-407 (n.d.)

McClelland, Muriel
Inequality in Industrial Authority,
Princeton Center for International
Studies (1969)

McCollum, Vashti Crowell
One Woman's Fight
Boston (1951)

McCullers, Carson
The Ballad of the Sad Cafe
adapted to the stage
by Edward Albee
Boston (1963)

McCullers, Carson
The Member of the Wedding
New York: New Directions
(1951)

McDonald, Ellen
"Educated Women, the Last
Minority?"
Columbia University Forum
(Summer 1967)

McGovern, James R.
"The American Woman's
Pre-World War I Freedom
in Manners and Morals"
Journal of American History
(December 1968)

McGuigan, Dorothy Geis
*A Dangerous Experiment: 100
Years of Women at the University
of Michigan*
Ann Arbor: Center for
Continuing Education (1970)

McKerron, Jane
"Abortion: Can Doctors Cope?"
New Statesman
(February 9, 1968)

McKinley, Donald Gilbert
Social Class and Family Life
New York (1964)

McMahon, Teresa Schmid
Women and Economic Evolution
Bulletin of the University of
Wisconsin, #496, Economics
and Political Science Series,
vol. 7, no. 2
Madison: University of Wisconsin
Press (1908)

McNetting, Robert
"Marital Relations in the
Jos Plateau of Nigeria"
American Anthropologist
(December 1969)

MacDonald, James Ramsey, ed.
*Women in the Printing Trades;
a Sociological Study*
London: P. S. King and Son
(1904)

MacDougall, Allan Rose
"Who was Isadora?"
Dance Magazine
(June, 1969)

McNally, Gertrude Bancroft
"Patterns of Female Labor
Force Activity"
Industrial Relations (May 1968)

MacNamara, Desmond
"Nin et Al" review of the
Journals of Anais Nin Vol. II,
by Anais Nin
New Statesman
(December 1, 1967)

McNulty, Donald
"Differences in Pay Between
Men and Women Workers"
Monthly Labor Review
(December 1967)

McVeety, Jean
"Law and the Single Woman"
Women Lawyers Journal, LIII, 10
(Winter 1967)

Mailer, Norman
The Prisoner of Sex
Boston (1971)

Mailer, Norman
"The Time of Her Time," in
Advertisements for Myself
New York (1959)

Mailer, Norman
An American Dream
New York (1965)

Mailer, Norman
The Prisoner of Sex
Boston: Little, Brown and Co.
(1971)

Mallet, Francoise
Joris, A Letter to Myself
New York (1964)

Malraux, André
The Temptation of the West
New York (1961)

Malraux, André
Man's Fate
New York (1961)

Mann, Arthur
*Yankee Reformers in the
Urban Age*
Cambridge: Harvard
University Press (1954)

Mansfield, Katherine
*The Short Stories of
Katherine Mansfield*
New York: A. A. Knopf (1937)

Man-u-code, Augtwofive, ed.
Rolla Rieder
Craig Ellis
212 Mt. Auburn St.
Watertown, Me. 02172
Maprix
ed. Rdell
Box 46067
Los Angeles, Ca. 90046

Marcus, Steven
*The Other Victorians; A Study of
Sexuality and Pornography in
Mid-Nineteenth Century England*
New York (1966)

Marcuse, Herbert
*Eros and Civilization; a
Philosophical Inquiry into Freud*
Boston (1955)

Marcuse, Herbert
"Love Mystified: A Critique of
Norman O. Brown"
Commentary
(February 1967)

Marder, Herbert
*Feminism and Art: A Study of
Virginia Woolf*
Chicago: University of Chicago
Press (1968)

Marr, Jean
Woman in Parliament
London (1962)

Marris, Peter
*Family and Social Change in an
African City*
Evanston, Ill.: Northwestern
University Press (1960)

Marshall, Paule
*The Chosen Place, the
Timeless People*
New York (1969)

Marshall, H. E.
*Dorothea Dix: Forgotten
Samaritan*
Chapel Hill: University of
N. C. Press (1937)

Marteneau, Harriet
Society in America
ed. and abridged by
Seymour Martin Lipset
Gloucester, Mass.: (1968),
(c. 1962)

Martinson, Floyd Mansfield
Family in Society
New York (1970)

Marx, Karl and Fredrich Engels
The Communist Manifesto
New York (1963)

Maslow, Abraham
"Dominance, Personality and
Social Behavior in Women
Journal of Social Psychology, X,
3-39 (1939)

Maslow, Abraham
"Self-esteem (Dominance
Feeling) and Sexuality in
Women"
Journal of Social Psychology,
XVI, 259-94 (1942)

Maslow, Abraham
Toward a Psychology of Being
Princeton, N.J. (1962)

Massey, Mary
*Bonnet Brigades: American
Women and the Civil War*
New York (1966)

**Masters, William H. and
Virginia E. Johnson**
Human Sexual Inadequacy
Boston (1970)

**Masters, William H. and
Virginia E. Johnson**
Human Sexual Response
Reproductive Biology Research
Foundation, St. Louis, Missouri
Boston (1966)

**Mattfeld, Jacquelyn A. and
Carol G. Van Aken, eds.**
*Women and the Scientific
Professions*
Cambridge, Mass.: Mass.
Institute of Technology Press
(1965)
A series of papers presented
at an MIT symposium on
American women in science

and engineering. The authors consider such topics as the problems women face in getting into scientific fields, staying in them, and eventually getting ahead in their careers. The contributors, including Jessie Bernard, Bruno Bettleheim, Erik Erikson, and Alice Rossi among others, see considerable hope for women in teaching in the sciences on the college level if they are willing to remain on the fringes of the profession. Leaving the research and publication to men would allow women to concentrate on rewarding relationships with students as well as satisfying home lives. The authors tend to ignore the fact that the system may need to be shaped to fit the people who work in it rather than vice versa.

Maulde la Clavière, Marie Alphonse Rene de
The Women of the Renaissance; a Study of Feminism
London: S. Sonnenschein and Co. (1900)

Mauriac, Claude
"Chinese Chastity for the Good of the Community" review of "The Arch" (film) by Shu Shuen
Atlas
(December 1969)

Maverick
P.O. Box 77, Agnew Station
Santa Clara, Calif.

May, Janice
"Equal Rights Amendment"
AAUW Journal, III (October 1970)

Mazzocco, Robert
"Swingtime" review of *Against Interpretation* by Susan Sontag
New York Review of Books
(March 13, 1969)

Mead, Margaret and Frances Kaplan, ed.
American Women: The Report of the President's Commission on the Status of Women
New York: Scribner (1965)
A study initiated by the President to investigate the status of American women in the sixties. The contributors show concern with educating women realistically, particularly in the opportunities and labor standards for women who work, the

realities of financial security (unemployment, maternity benefits), and the legal recognition of women (property rights, constitutional recognition). The book evaluates the situation of women and presents a variety of views on what is being done to solve the problems and how effective these programs are.

Mead, Margaret, ed.
Cultural Patterns and Technical Change
New York (1955)

Mead, Margaret
Male and Female: A Study of the Sexes in a Changing World
New York (1955), (c. 1949)

Media Women
G. P. O. 1692
New York, N.Y. 10001

Melder, Keith
"The Beginnings of the Women's Movement, 1800-1840"
(Unpublished dissertation)
New Haven, Conn.: Yale University Press (1963)

Melder, Keith
"Ladies Bountiful"
New York History, XLVIII, 231-255 (n.d.)

Melville, Robert
"Alma Without Gustav"
New Statesman
(August 11, 1967)

Melville, Robert
"Woman as Poison"
New Statesman
(July 25, 1969)

Mencken, H. L.
In Defense of Women
New York: Knopf (1922)

Mercer, Marilyn
"Is There Room at the Top?"
The Saturday Evening Post
(June 31, 1968)

Meredith, George
The Egoist
New York (1947)

Merriam, Eve
After Eve Slammed the Door: American Women in the 1960's
Cleveland (1964)

Merriam, Eve
After Nora Slammed the Door
A witty, but biting examination of woman's situation in modern America. Using Ibsen's Nora

as a kind of Everywoman, the author traces the possible routes she could take: 1/ retreat to safety in the doll's house, despite the frustrations; 2/ make it to the middle rung of the ladder with men to avoid competition with husbands and other; 3/ take up the life of the unmarried woman and learn to live in limbo. The author also exposes such myths as the "big, powerful Momma" who makes money for Madison Avenue, the "woman's place is the home" credo, and the stereotypes applied to women such as the total housewife, the shrew-wife in the suburbs and and the Venus-type. The book contends that all American women really want is a satisfying job and a homelife.

Metz, Tim
"Virility-Conscious Set at Dartmouth Decries the Advent of Co-eds"
Wall Street Journal
(October 1, 1969)

Meyer, Annie, ed.
Women's Work in America
New York: n.p. (1891)

Middleton, Putney
"Dominance in Decision in the Family: Race and Class Differences"
American Journal of Sociology, LXV (May 1960)

The Militant
873 Broadway
New York, N.Y.

Mill, John Stuart and Harriet Taylor Mill
Essays on Sex Equality
ed. Alice S. Rossi
Chicago: University of Chicago Press (1970)

Mill, John Stuart
The Subjection of Women
Philadelphia (1869)
A classic work of feminist literature in which the author pleads for an end to the enslavement of women. Arguing in philosophical rather than practical terms, Mill attempts to balance his belief that men and women are complementary to each other with his belief that the two sexes are equal. As a typical English liberal of his day, he based his belief in the

necessity of granting freedom to women on his more general conviction that the individual must have control over the affairs which concern him directly. Mill anticipated that granting full freedom to women would contribute to the "reformation of the human character," a goal which ranked as one of his most important.

Miller, Calvin
"St. Paul and the Liberated Woman"
Christianity Today
(August 6, 1971)

Miller, Henry
Tropic of Cancer
New York (1961)

Miller, Isabel
A Place for Us
n.p. (n.d.)

Miller, John N.
A World of Her Own: Writers and the Feminist Controversy
Columbus, Ohio (1971)

Millett, Kate
Sexual Politics
Garden City, N.Y. (1970)
Spends half the book on establishing and describing the existence of a patriarchy, half on literary exegesis of authors to which Mailer has addressed himself. The two in combination with works of the authors discussed, very interesting.

Millet, Kate
"Sexual Politics: Miller, Mailer, and Genet"
New American Review
(August 1969)

Millett, Kate
Token Learning: A Study of Women's Higher Education in America
New York: National Organization for Women (1968)

Mills, Nicolaus C.
"The Mothers Said No"
Nation
(November 25, 1968)

Mistral, Frédéric
Oeuvres Poetiques Complétes
Barcelona: Ramoun Berenguié (1966)

Mitchell, David J.
The Fighting Pankhursts; a Study in Tenacity
New York (1967)

Mitchell, David J.
Monstrous Regiment; the Story of the Women of the First World War
New York (1965)

Mitchell, Julian
"Grim Grin in the Gloom," review of *Frances with My Aunt* by Graham Greene
New Statesman
(November 21, 1969)

Mitford, Jessica
The American Way of Death
New York (1963)

Mitford, Jessica
The Trial of Dr. Spock, the Rev. William Sloane Coffin, Michael Ferber, Mitchell Goodman, and Marcus Raskin
New York (1969)

Mitscherlich, Alexander
Society Without the Father
New York (1969)

Moller, Herbert
"Sex Composition and Correlated Patterns of Colonial America"
William and Mary Quarterly, II, 113-153 (1945)

Montagu, Mary Wortley
The Complete Letters of Lady Mary Wortley Montagu
ed. Robert Halsband
Oxford: Clarendon Press (1965-1967)

Montgomery, Royal Ewart and Harry Alvin Millis
Organized Labor
3 vols.
New York and London: McGraw-Hill (1945)

Moody, Anne
Coming of Age in Mississippi
New York (1968)

Moran, Robert
"Reducing Discrimination: Role of the Equal Pay Act"
Monthly Labor Review (June 1970)

Morgan, Edmund
The Puritan Family; Essays on Religion and Domestic Relations in seventeenth Century New England
Boston, Mass.: The Trustees of the Public Library (1944)

Morgan, Edmund S.
The Puritan Family: Religion and Domestic Relations in 17th Century New England
New York (1966)

Morgan, Edmund Sears
Virginians at Home; Family Life in the 18th Century
Williamsburg, Va.: Colonial Williamsburg (1952)

Morgan, Robin, ed.
Sisterhood in Powerful
New York: Random House (1970)
One of the most comprehensive anthologies of writings from the Women's Liberation Movement. The work attempts to present a broad perspective on the problems of women by including the writings of women of all ages, professions, economic level, and ideological persuasions. The essays discuss such subjects as women in the professions; the psychological and sexual pressures put on women through social myths, literature, and the media; women in the black liberation movement; the problems of high school women and minority groups; the growth of ideological bases for women's liberation groups. The book is unique and particularly valuable because of the historical documents of the Women's Liberation Movement, an excellent bibliography, and information on liberation groups across the country.

Moriarty, Claire
"On Women's Liberation"
New Politics, II, ii (Spring 1970)

Morris, Richard B.
Government and Labor in Early America
New York: Columbia University Press (1946)

Morris, Robert K.
"Represses Consciousness," review of *The Collected Stories of Peter Taylor,* by Peter Taylor
Nation
(October 20, 1969)

Mortimer, Penelope
"Isadora Reborn"
Films Observer Review
(March 9, 1969)

Mortimer, Penelope
The Pumpkin Eater
New York: McGraw-Hill (1963)

Moses, Mary S.
"The Pioneer Woman"
Historian, II, 5-16 (n. d.)

Mother
P.O. Box 8507
Stanford, Calif. 94305

Mother Lode
334 Winfield St.
San Francisco, Ca. 94110

Mouat, Lucia
"Men favored in jobs,
Mrs. Griffiths says"
Christian Science Monitor
(August 9, 1969)

Mueller, Kate
Educating Women for a Changing World
Minneapolis: University of Minn.
Press (1954)

Murasaki, Shikibu
The Tale of Genji
Boston: Houghton, Mifflin (1925)

Murdoch, Iris
The Unicorn
New York (1963)

Murdoch, Iris, and J. B. Priestley
A Severed Head
London (1964)

Murray, Thomas J.
"It's Hell in Personnel"
Duns (March 1971) also
"Revolt of the Middle Managers"
Duns (Sept. 1969) and
"Executives in Ferment"
Duns (January 1971)

Murray, Pauli and Mary Eastwood
"Jane Crow and the Law: Sex Discrimination and Title VII"
George Washington Law Review,
XXXIV (1965)

Murton, Tom
"One Year of Prison Reform"
Nation
(January 12, 1970)

Mushroom Effect: A Directory of Women's
P.O. Box 6024
Albany, Ca. 94706

Myerson, Abraham
The Nervous Housewife
Boston: Little, Brown (1920)

Myrdal, Gunnar
The American Dilemma
New York: Harper (1962),
(c. 1944)

Myrdal, Jan
Report from a Chinese Village
New York (1965)

Myrid, Alva and Viola Klein
Woman's Two Roles, Home and Work
New York (1968)
A sociological study of the factors which affect women in deciding to pursue a career of homemaking or both. The authors discuss the phases in a woman's life and the problems she faces in a society in which everyone lives longer and therefore has much more time to occupy after the years of intensive childcare are over. Among the reasons women gave for going out to work were financial need (including supplementing a husband's income) and a sense of extreme isolation. Because the authors found that so many women wanted to work, they presented ways of reorganizing the labor situation to accommodate women; encouraging parttime work, reducing the work day to six hours to allow both parents to return home when the children return from school, encouraging middle-aged women to enter the labor force by offering equal advancement and pay, and so forth.

Nathan, Maud
The Story of an Epoch-Making Movement
n.p. (n.d.)

National Ad Hoc Committee for ERA Newsletter
c/o Flora Crater
2310 Barbour Rd.
Falls Church, Va. 22043

National Manpower Council
Womanpower
New York: Columbia University
Press (1957)

National Organization for Women
1952 E. 73rd St.
Chicago, Ill. 312-324-3067
Founded by Betty Friedan

National Woman's Party
144 Constitution Ave.
Washington, D.C. 20002

"Negro Women . . . in the Population and in the Labor Force"
U.S. Department of Labor; Wage & Labor Standards Administration
(December 1967)

Nelson, Truman
The Torture of Mothers
Newburyport: The Garrison Press (1965)

Neu, Charles
"Olympia Brown and the Woman's Suffrage Movement"
Wisconsin Magazine of History
(Summer 1960)

New Broadside
Box 390, Cooper Station, Dept. S
(41 Union Square W,
Room 1328)
New York, N.Y. 10003

New Broom Monthly Legislative News
Box 341, Prudential Center Station
Boston, Mass. 02143

New Carolina Woman
Box 1586
Fayetteville, N.C. 28302

New England Free Press
791 Tremont St.
Boston, Mass. 02118

"New Feminism: A Potent Force in Birthcontrol Policy"
Science (February 27, 1970)

The New Feminist
Box 597, Station A
(67 Huntly St.)
Toronto 116, Ontario, Canada

New Feminists Repertory Theater
c/o Dell Olio
43 West 54th St.
New York, N.Y.

New Mexico W.L. Newsletter
c/o Nancy Adair
804 Vassar N.E.
Albuquerque, N.M. 87106

News Women's Liberation of Louisville
1131 S. Brook, Apt. 1
Louisville, Ky. 40203

New Woman
Box 24202
Ft. Lauderdale, Fla. 33302

New York Feminist
20000 Broadway
New York, N.Y. 10023

Newcomer, Mabel
A Century of Higher Education for Women
New York (1959)

Newman, F. X., ed.
The Meaning of Courtly Love
New York: State University of New York Press (1968)

Newman, Randy
"Records: Rock, etc."
New Yorker
(April 18, 1970)

News and Letters
Detroit Women's Liberation
415 Brainard
Detroit, Mich. 48201

New York Radical Feminists
Box 621, Old Chelsea Station
New York, N.Y. 10011

New York Radical Women
Notes From the First Year
New York: NYRW 799 Broadway,
Room 412 (June 1968)

New Women's Paper
Media Center
2 Brookline St.
Cambridge, Mass.

Nimkoff, M. F.
Comparative Family Systems
New York (1965)

Nin, Anaís
The Diary of Anais Nin
New York: Swallow Press (1966)

No More Fun and Games
371 Somerville Ave.
Somerville, Mass. 02143

**"No Place for Women,
or Several?"**
Catholic World (February 1970)

Noble, Jeanne
Negro Woman's College
Education
n.p. (n.d.)

Nochlin, Linda
"Why Have There Been No Great
Women Artists?"
Art News, 69, 22-39, 67-71 (1971)

No More Fun and Games
A Journal of Female Liberation
16 Lexington Street,
Cambridge, Mass.

"Nonwhite Women Workers,"
U.S. Department of Labor
Women's Bureau
Washington, D.C. 20210

Nordhoff, Charles
Communistic Societies of the U.S.
New York: Harper and Brothers
(1875)

Notes on Women's Liberation
1900 E. Jefferson
Detroit, Mich. 48207

Notes from the Second Year
P.O. Box AA, Old Chelsea
Station
New York, N.Y. 10011

Nottingham, Elizabeth
"Toward an Analysis of the
Effects of the Two World Wars
on the Role and Status of
Middle Class Women"
American Sociological Review
(December 1947)

NOW
P.O. Box 114, Cathedral Station
New York, N.Y. 10025

NOW Acts
ed. Virginia Caralullo
1126 Hipoint St.
Los Angeles, Ca. 90039

NOW Chapter Newsletter
700 Penn Center Blvd., Apt. 207
Pittsburg, Pa.

NOW Newsletter
1952 E. 73rd St.
Chicago, Ill.

NOW Notes Atlanta NOW, YMCA
72 Edgewood Ave. N.E.
Atlanta, Ga. 30303

The NOW York Times
c/o N.Y. Women's Center
36 W. 22nd St.
New York, N.Y.

Noyes, John Humphrey
History of American Socialisms
New York: Dover Publications
(1966)

**Nye, F. Ivan and
Lois Wladis Hoffman**
The Employed Mother in America
Chicago (1963)

Oates, Joyce Carol
Expensive People
New York (1968)

Oates, Joyce Carol
A Garden of Earthly Delights
New York (1967)

Oates, Joyce Carol
Them
New York (1969)

Off Our Backs
P.O. Box 4859, Cleveland Park
Station
Washington, D.C. 20008

Off the Pedestal
376 Addison St.
Palo Alto, Ca. 94301

Older Women's Liberation
Women's Liberation Center
of N.Y.
36 W. 22nd St.
New York, N.Y. 10010

Oltman, Ruth M.
*Campus 1970: Where Do Women
Stand?*
Washington, D.C.: American
Association of University
Women (1970)

O'Brien, John A.
"Women in the Church: God's
Forgotten Children"
U.S. Catholic Jubilee (Jan. 1971)

O'Brien, Edna
Girls in Their Married Bliss
New York (1964)

O'Connor, Flannery
*A Good Man is Hard to Find and
Other Stories*
New York (1955)

O'Neill, Eugene
Desire Under the Elms, in *Nine
Plays,* selected by the author
New York: Liveright (1932)

O'Neill, William
Divorce in the Progressive Era
New Haven, Conn.: Yale
University Press (1967)
A study of the (moral)
conservative and (moral) liberal
approaches to the rising divorce
rate in the last part of the
nineteenth century. The author
sees the increase in divorces
as an index of the extreme
stresses placed on the solidarity
of the family by the growth of
industrial life. The changing
attitudes of the public toward
divorce reflect the changing
moral values of Americans,
particularly a shift from concern
for the general welfare to a
concern for civil liberties. The
author also contends that the
divorce issue was closely linked
to the feminist movement
because it reflected women's
concern for egalitarian
relationships with men.

O'Neill, William L.
Everyone Was Brave
Chicago: A Quadrangle
Paperback (1969)

O'Neill, William
*The Woman Movement: Feminism
in the U.S. and England*
New York: Barnes and Noble
(1969) also
London: Allen and Unwin (1969)
A history of social feminism and
the fight for suffrage in the
United States and Britain, with
a selection of documents from
the mid nineteenth century to
1929.

Opie, Iona and Peter Opie
*The Lore and Language of School
Children*
Oxford: Clarendon Press (1959)

Oppenheimer, Valerie Kincade
*The Female Labor Force in the
United States*
Berkeley: Institute of International
Studies
University of Calif. (1970)

Oppenheimer, Valerie Kincade
"The Sex Labeling of Jobs"
Industrial Relations (May 1968)

Ormsbee, Hazel
The Young Employed Girl
Bryn Mawr (1927)

Ossoli, Sarah Margaret (Fuller)
Woman in the Nineteenth Century
ed. Arthur B. Fuller
Boston: Brown, Taggard and
Chase (1860)

Ovington, Mary
*Half a Man; the Status of the
Negro in New York*
New York (1949)

Ovington, Mary White
The Walls Came Tumbling Down
New York (1947)

Owens, Rochelle
Futz and What Came After
New York (1968)

Paine, Thomas
"An Occasional Letter on the
Female Sex," in his Complete
Works.
Chicago: Belford, Clarke (1885)

Paley, Grace
The Little Disturbances of Man
Garden City, New York (1959)

Pandora
4224 University Way, N.E.,
Seattle, Washington 98105

Pandora's Box
Box 22094, San Diego,
California 92122

Pankhurst, Emmeline
My Own Story
New York: Hearst's International
Company (1914)

Pankhurst, Estelle Sylvia
*The Suffragette: The History of
the Woman's Militant Suffrage
Movement 1905-1910*
New York: Sturgis and
Walton Co. (1911)

Pankhurst, Sylvia
*The Suffrage Movement: An
Intimate Account of Persons and
Ideals*
New York: Longmans Green
(1931)

Papashvily, Helen
*All the Happy Endings: a Study of
the Domestic Novel in America,
the Women Who Wrote It, the
Women Who Read It in the
Nineteenth Century.*
New York (1956)

Park, Maud Wood
Front Door Lobby
Boston (1960)

Parker, Dorothy
*Here Lies: the Collected Short
Stories of Dorothy Parker*
New York: Literary Guild of
America (1939)

Parkman, Francis
Vassal Morton
Boston: Phillips, Samson (1856)

Parsons, Alice Beal
Woman's Dilemma
New York (1924)

Parsons, Talcott
"Age and sex in the social
structure of the United States"
American Sociological Review,
VII (October 1942)

Parsons, Talcott and Robert F. Bales
*Family, Socialization and
Interaction Process*
Glencoe, Ill. (1954)

Patai, Raphael
Women in the Modern World
New York (1967)

Patai, Raphael, ed.
Women in the Modern World
New York (1967)

Pathfinder Press
873 Broadway, New York.
They have a series of
pamphlets: "Problems of
Women's Liberation: A Marxist
Approach" "In Defense of the
Women's Movement" "Pioneers
of Women's Liberation"
"The Politics of Women's
Liberation" and others.

Patmore, Coventry Kersey Dighton
*The Angel in the House and the
Betrothal*
Boston: Ticknor and Fields
(1856)

Pavese, Cesare
Among Women Only
New York (1959)

Pearsall, Ronald
*The Worm in the Bud: the World
of Victorian Sexuality*
New York (1969)

Peck, Ellen
The Baby Trap
New York (1971)

**Pedestal Peak Publication
Society**
511 Carroll St. Vancourver 4,
C.C., Canada

**Pennington, Patience (pseud. for
Pringle, Elizabeth Waties)**
A Woman Rice Planter
ed. Cornelius O. Cathey
Cambridge: Harvard University
Press (1961)

Penny, Virginia
*Five Hundred Employments
Adapted to Women with Average
Rate of Pay in Each*
Philadelphia: n.p. (1868)

Perham, Margery Freda
Native Administration in Nigeria
London: Oxford University Press
(1962)

Persuasion
77 7th Ave., Apt. 16B, New York,
New York 10011

Perutz, Kathryn
*Beyond the Looking Glass:
America's Beauty Culture*
New York (1970)

Pickens, Donald D.
Eugenics and the Progressives
Nashville: Vanderbilt University
(1968)

Pifer, Alan
"Women in Higher Education",
speech: *Southern Association of
Colleges and Schools*
(November 29, 1971)

Pike, Edgar Royston
*Human Documents of the
Victorian Golden Age*
London (1969)

Pilati, Joe
"Five Women vs. The Draft
Board"
Village Voice
(January 10, 1969)

Pilpel, Harriet and Theodora Zavin
Your Marriage and the Law
New York (1965)

Pissed Off Pink
1404 E. Oakland, Lansing,
Michigan

Plath, Sylvia
Ariel
New York (1966)

Plath, Sylvia
*Crossing the Water: transitional
poems*
New York (1971)

Plath, Sylvia
The Bell Jar
New York (1966)

"Playboy Interview: Madalyn Murray"
Playboy
(October, 1966)

"PM"
Florida Free Press
Bob Broedel, 308 S. Macomb St.
Tallahassee, Florida 32301

Pogrebin, Letty Cottin
How to Make it in a Man's World
Garden City, N.Y. (1970)

Poirier, Richard
Reviews of *The Freudian Left* by
Paul Robinson and *Wilhelm Reich*
by Ilse Reich
New York Times Book Review
(October 26, 1969)

Poll, S.
*Hasidic Community of
Williamsburg*
New York (1962)

Pool, Rosey E., Ed.
Beyond the Blues
Lympne, Kent: Hand and
Slower Press (1962)

Porter, John
*The Vertical Mosaic: An Analysis
of Social Class and Power in*
Toronto: University of Toronto
Press (1965)

Porter, Katherine A.
*Flowering Judas and Other
Stories*
New York (1940)

Porter, Katherine A.
Pale Horse, Pale Rider
New York (1939)

Porter, Katherine A.
*The Leaning Tower and Other
Stories*
New York (1944)

Porter, Katherine A.
The Older Order
New York (1944)

Porter, Peter
"Death as Key" review of *The
Art of Sylvia Plath* by Charles
Newman, ed
New Statesman
(January 9, 1970)

Porter, Sylvia
"Maternity Leave Policies
Illegal, Employer to Find"
Atlanta Journal
(February 28, 1967)

Poussaint, Alvin F.
"The Stresses of the White
Female Worker in the Civil
Rights Movement in the South"
American Journal of Psychiatry,
CXIII
(October 1966)

Powell, Chilton
*English Domestic Relations 1487-
1653: a Study of Matrimony and
Family Life in Theory and Practice
as Revealed by the Literature,
Law and History of the Period.*
New York: Columbia University
Press (1917)

Powell, Chilton
"Marriage in Early
New England"
New England Quarterly I, 323-
334 (1928)

Praz, Mario
The Romantic Agony
New York (1951)

Pressman, Sonia, Senior Attorney
EEOC
"A Man and a Woman—Who
Gets the Job?"
(January 23, 1969)

Pressman, Sonia
"Sex Discrimination in
Employment and What you can
do about it"
Women Lawyers Journal, LIV, No.
4, 6 (Fall 1968)

**Prevost, Antonine Francois,
called Prevost d'Exiles**
Manon Lescaut
Trans. Helen Waddell
New York: Heritage Press (1935)

Pritchett, V. S.
"The Early Bourgeois World"
New Statesman
(September 1, 1967)

Professional Women's Caucus
P.O. Box 1057 Radio City
Station, New York, N.Y.

Pruette, Lorine
*Women and Leisure: A Study of
Social Waste*
New York: E. P. Dutton (1924)

**Pruette, Loraine and Iva Lowthers
Peters, eds.**
*Women Workers Through the
Depression*
New York: Macmillan (1934)

Pullen, Doris
"The Educational Establishment:
Wasted Women"
Voices of the New Feminism
edited by Mary Lou Thompson
Boston (1970)

Racine, Jean Baptiste
Andromaque
Baltimore (1967)

Racine, Jean Baptiste
Phedre
New York (1966)

Radical America
1237 Spaight Street,
Madison, Wisconsin 53703

Radical Lesbians
c/o Women's Center, 36 West
22nd Street, New York,
New York 10010

Rainbow Snake
San Diego Women's Poetry
Center for Women's Studies
and Services
San Diego State College,
San Diego, California 92115

Rainwater, Lee
"Crucible of Identity"
Daedalus, VC, (Winter, 1966)

**Rainwater, Lee and
Karol Weinstein**
And The Poor Get Children
Chicago (1960)

Rainwater, Lee and William Yancey
*The Moynihan Report and the
Politics of Controversy*
Cambridge, Massachusetts:
Massachusetts Institute of
Technology Press (1967)

**Rainwater, Lee and Coleman and
Handel**
Workingman's Wife
An objective study of lower-class
women which reveals marked
differences in their attitudes
toward the family and marriage
and the attitudes commonly
found among middle-and
upper-class women. The
authors found that, in general,
lower class women expected
life to be mundane, full of
endless, dull work. Their
children were bothersome to
them rather than the challenge
which middle-class women
found them. The women studied
showed little interest in going
out to work; they found the
traditional family pattern
acceptable even though they
complained a great deal about
boredom and their struggles
just to keep up with their
families' daily needs.

Ralph, C. H.
"The Tree of Knowledge" review
of *The End of Obscenity*
New Statesman
(April 11, 1969)

Randall, Ruth Painter
*Mary Lincoln: Biography of a
Marriage*
Boston (1953)

Rank, Otto
Will Therapy and Truth and Reality
New York (1945)

Ranzal, Ed
"Federal Court to Test
Constitutionality of States'
Abortion Laws"
New York Times
(November 6, 1969)

Rapoport, Rhona and Robert
"New Light on the Honeymoon"
Human Relations 17:1, 33-56
(1964)

Rapoport, Rhona
"The Transition from Engagement
to Marriage"
Acta Sociologica 8, 36-55 (1964)

Rapson, Richard
"The American Child as seen
by British Travellers 1845-1935
American Quarterly XVIII 520-534

Rat
241 East 14th St.
New York, New York

**Raush, H. W. Goodrich and
J. Campbell**
"Adaptation to First Years
of Marriage"
Psychiatry 26:4, 368-380
(November 1963)

Reage, Pauline
Story of O
New York (1965)

Red Star
Red Women's Detachment,
700 east 9th St.
New York, New York 10009

Redstockings
c/o The Group Center, 42½
St. Marks Place,
New York, New York 10003

Reed, Evelyn
*Problems of Women's Liberation:
A Marxist Approach*
New York (1971)
A collection of essays compiled
from speeches delivered by the
author on Marxist interpretations
of human development. Relying
on the work of Bachofen and
Briffault, the author argues
that women were the developers
of culture and industry and that
prehistorical society was
matriarchal-fratriarchal. She
contends that men eventually
achieved power through the
accumulation of capital and the
development of a class society.
The author lauds the work of
Betty Friedan and others of a
non-theoretical bent because
she sees potential for union
with sisters who can further the
revolution even though they
do not recognize the principles
involved. This is one of the
few recent works with a strong
theoretical orientation.

"Re-evaluating the Pill"
Newsweek
(January 12, 1970)

Reich, Ilse Ollendorf
*Wilhelm Reich: a Personal
Biography*
New York (1969)

Reich, Wilhelm
The Discovery of the Orgone
New York (1961)

Reich, Wilhelm
*The Sexual Revolution, Toward a
Self-Governing Character
Structure*
New York (1969)

Reik, Theodor
"Men and women speak
different language"
Psychoanalysis 1-2, 3-15 (Spring-
Summer 1954)

Reisig, Robin
"What Women Won May
Be Lost"
Village Voice
(July 23, 1970)

Remember Our Fire
Shameless Hussy Press,
2209 California Street,
Berkeley, California 94703

Renault, Mary
The Charioteer
New York (1959)

**Report of Governor Rockefeller's
Conference on the Status of Women.**
New York Women and
Their Changing World. (1969)

"Reporting the Movement"
Atlantic
(March 1970)

Reeve, Tapping
The Law of Baron and Femme
New York (1862)

Rheingold, J.
The Fear of Being a Woman
New York (1964)

Rhyne, Jennings Jefferson
*Some Cotton Mill Workers and
Villages*
Chapel Hill: University of
North Carolina Press (1930)

Rich, Adriene
"The Demon Lover"
New York Review of Books
(November 17, 1966)

Rich, Adrienne
*Necessities of Life: poems, 1962-
1965*
New York (1966)

Richardson, Bertha
*The Woman Who Spends: A Study
of her Economic Function*
Boston: Whitcomb and Barrows
(1910)

Richardson, Dorothy
*The Long Day: The Story of a
New York Working Girl as Told by
herself*
New York: The Century Co.
(1911)

Richardson, Dorothy
Pilgrimage
New York (1967)

Richardson, Samuel
Clarissa
New York (1950)

Riegel, Robert E.
American Feminists
Lawrence: University of
Kansas Press (1963)

Riegel, Robert E.
American Feminists
Lawrence, Kansas: University of
Kansas Press (1966)

Riegel, Robert Edgar
*American Women: A Story of
Social Change*
Rutherford, N.J.: Fairleigh
Dickinson University Press
(1970)

Riegel, Robert
"Women's Clothes and
Women's Rights"
American Quarterly (Autumn 1963)

Rimmer, Robert H.
The Harvard Experiment
New York (1967)

Rinehart, Mary
My Story
New York: Farrar and Rinehart,
Inc. (1931)

Roberts, Elizabeth Madox
The Time of Man
New York: Viking Press (1926)

Robertson, Andrew and Jean
"Faces their Fortune"
New Statesman
(May 30, 1969)

Robertson, Ross M.
History of the American Economy
New York (1964)

Robinson, Harriet
Loom and Spindle: or, Life Among the Early Mill Girls
New York: T. Y. Crowell and Co. (1898)

Robinson, Harriet
Massachusetts in the Woman Suffrage Movement 1774-1881
Boston: Roberts Brothers (1883)

Robinson, Lora H.
The Status of Academic Women
Review 5, Eric Clearinghouse on Higher Education
Washington, D.C. (1971)

Robinson, Paul
The Freudian Left
New York (1969)

Rockefeller, John D. III
"The New Chivalry"
Look
(October 7, 1969)

Rockwell, Jane
"Pity Revolutionary Women"
The Observer
(April 5, 1970)

Roddy, Joseph
"The Bernadette-Berrigan Encounter"
Look
(October 7, 1969)

Rogers, Katherine M.
The Troublesome Helpmate: A History of Misogyny in Literature
Seattle: University of Washington Press (1966)

Rolvaag, Ole Edvart
Giants in the Earth
New York: Harper (1927)

Rorem, Ned
"Woman: Artist or Artist-ess?"
Vogue
(April 1, 1970)

Rose, J. (ed.)
Technological Injury: The Effects of Technological Advances on Environment, Life and Society
London Gordon and Breach Science Publishers (1969)

Rosen, Gerald R.
"Business and the Radicals"
Duns
(June 1970)

Rosen, John
Direct Psychoanalytic Psychiatry
New York (1962)

Rosenbaum, Salo and Ian Alger, ed.
The Marriage Relationship
New York (1968)

Rosenbaum, Salo and Ian Alger
The Marriage Relationship: Psychoanalytic Perspectives
New York (1968)

Ross, Ishbel
Charmers and Cranks: Twelve Famous American Women Who Defied the Conventions
New York (1965)

Ross, Ishbel
Proud Kate: Portrait of an Ambitious Woman
New York (1953)

Rossi, Alice
"Abortion and Social Change"
Dissent, 338-346
(July-August 1969)

Rossi, Alice
"Abortion Laws and Their Victims"
Transaction
(September-October 1966)

Rossi, Alice
"Discrimination and Demography Restrict Opportunities for Academic Women"
College and University Business
(February 1970)

Rossi, Alice
"Job Discrimination and What Women Can Do About It"
Atlantic Monthly
(March 1970)

Rossi, Alice
"Naming Children in Middle Class Families"
American Sociological Review, XXX, IV
(August 1965)

Rossi, Alice
"Sex Equality: The Beginnings of Ideology"
The Humanist
(September-October 1969)

Rossi, Alice
"Transition to Parenthood"
Journal of Marriage and the Family, 30:1, 26-39
(February 1968)

Rossi, Alice
"Status of Women in Graduate Departments of Sociology 1968-69"
American Sociologist
(February 1970)

Rossi, Alice
"Transition to Parenthood"
Journal of Marriage and the Family
(February 1969)

Rossi, Alice
"Women in Science: Why so Few?"
Science
(May 28, 1965)

Roth, Philip
Goodbye, Columbus and Five Short Stories
Boston (1959)

Roth, Philip
Letting Go
New York (1962)

Roth, Philip
Portnoy's Complaint
New York (1969)

Rougemont, Denis de
Love in the Western World
New York (1956)

Rousmaniere, John
"Cultural Hybrid in the Slums"
American Quarterly
(Spring 1970)

Rousseau, Jean Jacques
Emile (Book V)
London: Dent (1911)

Rowson, Susanna
Charlotte Temple
New York
Evert Duyckinck (1814)

Roy, Rustum and Della
"Is Monogamy Outdated?"
The Humanist
(March-April 1970)

Roszak, Betty and Theodore, ed.
"Masculine/Feminine"
Readings in Sexual Mythology and the Liberation of Women.
New York (1969)
A relatively staid collection of essays and statements, including essays by male enemies and allies of women, essays "toward liberation," and a collection of women's liberation manifestoes. Selected annotated bibliography.

Rubin, Alan Miles and Betty J. Willis
"Discrimination Against Women in Employment in Higher Education"
Cleveland State Law Review 20, 472-491 (1971)

Ruben, David
"Dr. Ruben Answers Your Questions About Women's Liberation"
McCalls
(September 1971)

Rubin, Theodore Isacc
"What Makes a Man Lovable?"
Reader's Digest
(January 1970)

Ruether, Rosemary
"Women's Liberation in Historical and Theological Perspective"
Soundings
(Winter 1970)

Ruskin, John
Sesame and Lilies
Boston: Gini and Co. (1927)

Russell, Dora
Hypatia, or, Woman and Knowledge
New York: E. P. Dutton (1925)

Sade, Donatien Alphonse Francois, comte called marquis de.
Justine: or the Misfortunes of Virtue
Compiled and trans. by Richard Seaver and Austryn Wainhous.
New York (1966)

Safilios-Rothschild
"Family Sociology or Wives' Sociology? A Cross-Cultural Examination of Decision Making" *Journal of Marriage and Family,* 31:2, 290-301
(May 1969)

Safilios-Rothschild
"Family Sociology or Wives' Sociology? A Cross-Cultural Examination of Decision Making"
Journal of Marriage and Family, 31:2, 290-301
(May 1969)

St. Andre, Lucien
The American Matriarchy
Madison, N.J.: The Florham Park Press (1970)

St. Joan's Bulletin
Jinny Finn, 1941 N. 36th St., Milwaukee, Wisconsin 53208

Salamanca, J. R.
Lilith
New York (1961)

Sampson, Ronald V.
The Psychology of Power
New York (1966)

Sanchez, Sonia
We a BaddDDD people
Detroit (1970)

Sanchez, Vilma
"Women unite in support of strike"
Guardian
(November 8, 1969)

Sandler, Bernice
Testimony in *Discrimination Against Women.* Hearings before the Special Subcommittee on Education of the Committee on Education and Labor, House of Representatives, 91st Congress, 2nd Session, June and July (1970).

Sanger, Margaret
Margaret Sanger: An Autobiography
New York: W. W. Norton and Co. (1938)

Sappho
Poems and fragments
trans. Guy Davenport
Ann Arbor: University of Michigan Press (1965)

Sarris, Andrew
"Films—Sweet Charity"
Village Voice
(April 17, 1969)

Sarton, Mary
The Small Room
New York (1961)

Sartre, Jean-Paul
Anti-Semite and Jew
New York (1948)

Sartre, Jean-Paul
The Flies in *The Flies and In Camera*
London (1946)

Sartre, Jean-Paul
Nausea
New York (1969)

Saveth, Edward
"The Problem of American Family History"
American Quarterly
(Summer 1969)

Scanzoni, John H.
Opportunity and the Family
New York (1970)

Scarlet Woman
c/o Women's Liberation Group, Derwent College, University of York, Heslington, York, England

"Scenes"
Village Voice
(March 13, 1969)

Scheff, Thomas J.
Mental Illness and Social Processes
New York (1967)

Scheinfeld, Amram
Women and Men
New York (1943)

Schlegel, Friedrich von
Lucinde
Jena: E. Diederichs (1907)

Schlesinger Library
c/o Radcliffe College, 3 James St., Cambridge, Mass. 02138
An Extensive collection on women.

Schmalhausen, Samuel and V. F. Calverton, ed.
Woman's Coming of Age
New York: H. Liveright (1931)

Schneider, David and Kathleen Gough, eds.
Matrilineal Kinship
Berkeley: University of California Press (1967)

Schneiderman, Rose, with Lucy Goldthwaite
All for One
New York (1967)

Schneir, Miriam, ed.
Feminism: The Essential Historical Writings
New York (1972)
A collection of essays, letters, and memoirs from major contributors to feminist literature, beginning with Abigail Adams and ending with Virginia Woolf. The book includes excerpts from the writings of such people as Wollstonecraft, the Grimkes, Truth, Mott, Stanton, Anthony, Mill, Engels, Goldman, Ibsen, Bebel, Wrodhull and Claflin, Gilman, Putnam, Sanger and Catt. The author has deliberately omitted excerpts which refer solely to the suffrage movement, choosing to emphasize feminist questions which she considers pertinent to the modern movement, such as the oppressive character of marriage, sexual freedom, the economic dependence of women, and the problems of achieving selfhood in a society in which women define themselves by their relationships to other people.

Schraner, Olive
Woman and Labor
London: T. F. Unwin (1923)

Schreiner, Olive (pseud. Ralph Iron)
The Story of an African Farm
Boston: Roberts Bros. (1893)

Schuck, Victoria
"Reports of the APSA Committee: Part II of the Committee Report; Some Comparative Statistics on Women in Political Science and other Social Sciences"
Political Scientist (1970)

Schuck, Victoria
"Women in Political Science: Some Preliminary Observations"
Political Scientist, 2, 642-643 (1969)

Schucking, Levin Ludwig
The Sociology of Literary Taste
Chicago: University of Chicago Press (1966)

Schulder, Diane and Kennedy, Florynce
Abortion Rap
New York: McGraw-Hill Book Company (1971)

Schur, Edwin, ed.
The Family and the Sexual Revolution
Bloomington, Indiana: University of Indiana Press (1964)

Schwartz, Eleanor Brantely
The Sex Barrier in Business
Atlanta: Georgia State University (1970)

Scott, Anne Firor
"After Suffrage: Southern Women in the Twenties"
Journal of Souther History, XXX, 45-66 (August 1964)

Scott, Anne Firor
The American Woman: Who Was She?
Englewood Cliffs, N.J. (1971)

Scott, Anne Firor
"The 'New Woman' in the New South"
South Atlantic Quarterly, LXI, 473-83 (August 1962)

Scott, John Finley
"The Role of the College Sorority in Endogamy"
American Sociological Review, 30:4, 514-527 (August 1965)

Scudder, Vida
On Journey
New York: Dutton (1924)

Seattle Radical Women
2940 36th Avenue South
Seatle, Washington 98114

Seawell, Molly
The Ladies' Battle
New York: Macmillian (1911)

The Second Wave
A magazine of the New Seminism
Harwich Press, Box 303,
Kenmore Square Station
Boston, Mass. 02215

Seehy, Gail
"A City Kind of Love: A Report on the State of the Art"
New York Magazine (February 16, 1970)

Segal, Bernard E.
Racial and Ethnic Relations
New York (1966)

Seward, Georgene H. and Robert C. Williamson, eds.
Sex Roles in Changing Society
New York (1970)

"Sex and Equal Employment Rights"
Monthly Labor Review (August 1967)

"Sex and the Contemporary American Scene"
The Annals of the American Academy of Political and Social Science (March 1968)

Sexton, Anne
All My Pretty Ones
Boston (1962)

Sexton, Anne
Live or Die
Boston (1966)

Sexton, Anne
Love Poems
Boston (1969)

Sexton, Patricia
The Feminized Male: Classrooms, White Collars and the Decline of Manliness
New York (1969)

The Sexual Barrier Legal & Economic Aspects of Employment
Marija Hughes, 2422 Fox Plaza,
San Francisco, Calif. 94102

"The Sexual Renaissance in America"
Journal of Social Issues (April 1966)

Shanas, Ethel and Gordon Streib, ed.
Social Structure and the Family:

General Relations
Englewood Cliffs, N.J. (1965)

Shaw, Anna Howard with the collaboration of Elizabeth Jordan
The Story of a Pioneer
New York: Harper (1915)

Shaw, George Bernard
The Intelligent Woman's Guide to Socialism and Capitalism
New York: Brentano's (1928)

Shaw, George Bernard
Major Barbara
Baltimore (1959)

Shaw, George Bernard
Saint Joan
Baltimore (1952)

Shearer, Lloyd
"Mini-Midi-Maxi—How Ridiculous Can Fashion Get?"
Parade (carried in Sunday papers) (March 29, 1970)

Shearer, Lloyd, and Dunlap, Carol
"The First Woman President of the U.S.—Why Not and When?"
Parade (February 7, 1971)

Sheehy, Gail
"The Great St. Valentine's Day Uprising"
New York Magazine (February 16, 1970)

Shelton, Elizabeth
"Civil Rights Act Opens More Jobs for Women"
The Atlanta Journal (November 27, 1966)

Shelton, Elizabeth
"Few Women Hold Key Jobs"
Washington, D.C. Post (September 2, 1968)

Sherriffs, A. C. and John P. McKee
"Qualitative aspects of beliefs about men and women"
Journal of Personality XXV, 451-464 (1957)

Shrew
9 Stratford Villa, London NW 1,
England or 127 Lower Marsh,
London SE 1, England

SIECUS Newsletter
Sex Information & Education Council of the U.S., 1825 Willow Road, Northfield, Ill. 60093

Sillen, Samuel
Women Against Slavery
New York: Masses and Mainstream (1955)

Simons, H. J.
African Women: Their Legal Status in South Africa
Evanston: Northwestern University Press (1968)

Simpson, Lawrence A.
"A Myth is Better Than A Miss"
College and University Business,
48, 72-73 (1970)

Sinclair, Andrew
The Emancipation of the American Woman
New York (1969)
A historical study of the feminist movement as it developed out of the changing American culture.
The author sees an important link between the growth of cities and towns, the increasing leisure time of upper-middle class women, and the growing agitation for women's rights. He also links the women's movement to the whole spectrum of reform movements which developed during the Progressive Era.
The author contends that the keys to woman's success in obtaining the vote were "the advance of technology and urbanization," because they allowed her the time to desire and work for liberty.
The book is sympathetic in its treatment of women and it includes helpful chapters on the slave status of colonial and pre-abolition women. The author concludes his study with the thesis that modern men and women have a strong connection with the Victorians among whom women were reluctant to give up their leisure, while their men fought to earn it.

Singer, Daniels
My Mother, the Doctor
New York (1970)

Sisters
1005 Market, Room 208, San Francisco, Calif. 94103

Sisters in Poverty Newsletter
1712 Gold SE, Albuquerque, N.M. 87106

Skard, Aase Gruda
"Maternal Deprivation: The Research and its Implications"
Journal of Marriage and the Family, XXVII, No. 3
(August 1965)

Skirting The Capital

P.O. Box 4569, Sacramento, Calif. 95825

Sklar, Robert
"Consciousness Confrontation" review of *Styles of Radical Will,* by Susan Sontag
Nation
(June 2, 1969)

Slater, Philip E.
The Glory of Hera, Greek Mythology and the Greek Family
Boston (1968)

Smelser, Neil Joseph
Social Change in the Industrial Revolution
London (1959)

Smith, A. E.
Colonists in Bondage: White Servitude and Convict Labor in America
Chapel Hill: University of North Carolina Press (1947)

Smith, Florence
Mary Astell (1666-1739)
New York: Columbia University Press (1916)
Includes her early works on women's rights.

Smith, Georgina M.
Help Wanted—Female: A Study of Demand and Supply in a Local Job Market for Women
Rutgers, N.J.: Institute of Management and Labor Relations of Rutgers University (1964)

Smith, Julie
"What They Want: A Survey of Campus Liberation Movement"
California Monthly
(June-July 1970)

Smith, Lillian
Killers of the Dream
New York (1961)

Smith, Lillian
Strange Fruit
New York: Grosset and Dunlap (1944)

Smith, Page
Daughters of the Promised Land, Women in American History
New York (1970)
An extremely valuable history of women in America. The author's approach is straightforward and fairly objective except when he succumbs to the temptation to include a chapter on the nature of women. The rest of the book gives a superb account of American women and the movements in which they were involved. The book includes chapters on such subjects as the spread of poor health among nineteenth century American women, the growing demand for sexual rights, the missionary movement, the role of women in settling the west, the effects of capitalism on women, the theories of Ellis, Freud and Marx, and the proliferation of women's organizations following the last successful drive for the vote. The author also discusses the standard questions of prohibition and the suffrage movement, but his unique contribution to feminist literature lies in the diversity of his coverage and his comprehensive discussion of the less widely known ways in which women shaped American culture.

Smuts, Robert W.
Women and Work in America
New York (1959)

Snow, Helen
Women in Modern China
New York (1968)
A popular approach to the role of women in recent Chinese history. The author traces the traditional attitudes held by the Chinese concerning women (woman as a sort of goddess, etc.). The book also presents the biographies of the ten most influential women in Chinese history during this century.

Snowden, Frank M., Jr.
Blacks in Antiquity, Ethiopians in the Greco-Roman Experience
Cambridge, Mass.: Harvard University Press (1970)
Socialist Woman
16 Ella Road, West Bridgeford, England or 21 Watcombe Circus, Carrington, Nottingham, England
Society For Humane Abortion Newsletter
P.O. Box 1862, San Francisco, Calif. 94101

Soehngen, Sandra
"Films for Consciousness Raising"
Media & Methods (March 1972)

Solotaroff, Theodore
"Death in Life"
Commentary
(November 1967)

Sontag, Susan
Against Interpretation and other essays
New York (1966)

Sontag, Susan
Deathkit
New York (1967)

Sophia Smith Collection
Greenwood Press: 51 Riverside Ave., Westport, Conn. 06880
A project to reprint in a multivolume set the classic out-of-print works on feminism.

Source Catalog
Source Coalition, 2115 "S" Street, Washington, D.C. 20008

Southern Journal of Female Liberation
Box 30087, Lafayette Square Station, New Orleans, La. 70130

Soviet Woman
c/o Northern Book House, Box 1000, Gravenhurst, Ontario, Canada

Spain, Jayne Baker
"A Woman Could Be President"
Vital Issues and Speeches of the Day (April 1, 1971)

Spalletta, Matteo
"Divorce in Colonial New York"
New York Historical Society Quarterly, 422-440
(1955)

Spark, Muriel
The Prime of Miss Jean Brodie
London (1961)

Spazm
Women's History Library, 2325 Oak St., Berkeley, Calif. 94708
An Out-of-print journal from the early years of the movement.

Spear, Allan
Black Chicago: The Making of A Negro Ghetto 1890-1920
Chicago: University of Chicago Press (1967)

Spencer, Anna Garlin
Woman's Share in Social Culture
Philadelphia: J. B. Lippincott (1925)

Spero, Sterling D. and Abram L. Harris
The Black Worker: The Negro and the Labor Movement
New York: Columbia University Press (1931)

Spiegel, Jeanne, ed.
Career Counseling: New Perspectives for Women and Girls
Washington, D.C. Business and Professional Women's Foundation (1972)
a selected and annotated bibliography

Spiegel, Jeanne, ed.
Continuing Education for Women
Washington, D.C. Business and Professional Women's Foundation (1967)
a selected and annotated bibliography

Spiegel, Jeanne, ed.
Sex Role Concepts
Washington, D.C. Business and Professional Women's Foundation (1969)
a selected and annotated bibliography

Spiegel, Jeanne, ed.
Women Executives
Washington, D.C. Business and Professional Women's Foundation (1970)
a selected and annotated bibliography

Spiegel, Jeanne, ed.
Working Mothers
Washington, D.C. Business and Professional Women's Foundation (1968)

Spiro, Melford E.
Children of the Kibbutz: A Study in Child Training and Personality
New York (1965)

Spock, Benjamin
"Should Girls Expect to Have Careers?"
Redbook
(March 1972)

The Spokeswoman
Urban Research Corporation, 5464 South Shore Drive, Chicago, Ill. 60615

Spruill, Julia Cherry
Women's Life and Work in the Southern Colonies
Chapel Hill: The University of North Carolina Press (1938)

Squire, Belle
The Woman Movement in America (n.p.) (n.d.)

Stabile, Toni
"Adventures in the Skin Trade"
The Nation
(Jan. 1, 1968)

Stade, George
"Commonplaces About Women"
Review of *Thinking About Women*
by Mary Ellman
Nation
(February 17, 1969)

Stafford, Jean
Collected Stories
New York (1969)

Stambler, Sookie, ed.
Women's Liberation: Blueprint for the Future
New York: Charter Communications, Inc. (1970)
A collection of writings by women who are active within the Women's Liberation Movement. Called a "showcase of our work" by the editor, the essays present strictly female opinions on such subjects as the temptations women face to resort to the feminine stereotypes, the abortion issue and the courts, the status of women before the law, the problems of high school women and curriculum structuring, lesbianism, the political goals of women within the Movement, and the women's struggle in historical perspective. A particularly interesting and valuable feature of the book is the section on women in the arts, including some criticism of films, the theater, and the music scene, as well as a few pieces of fiction by women writers within the Movement. A very extensive and valuable authology.

Stanton, Elizabeth Cady
Eighty Years and More
New York: European Publishing Co. (1898)

Stanton, Elizabeth C., Susan B. Anthony, Matilda J. Gage, and Ida H. Harper
History of Woman Suffrage 6 vol.
New York: Fowler and Wells (1881-1922)

Stanton, Theodore, ed.
The Woman Question in Europe
New York: George P. Putnam's and Sons (1884)

Starkey, M.
The Devil in Massachusetts, a Modern Inquiry into the Salem Witch Trials
New York (1949)

Statues of Liberty
c/o Women's Liberation, 8 Harvard Street, Rochester, N.Y. 14620

Stead, Christina
The Man Who Loved Children
New York (1965)

Stegner, Wallace Earle
The Big Rock Candy Mountain
New York: Duell Sloane (1943)

Stegner, Wallace Earle
The Sound of Mountain Water
Garden City, N.Y. (1969)

Stein, Gertrude
Autobiography of Alice B. Toklas
New York: Random House (1933)

Stein, Gertrude
Lectures in America
Boston: Beacon Press (1935)

Stein, Gertrude
Three Lives
Norfolk, Conn.: New Direction
(1933)

Stein, Robert L.
"The Economic Status of
Families Headed by Women"
Monthly Labor Review, XCIII, 3-10
(December 1970)

Stein, Ruthe
"The Loves of Isadora" film rev.
Cineaste, III, i
(Summer 1969)

Steinem, Gloria
"Hormones in the White House"
Time (August 10, 1970)

Steinem, Gloria
"The City Politic"
New York Magazine
(April 7, 1969)

Steinem, Gloria
"Laboratory for Love Styles"
New York Magazine
(February 16, 1970)

Steinem, Gloria
"What *Playboy* Doesn't Know
about Women Could Fill a Book"
McCalls
(October 1970)

Steinem, Gloria
"Woman President in 1976"
Look (January 13, 1970)

Stendahl, Kister
The Bible and the Role of Women
Philadelphia: Fortress Press
(n.d.)

Stendahl, Krister
"Women in the Churches:
No Special Pleading"
Soundings
(Winter 1970)

Stenton, Doris Mary
The English Woman in History
New York (1957)

Stephens, William N.
*The Family in Cross-Cultural
Perspective*
New York (1963)

Stern, Karl
The Flight From Woman
New York (1965)

Stern, Madeleine
The Life of Margaret Fuller
New York: E. P. Dutton and Co.
(1942)

Stern, Paul
"When's It Going to be
Ladies Day?"
New Republic
(July 5, 1969)

Sterrett, Mary
*Pioneer Women of Western
Pennsylvania*
Pittsburgh: University of
Pennsylvania Press (1931)

Stevens, Barry and Carl Rogers
*Person to Person: the Problem of
Being Human; a New Trend in
Psychiatry*
Walnut Creek, California:
Real People Press (1967)

Stevens, Doris
Jailed for Freedom
New York: Boni and Liveright
(1920)

Stewart, Elinor Pruitt
Letters of a Woman Homesteader
Boston and New York:
Houghton, Mifflin (1914)

Stoodley, Bartlett H., ed.
Society and Self
Glencoe, Ill. (1962)

Stowe, Harriet B.
Uncle Tom's Cabin
Cambridge, Mass.: Harvard
University Press (1962)

Suelzle, Marijean
"Women in Labor"
Trans-action 8, 50-58 (1970)

Suhl, Yuri
*Ernestine Rose and the Battle for
Human Rights*
New York (1959)

Sullerot, Evelyne
Women, Society and Change
New York (1971)

Sumner, W. G.
Folkways
Boston: Ginn and Company
(1940)

The Survey
(December 1, 1926)
entire issue devoted to women

Sussman, Marvin B.
*Sourcebook on Marriage and the
Family*
New York (1968)

Swidler, Leonard
"Jesus Was A Feminist"
Catholic World
(January 1971)

Swisshelm, Jane Grey
Half a Century
New York: Source Book Press
(1970) (c. 1880)

Sydney, Women's Liberation
Newsletter
Women's Liberation, 67 Glebe
Point Road, Glebe 2037,
New South Wales, Australia

Taft, Julia Jesse
*The Woman Movement from the
Point of View of Social
Consciousness*
Chicago: University of Chicago
Press (1916)

Taft, Philip
*Organized Labor in American
History*
New York (1964)

Tagore, Rabindranath
Collected Poems and Plays
New York (1949)

Tait, Marjorie
*The Education of Women for
Citizenship*
Paris: UNESCO (1954)

**"Take Them They're Yours: Six Jobs
in Search of Truly Liberated Women"**
Esquire (February, 1970)

Tannenbaum, Frank
*Slave and Citizen; the Negro in
the Americas*
New York (1946)

Tanner, Leslie B., ed.
Voices from Women's Liberation
New York (1971)

Tarbell, Ida
*All in the Day's Work; an
Autobiography*
New York: MacMillan Co. (1939)

Tarbell, Ida
The Business of Being a Woman
New York: MacMillan (1912)

Tarbell, Ida
The Ways of Woman
New York: MacMillan Co. (1915)

Taylor, Angela
"She Used to Model but
Now She Paints"
New York Times
(November 6, 1969)

Taylor, Elizabeth
In a Summer Season
New York (1961)

Taylor, Gordon R.
Sex in History
New York: Vanguard Press
(1954)

Taylor, Orville
"Jumping the Broomstick"
Arkansas Historical Quarterly,
XVII, 217-231 n.d.

Taylor W. and C. Lasch
"Two 'Kindrel Spirits' Sorority
and Family in New England,
1839-1846"
New England Quarterly (March,
1963)

Taylor, William R.
*Cavalier and Yankee; the Old
South and American National
Character*
New York (1961)

Tennyson, Alfred, Lord
The Princess and other Poems
New York: F. A. Stokes (1890)

Terry, Walter
*Isadora Duncan: Her Life, Her
Art, Her Legacy*
New York: Dodd, Mead (1964)
(c.1963)

Theodore, Athena, ed.
The Professional Woman
Cambridge, Mass. (1971)

TFWL
c/o Ceballos, 148 W. 58th St.,
New York, N.Y.

TWWA
346 W. 20th St., New York, N.Y.

Thomas, Edith
The Women Incendiaries
New York (1966)

Thompson, Mary Lou, ed.
Voices of the New Feminism
Boston (1970)

Thomson, George
*Studies in Ancient Greek Society:
The Prehistoric Aegean*
New York (1949)

Thomson, Patricia
*The Victorian Heroine, A
Changing Ideal, 1837-1873*
New York: Oxford University
Press (1956)

Thompson, Clara
"Cultural Pressures in the
Psychology of Women"
Psychiatry, V, 331-339 (1942)

Thomspon, Eleanor Wolf
*Education for Ladies, 1830-1860,
Ideas on Education in Magazines
for Women*
New York: King's Crown Press
(1947)

Thompson, Mary Lou, ed.
Voices of the New Feminism
Boston (1970)

Throb
ed. F. A. Nettelbeck
3808 Laurel Ave., Manhattan
Beach, Calif. 90266

Tiger, Lionel
"The Possible Biological Origins
of Sexual Discrimination"
*The Other Half: Roads to Women's
Equality*
eds. Cynthia Epstein and
William Goode
Englewood Cliffs, N.J. (1971)

Tiger, Lionel
Men in Groups
New York (1969)

Tim, Tiny
"The Percect Mother"
Esquire (Dec., 1970)

Time
"Madam President,"
(March 20, 1972)

TCP
1023 Sixth Ave., New York,
N.Y. 10018

Tims, Margaret
*Jane Addams of Hull House,
1860-1935*
London (1961)

Tindall, Gillian
"Beware the Love Prigs"
New Statesman (June 14, 1968)

Tindall, Gillian
"On the Frontier of Time" review
of *The Four-Gated City* by Doris
Lessing
New Statesman (July 4, 1969)

Tindall, Gillian
"Sequestration", Review of
*Locked-Up Daughters: a Parent's
Look at Girls' Education and
Schools*, by Felicia Lamb and

Helen Pickthorn
New Statesman (March 15, 1968)

Tindall, Gillian
"A Shared Predicament"
New Statesman (January 10, 1969)

Tobias, Shelia
Female Studies No. 1
Pittsburgh, Pa.: Know, Inc.
(1970)

Tolstoy, Leo Nikolaevich, graf.
"Family Happiness" in *A Russian
Proprietor and other Stories*
New York: C. Scribner Sons
(1970)

Tomalin, Claire
"Broody", review of *Women's
Magazines 1693-1968*, by Cynthia
White
New Statesman (March 13, 1970)

Toomer, Jean
Cane
New York: Harper and Row
(1969) (c. 1923)

TAN
1800 Prince St.,
Berkeley, Calif. 94704

Trager, George L.
"A Scheme for the Cultural
Analysis of Sex."
*Southwestern Journal of
Anthropology*, 18.2 114-118
(Summer, 1962)

Transition
c/o The Women's Liberation
Center of New York,
36 W. 22nd St., New York, N.Y.

Transvestia
The Chevalier Publ. Co.,
Box 36091, Los Angeles, Calif.

**"Trends in Educational Attainment
of Women"**
U.S. Dept. of Labor,
Washington, D.C. 20210

Treudley, Mary
"The Benevolent Fair"
Social Service Review, 509-522
(1940)

Tribal Sisters Collective
419 Locust St., Kalamazoo, Mich.

"Triumph of Irrelevance"
Nation (May 12, 1969)

Trollope, Frances Milton
*Domestic Manners of the
Americans*
London: Routledge (1927)
from 5th edition prtd. (1839)

True to Life
Box 26003, 80 Butler St.,
Atlanta, Ga. 30303

Tryon, Rolla Milton
Household Manufacturers in the U.S. 1640-1860; A Study of Industrial History
Chicago: University of Chicago Press (1917)

Turn of the Screwed
3601 Glacier, Garland, Tex. 75040

Tweedie, Jill
"Liaison"
New Statesman (March 8, 1968)
"The Underdeveloped Sex"
The Economist, p. 18 (April 3, 1971)

Underground Woman
c/o Kathy Frederick,
2505 St. Louis Ave.,
St. Louis, Mo.

Undset, Sigrid
Kristin Lavrensdatter
New York (1946) (c. 1923)

United Nations, Sect. General (Thant)
Participation of Women in the Economics and Social Development of Their Countries
Report of the Secretary General
New York: United Nations (1970)

"United States: Leading Lady"
Newsweek (September 29, 1969)

U.S. Dept. of Labor, Wage and Labor Standards Admin., Women's Bureau
American Women: 1963-1968
Washington, D.C.:
Government Printing Office n.d.

U.S. Dept. of Labor, Women's Bureau
"Background Facts on Women Workers"
Washington, D.C.:
Government Printing Office (1970)

U.S. Dept. of Labor, Women's Bureau
"Day Care Facts"
Washington, D.C.:
Government Printing Office (August, 1969)

U.S. Dept. of Labor, Women's Bureau
"Fact Sheet on the Earnings Gap"
Washington, D.C.:
Government Printing Office (Feb., 1970)

U.S. Dept. of Labor, Women's Bureau
"Facts About Women's Absentism and Labor Turnover"
Washington, D.C.:
Government Printing Office (August, 1969)

U.S. Dept. of Labor, Women's Bureau
Handbook on Women Workers
Washington, D.C.:
Government Printing Office (1965)

U.S. Dept. of Labor, Women's Bureau
"Labor Dept. Guidelines to Bar Sex Discrimination on Government Contract Work"
Washington, D.C.:
Government Printing Office,
11–265 with Title 41,
Chap. 60, Part 60–20

U.S. Dept. of Labor, Women's Bureau
"Laws on Sex Discrimination in Employment"
Washington, D.C.:
Government Printing Office (1970)

U.S. Dept. of Labor, Women's Bureau
"Negro Women . . . in the Population and in the Labor Force"
Washington, D.C.:
Government Printing Office (October, 1969)

U.S. Dept. of Labor, Women's Bureau
"A Report of the President's Task Force on Women's Rights and Responsibilities"
Washington, D.C.:
Government Printing Office (April, 1970)

U.S. Dept. of Labor, Women's Bureau
"Underutilization of Women Workers"
Washington, D.C.:
Government Printing Office (August, 1967)

U.S. News & World Report
"A Woman for President? Hurdles in the Path of Margaret Chase Smith"
(February 10, 1964)

Up from Under
399 Lafayette St.,
New York, N.Y. 10012

Updike, John
Couples New York (1968)

Utley, Francis
The Crooked Rib, an analytical index to the argument about women in English and Scots literature to the end of the year 1568
Columbus:
Ohio State University Press (1944)

Valency, Maurice Jacques
In Praise of Love; an Introduction to the Love Poetry of the Renaissance
New York (1958)

Van Riessen, H.
The Society of the Future
Philadelphia (1958)

Van Vorst, Bessie and Marie Van Vorst
The Woman Who Toils
New York:
Doubleday, Page & Co. (1903)

Vayda, Andrew P.
Environment and Cultural Behavior: Ecological Studies in Cultural Anthropology
New York:
The Natural History Press (1969)

Veblen, Thorstein
The Theory of the Leisure Class
New York (1953)

Velvet Fist
Toronto Women's Caucus,
Box 808, Street F.,
Toronto, 5, Ont.

Velvet Glove Magazine
P.O. Box 188,
Livermore, Calif. 94550

Vidich, Arthur J. and Joseph Bensman
Small Town in Mass Society; Class, Power, and Religion in a Rural Community
New York (1958)

Vigman, Fred K.
Beauty's Triumph
Boston: Christopher Publishing House (1966)

Viorst, Judith
"A Women's Liberation Movement Woman"
New York Magazine (February 16, 1970)

Voice of Women
811 Washington St.,
Newtonville, Mass. 02160

Voice of Women's Liberation
1545 Claremont, Chicago, Ill.

Voices for Children
Day Care & Child Development Council of America
1426 H St. NW,
Washington, D.C. 20005

Von Mering, Faye Higier
"Professional and non-professional Women as Mothers"
Journal of Social Psychology, XLII, 21-34 (1955)

Vonnegut, Kurt
Welcome to the Monkey House
New York (1970)

Vorse, Mary Heaton
A Footnote to Folly
New York:
Farrar and Rinehart (1935)

Waddington, Mary
　　Letters of a Diplomat's Wife,
　　1883-1900
　　New York:
　　C. Scribner's Sons (1903)

Wade, Mason
　　Margaret Fuller: Whetstone of
　　Genius
　　New York: Viking Press (1940)

Wade, Mason
　　The Writings of Margaret Fuller,
　　2 vols.
　　New York: Viking Press (1941)

Wakefield, Dan
　　Going All The Way
　　New York (1970)

Wakowski, Diana
　　Inside the Blood Factory
　　Garden City, N.Y. (1968)

Wald, Lillian
　　House on Henry Street
　　New York: H. Holt (1915)

Wald, Lillian
　　Windows on Henry Street
　　Boston: Little, Brown (1934)

Waldman, Elizabeth
　　"Changes in the Labor Force
　　Activity of Women"
　　Monthly Labor Review (June, 1970)

Waldman, Elizabeth
　　"Marital and Family
　　Characteristics of the U.S.
　　Labor Force"
　　Monthly Labor Review (May, 1970)

Walton, Cynthia
　　"Growth of Family Planning"
　　New Statesman (June 17, 1966)

Ward, Barbara, ed.
　　Women in the New Asia UNESCO
　　(1963)

Ware, Caroline
　　Early New England Cotton
　　Manufacture
　　Boston and New York:
　　Houghton, Mifflin (1931)

Ware, Cellestine
　　Womanpower New York (1970)

Ware, Norman
　　The Industrial Worker, 1840-1860
　　Boston: Houghton, Mifflin (1924)
　　Washington Newsletter for Women
　　1730 M St., N.W.,
　　Washington, D.C. 20036

Washington Opportunities for Women (WOW)
　　Christine Nelson,
　　Rm. 101, Vanguard Bldg.,
　　1111 20th St., Washington, D.C.

Wasilewska, Wanda
　　The Rainbow
　　New York: Simon and Schuster
　　(1944)

Watkins, Alan
　　"The Battle for Barbara's Bill"
　　New Statesman (February 23,
　　1968)

Watt, Ian
　　The Rise of the Novel
　　London: Chatto and Windus
　　(1957)

Weal Word Watcher
　　P.O. Box 30142, Midpoint P.O.,
　　Middleburg Hts., Ohio

Webb, Beatrice
　　My Apprenticeship
　　London: Longmans (1926)

Webster, Dayard
　　"Overpopulation Unites 2 Groups"
　　New York Times (October 2, 1969)

Weil, Mildred
　　"An analysis of the Factors
　　Influencing Married Women's
　　Actual of Planned Work
　　Participation"
　　American Sociological Review
　　(Feb., 1961)

Weil, Simone
　　Gravity and Grace
　　New York (1952)

Weil, Simone
　　The Need for Roots
　　New York (1955)

Weiss, Samuel Abba, ed.
　　Drama in the Modern World
　　Boston (1964)

Weisstein, Naomi
　　"Kinder, Kuche, Kirche
　　as Scientific Law: Psychology
　　Constructs the Female"
　　Boston (1968)

Weisstein, Naomi
　　"Woman as Nigger"
　　Psychology Today (October, 1969)

Welter, Barbara
　　"Anti-intellectualism and
　　the American Woman"
　　Mid-America 258-270 (1966)

Welty, Eudora
　　Short Stories
　　New York (1950)

Welter, Barbara
　　"The Cult of True Womanhood"
　　American Quarterly, XVIII, 151-175
　　n.d.

Wells, Mildred White
　　Unity in Diversity
　　No Place. n.d.

Wembridge, Eleanor
　　"Petting and the Campus"
　　Survey (July 1, 1925)

Wesley, Charles S.
　　Negro Labor in the U.S. 1850-
　　1925; a Study in American
　　Economic History
　　New York: Vanguard Press
　　(1927)

West, Anthony
　　"Who Takes Advantage
　　of American Women?"
　　Vogue (May, 1968)

Westermack, Edvard Alexander
　　A Story History of Marriage
　　New York: MacMillan Co. (1926)

Wack Newsletter
　　P.O. Box 1595,
　　Anniston, Ala. 36201

Wharton, Edith
　　Age of Innocence
　　New York: Modern Library (1920)

Wharton, Edith
　　The House of Mirth
　　New York: Scribner (1951)

Wharton, Vernon
　　The Negro in Mississippi, 1865-
　　1890, ed. Albert Ray Newsome
　　Chapel Hill: University
　　of North Carolina Press (1947)

"What are You Supposed to do if You Like Children?"
　　Atlantic (March, 1970)

"Where Are They Now?"
　　Newsweek (March 23, 1970)

Whicker, George F.
　　This Was a Poet: A Critical
　　Biography of Emily Dickinson
　　Amherst, Mass.: The Jones
　　Library, Inc. (1930)

Witch (New York Covens)
　　Box 694, Stuyvesant Station,
　　New York, N.Y. 10009

White, James J.
　　"Women in the Law"
　　Michigan Law Review (April,
　　1967)

White, Wm.
　　"O Caeca Nocentum Consillia"
　　Mensa Interloc (Sept., 1969)

White, Wm.
　　"Psychology, the new Witchcraft"
　　Mensanity (May, 1969)

White, Wm.
　　"The American Sexual

Revolution"
Proteus (Nov., 1968)

"Why Women Work"
U.S. Dept. of Labor,
Women's Bureau
Washington, D.C. 20210

Whyte, William Foote
*Street Corner Society; the Social
Structure of an Italian Slum*
Chicago: University of Chicago
Press (1943)

Wieth-Knudsen, K. A.
*Understanding Women: A
Sociological Study of the Woman
Question from Ancient Times to
the Present Day*
trans. by Arthur G. Chater
New York: E. Holt (1929)

Wilensky, Harold
"Women's Work: Economic
Growth, Ideology, Structure"
Industrial Relations (May, 1968)

**Willacy, Hazel M.
and Harvey J. Hilaski**
"Working Women in Urban
Poverty Neighborhoods"
Monthly Labor Review (June,
1970)

Willard, Frances
*Glimpses of Fifty Years. The
Autobiography of an American
Woman*
Chicago: Women's Temperance
Publication Assoc. (c. 1889)

Williams, David
"The Politics of Seminism in the
French Enlightenment", P. Hughes
and D. Williams eds. *The Varied
Pattern: Studies in the Eighteenth
Century*
Toronto (1971)

Williams, John Alfred
Sissie
New York (1963)

Williams, Tennessee
Baby Doll
New York (1956)

Williams, Tennessee
A Streetcar Named Desire
New York (1947)

Williams, Tennessee
Suddenly Last Summer
New York (1958)

Willis, Alice
"See America First",
film review of "Easy Rider"
and "Alice's Restaurant"

New York Review of Books
(January 1, 1970)

Willis, Ellen
"The Lessons of Chicago"
New American Review (April,
1969)

Willis, Ellen
"What Ever Happened to
Women, Nothing—That's
the Trouble"
Mademoiselle (September, 1969)

Wilson, Dorothy, Clark
*Lone Woman, the Story of
Elizabeth Blackwell, the First
Woman Doctor*
Boston (1970)

Wilson, Edmund
*Patriotic Gore; Studies in the
Literature of the American Civil
War*
London (1962)

Wilson, Robert McNair
Women of the French Revolution
Port Washington, N.Y.:
Kennikat Press (1970)

Winch, R., S. Greer and Blumberg
"Ethnicity and Extended
Familism in an Upper Middle
Class Suburb"
American Sociological Review,
82:2, 265-272, (1967)

Winch, Robert
The Modern Family
New York (1963)

**Winch, Robert F., Robert McGinnis
and Herbert R. Barringer, eds.**
*Selected Studies in Marriage and
the Family*
New York (1962)

Wishy, Bernard
*The Child and the Republic; the
dawn of Modern American Child
Nurture*
Philadelphia: University
Pennsylvania Press (1967)

Wister, Owen
The Virginian
New York: Grosset and Dunlap
(1929)

**"The Witness a Prophet" review of
The Four Gated City, by Doris Lessing**
Time (July 25, 1969)

Wolfe, Helen Bickel
Women in the World of Work
Albany: N.Y. State Dept. of Educ.,
Div. Research (Sept. 1969)

Wolff, Janet
What Makes Women Buy?
New York (1958)

Wolfson, Theresa
*The Woman Worker and the
Trade Unions*
New York: International
Publishers (1926)

Wollstonecraft, Mary
*A Vindication of the Rights of
Women*
New York: W. W. Norton
(1967) (c. 1792)

Woman: a Bibliography
St. Paul, Minn.: College
of St. Catherine (1967)

Woman Activist
2310 Barbour Rd.,
Falls Church, Va. 22043

Womankind
c/o Chicago Women's Liberation
Union, 852 West Belmont,
Chicago, Ill. 60657

Woman West
P.O. Box 2335, Toluca Lake Sta.,
N. Hollywood, Calif. 91602

Woman Worker
P.O. Box 26605,
Los Angeles, Calif.

Woman's Journal
Boston and Chicago:
NAWSA, 1870–1917
Title Varies: *The Woman Citizen*
between June, 1917 and
December, 1927

**A Woman's Liberation Address
Booklet**
Female Liberation of
Durham-Chapel Hill, Box 954,
Chapel Hill, N.C. 27514

Woman's Struggle
3 Rona Rd.,
London, N.W. 3, England

Women
Rm. 333, 225 Park Ave.,
New York, N.Y.

Women: A Bibliography
c/o Cisler, 102 W. 80th St.,
New York, N.Y. 10025

Women
c/o Women's Liberation,
2011 Guilford Ave.,
Baltimore, Md. 21218

Women & Religion
F. J. Farians,
6825 North Sharidan,
Chicago, Ill. 60626

Women in Struggle
Box 324,
Winneconne, Wis. 54986

Women Speaking
The Wick, Roundwood Ave.,
Hutton, Brentwood,
Essex, England

Women: to, by, of, for and about
New Moon Publishers,

Dept. V-al, Box 3488,
Ridgeway Station,
Stamford, Conn.

Women Today
Today Publications,
ed. Barbara Jordan Moore
1132 National Press Bldg.,
Washington, D.C. 20004

Women's Caucus
307 W. Broadway,
Vancouver, B.C., Canada

Woman's Education Newsletter
University of Wisconsin Extension,
432 North Lake St.,
Madison, Wis.

Women's Equity Action League
Mrs. Elizabeth Boyer,
765 Dines Rd., Novelty, Ohio

Women's History Research Group
2325 Oak St.,
Berkeley, Calif. 94708

Women's Liberation Committee
1900 E. Jefferson,
Detroit, Mich. 48207

Women's Liberation Newsletter
Box 116, Cambridge, Mass.

Women's Liberation
Box 13098, "T" Station,
New York, N.Y. 10009

Women's Liberation
New Haven, Conn.

Women's Liberation Center of N.Y.
36 W. 22nd St.,
New York, N.Y. 10010

Women's Liberation Newsletter
c/o Judy Walther, 6090 Oakland,
Austin, Tex.

Women's Liberation
Rm. 101, 1380 Howard St.,
San Francisco, Calif.

Women's Liberation
c/o Thomas Outpost,
13037 Euclid Ave.,
E. Cleveland, Ohio

**Women's Liberation of Mich.
Newsletter**
2230 Witherell,
Detroit, Mich. 48202

Women's Liberation League Newsletter
c/o Peggy Morton, 52 Elgin St.,
Toronto, Ont., Canada

Women's Liberation Union
Info. Center, 2875 W. Cermak Rd.,
Chicago, Ill.

Women's Liberation
c/o Joan Pitkin, P.O. Box 22094,
San Diego, Calif. 92122

Women's Page Newsletter
1227 37th Ave., San Francisco,
Calif. 94122

Women's Rights in Employment
Calif. State Library, Law Lib.,
Sacramento, Calif.

Women's Rights Law Reporter

Ann Marie Boylan,
School of Law, Rutgers Univ.,
180 University Ave.,
Newark, N.J. 07102

Women Speak Out
1376 Hollister Rd.,
Cleveland Hts., Ohio

Women and the Law
Valparaiso Univ., Law Review,
Valparaiso Univ. School of Law,
(1971)

**"Women in Higher Education:
Challenging the Status Quo"**
The Chronicle of Higher Education,
2-5 (Feb. 9, 1970)

**"Women in Love", review of film
based on novel of same title**
by D. H. Lawrence
Look (February 24, 1970)

**"Women's Lib: The War of Sexism,
with Views of Social Scientists"**
Newsweek (March, 23, 1970)

**"Women's Lib in Russia: the myth
and the reality"**
U.S. News and World Report, 74-
75
(November 16, 1970)

"Woman's Place in the Church"
America (February 28, 1970)

Woman's World
P.O. Box 694, Stuyvesant Station,
New York, N.Y. 10009

Wood, H. Curtis
"The Case for Voluntary
Sterilization"
The Humanist (August, 1969)

Wood, Robert Coldwell
*Suburbia, Its People and Their
Politics*
Boston: Houghton-Mifflin
(1959) (c. 1958)

Woody, Thomas
*A History of Women's Education
in the United States*
New York and Lancaster, Pa.:
The Science Press (1929)

Woolf, Virginia
*A Haunted House and other Short
Stories*
London: Hogarth (1953)

Woolf, Virginia
A Room of One's Own
New York (1920)

Woolf, Virginia
A Writer's Diary
London: Hogarth Press (1953)

Woolf, Virginia
Mrs. Dalloway
New York: Harcourt, Brace & Co.
(1925)

Woolf, Virginia
Night and Day
London: Hogarth Press (1919)

Woolf, Virginia
Orlando
New York (1960)

Woolf, Virginia
The Voyage Out
London: Hogarth Press (1929)

Woolf, Virginia
Three Guineas
New York: Harcourt, Brace
& World (1938)

Woolf, Virginia
To the Lighthouse
New York: Modern Library (1937)

**"Working Wives: Revolution in
American Family Life"**
U.S. News and World Report
(November 17, 1969)

**"Working Wives—Their Contribution
to Family Income"**
U.S. Dept of Labor—
Wage Standards Adm.,
Women's Bureau
Washington, D.C. 20210

Wright, Frederick Adam
*Feminism in Greek Literature
from Homer to Aristotle*
New York:
E. P. Dutton & Co. (1923)

Wright, Louis B.
*Middle Class Culture in
Elizabethan England*
Chapel Hill: University
of North Carolina Press (1935)

Wylie, Philip
Generation of Vipers
New York: Rinehard and Co.
(1955)

Whyte, William H.
"The Wife Problem"
*The Other Half: Roads to Women's
Equality*
edit. Epstein and Goode
Englewood Cliffs, N.J. (1971)

Yang, C. K.
*Chinese Communist Society: The
Family and the Village*
Cambridge, Mass.:
Mass. Inst. of Technology Press
(1965) (c. 1959)

Zakrzewska, Marie
A Woman's Quest
New York:
D. Appleton & Co. (1924)

Zapoleon, Marguerite Wykoff
Occupational Planning for Women
New York (1966)

Zweig, F.
Women's Life and Labour
New York (1952)

Trispect Reference/Index